CULTURAL CHANGE AND CONTINUITY IN CENTRAL ASIA

CULTURAL CHANGE AND CONTINUITY IN CENTRAL ASIA

Edited by

SHIRIN AKINER

KEGAN PAUL INTERNATIONAL

London and New York

in association with the

CENTRAL ASIA RESEARCH FORUM

School of Oriental and African Studies, London

First published in 1991 by
Kegan Paul International Ltd
PO Box 256, London WC1B 3SW, England

Distributed by
John Wiley & Sons Ltd
Southern Cross Trading Estate
1 Oldlands Way, Bognor Regis,
West Sussex PO 22 9SA, England

Routledge, Chapman & Hall Inc
29 West 35th Street,
New York, NY 10001, USA

© Kegan Paul International 1991

Phototypeset in Linotron Palatino 10 on 12pt
by Intype, London

Printed in Great Britain by TJ Press (Padstow) Ltd, Padstow,
England

British Library Cataloguing in Publication Data
Cultural change and continuity in Central Asia.
1. Central Asia. Cultural processes
I. Akiner, Shirin
306'.0958

ISBN 0–7103–0351–3

Library of Congress Cataloging-in-Publication Data
Cultural change and continuity in Central Asia / edited by Shirin
Akiner.
387 pp. 234 cm.
ISBN 0–7103–0351–3
1. Asia. Central—Civilization. 2. Soviet Central Asia—
Civilization. I. Akiner, Shirin.
DS328.2.C85 1991
303.4'0958–dc20   90–43441
                                                        CIP

CONTENTS

v

CONTENTS

FOREWORD

Central Asia is a vast sprawling territory with no precise boundaries, no precise geographic definition. The term has sometimes been used rather narrowly, to refer to a circumscribed area such as Transoxiana, sometimes very broadly to include the whole of the land mass at the heart of Asia, from Siberia in the north to the Pamirs in the south, from Mongolia in the east, westwards across the steppes of Kazakhstan, to the Volga. Culturally and linguistically the divisions are blurred: different traditions intermingle, different influences predominate, yet underlying the diversity there is a perceptible framework of shared traditions.

There is much detailed, closely focused research that remains to be done on every part of Central Asia. Sometimes, however, it is illuminating to stand back and look at the region as a whole, seeking similarities as well as contrasts. It was with this aim in mind that a conference on *Tradition and Change in Central Asia* was held at the School of Oriental and African Studies, University of London, in April 1987. Over a hundred papers were presented, covering a wide range of topics, a number of disciplines and several different regional interests. It would, of course, be an exaggeration to say that this 'brainstorming' approach produced a sudden revelation of the innate unity of Central Asian culture, but it certainly did highlight a surprising number of common features. This in turn stimulated animated discussion on questions of shared genealogies, cross-cultural fertilization and the role of coincidence.

It is impossible to reproduce this aspect of a conference in book form – the excitement of shared views, of hotly disputed opinions – the mortar of debate that binds the different contributions into a coherent whole. Nevertheless, even without this unifying force, it is often valuable to bring together a collection of such papers in order to present a more diverse picture of the region than would otherwise be possible. It is for this reason that the present selection of contributions has been made. The chapters included here were originally given as papers at the conference in 1987, but in a number of cases they have been somewhat reworked in the light of discussions that took place on that occasion.

The theme of 'tradition and change' is illustrated in a number of ways. The essays on literature examine various aspects of the transition from older traditions to a modern form. David Montgomery, Eden Naby and Ingeborg Baldauf look at change that is politically motivated, whereas Irena Jeziorska examines one writer's personal search for a means of integrating the past with the present, and also with the future. This study of Chingiz Aitmatov provides a revealing analysis of the way in which this highly sophisticated, 'westernized' writer draws on traditional images, and symbols and myths – Christian as well as Islamic and shamanistic – to create his artistic world.

There has been a conscious effort to direct language development in both Chinese and Soviet Central Asia. The authors of three chapters examine manifestations of these language planning policies. Ildikó Bellér-Hann traces the history of the script changes in Xinjiang and draws comparisons with similar developments in Turkey and in Soviet Central Asia; she sets these changes in a wider cultural context than that of orthography alone. Simon Crisp gives a detailed and carefully argued assessment of language affiliation in Soviet Central Asia today. His critical evaluation of census data is an important contribution to research in this field. An interesting complement to this chapter is provided by Mike Kirkwood's study of Russian language teaching policy in Soviet Central Asia. He examines the role of Russian within the school system and considers the successes and shortcomings of the policy.

Among the most fruitful areas of research in the quest for examples of 'tradition and change' are those concerned with ritual. Ewa Chylinski provides an interesting account of the modern practice of one of the most tenacious life cycle rituals, that of circumcision; she places it within the social context of the family unit. A fascinating study of the beliefs and rituals of Central Asian craftsmen is given by Zbigniew Jasiewicz. His research was carried out in Afghanistan, but, as he points out, similar practices were no doubt common among the craftsmen of what is today Soviet Central Asia in the pre-revolutionary period. His work gives a rare insight into a lost aspect of life in the modern Central Asian republics. Nancy Tapper and Richard Tapper also look at aspects of change and tradition in Afghanistan. The former considers the role of women in Afghan Turkistan among the Durrani Pashtuns, examining aspects of conformity and non-conformity. Nomadism, in the traditional sense, has disappeared from many parts of Central Asia in this century. Richard Tapper discusses the effect of this change on the Afghan nomads' sense of identity; he also looks at the relationship between settled households and nomads and shows that the distinction between them is some-times not as clear-cut as might be expected.

Innovation and tradition in sport, the arts and aspects of personal adornment are discussed by Chris Hann, Jennifer Scarce, Firuz Ashrafi and John Baily. A historical perspective is given in the last four contributions. A small but intriguing chapter of Central Asian history is that of the Baha'i community of Ashkhabad. Moojan Momen draws together a number of sources to reconstruct this extraordinary flowering of Baha'i culture in Turkmenia. Jacques Waardenburg gives a masterly survey of Islam in China and analyses western interpretations of this phenomenon; he indicates the direction that future research in this field should follow.

There are still many 'blank spots' in Central Asian history, especially on the Soviet side of the border. Alan Bodger draws attention to one, the sensitive subject of the submission of the Kazakh khans to Russian authority in the eighteenth century. Much about this period is still obscure; even today, in the new atmosphere of 'openness', it has yet to be examined in full by Kazakh scholars. Finally, Andrew Forbes looks at ethnic tensions in Xinjiang. The period under discussion is the first half of the twentieth century, the Republican period, but much of what he recounts is of relevance today.

Shirin Akiner
London, 1990

ZAYNAB AND AMAN: LOVE AND WOMEN'S LIBERATION ON A SOVIET UZBEK COLLECTIVE FARM IN THE 1930s, A STORY POEM BY HAMID ALIMJAN

David C. Montgomery

Introduction

Zaynab and Aman, a story poem written by the Uzbek poet, Hamid Alimjan, in 1938, is a noteworthy example of the inter-action between literature and politics in Soviet Uzbekistan during the 1930s. The poem uses courtship on an Uzbekistan cotton growing collective farm to lend literary support to Soviet style modernisation of a traditional Muslim society. The plot is about the efforts of a girl, Zaynab, and a young man, Aman, to have the right to choose each other as husband and wife, despite the continuing practice of arranged marriages.[1]

After Tsarist Russia had incorporated the area of Uzbekistan into its empire during the 1860s, a large measure of political and cultural autonomy was allowed. However, with the con-solidation of Soviet Russian power in the 1920s the Uzbeks were organised into their own Soviet Socialist Republic and in the following decade steadily urged towards modernisation and sovietisation through the processes of secularisation, col-lectivisation, industrialisation and education. The poem, *Zaynab and Aman*, is set during the transition period toward modernisation.

The Author

The poem was written by Hamid Alimjan, an Uzbek poet, who was born in 1909 and died in 1944 (Montgomery, 1975, pp. 492–509). The short thirty-five year life of Alimjan coincided with the fall of the Tsarist government and the rise of the Soviet regime. As a child he lived through rebellion, revolution and civil war; he grew up during the difficult years of collectivisation, industrialisation and secularisation. His adult years saw political turmoil and war.

Alimjan was born in Jizzak near the great and age-old centre of Samarkand. The household in which he grew up was presided over by his grandfather, a man of moderate means and some education. From his mother and grandmother the boy received a knowledge of Uzbek-Turkic and Tajik-Iranian folk traditions. Largely from his grandfather young Hamid received an early educational start, including a knowledge of the Russian language.

With this background young Alimjan was in a position to take full advantage of the educational opportunities offered by the new Soviet regime. In 1923, having completed basic schooling in his home town of Jizzak, he went away for higher education in Samarkand. In 1928 he completed high-school level training and in 1931, at the age of twenty-one, graduated from the Literature and Language Faculty of the Uzbek Pedagogical Academy.

While in his early teenage years Hamid Alimjan had begun to write poetry; by the age of seventeen his poems and also articles about political and social themes were regularly appearing in local publications. During his college years he became active in literary organisations. By the time of his graduation two volumes of his poetry had already been published. Much of his early poetry was on love and nature themes, but also present were many verses extolling the Soviet government and the new transformation of Uzbek life. By the 1930s Uzbek literary activity was becoming increasingly politicised. Alimjan's career progression reflects a successful blend of political conformity and timing with literary talent.

Having completed his schooling, in 1931 Alimjan went to Tashkent, the capital of Uzbekistan, where he began work as a writer for various newspapers and journals. By the mid–1930s he had established for himself a reputation for both literary talent and political astuteness; his career progressed as accused nationalist writers were denied publication opportunities and removed from positions in literary organisations. Alimjan perilously survived the 1937–38 period of the purges, which shook all segments of Soviet society. In 1939, at the age of twenty-nine, he was appointed chairman of the Union of Soviet Writers in Uzbekistan.

Despite the atmosphere of political tension during the latter half of the 1930s, these were Alimjan's most productive years. He wrote a large body of lyrical poetry about love and nature and several story poems based on folklore themes. Oral epic poetry was written down and edited for publication; Russian literature was translated into Uzbek. He wrote articles about current Soviet literature and the classical literature of Uzbekistan. The lengthy story poem, *Zaynab and Aman*, the subject of this paper, appeared in 1938.

During the Second World War Hamid Alimjan continued as head of the Uzbek Writers' Union. He produced a great number of poems in support of the war effort. He also wrote essays and stage plays. He visited the battle front as a civilian correspondent during 1943. Hamid Alimjan was killed in a Tashkent traffic accident in 1944.

Although more than forty years have passed since Alimjan's death, he continues to be considered a prominent figure in twentieth-century Uzbek literary development. His works are widely read and appreciated and have been frequently republished. Much of his production has been translated into Russian.

Alimjan and other Uzbek authors of the period had the difficult and delicate task of urging their countrymen toward accepting and understanding the Soviet-led modernisation of a traditional Muslim society. His life and works are examples of the cooperation and compromise which were necessary for career success and literary acceptance during a transitional period. He and others like him, who emerged on the side of the Soviet authorities, can be viewed from a historical perspective as being 'constructive collaborationists', whose efforts were positive in that they aided in the eventual stabilisation of social, economic and political life in Uzbekistan and thereby accelerated the pace of modernisation, which has made the

3

Uzbeks a populous and progressive nation within the Soviet Union.

Zaynab and Aman is a work of Uzbek literature which advocated social change during the transition toward modernisation.

The Story of the Poem

The plot of *Zaynab and Aman* is simple, ordinary and universal. A boy and a girl meet, fall in love, overcome obstacles and finally marry.[2] The details, to the Western reader at least, may be somewhat unusual. The story takes place on a cotton growing collective farm in Soviet Uzbekistan during the mid-1930s. Zaynab, a girl in her late teens, is a field worker on the collective farm. She is an orphan, her parents having perished, presumably in the turmoil of the civil war period, a decade before. As a child she was taken in by Anar, an old woman with no children. Zaynab worked as a chore-girl for Anar; when the village was formed into a collective farm, she also worked in the fields and attended school. Her life has been hard, but happy. She has a best girlfriend, Khuri, who is also a village resident and collective farm worker.

For the first time in her life Zaynab is in love. The object of her love is Aman, a young man on the collective farm. Aman does not know about Zaynab's love, because custom prohibits the mingling of young people. Zaynab loves Aman secretly and at a distance. Her sleepless nights are filled with thoughts of Aman. Boldly she writes a letter to him, declaring her love; then she tears it up. Often she wants to tell her stepmother, Anar, about her feelings, but hesitates; only to her girlfriend, Khuri, does she confide her love. Khuri, who knows Aman, introduces the two. Emboldened by her friend, Zaynab decides to tell her stepmother about her love for Aman.

Together with Khuri, Zaynab goes to Anar; however, before she can tell about Aman, her dreams are shattered by old Anar's announcing that the time has come to fulfil the marriage arrangements made by Zaynab's parents when she was an infant in the cradle. Zaynab had been promised to a young man named Sabir, who is away studying at the university. All of this had been unknown to Zaynab, who is struck speechless by the unexpected turn of events. However, her friend Khuri,

4

who is not at a loss for words, tries to dissuade Anar from honouring the marriage agreement; she tells about Zaynab's love for Aman. Anar becomes enraged and drives Zaynab from the household. Zaynab goes to live with Khuri.

On an evening soon afterwards, when the saddened Zaynab is strolling near the river, she meets Aman. The two for the first time have a chance to talk with each other alone. In the conversation Aman reveals his life story. He also is an orphan; his parents likewise disappeared during the turbulent period of revolution and civil war. His difficult youth toughened him, but did not embitter him; having no family with which to identify, he considers himself to be a son of the Uzbek people and a child of the collective farm. The two young people, who until this point have had separate, but similar and parallel lives, reveal their love for each other. They kiss for the first time.

The next morning Zaynab and Khuri boldly go to the house of Sabir, who recently has returned from the university. Although Sabir's parents are present, Zaynab speaks directly; she tells him about their childhood engagement and her love for Aman; she asks to be released from the betrothal. Sabir is stunned; he also did not know of the long past arrangement. Nor is he happy with the situation. He disclaims the traditional practice to his parents and asserts the right of young people to find marriage by the dictates of their own hearts. Sabir reveals that there is someone else whom he loves and releases Zaynab from the engagement.

Word about the new situation between Zaynab, Sabir and Aman rapidly spreads throughout the village. Their actions have met with approval, and a wedding is planned, which takes places in the assembly square of the collective farm. All attend. After much feasting, singing and dancing, a joyful procession conducts the newlyweds to their new home, in which, presumably, they live happily ever after.

Soviet Commentary

This simple and straightforward rural romance has been well received since it first appeared in 1938. Later commentators have called it the 'peak of Hamid Alimjan's creative achievements in the 1930s' (*Istoriya*, 1967, p. 518) and the most outstanding of his works about Soviet reality (Abdulmavlyanov 1966, p. 142). The poem has been interpreted as showing 'with great artistic expression the creation of new family relations and the victory of communist morality over remnants of the past' (*Istoriya* 1967, p. 517). The poem portrayed the very real clash between new social concepts and the traditional way of life and between the aspirations of the older and younger generations. 'The conflict between these two groups brought about the creation of a new people. There is no greater interest for the happy generation which grew up with Soviet development than interest in the people and the collective' (*Istoriya* 1967, p. 517). The poem is viewed as an illustration of the increased freedom for the individual offered by a modernised society, not only freedom of person, but also freedom of emotion. 'In our time love has found its true value. Sincerity and loyalty have triumphed in the relations between those in love, embodying humanistic efforts in the lives of a new people' (*Istoriya* 1967, p. 517). ' "Zaynab and Aman" is not just a poem about two people in love; it is a work which represents the great revolutionary power of the socialistic collective in which brotherhood, friendship and the spirit of creativity have dominion' (*Istoriya* 1967, p. 517).

Zaynab, the farm girl, is the poem's focus. To Soviet commentators she is a model and example for the new Uzbek woman: progressive, independent and hardworking. 'The poet has utilised basic and concrete facts of life, to which he has been able to give wide and general significance, having created the typical image of workers in an Uzbek collective village. . . . In the image of Zaynab are manifest many characteristics of an Uzbek Soviet woman. . . . Zaynab breaks with the old customs and disregards the prejudices of the feudal past. She struggles for the freedom and independence of the human personality. Zaynab is a person of the new world, and her victory is secured by life itself and by Soviet actuality' (Babayev 1959, p. 134). Thus, although Zaynab is only a young girl emboldened by love, her struggle and victory become a type of mini-epic. The author 'embodied in Zaynab the features of a hero of our time. The poet, in expressing his own aesthetic principles, combines the high moral qualities of the Soviet people with the spirit and make-up of the new era. . . . The poem shows the birth of a new person: richly spiritual, sensible and humane' (*Istoriya* 1967, p. 517). It is implied that the poem illustrates the correct Marxist historical development of a society. 'The unavoidable dramatic hindrances, which in these events stand in the way of the lovers, and the obstacles, which would have been insurmountable in Uzbekistan just a quarter of a century ago, now have fallen, shattered by the push of life, just as an old mud wall falls under the action of the sun and the rain.' (Babayev, 1959, p. 134).

Briefly, with respect to comparative literature, this poetic work, which shows the clash of generations and traditional and modern values, as well as great emotional feeling, is linked with both the classical Russian authors and with the classical literature of the Muslim East. The theme of social conflict is one of 'fathers and sons', an obvious reference to the novel by Turgenev (Abdulmavlyanov 1966, p. 143). The poem *Zaynab and Aman* is 'an example of the fruitful synthesis of the traditions of Russian literature and classical oriental poetry. Hamid Alimjan, who translated Pushkin's "Prisoner of the Caucasus" [into Uzbek], finds a source of artistic inspiration in the romantic poems of Pushkin and Lermontov, which have romantic perceptions of the Orient with their lyrical feelings about nature and love romantics. While reading Zaynab's letter to Aman, we recall . . . the letter of Tatyana to Onegin and also the love letters of Shirin and Layla (heroines of Iranian and Arab legends) to their beloveds. This fertile synthesis is a characteristic phenomenon for the best achievements of Uzbek poetry in the Soviet epoch and most of all for the poetry of Hamid Alimjan' (Babayev 1959, p. 133).

A History of the Poem

Hamid Alimjan's poetic presentation about the progress of Soviet Uzbek women is, of course, not unique. Other Uzbek authors of the same period also dealt with the theme, which was of sincere concern to the government. Literary attention to the role and status of Uzbek women pre-dated the Soviet period, when a progressive Muslim group in Russian Turkistan, the Jaddidists, were dealing with the topic (Allworth 1964, pp. 31–40).

With regard to Hamid Alimjan's other works up to 1938, when *Zaynab and Aman* appeared, the poem is a dovetailing of two themes, rural development and the status of women, about which he had been writing for a decade. Rural development is the theme of a series of lengthy poems which had been written by him since the early 1930s.[3] In each of these poems the shortcomings of the past are contrasted with developments during the Soviet period. None of them are of such a specific story nature as is *Zaynab and Aman*. While yet a teenager, Alimjan had begun to write poems about the changing roles of women in society. Several such poems had been produced prior to *Zaynab and Aman*.[4] Women also had been given increased status in folklore-type productions.[5]

Zaynab and Aman is based on a real person. In 1935 a collective farm worker, Zaynab Amanova, was awarded the Order of Lenin for her self-sacrificing labour during the cotton harvest (Babayev, 1959, p. 132). Her story was written in a prose narrative by Alimjan and published in 1937 (Olimjon 1972, p. 69). The real Zaynab was married to a man named Aman.

The poem not only incorporates themes and subjects about which Alimjan had written previously, but also contains many passages quite similar to poems which he had written before. Thus, Soviet commentators correctly say, 'The poem "Zaynab and Aman" is the synthesis and peak of Hamid Alimjan's creative work in the 1930s' (*Istoriya* 1967, p. 518). 'It seemingly incorporates into itself the ideas and motifs in many of his preceding poems; in it are disclosed the most treasured thoughts and feelings of the poet; they receive their own artistic embodiment, the ultimate stamp of form to which his poetry always strove' (Abdulmavlyanov 1966, p. 142).

After its first publication in 1938 the poem has been republished in Uzbek many times up to the present (Olimjon 1979, p. 131). In 1943 the poem was translated into Russian for distribution to both civilians and soldiers. It was immediately popular; in many ways it was a welcome contrast to the usual patriotic literature of the war years; it was 'not about war heroics, but full of the light and happiness of prewar Uzbekistan' (Allworth 1964, p. 205). The Russian translation was republished in 1971 and perhaps even more recently (Alimjan 1971, p. 208). In 1958 the Uzbek poetess, Zulfiya, Alimjan's widow, used the text of the poem as the basis for the libretto of an opera by the same name, thus even more establishing

Zaynab and Aman as a popular work of Uzbek Soviet literature (Baybekova 1963, p. 233).

An Analysis of the Topic and Contents

Zaynab and Aman describes in a poetic manner the triumph of modernism over traditionalism and the triumph of youth and reason over intransigent and repressive customs. The poem's specific theme of rights and status for women was a valid issue in the mid-1930s. Since Soviet power had been established in Central Asia during the early 1920s several laws had been promulgated to raise the status of women in society, and a vigorous propaganda campaign on behalf of women had been conducted. The veil had been banned; bride prices and the seclusion of women were discouraged; education was made available; women were allowed to vote and hold responsible work and administrative positions outside of the household. Nevertheless, change was slow, and laws did not rapidly become the lifestyle.

Alimjan was a realist when he discussed conditions in the countryside. He recognised that even though the Soviet regime had brought about major political and economic changes, it had not been as effective in the area of social relationships. Many old ways persisted; among them was the status of women. Alimjan in most of his works demonstrated an admiration and respect for many aspects of the historical and cultural traditions of Uzbekistan. He was, however, a modernist, who felt that there could be a selective continuity of the past. Alimjan realistically recognised the dominant position of the Russians in the modern world as it was presented to him. But, politically minded as he was, he was not a 'Russianiser'. On the other hand, despite his great love for the Uzbek land, he was not a nationalist; he can best be classed as a 'sovietiser'.

Alimjan tactfully presented the problem and the solution. Though the poem was written during a period of political turmoil, when both careers and lives were often at stake, and many writers, including Alimjan, often were slavishly producing politically motivated works praising the Revolution, Lenin, Stalin and the Communist Party, *Zaynab and Aman* is for all practical purposes a totally apolitical poem, at least on the surface. The poem is devoid of any ideological rhetoric; there

9

is no mention of Communism or Marxism-Leninism; though the action occurs on a collective farm, collectivisation was already a fact of recent history. As much as is revealed in the poem, the basis for Zaynab's actions in acting contrary to the traditional ways are the promptings of the heart and the mind. She is a young girl emboldened by love, not a pushy *Komsomolka* or representative from the *Zhenotdel* armed with the ideology and the power of the state.

Much as Alimjan presents a humanistic solution to the problem of making dreams of love come true, he also presents a national, or better stated — ethnic, cast of characters. All figures are Uzbeks; there are no Russians in the poem; neither is Russia nor the Soviet Union mentioned. Though Zaynab is the heroine, and Aman is the hero, there is neither a villain, nor even a real negative character. Stepmother Anar, despite the fact that she has used Zaynab more as a servant than as a daughter and attempted to block her love for Aman, is nevertheless presented sympathetically; she herself is not bad and also had suffered from an arranged marriage. Only the way of life which she is attempting to maintain is bad. Thus is presented a tactful exculpation for those yet adhering to the old ways.

The heroine Zaynab is a model young Soviet woman. She is modest in her conduct. She is literate. She receives great satisfaction from working in the fields of the collective farm. Aman, the hero, has similar characteristics. Sabir, the childhood fiancé of Zaynab, is also a positive character; not only does he nobly release Zaynab from the engagement, but he is one who is destined to become one of the newly emerging rural intelligentsia; he is a student of agricultural science. The combination of his urban acquired modern skills (learned from the unmentioned Russians) with the land-rooted virtues of hard-working collective farm workers such as Zaynab and Aman will build a new Uzbekistan.

An issue which the author does avoid, however, is that of family ties, which are very strong among the Uzbeks. Perhaps Sabir, a lesser character, could act contrary to his parents' wishes, but such would not be appropriate for Zaynab and Aman, who are intended to be totally positive figures. By having both be orphans, some difficult issues are avoided. On the other hand, in this way each is possibly more representative of the new Soviet citizen without strong ties to the encumbering past. As stated above, Aman styles himself a son of the Uzbek people and the collective farm, a wedding of old and new.

Alimjan acknowledges that innovation and change can be misunderstood. As in many areas of the world what is contrary to traditions is associated with immorality. Thus, when Zaynab tells about her love for Aman, her stepmother shouts in a rage, 'You no-good! Here, this is the attitude you've acquired at this collective farm. This is the work you did during the summer. You found a lover for yourself! Shameless one! in my own family, a loose woman. That you should so shame yourself in front of people. Ach, strumpet, wretch, animal!' . . . 'Who is he, this damned devil who slept in your embrace?'

The author is somewhat inconsistent when he portrays the repressive influence of the traditional ways. Early in the poem Zaynab fears to reveal her love for Aman, lest the people condemn her for immorality. Yet at the end, when their love has been revealed, and old customs have been put aside, everyone seems to approve.

The Islamic religion is presented as a crushing burden of the past, particularly for women. The women's section of the household is an area where 'following grey-haired custom, the *sura* (chapter of the *Koran*) ruled over the heart.' The prophet Muhammad is portrayed in a negative light with regard to his child bride; he 'took Aysha to wife when she was nine years old, and since then the prophet's decree controls the whole world under the crescent (of Islam).'

Not only religion specifically, but also all the old ways, which kept women in a repressed social status, are bad. Zaynab's confrontation with the past is ominously presented. 'The black and evil raven of the old ways pulled Zaynab to itself. It flew at her like a night phantom to plunge its claws into her heart, peck out her living eyes and to decide her fate in the old way.' 'A past age, when carefree and proud man was pitiless and lawless, when pretty girls did not dare to open their almond shaped eyes. . . . The past, forgotten in some crack, now and then throws itself at us. Zaynab did not guess and did not know, that somewhere behind her back the past was spinning a net for her and was preparing another path

11

for her, and that someone, against her wish, had already decided her fate, and that the old custom would cause so much new suffering.'

The dark forces of the past were overcome. By the strength of love and a sense of her heartfelt individual rights Zaynab was able to achieve her goal, thus becoming a model for the youth of her time and for those of the following years.

Conclusion

The continuing popularity of Hamid Alimjan's *Zaynab and Aman* is in part based on the fact that, though a politically desirable goal of modernisation is achieved in the end, it is accomplished in a non-political manner. Also in large part the poem's popularity can be attributed to the literary craft of the author. Word, rhythm and rhyme are skilfully and charmingly combined into descriptions of the countryside, of personalities and of emotions. The message of the poem is not unique, but the presentation has given to it a singular quality and effectiveness.

Notes

1 This chapter has its origin in a paper of similar title which was presented at the annual meeting of the Western Conference of the Association for Asian Studies; Tempe, Arizona; 6 December, 1974. Since that time the author has resided in Uzbekistan on two occasions for a total of six months (1977/1978 and 1982). Each experience not only gave to him an increased understanding of Uzbek life, but also additional literary sources.

2 The present discussion of the poem is based on the Uzbek language version found in Olimjon, Hamid. *Besh tomlik asarlar majmuasi: ikkinchi tom — balladalar, poemalar, tarjima.* Tashkent, 1971. The initial 1974 version was based on a Russian language translation found in Alimdzhan, Khamid. *Stikhi o lyubimoi zemle.* Moscow, 1944.

3 'Shakhimardon' (1932), 'The valley of happiness' (1932), 'The life of an old man' (1934).

4 'The village girl' (1927), 'The Komsomol girl' (1927), 'Sharafat' (late 1920s), 'Bakhri' (1935), 'The story of two girls' (1935–1937), 'The girl' (mid–1930s); the latter is about the first Uzbek woman parachutist, Basharat Mirbabayeva.

5 For example, in 'Aygul and Bakhtiyar' (1937), which is about a slave rebellion, a girl, Aygul, plays a leadership role.

References

Abdulmavlyanov J A and Babakhanov A A (1966), *Istoriya uzbekskoi literatury*. Tashkent.

Alimdzhan Kh (1944), *Stikhi o lyubimoi zemle*. Moscow.

Alimdzhan Kh (1971), *Izbrannye proizvedeniya*. Tashkent.

Allworth E (1964), *Uzbek Literary Politics*. Mouton, The Hague.

Babayev E G (1959), *'Put' poeta'*, *Voprosy uzbekskoi literatury*. Tashkent, pp. 120–44.

Bacon E (1966), *Central Asians under Russian Rule*. Cornell, Ithaca.

Baybekova F, Sultanova M, Nosirova M and Alimhujayeva M (1963), *Özbek adabiyoti (1940–1958) — bibliografiya*. Tashkent.

Istoriya . . . (1967), *Istoriya uzbekskoi sovetskoi literatury*. Moscow.

Montgomery D C 'Hamid Alimjan (1909–1944): a Soviet Uzbek poet and publicist', *Canadian Slavonic Papers* Vol. 17, nos. 2 & 3, pp. 492–509.

Olimjon H (1971), *Besh tomlik asarlar majmuasi: ikkinchi tom — balladalar, poemalar, tarjima*. Tashkent.

Olimjon H (1979), *Mukammal asarlar töplami: ikkinchi tom — balladalar, dostonlar, she' riikhat*. Tashkent.

2

UIGHUR LITERATURE: THE ANTECEDENTS

Eden Naby

With the administrative division of the population of Central Asia into ethnic groupings during the early twentieth century, much energy was devoted to the development of separate cultures for the major ethnic groups living in the area. Although most of the groups fall within the Turkic language family, smaller groups such as Iranians and Mongols faced similar problems. The chief problem to be resolved stemmed from the common underpinnings of local culture which were strongly influenced by religion. For the Turkic and Iranian peoples of the area, the religious influence on culture was Islamic and therefore tied closely to general Middle Eastern culture. Additionally, educated persons of sedentary Turkic culture were steeped in Persian literature. Thus sedentary Turkic cultures, from those of the Azerbaijanis to the Uzbeks to the Uighurs faced a twofold problem: to extract Turkic culture from Iranian culture, and at the same time, create separate Turkic contemporary cultures. Added to these formidable problems arose a third: how to deal with the antecedents to contemporary culture. In this chapter I would like to examine the case of the Uighurs in China who, having passed through several cultural phases, have established the structure for the development of a modern literature and have now begun the task of gathering together the antecedents to that literature.

Specifically, the Uighurs have shared a long and close relationship with what is today Uzbek culture. In order to create antecedents, Uighurs need to decide how much of that shared culture to admit and how much of it to claim as being exclusively Uighur. As this kind of problem is common to the entire Central Asian area, by studying Uighur literature I hope

14

to provide some insight into the mechanisms and choices that are made as well as their results.

The study will be based on Uighur materials, both from Urumchi and from provincial areas, as well as interviews. Comparisons with developments among the Tajiks and Uzbeks will be drawn where parallels are significant.

Models for Literary Antecedents

At various times during the period of transition from traditional into the mainstream of nationally oriented world cultures, among all of the various officially recognised ethnolinguistic cultures of Central Asia stocktaking of the past has occurred. Setting aside the entire issue of revisionist history and ideology, the process of stocktaking and assessing the value of the past literary tradition has led to periodisation of literary history. Certainly political justification has entered into periodisation but this approach has not provided the main impetus for periodisation. Rather, the impetus has come from a genuine attempt to distinguish that part of the past which was held in common among all Central Asians from that part that provided the specific background for the particular recognised group in existence today.

In the twentieth century, three Central Asian ethno-linguistic groups, all with traditional sedentary cultures, have emerged as demographically, politically and culturally important. These are the Uzbeks — 13 million in the USSR mainly living in their own Republic but also in the Tajik SSR, the Tajiks — about two million living in their own Republic and in the Uzbek SSR, and the Uighurs of China's largest administrative area, the Xinjiang Uighur Autonomous Region.

By virtue of their early administrative organisation into nationality units under the Soviet regime, cultural leaders in West Central Asia embarked on the process of establishing their cultural links with the past and periodising that past earlier than those in the east or even the south. Tajiks and Uzbeks, belonging to Iranian and Turkic linguistic groups were among the first to embark on setting the parameters for their cultural antecedents and creating sets of politically acceptable pasts.[1] However many times the ideologically acceptable version of past cultural heroes may have been modified in succeeding years, the publication of Abdur Rauf Fitrat's *Eng Eski Turk Adabiyati Namunalari: Adabiyatimiz Tarikhi Uchun Materyallar* ('Specimens of the Oldest Literature of the Turks: Materials for our Literary History') (Tashkent-Samarkand, 1927) and Sadriddin Aini's *Namuna-i Adabiyat-i Tajik* ('Specimens of Tajik Literature') in three volumes, Moscow, 1926, established the overall model for exploration of the cultural past.[2] A third possible model, Fitrat's *Ozbek Adabiyati Namunalari* ('Specimens of Uzbek Literature'), cited in Edward Allworth's *Uzbek Literary Politics*, followed Aini's publication by two years. Yet it proved extremely controversial and is now not readily available.[3]

In the works here examined, the editors list the writers or anonymous works that form part of their respective cultural traditions. They approach their task with two basic premises: that language is the most important determinant of whether the work or writer belongs in the cultural tradition, and that whether the work or writer lived within the geographical boundaries of the present national territory is immaterial to his or its being part of the tradition. Exceptions to these premises arise in the case of writers who were born in the present national territory but wrote elsewhere and those who either wrote in a language other than their mother tongue or in two languages, usually a Turkic one and Persian. The question of whether the work had been a recognised part of the culture over past centuries by the people, elite or common, did not seem to affect inclusion. Moreover, when compiling their trend-setting anthologies or specimens, both Fitrat and Aini were concerned with written, high culture rather than with oral or folk literature. Thus for example, Fitrat includes the *Kutadgu Bilig* ('Auspicious Knowledge'), a didactic work written about 1069 in the Kashgar area by a man from Balasaghun (location north of the Syr Darya), as well as Mahmud al-Kashqari's *Divan-e Lughat-e Turk* ('Collection of Turkic Dialects').[4] In the same manner, Aini includes in his array of Tajik literary antecedents not only Ali Shir Nawa'i (born and buried in Herat)[5] but also writers such as Kamaluddin Khojandi, a fourteenth-century poet born in Khojand but living mainly in Tabriz and Saray.[6]

The necessity to create a separate heritage for each recognised ethno-linguistic group has resulted in claims that must bow to the shared culture of all Central Asians. For political reasons that have been more or less strongly enunciated in the past, especially in Stalinist USSR, the explicit statement of shared culture has had to be muted. Just as in European cultural history Greek and Latin literary works naturally serve as the antecedents of French, English, German and other cultures, so the cultural heritage of Central Asia must include the great literary monuments, from within the region as well as without that influenced its development. The distortion in the process of tracing the heritage occurs when political parameters limit inquiry and alter historical reality. Soviet Central Asians, especially during the early 1920s when military and political priorities dictated Moscow's attitudes toward culture, labored under two specific limitations on intellectual inquiry. First, they had to tread carefully to avoid accusations of political deviation stemming from advocacy of any of the various pan-movements viewed as subversive (pan-Islamic, pan-Turkic, pan-Turanian).[7] Second, they had to discuss past culture in terms of the then emerging nationality structure.[8]

Fitrat divides his *Specimens of the Oldest Literature of the Turks* into three parts. In a lengthy introduction he discusses the various theories of the divisions among Turkic people. For our purposes, of interest is the view that the language of the Central Asians falls into the same category: he defines Central Asians as Sarts, Uzbeks, and Taranchis.[9] In today's political Soviet terminology, the first two have merged together as Uzbek, and the Taranchis are called Uighur-speaking. Thus, Fitrat recognised contemporary Uzbek and Uighur literature as belonging to the same tradition and linguistic grouping. On the basis of this introduction, the author takes the well-known monuments of Turkic literature and analyses them in terms that would make them appealing and useful to his contemporaries.

While this first work may be viewed as scholarship that reinforced Turkic nationalism, Fitrat's second work *Specimens of Uzbek Literature* opened him for attack as a nationalist. Yet this work follows in style and format the anthology published by Aini in 1926. Aini was lauded for his work, while Fitrat was denigrated. It is not our purpose here to examine the reasons why nor to make a comparison of the Tajik with the Uzbek anthology. Rather, we want to examine the possible motivation for the creation of the anthologies and their effects on cultural pride and consciousness in order to draw some lessons for the Uighur anthologies.

Aini's *Specimens of Tajik Literature* covers the entire time span of Persian literature beginning with Rudaki. Unlike the Uighur anthology, he does not confine himself to 'classical' authors but provides samples through to the 1920s. He includes in his list of over 300 poets, both Turkic and Iranian poets, as long as the works were in Persian. As a bilingual author himself, Aini accepted multilingualism as the condition of sedentary literary creation in Central Asia. Ali Shir Nawa'i, the fifteenth-century poet-statesman of Timurid Herat, holds a place in Aini's anthology as he does in Turkic anthologies (of Uzbeks and Uighurs) but here he is almost dwarfed by the great classical Persian writers of which he is the Turkic examplar. Collected from the many *tadhkira*'s ('anthologies') private and public libraries of Samarkand, Bukhara and elsewhere, Aini enriched what he called Tajik literature with the writings of all but the most clearly Iranian (from Iran) writers. He did not include in this heritage Sa'adi and Hafiz (of Shiraz) for reasons that have yet to be explained. He does include other important mystical poets such as Jami (of Herat) and even a contemporary Iranian, Abul Qasem-e Lahuti.[10]

Having discussed elsewhere the problem of separating Tajik culture from Uzbek and Iranian,[11] the purpose in discussing Aini is to focus on the model that his anthology set for related nationality cultures of the area. Aini contributed in two ways to the creation of a pattern for claiming antecedents for a culture: first he included every writer who wrote in Persian within the wide radius of Central Asia. Second, to the extent possible, he set each writer within a socio-economic context and by selecting examples of their work that documented any social concerns of the writers, he lent legitimacy (in proleterian-oriented critics' eyes) to the value of the past Tajik culture. Having explained these two reasons however, one must also recall that Tajiks in Central Asia have formed the means of dividing a possibly threatening Turkic population. Thus the critic's focus was rarely the Tajik intellectual but rather the Uzbek intellectual from whom dangerous nationalist tendencies were expected. While Aini's anthology set a precedent, it could not necessarily be imitated in other communities with impunity: this lesson was made clear in the case of the Uzbeks with the treatment meted to Fitrat.

As a corollary, claims to literary works that fall outside the language group of the claimant nationality (but inside its territory) have led to the necessity of translation of original works into the language of the claimant nationality.

Establishing antecedents to their written literary culture has created for Central Asians an entire set of problems that raises questions of the validity of separation of cultures, the identification of languages and the naming of the languages of various periods, as well as the problem of making the language of the past relevant and readable to present generations. Political ideology as well as international friction add further complexity to the problem.

Establishing the Uighur Literary Antecedents

With the example of how the two leading west Central Asian sedentary cultures have attacked the issue of creating antecedents to their literary cultures, we now turn to the remaining major sedentary culture of Central Asia, that of the Uighurs. Uighurs are the major eastern extension of the Turkic-speaking people and form the major Turkic population of China. To the roughly seven million living in China may be added another 220,000 scattered in and around Alma Ata, Frunze and Tashkent who have settled in the Soviet Union as refugees from China. As a recognised nationality of certain political significance in the Sino-Soviet border dispute, Soviet Uighurs enjoy some opportunity for cultural autonomy. Their importance to this study lies in the insights that comparing Soviet Uighur treatment of the cultural heritage with that of the Uighurs in China provide.[12]

In examining Uighur literary heritage studies, I have relied on two works of recent publication without, in this study, attempting to trace the historical development of the heritage issue during the entire Communist period since 1949 or drawing comparisons with the period of the 1930s. In fact, the 1930s would provide a political background more comparable to the period in which the two works (by Fitrat and Aini) mentioned above were produced. It was in the 1930s that cultural divisions among local inhabitants of Chinese Central Asia were introduced in a bid to transfer Soviet nationality policy eastward.[13] Nonetheless, the dearth of available Uighur publications from the 1930s and the intervening political dislocations caused by secessionist movements and the imposition of Communist Chinese rule in Xinkiang make the contemporary period the only time of relative calm, in recent history, that allows the opportunity for Uighurs to produce cultural materials.

The chief Uighur work that parallels the anthology of Fitrat here examined is the compilation *Qadimi Uighur Yazma Yadgarliqlardin Tallanma* ('A Collection of Ancient Uighur Written Remains') published in Urumchi in 1984.[14] The work is compiled by three Uighurs trained in Beijing (Abiduqayum Khoja, Tursun Ayup and Israpil Yusup) and appears in a large printing of 12,400 copies. Included in the 417 pages are descriptions and translations beginning with the Orkhon inscriptions down through Manichaean, Buddhist and Nestorian religious writings, as well as discussions of the origins of the Oghuz Nama, especially the thirteenth-century Turpan manuscript of which the only known copy in the Uighur script is at the Bibliotheque Nationale.

The orientation of the compilers is historically linguistic. They are competent in analysis of the pre-Islamic Uighur alphabet (based on Aramaic through a Sogdian intermediary) that was in use for eastern Turkic from the ninth through the seventeenth century.[15] Other than a few photo reproductions of inscriptions and scrolls, no original facsimiles are produced in this book. Instead, the editors have transcribed the original materials into the contemporary Uighur alphabet. In providing line-by-line translations of samples of various written remains, the editors apparently have in mind the literate Uighur lay person who, prior to this work, had no single available source of information about the Uighur cultural heritage in his own language. To interest their audience in the transcriptions, the editors have painstakingly worked out an extensive (48-page) glossary of terms. Interestingly, other than facsimiles or originals of the ancient works, the editors relied only on Chinese authors writing on these subjects. None of the extensive Western analysis on this subject was apparently available, possibly for linguistic reasons.

The second Uighur anthology aimed at introducing the past literary heritage to contemporary Uighurs parallels the anthology of Aini for the Soviet Tajik heritage. *Uighur Klasik Adabiyatidin Namunalar* ('Specimens from Classical Uighur Literature') was published in Urumchi in 1981. It is among the first publications to appear during the politically relaxed period in recent Chinese history. Its influence may be measured in part by the large first issue (25,000) and by the fact that it can be seen even in village homes.[16] The compilers of the work, Tiyipjan Aliyop and Rahmitulla Jari, provide a ten-page introduction (penned by Jari), brief introductions to seventeen authors or works, and samples of the writing that are accompanied by translation into the contemporary literary vernacular. All of the writing, whether from the widely known eleventh-century *Divan-e Lughat-e Turk* or lyrical verse from the nineteenth-century poet Tajalli, appear in the officially sanctioned modified Arabic alphabet of today.

The *Uighur Klassik* . . . differs from the *Qadimi Uighur* . . . in that it includes works that have been a part of the living tradition of Uighurs. These works are all from the Islamic period. Unlike the Orkhon inscriptions or Buddhist cave scrolls, the literate and even many among the non-literate are familiar with the forms and the content of the writing. Contemporary writers often write in the same *'arudh* (prosody) mold and the images and metaphors of the Islamic past form the main base of present culture. From their reference in the introduction to the harmful influence of the 'Gang of Four',[17] the editors apparently wish to restore to legitimacy not only pride in Uighur culture but also individual writers who criticised the Chinese conquest of Central Asia. Inclusion of Mulla Bilal (1823–99), and in particular, mention of his work *Kitab-e Ghazat dar Mulk-e Chin* ('The Book of Rebellion in China'), based partially on his own experiences as participant in the 1867 rebellion against the Chinese, marks the legitimisation of this author for Uighurs in China.[18] The mention of his book on the 1867 rebellion (associated with the short-lived independent state led by Ya'qub Beg [d. 1876]) has opened the way for the future publication of this book in China, access to which had long been denied to Uighur scholars. Interestingly, this work has been available in the West since it was published by N. N. Pantusov.[19]

Literary histories abound in every modern western culture with a literary tradition. In non-western cultures however, they are a hallmark of national consciousness, if not in the sense of political consciousness, then certainly as indicators of cultural separateness (and equality or superiority). Given the unimportance of nationalism among politically uninvolved people in traditional Muslim culture, the scramble to establish national cultural turf may be taken as both an indication of the cultural significance of the administrative division of Central Asian people and a reaction against the chauvinism of the politically empowered majority. Put simply, Uighurs, Tajiks and Uzbeks have needed to justify their cultural autonomy and the value of the continuation of their language and literary traditions by pointing to a rich past. For this reason alone, the anthologies have circulated widely. As in the case of the Tajiks, the Uighur anthologies, particularly the one on the Islamic period, set the parameters for what legitimately can be included in Uighur literary culture. Classroom texts and literary analysis together with the whole range of cultural activities that arise from a literary base such as drama, opera, ballet, historical novels, anniversary celebrations, the naming of buildings, streets, institutions and so forth stems from establishing a cultural heritage. For examples of how entire cultural structures can be built on an established literary base, we need only look at Uzbekistan, Tajikistan and to some extent also Iran and Pakistan. That Afghanistan had not been able to draw together an agreed upon cultural heritage made up of the combined cultures of the major traditions of the area, Persian, Pushtu as well as Turkic, probably hindered national consciousness as much as any other social and political factor.[20]

The Periodisation of Literature

The editors of the anthologies here examined, together with most literary historians, organise content chronologically. Periodisation of literature, however, means taking one step beyond simple chronology to separate literary production into sections that relate to political and social history. Moreover, in such works milestones in literary history do not simply receive more space and praise, but are accompanied by discussions of the reasons and circumstances under which certain milestones were produced and their effects.

Although periodisation originally developed under Hegelian

22

and especially Marxist ideas for historical development, the acceptance of the significance of major shifts in societal paradigms has come into general practice. Broadly speaking, the high literature of the Muslim people has been periodised traditionally into pre-Islamic, Islamic and now also modern or contemporary, meaning secular literature. The rationale for this pattern of periodisation lies in the fact that the spread of Islam brought with it two elements basic to subsequent literary output: Arabic prosody (*'arudh*) and the Arabic alphabet. Modified though both elements were in the Iranian and Turkic linguistic context, nonetheless, they formed the basis of high literature for the millenium following the spread of Islam. Reluctant to accept religion as the basis for periodisation, Soviet-oriented scholars of Central Asian literature have either retained simple chronology or they have introduced periodisation based on fairly artificial factors. Complicating the study of Uzbek, Tajik and Uighur culture has been the attempt to project on the historical period current political ethnic divisions. Thus, in Soviet sources, we have the use of a whole series of terms, associated with periodisation, that are clearly artificial. These include 'old Uzbek' for Chagatay, and the 'Uighur-Karluq,' and 'old Uighur' (as opposed to ancient Uighur, a widely accepted term for the pre-Islamic language) for the language (and dialects) locally known simply as 'Turki' on the east and west sides of the Tien Shan throughout the Islamic period.[21] Indeed the use of the term Uighur for the current language of the sedentary Turkic population of Xinjiang is a direct creation of Russian scholars and administrators in Tashkent in 1921 when other ethno-linguistic designations were being made.[22]

Unlike Aini's anthology of Tajik literature which, in chronological fashion, and much like the *'tadhkira'*s of traditional Muslim society, mentions poems by certain contemporary writers, the editors of the Uighur anthology pick and choose even among the wide range of authors from which they could draw. Very useful is the biographical account provided for each author. The Uighur anthology treats seventeen topics, sixteen of them authors and one, the *Oghuz namah*, an anonymous work. The following is a list of the writers, their dates and the town or region with which they are associated:

	Name	Date	Place
1	Mahmud al-Kashqari	(11th C.)	
2	Yusup Khas Hajip	(11th C.)	
3	Ahmad [ibn Mahmud] Yugnaki	(12th–13th C.)	
(4	the Oghuz namah)		
5	Ata'i	(15th C.)	Herat or Balkh
6	Sakkaki	(14th–15th C.)	
7	Lutpi*	(15th C.)	Maveralnahr
8	Ali Shir Nawa'i*	(1441–1501)	Herat
9	Mohammad Amin Khirqati	(1634–1724)	
10	Zalili	(17th–18th C.)	Southern Xinjiang
11	Nowbati	(18th C.)	Khotan
12	Abid ur Rahman Nizari	(1770–1840)	Kashqar
13	Qalandar	(19th C.)	Khotan
14	Gumnam	(19th C.)	Kashqar
15	Amir Hussein Suburi	(18th–19th C.)	Kashqar
16	Mulla Bilal	(1823–1899)	Khulja
17	Tajalli	(1850–1930)	Qaghliq

* indicated to be bilingual in 'Uighur' (not Uzbek or Turki) and Persian.

All of the writers up to and including Ali Shir Nawa'i appear as antecedents of the separate Uighur and Uzbek literatures. The notable exception to this pattern emerges in the claimed antecedents to *Soviet* Uighur literature, where, in apparent deference to the sensibilities of the powerful Uzbeks, Nawa'i is deleted from the Uighur heritage.[23] After Nawa'i, a breaking away of the joint tradition into two parts may be observed.

The editors of the Uighur anthology do not attempt to explain or take note of any sharing with the Uzbeks of any of this past. They also appear oblivious to the fact that, with the exception of the first two writers, al-Kashqari and Hajip, the others appear to have made their home in areas other than Xinjiang. Nor do Uzbek accounts of the claimed heritage care to attempt explanations of such facts that might entangle them in questions of the common heritage of the two major sedentary Turkic people. That Nawa'i, clearly the star of the anthologies, lived in present-day Afghanistan appears to be no obstacle to his dominant position in both Uighur and Uzbek literary histories. In fact, he is claimed as being within the heritage of even the Afghans and the Tajiks despite the fact that his best poetry was written in 'Turki' and his lesser poetry in Persian (under the pen-name of Fani).[24]

Why is Nawa'i such a dramatic turning point in the perception of the development of four major Central Asian literary cultures? Some of the explanation is certainly historical. After Nawa'i, the coming of the Uzbeks to Transoxiania (sixteenth century) marks a break in much of the unity of the area, both cultural and political. The competing Timurids are swept away and replaced by an essentially tribal and partly nomadic, but mainly unPersianised ruling clique. Moreover, because of the cleavage with Safavid Iran over the issue of Shi'ism, the cultural unity of the area also became upset. Although bilingualism in Persian and Turki continued among urban dwellers, the deciding political role of the Uzbeks plus the diminished cultural role of Iran reduces the role of Persian in Central Asia.

Part of the answer to the pivotal role of the poet certainly lies in his own achievements. The conviction of his contemporaries and followers as well as popular perception held that Nawa'i elevated Turki into a literary language. He made composing in Turki respectable. Thus Turki could aspire to compete with Persian in the area of high literature. Coupled with the emerging political dominance of the Uzbeks and their eventual sedentarisation, the high literary niche created for Turki by Nawa'i accounts for what appears to be the beginning of the separation between Persian and Turki culture.

Whatever the answer to questions about the change after the fifteenth century, it is clear that from the period following the age of Nawa'i the three sedentary cultures of Central Asia follow different paths. Tajik literature relies more heavily upon exchange with the Moghul Persian culture of India; Uzbek literature, after a lapse of some decades, re-emerges as a religiously pre-occupied literature with a minor bilingual strain, and Uighur literature appears to lapse into its own reverie, drawing on its own regional resources. After the forcible relocation of many Uighurs from the south to the Khulja area by the Chinese in the eighteenth century, a new Uighur culture emerges from this nomad-dominated area as well, as represented by Mulla Bilal.

The last entry in the Uighur anthology, that of Tajalli, marks the beginning of another drastic change. For with Tajalli we see the commencement of the introduction of technology even into East Turkestan and the effect of this on culture. Tajalli benefited from three 'modernising' factors: he was able to attend modern schools in India, he benefited from increased travel opportunities, possibly by train, and he was even able to see his works printed, albeit on lithograph presses, in the Kashqar of the turn of the century.[25] These increased opportunities resulted in bringing out some of those attributes of the writers of Central Asia of the time of Nawa'i and before: Tajalli wrote poetry in four languages (Uighur, Arabic, Persian and Hindustani), he was read in west Turkestan as well as East Turkestan, and he was a scientist. His works were published in Tashkent where they appeared under the pen-name 'Ayar'.[26] He died in 1930, the year in which major political and cultural changes began in Xinjiang.

For the editors of the Uighur anthology, the classical period has three turning points: the commencement of Islamic Uighur literature with the *Divan-e Lughat-e Turk*, the widespread use of Arabic prosody models for the local language, a trend that culminates with Nawa'i, and the turning toward international literary models, especially through the adoption of the prose genre after the 1930s. While it is clear from the catalogue of Uighur manuscripts published in 1957[27] in China that the sixteen poets included in this anthology do not represent the entire spectrum of classical Uighur literary accomplishment, nonetheless, the editors have offered a glimpse into the little known history of their own literary heritage. In its own modest way, the anthology of classical Uighur Literature serves to encourage preservation of a distinct Uighur culture while at the same time drawing attention to those parts of the culture that are held in common with the other major Turkic culture of the area.

Notes

1 For English language studies of Tajiks see Jiri Becka, 'Tajik Literature from the 16th century to the Present', in *History of Iranian Literature* ed. Jan Rypka (Dordrecht, Holland, 1968) pp. 483–606 and Ibrahim V. Pouhadi, 'Soviet Tajik Literature', *Middle East Journal* no. 20, 1966 pp. 104–114. For similar studies of Uzbek literature see Edward Allworth's *Uzbek Literary Politics* (The Hague, 1964).

2 Cited in Edward Allworth, *Nationalities of the Soviet East: Publications*

and Writing Systems (New York, 1971). All three volumes may now be found at the Library of Congress, Washington, D. C.

3 Allworth (1964) pp. 53–55, 83.

4 Abdur Rauf Fitrat, in his *Eng Eski Turk Adabiyati Namunalari: Adabiyatimiz Tarikhi Uchun Materyallar* (Tashkent-Samarkand, 1927), draws on both these authors for examples of vocabulary, etc.

5 Sadriddin Aini, *Namuna-i Adabiyat-i Tajik* (3 vols.) (Moscow, 1926), p. 96.

6 Aini, p. 47.

7 Fitrat was among the intellectuals who was attacked in the press for pan-Turkism and Uzbek nationalism and disappeared in the 1930s.

8 For the problem of reconciling the past with proletarian ideals, see Allworth (1964), pp. 48–55.

9 Fitrat, p. 4–5.

10 Aini, p. 1887.

11 See my two articles, 'Tajik and Uzbek Nationality Identity: the Non-Literary Arts', in *The Nationality Question in Soviet Central Asia,* ed. Edward Allworth (New York, 1973), pp. 111–22 and 'The Literary Culture of the Tajiks', in forthcoming volume *Politics and Literature in Central Asia* ed. Wm. Fierman.

12 The work used here about Soviet Uighurs is M. R. Ruziev, *Vozrozhdennyi Uigurskii Narod* ('The Rebirth of the Uighur People') (Alma Ata, 1982 [second edition]).

13 See Andrew D. W. Forbes, *Warlords and Muslims in Chinese Central Asia: A Political History of Republican Sinkiang 1911–1949* (London, 1986).

14 All Uighur material now published in China appears in a modified Arabic alphabet similar to, but not the same as that used for Uighur in the Soviet Union in the 1920s. See Allworth (1971) p. 372 for the transliteration chart of the alphabet prior to 1928.

15 The last known printing done in the old Uighur alphabet was in 1687 and was found among the Sarigh Uighurs of Kansu province. The content was Buddhist. Other texts also date from the Ming period (1368–1644). During the fourteenth to fifteenth centuries, other examples also appear throughout sedentary Turkic areas, probably in the aftermath of Timur's order to go back to the old script. See J. Kalproth, *Abhandlung und Schrift der Uiguren* (Paris, 1820). I am grateful to Kahar Barat (Harvard University) for these details.

16 Personal observation during August 1985 in Uighur villages in Xinjiang.

17 Tiyipjan Aliyop and Rahmitullah Jari, *Uighur Klasik Adabiyatidin Namunalar* (Urumchi, 1981), p. 1.

18 op. cit., p. 576.

19 *Voina Musul 'man Protiv Kitaitsev,* 2 vols. (Kazan, 1880–81). Another local history of nineteenth-century Muslim wars against the Ch'ing, Mulla Musa Sairami's *Tarikh-i Amniyya* is not mentioned in this anthology but has also been published. See Kim Hodong,

The Muslim Rebellion and the Kashgar Emirate in Chinese Central Asia, 1864–1877 (PhD Thesis, Harvard University, 1986) p. xiii.

20 The attempt to elevate Pushtu in prestige in opposition to Persian led to forgery of manuscripts that would serve in place of a literary heritage to vie with Persian. The best known case is that of Abdul Hai Habibi's production of *Khazana*, published in Kabul.

21 Janos Eckman discusses the various designations of pre-modern eastern Turkic literary languages in *Chagatay Manual* (Bloomington, 1966) pp. 1–13. Ruziev deals with Uighur literary language but follows the Soviet model in using the term 'Uighur' for the Islamic period as well as the pre-Islamic. Allworth (1964) discusses the issue of language designation on page 83, ft. 3.

22 Ruziev, op. cit.

23 Ruziev does not include Nawa'i and neither do the articles on Uighur literature in the *Bolshaia Sovietskaia Entsiklopedia*. In the latter Rabghuzi is included for the fifteenth century from whence the jump to Khirqati in the seventeenth century.

24 For limited discussion of Nawa'i within the Afghan context, see Eden Naby, 'The Ethnic Factor in Soviet Afghan Relations', *Asian Survey*, March 1980.

25 Aliyop and Jari, p. 613.

26 Ibid.

27 Yusuf Beg Mukhlisov, ed. *Uighur Klassik Edibiyati qol Yazmiliri Katalogi* (Catalogue of manuscripts of Uighur classical literature) mentioned, but not seen by Kim, p. 287. According to Kim, Mukhlisov includes historians in the catalogue. These do not appear in the anthology at hand with the exception of Mulla Bilal who versified parts of his history.

3

A LATE PIECE OF *NAZIRA* OR A SYMBOL MAKING ITS WAY THROUGH EARLY UZBEK POETRY

Ingeborg Baldauf

The *nazira*, as in all classic Middle Eastern literature, was a highly esteemed genre in the Chaghatai and Persian-Tadzhik literature of Central Asia across the centuries. The genre as such continued to exist after the revolutionary events of the early twentieth century. However, the social and cultural changes the revolution brought about did leave their traces upon the *nazira*: It was used primarily as a means of literary criticism and, consequently, as a weapon in the 'ideological fight' (*mafkuravij kurash*) that determined the atmosphere of early Uzbek literary life. The inherent qualities of the *nazira*, of course, tempted the writers of the flourishing ironic-satirical journals to produce *nazira*-like literary parodies. Some of these parodies were quite successful.[1] I shall nevertheless skip this sector and turn to a poem and two *nazira*s by no means meant to be humoristic — just the contrary. I shall deal with a poem by Chölpon, followed by one *nazira* by Gajratij and another one by Saloh Sasan.[2] Investigating these examples, we are not only likely to trace the literary (and personal?) enmity of two prominent members of the early Uzbek literary community, but we will also be able to examine features of 'symbolism' and 'vulgar sociologism' as well as the timid awakening of 'socialist realism' in Uzbek poetry from the twenties up to the early thirties.

Before turning to the poems, we should consider their background, that is, the counterrevolutionary movement in Farghona and the *bosmachi* activities that caused an intervention of the Red Army and led to a civil war which lasted for half a decade and left the Farghona Valley in a state of utter devastation. This is not the place to discuss the historical facts. All that can be said here is that the Farghona events have been translated into poetry by many an Uzbek writer. Apart from the poem that we are going to consider, the best-known example, dating from the days of the civil war, is probably Shokir Sulajmon's *Parghona*.[3] It was written in free verse (*sochma-nazm*), which was quite innovative at that time. Its plot is based on the theme of the Angel of Death haunting Farghona, obviously an allusion to the ferocious *bosmachi* gangs.[4] However close to an objective reality his description of the devastation may have been, the poem is today criticised for stressing the pessimistic motifs instead of dealing with the revolutionary life of the people and calling upon people to fight the class enemy.[5]

When finally, in 1923, Chölpon openly joined the propagandistic supporters of the counterrevolutionary movement and even went to Andidzhon, a flood of literary and para-literary comments swamped the newspapers and the satirical gazettes.[6] This flood reached such a level that finally in the fall of 1924 a critic remarked that 'the events of Farghona were too narrow in inspiration to base the entire literature on.'[7]

However, Chölpon's greatest provocation was the *doston Buzilgan ölkaga* ('Poem to a Devastated Land') that came forth in late 1923 in the volume *Buloglar* ('Springs'). This poem has (except for the era from 1932 to 1956 when the taboo was paramount) stirred the emotions of literati and literary critics in a way unequalled by any other product of early Uzbek literature. The fact that *Buzilgan ölkaga* has not yet been shelved encourages me to take it up once more and to try to discover what rendered it so abominable. The *nazira*s by Gajratij[8] and Saloh Sasan,[9] both composed in strict opposition to Chölpon's poem, can provide valuable guidelines to a solution to this question.

Our examples are, in accordance with the demands of social-ist realism (though this theory was only fixed a couple of years later), functional and tendencious. They were intended as weapons in the ideological fight, and their efficacy depended on how well-sharpened the weapon was. We remember Majakovskij's thesis: the poet's material is words; he has to choose the most significant terms which, in turn, are to be at hand in a given poetic language to meet the needs of the poet.[10] So what were the whetstones an Uzbek poet of the early twenties could make use of to sharpen his tongue?

We must not forget that the whole Uzbek language was still in its developmental stage during those years. The former literary language was outdated and far from being intelligible to the people. The puristic words and constructions invented and promoted by jadidist and pan-turkist circles were probably no more intelligible, but were nonetheless just about to take root in newspapers and journals. The local Uzbek dialects were certainly a source of inspiration, yet were still far from being a compulsory and therefore reliable base.

From these facts, we can guess what difficulties a poet faced in this situation: Not even the language he should use was fixed, let alone a stock of poetic devices such as Majakovskij calls for. The choice of means largely depended on a poet's educational and literary background and on his personal taste.

As for Chölpon, neither his educational nor his literary background can easily be fixed to one single model. Up to the years that concern us here he had attended both Russian and local schools and had learned the local literary tradition as well as at least Russian and Ottoman literature. The fact that he successfully made use of the *barmoq vazni* (form of syllabic metre) is evidence of a certain familiarity with folk poetry. Of special importance is of course the inspiration he took from modernist tendencies in Russian literature. His closest contact with one of these tendencies occurred only some years after the period that interests us — that is when he accompanied the *davlat dram truppasi* ('state drama troupe') to Moscow and came into contact with the Vakhtangov theatre school. Nevertheless, his contemporaries, when trying to discredit him, used to label him a symbolist. Modern academic literary scholarship has not yet studied Chölpon's work thoroughly enough to prove or reject these statements,[11] nor would I dare to answer the question myself. But I suppose that calling him a symbolist is exaggerated, to say the least.

The pretext to call him a symbolist, which at times was quite a dangerous accusation, could be found in his deliberate use of rhetoric figures, among them both symbols and simple metaphors. A metaphor he used in *Buzilgan ölkaga*, an image that is also well-known as a symbol, will be the subject of our special interest here, and we will compare the corresponding words in the *nazira*s as well: In the second line of Chölpon's poem appears a 'dark cloud' that casts, or to be more exact, *is* 'a shadow' over the mighty land's head. An implication following from the use of this metaphor: the cloud, at the same time shadow, deprives the land of the sun, more generally of the light, and (cf. last line) is throttling the land.

The corresponding line of Gajratij's *nazira* reads 'Today the cloud of freedom is shadow above your head'. The revised editions, however, give an entirely different second line, saying 'A black cloud does no longer cast shadow upon your head now'.

The corresponding line of Saloh Sasan's poem, finally, reads 'Over her head there is no shadow any more, not a bit'. By replacing the original first line with 'Free land that hath drunk sun and become free' — the Uzbek text sounds much better because of the use of two synonyms for 'free' — Saloh Sasan deliberately enlarges the figure and adds a non-metaphoric element to it.

The fact that Gajratij composed a second line and recomposed it in an entirely different way attracts our attention. What could the reason for this change have been?

Literary criticism is assigned a prominent role in the method of socialist realism. The 'ancient elites' dominated the first years of literary criticism during the first years of Soviet reign in modern Uzbekistan. As late as 1928, coinciding approximately with the constitution of the Writers' Union Qizil Qalam, the basic principles of what was to be socialist realism were (on an all-Soviet scale) developed highly enough to set a general and reliable standard for the writers who were 'on the socialist platform' — and what was more important: from that time on, there were Uzbek critics who mastered their task.[12] Before 1928, criticism had existed without a compulsory theoretical base and thus was often abused as a mere playground of personal animosities. The impressionistic style of criticism, however, remained for some time longer. Nevertheless such impressionistic essays obviously served their purpose. A brief review of Gajratij's booklet *Jashash taronalari* ('Melodies of Life'), written by a critic using the pen-name Orif,[13] gives proof of the skill of even low-rate criticism in those 'flamboyant years'.

Orif comments upon some of Gajratij's poems, most of them owing inspiration to some other poet's lines. With regards to *Tuzalgan ölkaga* ('To the Cured Land'), the critic approves of the content, the ideological element, and the 'genius of creation' (*idzhod ruhi*), but feels compelled to say that 'from the point of view of artificial finishing' it 'falls short of the other one' (i.e. Chölpon's poem).[14] — What evidence does he build his judgement upon, then? Citing the second line, he states that 'using the cloud as a metaphor (*ramz*) for freedom here offends the feelings of the reader'.

Unfortunately, I have not yet been able to trace the earliest revised version of Gajratij's poem; some of the expressions used in it (e.g., *gigant qurilishlar* 'gigantic constructions', *kollektiv kuch* 'collective strength' and *proletarning pölat qöli* 'the proletariat's steel arm') point to the era of the first five-year plan. However, the fact that the poem has been taken up and worked through once more shows how seriously literary criticism was taken and how normative and prescriptive it could be.

What was Gajratij's error in the second line? He had used 'freedom' together with 'shadow', the word appearing in Chölpon's second line, to inverse and distort the picture made up of metaphors, a picture that had been consistent, but of course unacceptable for Gajratij. Shadow, in traditional oriental metaphorical language, is something agreeable — what else could it have been in a region that suffered much more from the sun than from its being hidden behind clouds! The 'shadow' a high person casts is a blessing for the one on whom the shadow falls. In this sense, Gajratij's distortion of Chölpon's picture was a witty, ingenious device — a device worthy of a *nazira*. But unfortunately this kind of wit was not appreciated any more in 1928. Gajratij, one of the truest followers of the new life, had fallen guilty of a *lapsus* that clearly shows how delicate the membrane between the 'acceptable' part of tradition and the part of tradition that could not be evaluated for innovation still was in those times. His 'cloud of freedom' is exactly what has been classified as 'inappropriate metaphors' which produce '. . . shallow works that have not been able to leave the circle of pictures of Eastern poetics' — as Mahmudali Junusov puts it in his study *Traditsija va novatorlik problemasi* ('Tradition and the Problem of Innovation') (Tashkent 1965, p.

116). The metaphoric language must be understood within a historical and cultural framework.[15] The new social situation called for new pictures. Gajratij understood the hint of the critic and rewrote the second line, thus giving up his witty distortion of Chölpon's picture for a rather insipid 'no longer does a black cloud cast shadow on your head'. This expression, however, had a safe place within the newly established metaphoric language.

Saloh Sasan in his turn found himself in a much easier situation than Gajratij did, when he created his poem in 1930: By that time the important discussions had already been carried out and the dangerous battle for a new understanding of literature on the whole and new poetic means in particular had been more or less fought. In 1930 the raw material, the means that Majakovskij demands as a sound base for literary production was at hand. Saloh Sasan moved on safe ground. Nonetheless, he felt the need to be unmistakable, as did many writers of the beginning of the thirties.[16] Therefore he not only enlarged the picture of the land freed from shadows by adding the affirmation that she had imbibed the light of the sun (*gujosh ichgan*), but he even provided the explanation: *ozod bölgan* 'having gained freedom'.

The symbol of the sun, and following from it, the symbol of the darkness (be it the darkness of the night or the darkness caused by clouds or fog hiding the sun) had been used in all literature that we may assume to be sources of inspiration for the Uzbek poets.

Classical Islamic poetry uses the sun as a symbol for the beloved one, be it the *ephebe* or be it God. This understanding of the sun appears time after time, even in the poetry of Uzbek writers like Elbek who certainly had no mystical touch and struggled hard for a place on the 'platform'.[17] However, the symbol seems to have been overcome by the late twenties.

The enlightenment understands the sun as a symbol for education in the modern sense of the word, and more generally as a symbol for the new life. Conversely, darkness is the old way of life. Clouds (or, more often, curtains) that block the sunrays symbolise the conservatives and reactionaries, i.e., in general, the clerical circles and their followers. This understanding of the symbol of the sun predominates in early Uzbek poetry, remaining valid up to the *hudzhum* period of 1927–29 when the traditional attitude towards women was assaulted.

Wherever the Uzbek enlightenment may have gained inspiration — Tatar and Ottoman influence are most plausible, but we should not deny the Russian element either — the symbol of the sun is present in each of them. Jadidis and 'democrats' made use of it to an extent that must have been quite boring for the public. We may content ourselves with a single example here: a stanza from Hamza's *Ilm usta* ('About Knowledge') (1914):[18]

olaming khurshidi kundir, odaming khurshidi ilm
olaming zulmoti tundir, odaming nodori ilm
'The sun of the world is the bright day, mankind's sun
is knowledge. The darkness of the world is (caused by)
the night, (while) mankind's is (caused by) lack of knowledge.'

The jadidi-dominated press of the years following the Revolution provides another flood of poems devoted to the picture of the sun bringing enlightenment. Most of them are very plain and of no interest for our purpose. There are some though, which cannot easily be labelled as 'late jadidi' and therefore deserve to be mentioned.

First, there is the poem *Ögit*[19] 'advice', whose author (probably Oltoj) tried to imitate the futuristic manner of writing — not all too successfully, because his 'futurism' is confined to repeatedly advising the acceleration of life for the sake of progress. The lines including the symbol of the sun read as follows:

. . . kishilik dunjosi
qujosh, nur istar;
kishilik
kökarmoq,
unmoq istar,
qujosh bulutdan
qutilmoq istar
nur bilan dunjoni
bezamoq istar; . . .
'Mankind's world needs the sun, the light; mankind's
world wants to flourish and prosper, the sun wants to

35

be freed from clouds and to embellish the world with light.'

Of course, nothing in these lines precludes an interpretation along the well-known path of enlightenment. The regularly repeated allusion to progress in civilisation, however, allows a more narrow understanding as well: the sun as a symbol for education no longer following the outdated jadidi ideal, but a more progressive one, curious for the *dernier cri* in technology, as opposed to the 'clouds' of conservativism.

The second example is more traditional in shape. It is dedicated to the *chetdan kelgan öquvchilar* ('readers who come from afar') an interesting dedication, as we will see. But first of all the lines that concern us most:

Uchqunlar[20] (Asl)
(chetdan bizga kelgan öquvchilarga baghishlab)
mana bugun qarshimizda uchqunlar, . . .
. . . shu tomonga qanot jasab ucharlar
qoronghiliq zulumotin jiqarlar! . . .
. . . nurlar sochib jangi 'hajot' qururlar!
uzoqlardan nurlar sochgan qujoshdek
bezatarlar jurtimizni, borliqni!
qörqmajdirlar kökrak kerib arslondek
jöq qilarlar saltanatlar, takhtini! . . .
'Sparks (dedicated to the readers who have come to us from afar) — Look: today we are confronted with sparks (. . . that) tie wings and fly here and pull down the darkness! (. . .) They shed light and build up a new "life"! Like the sun, shedding light from far away, they embellish our land, the universe! They know no fear: Presenting their broad breast, like lions, they destroy the throne of kingdoms.'

We are not going to judge the literary merits of this poem here; its insights into the understanding of a metaphoric scenario are doubtlessly interesting. The sparks form the centre of the poem: They defend darkness and help to build up a new life, i.e., a life free of fatal unconsciousness. On the other hand, they grant their light *like the sun*, fearlessly, thus overthrowing thrones. The 'sparks' are charged with a double function — the function of enlightenment and of revolution.

When the author hints at the revolutionary moment, he shifts away from the 'sparks' and makes use of the 'sun'. The author's understanding of the 'sun' is obviously two-sided, including both 'enlightenment' and 'revolution', the first one being a step towards the second one.

Unfortunately, I am not able to tell to whom the allusion refers. Of course, the first thought goes to the Tatars volunteering in Turkistan, later Uzbekistan, to whom the party owes many of the successes in the field of education, especially in the women's liberation movement. But why should they be addressed as *öquvchilarimiz* which means 'our readers'? How could the writer of these modest lines address them as if he spoke on behalf of the journal, or even more extremely, the *özgarishchi joshlar*, that is to say the komsomol?! On the other hand, interpreting *öquvchilarimiz* as 'our students' doesn't lead any further. A solution would be to suppose that a *t* has been omitted in the print which would have made a 'teacher' out of the 'reader' or 'student' — misprints are an every day feature of the journals throughout the twenties, but of course relying on misprints is a doubtful solution.

Anyway, the poem provides us with the insight into another feature of the symbol of the sun: 'sun' in connection with revolutionary events.

As we have already seen in the poem cited just before, the images of enlightenment and of revolution tend to merge. In pre-revolutionary poems it is not easy to decide which aspect of the image prevailed; interpretation usually depends on the author's attitude towards revolution *ex post festo*. (If, for example, the 'sun' in Tevfik Fikret's poem *Sabah olursa* ('If morning comes') can be understood as hinting at a revolutionary situation, this is due doubtless to the statement given in *Rucû^c* three years later under the impact of the 1908 events. Uzbek literary scholarship and criticism applies this method of inductory demonstration to the works of pre-revolutionary Hamza and khurshid, for instance.)

A poet who had enlightening and revolutionary moments merge in his personality, that is to say, had them follow one another, is Hamza. He is credited with being the first Uzbek poet to develop a revolutionary metaphorical system that includes the sun. In his song *Ishchi bobo* ('Labourer') (1918) he succeeds in creating an image that is at the time consistent and convincing:

> guldur etib bulut tarqab
> jalt-jult etib chaqmoq chaqdi,
> ishchi bobo seskansangchi
> sharqqa qujosh chinlab chiqdi . . .[21]
> 'With a grumbling of thunder, breaking the clouds, the lightning flashed. Labourer, hurry up! The sun has truly risen above the East!'

Hamza uses the 'sun' not only for Revolution itself, but also, as is the case in this poem, for the bright life that results from it. Many writers throughout the twenties followed his example. Especially in connection with women's liberation, the metaphor of the sun had to serve as an inexhaustible source of inspiration. Any choice of examples from the wealth of eulogies on the October Revolution, the 1st of May, women's liberation, would be arbitrary. There are no outstanding highlights within this genre of early Uzbek poetry. (Had there been an Uzbek poet of Majakovskij's satirical qualities, the 'guide to the drawing-up of poems to the 1st of May' would have been written in Uzbek.) Let us nevertheless consider two or three representatives of the genre.

One of Shokir Sulajmon's less successful poems directed to the Uzbek girl and woman is *Inqilob qizi* 'Revolutionary girl' (1924).[22] It is written in his favourite verse, the *sochma-nazm*. I quote a few lines only:

> . . . nega endi örtoqlaring ukhlajlar
> qujosh chiqqan,
> tang otganin sezmajlar.
> nega sendaj kurashchi qiz bölmajlar?
> — inqilobdan tughmajlar!
> '. . . Why are your girl-friends sleeping, why do they not realise that the sun has risen and dawn has broken. Why are they not fighters like you? — Why are they not born out of the Revolution!'

He equates 'sun' and 'revolution', as we can hear: Botir, from whom I quote another example, was less interested in finding new poetic means than Shokir Sulajmon. He was content with a mixture of several syllabic metres when composing the poem *Nur qöjnida* 'At the bosom of the light' (1929):[23]

... dard sochib chiqdi qujosh
borliqni nurga gharq etib
tökhtadi mazlumda köz josh
ötdi tunlar qon jutib. (. . .)
... qipqizil sop nur butun
dunjoni endi qoplagaj (. . .)
'. . . The sun rose, scattering sorrows, flooding all the world with light. The tormented people's tears dried up, the days of bloody grief had gone. (. . .) Clear red light will now embrace the world.'

In this poem the 'sun' is definitely assigned to the Revolution. As has been mentioned before, in the period of APP (Association of Proletariat Writers)'s power poetic utterances had to be as unmistakable as possible. The refrain line of a poem that appeared in 1931, as well as the title, reads

Öktabir qujoshi kularkan
'While the sun of the October (Revolution) smiles.' In this poem the 'sun' denotes the fruits of the revolution, the soviet reality.[24]

As we can see from these examples, the meaning of 'sun' shifts to and fro between 'revolution' and 'new life after the Revolution'. But the general idea remains the same in both cases.

Saloh Sasan's *nazira* — to return to our initial texts — is in full accordance with the approved metaphorical imagery: *qujosh ichgan ölka* 'land that has drunk (light from the) sun' is obviously to be understood as 'land that has benefited from the blessings of the Revolution'. Gajratij's revised version fits the imagery as well: 'No longer does a black cloud cast shadows on your head' — 'no longer are you deprived of the blessings of the Revolution'.

Chölpon's image, however, does of course not fit the post-revolutionary imagery. Judging from the historical situation in which he composed the *doston Buzilgan ölkaga* and from what we know about his political intentions in 1922, we may easily guess that his 'sun' was the ideal of an autonomous state for his *millat* ('nation'); consequently, the 'dark cloud' must denote the ones whom he accused of hindering the realisation of his ideal: namely, the Russians. So his imagery does not conform to the jadidist-enlightening one, either. Did he really use an egocentric metaphoric language, then, a shortcoming which he is always accused of when his affinity to symbolism is stressed? In fact he does use a puzzling set of symbols in some of his poems, but not in the one we are talking about.

We may call it a quirk of fate that of all the Uzbek poets Gajratij is the one to correct the often-heard statement that Chölpon's imagery was fruit of his very own literary genius. The symbol of the Russians as a black cloud turns up in one of the late *dostons* of Gajratij's, namely the work *Shoir* ('Poet') that I quote from the little volume containing his last poems, the booklet *Qujosh mehri* ('Love of the sun') (Tashkent 1980).

The *doston* sketches Zavqij's benevolent helping hand in intimately personal matters as well as in matters of highest social relevance during the period from the eve of the Revolution up to the end of the *bosmachi* events. In the preamble to the *doston*, we are introduced to how the people suffered under the Russian, that is to say Tsarist, yoke. The title of the preamble is *Qora bulut* 'The black cloud'. I will quote a few lines only:

joz chillasi, nafasni
böghar harorat.
tabiatda hasratli
böghiq bir holat. (. . .)
. . . oghir ghamga burkangan
vajrona bu jurt. (. . .)
. . . ikki boshli burgutning
oghir sojasi
elning boshiga tushgan
jöq nihojasi. (. . .)
. . . feruza kökni bosgan
qop-qora bulut.
'The dog-days of summer: heat takes the breath away. Nature in a yearning, choked state. (. . .) Grief is weighing heavy on this devastated land. (. . .) The heavy shadow of the double eagle has fallen on the people's head — no end. (. . .) A cloud as black as coal is covering the turquoise sky.'[25]

These lines clearly prove that Gajratij was familiar with the metaphor of the black cloud for the Tsarist Russian regime. With this in mind, we should look at his *nazira* again: maybe the revised version, which contains the metaphor of the black cloud, can (or even must) be interpreted another way round. The line was 'No longer does a black cloud cast shadow upon your head', and we understood it as 'No longer are there obstacles that deprive the land of the light of the Revolution'. Knowing what we know now, we may try another interpretation: 'There is no Russian hegemonism any more that might deprive the land of the benefits of the Revolution'.

If this interpretation is right, much of the bitter criticism Gajratij had earned for 'lacking poetic abilities' before the aura of the People's Poet of the UzSSR safeguarded him from such attacks can be removed posthumously. By making allusion to the 'Russian hegemonism' that now (1927), in contrast to Tsarist days, no longer existed, he replaced his first, witty inversion of Chölpon's 'shadow' that had brought out the positive aspects of this very shadow with an even more ingenious distortion: He rejected Chölpon's nationalist attack that was disguised in a poetic symbol and which in those days could not be openly discussed.[26] He employed the reverse of the same weapon, namely a disguised allusion to a political strategy that was new in those days — the rejection of 'narrow local chauvinism' as well as 'great power hegemonism'. The taboo on all these matters was quite strict.[27] In a poetic disguise that can well be called a 'double disguise', Gajratij was again able to prove that he was not only the 'zealot' some circles wanted to make of him, but that by now he had mastered the whetstones at hand well enough to draw the sword of a *nazira* successfully in view of a great antagonist.

Notes

1 E.g. Mullo Dzhunbul (A. Qodirij?)'s little *nazira* on Ni'mat Hakim's eulogy upon the newly proclaimed UzSSR (in: *Qizil Özbekiston* no. 1, 5 Dec. 1924) written for the satirical journal *Mashrab* (no. 12, 12 Dec. 1924) which, by the way, might serve as an introduction to the poems dealt with here:
(texts quoted from *Mashrab*, p. 3)

original
(Özbekiston dzhumhurijatiga baghishlab)
qum dalasi Turkiston

örtasida bogh-böston
dehqoniston, pakhtaston,
guliston — özbekiston . . .
ul endi
dzhumhuriston! . . .

nazira

ahmoqiston Turkiston,	tarbijatsiz Turkiston,
avval edi khoniston,	nodoniston — khoriston,
shundaj ölkani ruslar	Ni'mat Hakimla böldi:
qildi jer bilan jakson.	shoiriston — guliston! . . .
ja'ni böldi Turkiston	hoj hoj ana she'riston! . . .
ölukiston, göriston.	
özgarishdan kejin ul,	
böldi birdan guliston.	
endi unga qarangiz;	
dzhumhuriston, hurriston!	shoirlar dösti: Mullo Dzhunbul

2 The name quoted as *Sasan* here is probably misprinted. A poet of that name does not appear in any familiar reference work.

3 in: *Ormughon* (1922), Tashkent, 8 April, p. 13.

4 Note the line *öz elin öz jurtin ohi zorin tinglamagan jirtqichlar hukm suradi* 'Brutes are reigning that won't listen to the grief and lamentations of *their* people and *their* land'!

5 M. Bobokhödzhaev (1929), *Kurash poezijasi. (1917–1929 jillar özbek sovet poezijasi materiallari misolida)*, Tashkent p. 22.

6 E.g. Mullo Chöqmor (Ġozi Junus) in *Mushtum* no. 2. 1923, proposed to slaughter among others a 'lightless enlightener' (*zijosiz zijoli*) as a sacrifice to the evil spirits haunting Farghona (p. 2); in no. 13 of the same journal Chölpon was made the 'crow' of a burlesque quatrain imitating Elbek's *style folklorisant*, the last line of which goes *bari körsa bir ölumtuk unga sevinib sajrar* 'Just when (the crow) makes out some carrion it will rejoice at it and sing'; even a principally friendly review of Chölpon's recent poetic volume in *Özgarishchi joshlar* no. 1. 1923 remarked that the poet's way had reached a deadlock.

7 Abdurrahmon Sa'dij in: *Özgarishchi joshlar* 1924 no. 7, p. 54.

8 *Tuzalgan ölkaga.* in: Ġajratij: *Jashash taronalari. She'rlar töplamidan II. bölak* (1928), Samarqand-Tashkent (Özbekiston davlat nashrijoti) pp 8–10.

9 *Bu ölka.* in: *Jangi jöl* 1930 no. 12, p. 11.

10 *Vladimir Majakovskij. Polnoe sobranie sochinenij v 13 tomax* (1959), t. 12. Moscow p. 87.

11 As far as I know, the first Phd dissertation to deal, among others, with Chölpon, is being written now in Moscow.

12 For a valuable survey of Uzbek literary criticism, see Homil Joqubov 'Tanqid va adabijotshunoslik tarikhiga bir nazar', in: *Adabijotimizning jarim asri. Maqolalar töplami*, (1967), t. 1 Tashkent, pp. 339–408.

13 in: *Qizil Tamgha* (1928), no. 4, 7 Sept, p. 4.

14 Saying so, he of course falls prey to the same 'vulgar sociologism' which Ojbek was accused of in connection with his famous article *Chölpon. Shoirni qandogh tanqidlash kerak*, and which he later on admitted to be due to a misunderstanding on his part. Orif's error was, as it is exactly the reverse of Ojbek's, not so disapproved of, and has not been discussed publicly, as far as I know.

15 Asqarali Sharapov is not precise enough when he points to the 'historical and national peculiarities' (*tarikhij va millij khususijatlar*) of the poetic repertoire: the traditional Uzbek poetic language can not be understood as separate from, e.g., the Persian-Tajik one. (*Olamlar ichra olamlar* (1978) Tashkent, p. 51).

16 The mode of those years was to explain everything that might have served a malevolent critic as a pretext to doubt the writer's sound intentions by footnotes; one could interpret these footnotes as a means of making the work intelligible for everybody — which was the great claim of the APP, but we may well assume that the more important reason for leaving not the slightest possibility of being misunderstood was the writers' only weapon against the machinations of exactly that APP.

17 cf. Sharapov, *Olamlar . . .* p. 154 et al.

18 Text quoted from *Hamza Hakimzoda Nijozij. She'rlar* (1964), Tashkent p. 39.

19 In: *Özgarishchi joshlar* (1924) no. 5, 30 July, pp. 36–37. (The poem dates from 24 Sept 1923 and was written in Moscow.)

20 id. p. 38.

21 *Hamza Hakimzoda Nijozij. Asarlar.* t. 1, (1960), Tashkent, p. 153.

22 In: *Özgarishchi joshlar* (1924) no. 7, pp. 33–35.

23 In: *Alanga* (1929) nos. 2–3, p. 8.

24 N. Rahimij: *Juksalish qöshiqlari. She'rlar IV* (1931), Tashkent 1931. pp. 20–23.

25 The image, as the reader sadly realises, is not quite consistent: The poet is obviously trying to draw a parallel between nature and human life. If so, he might have considered that a 'heavy shadow' and a 'black cloud' do not really torture folks otherwise pestered by the merciless sun of the dog-days.

26 Throughout the discussion of Chölpon's and Ġajratij's poems (Saloh Sasan's 'nazira' is disregarded for good reasons — in fact it does not add anything important to the preceding poems and can be interesting, if at all, only from the point of view of documentation to the manner of writing of the years of 'self-criticism' and the Stalinist purges) up to the very recent publications on the subject, there is no mention of the subject Chölpon referred to. The poet is accused of 'utter nationalism', but the taboo on the 'Russian hegemonism' seems to be paramount up to our days. On the contrary, many a critic as well as most of the scholars try to transfer the whole discussion to an entirely different — and obviously less risky — level by only stressing the fact that Chölpon humiliated his country when drawing a description of the devastations, whereas Ġajratij restored the land's honour, pointing out

the obvious welfare and progress (thus not only disregarding the poets' intentions, but the historical facts as well).

27 An interesting fact is, that the taboo obviously dominated the literary production only. On the level of literary politics discussion took place in a much more open atmosphere, see e.g. Akmal Ikromov's speech *Sotsializm madanijati uchun, ötmishning meroslarini tanqidij ishlash uchun*, published in *15 jilga Al'manakh* (1932), Tashkent.

4

RELIGIOUS THEMES IN THE NOVELS OF CHINGIZ AITMATOV

Irena Jeziorska

The purpose of this paper is to examine the literary treatment of religious experience in three of Chingiz Aitmatov's best known novels: *The White Steamship* (*Belyy parokhod*), 1970, *The Day Lasts More than 100 Years* (*I dol'she veka dlitsya den'*), 1980, and *Scaffold* (*Plakha*), 1986. It is suggested that, when read consecutively, these works illustrate an intriguing shift in Aitmatov's thinking: passing from a sympathetic preoccupation with individualism of spirit and the values associated with it, through a growing concern about collective integration between man, the social unit and the natural environment, towards an affirmation of social and moral collectivism as the highest value. This shift is considered with reference to some of the religious forms prevalent in Central Asian and specifically Kirghiz culture including animism, totemism, shamanism, and polytheistic cults, as well as Islam and Russian Orthodox Christianity.

Animism is generally understood to be a belief in personalised spirits which inhabit features of the natural environment. There is a school of thought, associated with the anthropologist Edward B. Tylor, which holds that this is the essence of primitive religious feeling. Tylor maintains that man has a tendency to imagine the world in his own image and, since animals, plants and objects move, act, behave and help or hinder him, primitive man will naturally assume that they are endowed with souls or spirits. Animism is an expression of something which may be termed the religious 'urge': the drive to determine and systematise the nature of ultimate reality and its relation to the universe and to man.

Totemism is a cult which reflects a special, intimate relationship existing between a group of kindred people on the one hand, and totem — which can be a species of natural or artificial object — on the other. The totem is usually regarded as the ancestor of the clan or group, gives its name to it, and is venerated as a guardian spirit which directs the pattern of behaviour of the society. Every individual specimen of the totem object belongs to the clan and is often the subject of taboos or prohibitions: it may not be injured, killed or eaten. One interesting point is that, as Emile Durkheim and Bronislaw Malinowski have both noted, totemism is a tradition above all bound up with the preservation and organisation of society. Malinowski[1] points out that it possesses a utilitarian quality, which is stronger perhaps than any urge to speculate about religious phenomena.[2] Durkheim also argues that the tradition is based on an anonymous and impersonal force, 'mana', conceived of as the totemic principle in whatever form, which is identified as the god of the clan and so closely associated with it that it can be nothing else than the clan itself.[3]

Shamanism has been defined by Mircea Eliade as 'one of the archaic techniques of extasy — at once mysticism, magic and religion in the broadest sense of the term'.[4] It is a religious system which was widespread in Central and Northern Asia until as late as the nineteenth century, despite pressures to convert to Islam. The shaman is a medicine-man and a healer, but he is also a magician, a priest and a mystic who, as a consequence of overcoming a violent physical and psychological crisis has gained a certain power over nature which he can use to benefit or harm his fellow men. In the shamanistic trance he communicates with spirits, he has mastery over fire, and he can take different animal forms to span the three cosmic zones: the sky, the earth and the underworld. The shaman is much more than a quack: he is one of the elect, a man who can see further into the nature of things and into the human soul because he is directly in touch with the sacred. He is, in fact, the prophet of God.[5]

The question of the amalgam of monotheism and polytheism among primitive peoples has been hotly debated by anthropologists; but among the Turkic and Mongolian tribes, Jean-Paul Roux has recently argued, belief in the existence of a supreme God — the God of the Sky (*Tengri*) — was prevalent in pre-Islamic times.[6] In addition, gods and spirits of earth and water, object and place were venerated to a greater or lesser degree in different areas.

The references to and images from pre-Muslim and pre-Christian religious traditions, and the ways in which they are introduced and treated in the three works discussed here, reflect certain assumptions about the nature of the world we live in and about man's relationship with the environment, which are important for a fuller understanding of Aitmatov's writing. They are the means by which his attitudes towards religious experience are codified, and perhaps may reflect a tension between the personal urge to determine and touch the essence of things, and the demands of the Soviet collective, with its particular social and ethical assumptions and its emphasis on the conservation or protection of group cohesion. The personal religious urge, I suggest, is associated most closely with the use of images related to animism and shamanism, the call of the social collective — with totemism. It is my view that the increase in totemic references in the later works (*The Day Lasts More than 100 Years*, and particularly *Scaffold*) indicates that over the years Aitmatov has come to lay greater emphasis on issues related to the cohesion and protection of society, which in *The White Steamship* are treated as subordinate to the spontaneous religious drive.

Islamic references have not been fully covered in this paper, although it is noted that Muslim traditions and forms are touched upon in *The Day Lasts More than 100 Years*.

The Christian tradition is arguably reflected to some degree in *The White Steamship*,[7] but it is handled with striking directness in *Scaffold*, in a way which has stimulated considerable controversy among Soviet critics. I shall be discussing the implications of this in the final section of the paper.

The White Steamship (1970)[8] tells the story of a kindly but ineffectual old man, Ded Momun, and his 7-year-old grandson, who is an orphan. It is about the incompatibility of the ways in which they see the world, and about the tragic consequences this clash of perception brings.

Ded Momun's greatest concern in life is his tribal identity and the preservation of the ancient tradition of his once powerful clan, the Bugu of northern Kirghizia. In order to comfort and reassure his grandson, he tells the boy a version of the traditional myth of origin of the Bugu tribe which describes how in years gone by, on the banks of the River Yenisey — where the Kirghiz are said originally to have had their settlements — two children survived the massacre of their tribe, and were rescued and nurtured by a deer who led them to the banks of Issyk Kul', where they were able safely to settle and multiply. The stag became the surrogate mother of the Bugu tribe,[9] and was properly venerated until the day when younger members of the clan decided to glorify their dead by killing deer and crowning the graves of ancestors with their horns. The totemic ancestor of the Bugu ('the Horned Deer Mother', Aitmatov calls her) was thus debased into an object of thriving trade, to be hunted and possessed as a mark of social status. Because of this, she departed from Issyk Kul', never since to return.

The little boy takes the myth literally. His understanding is coloured by an animist perception of things. To him, animals, plants and objects are in any case personalised, and he is quite content to apply Ded Momun's story to the world as he has experienced it. Later, deer are sighted in the area. Momun's family go out hunting; they kill a deer and feast on it, with Ded Momun taking part in the sacrilege. Seeing this, the boy withdraws into his personal fantasy of transforming himself into a merman and swimming out into the waters of Issyk Kul' to meet the white steamship he has watched pass by from the shore. There, he believes, he will find his rightful father and the resolution to the puzzle of his existence. But alas, he drowns.

Aitmatov's novella reveals a tension between two forms of perception, one which is totemic and another which is animist. To Ded Momun, the myth of the Deer Mother is a point of reference by which he can define his own identity and his relationship with the collective and the environment. His view of the world is totemic not only in that he likes to associate his experience and understanding of things with a totemic myth telling of the ancestral origin of his tribe, but particularly because for him the clan and the preservation of its traditions and rites are of prime importance. His perspective on life falls well in line with Durkheim and Malinowski's interpretation of the totemic tradition as one which looks less to the understanding of transcendent realities than to collective survival.

In the light of these points, the implications of Aitmatov's story are very interesting. For it is suggested that the totemic principle, the essentially impersonal principle of the clan, fails in practice to satisfy the personalist religious urge inherent in the unspoilt human psyche. Ded Momun's absolute, the clan, proves to be in conflict with the animist urge which, Aitmatov shows, is a part of the innocent, child-like experience of reality. The little boy takes his grandfather's myth as a reality to be lived, and as knowledge to satisfy his instinctive, personalist religious and moral cravings. It becomes, for him, a prescriptive codification of the religious urge and therefore a source of motivation and action. It inspires his ultimate act of disengagement from the way of the world which is tragic at the temporal level because he must die, but a triumph at the moral level — as Aitmatov indicates in the last few lines of his story:

> You rejected what your child's heart could not reconcile itself to. And that's my consolation. You lived like a bolt of lightning which once — and only once — flashed and expired. But lightning strikes from the sky. And the sky is eternal. That too is my consolation. And that a child's conscience in a person is like an embryo in a particle of grain: the grain won't grow without the embryo. That whatever awaits us on earth, truth will endure forever as long as people are born and die.[10]

If the brief life of Aitmatov's nameless little boy is like a flash of lightning born of the eternal sky, then in terms of the Kirghiz tradition he is a child of the Supreme God, *Tengri*. He has a particularly close rapport with clouds: they are his special friends and he shares with them his secret desire to flee the world, to be transformed into a fish-like creature and take to the water[11] so that he may reach his unknown, omniscient father. His greatest aspiration then, is a metamorphosis which will take him on something akin to a shamanistic journey into another sphere of existence.

There are a number of features in *The White Steamship* which suggest that the boy is not only a personification of the innocent soul, but an unrecognised shaman or prophet,[12] whose experiences may be related to initiation rites performed towards the fulfillment of his vocation. He has been abandoned by his father, just as the shaman is abandoned in some traditions.[13] He takes the mythical stag to be his mother, just as the shaman is said to have an animal mother, often pictured in the form of an elk embodying the prophetic gift.[14] Above all, however, he seeks to communicate with another world. He regularly climbs a hill overlooking Issyk Kul' to contemplate the white steamship and hold imaginary conversations with his father, rather like the shaman who climbs the Cosmic Mountain to reach the higher cosmic zone. He also keeps company with a stray dog; the dog is the shaman's traditional companion during his descent into the underworld.[15] And ultimately, of course, the boy seeks to take on a new form which will allow him to make the transition into another field of life.

The shamans of western and central Siberia are generally recognised by exceptional traits shown during adolescence (nervousness or epilepsy are typical), but the vocation may also be revealed through attitude rather than sickness.[16] Like Aitmatov's hero, the shaman may be a meditative, solitary, apparently absent-minded child, with a tendency to dream. His vocation is confirmed by a crisis, a form of mental illness or breakdown, during the course of which he experiences a shift of reference from the family or clan to the universe as a whole. This leads, Joseph Campbell writes,[17] to the realisation of 'something far more deeply interfused' inhabiting both the earth and one's own interior which gives the world a sacred character. The shaman emerges from his ordeal, as it were, delivered from the human condition, ready to take on his role as mediator between the worlds.

The little boy in *The White Steamship* also has a crisis which is diagnosed as a feverish cold, during which he converses with the Horned Deer Mother, bathes in hot water (Eliade makes reference to the function of heat in the process of the shaman's mutation from body to body[18]) and performs superhuman feats: he fights monsters in a blizzard, he leaps from mountain to mountain and rescues people from burning and drowning, ever watched and protected by the white stag. He then returns to the world of men to witness the savage dismemberment of his incarnate godhead, the deer, and to see her being devoured by members of his clan. Only then does he perform the act which must confirm his vocation as a shaman: the actual, unimagined acquisition of an animal body to cross over into a new dimension.

However tragic the consequences of this may be in temporal

terms, Aitmatov makes it quite clear that the child's animist experience, his personalist religious urge, and his shaman-like vocation, all positively motivate, while Ded Momun's totemic beliefs lead only to his capitulation before the will of the clan. The one provides scope for total consistency in action, even at the cost of disengagement from life itself, while the other does not, at the cost of the debasement of human stature. Because he worships the principle of the clan, and not a personalised deity, he is forced in the end to follow the ways of the clan. He sacrifices his totem to the pragmatic necessity to conform and shares in the feast which celebrates the killing of the deer in order not to offend, and out of a fear of his ambitious, autocratic and violent son-in-law, Ozorkul. For his part, Ozorkul evidently has no god other than personal glory, and this is the deity which triumphs in the temporal conflict Aitmatov depicts. If there is any comfort in all this, it must lie only in the capacity of the child to disengage himself from that victory, and to act in consistency with his faith in the possibility of transfiguration, and of finding a better way of living by taking on another form.

When *The White Steamship* was published in *Novyy mir* in 1970, the Soviet press seems to have reacted critically. The work was declared to be 'pessimistic', and disappointment was expressed that the novella did not, like earlier works for which Aitmatov had received the Lenin Prize in 1963, 'illuminate the social significance of events' and inspire the reader with 'hopes and dreams'. The author was charged with deviating from historical and social roots and from 'reality'.[19] However, in a full critical assessment of Aitmatov's work published in 1982,[20] the Soviet critic, G. Gachev, treats *The White Steamship* as a landmark in Aitmatov's literary development, and goes on to comment on Christian imagery in the work. He associates the boy's lost father with God the Father, the Deer Mother with the Virgin, and the boy with Christ. Momun, he argues, plays a role similar to Judas in betraying his Deity.[21] Gachev sees the Christian features as part of the mythological structure of the story, and essential to its meaning. He gives *The White Steamship* a proper critical acknowledgement which it initially apparently failed to inspire.

The Day Lasts More than 100 Years,[22] published ten years later in 1980, could also be called pessimistic, and arguably with more justification. It is a novel which exposes the dangers of losing touch with memory, tradition and cult. It is about ways in which modern man has come to stunt or maim his personality, his mind and his potential; and implies that he is continuing to do so by refusing to acknowledge the possibility of reaching beyond the knowable as much as the known.

In Boranly-Burannyy, a settlement in the Sarozek steppes of Kazakhstan, an old and honoured member of the village community has just died. His long-standing friend, Yedigey, takes it upon himself to ensure that he receives a proper, traditional rite of burial, despite all the inconvenience and the reluctance of younger members of the family to co-operate. Yedigey insists that the body should be transported to the ancient cemetery of Ana-Beyit, thirty kilometres away, where the ancestors of the steppe peoples lie. The bulk of the novel describes Yedigey's experience of the funeral procession across the steppe, which he leads by camel with a tractor bearing the body and a stray dog following in tow. The journey appears to draw together in his mind the most important things he has heard, seen and felt in the sixty years of his life. It is a period of reflection and recollection.

Interwoven with this is a curious and apparently unconnected science-fiction story. As Yedigey arranges the burial of his friend, two space rockets — one Soviet, one American — take off to unravel a problem which has arisen aboard their jointly owned space station. The astronauts based there have discovered the existence of another planet populated by anthropomorphic, intelligent beings who are concerned about the long-term effects of dehydration on their environment, and are seeking to make contact with Earth in the hope of working jointly on a problem which in the long run could affect the human race as well. The authorities on Earth, however, cannot accept the implications of extra-terrestrial life, and when the astronauts leave the space-station to explore their discovery further, they are forbidden to return. Steps are taken to ensure that no further contact with the other planet can take place, and the Earth is cordoned off with circling defence rockets to protect or isolate it from the rest of the cosmos for fear of the imminent threat to the limitations of earthly consciousness and its possible implications for the human race. And so, as Yedigey and the little funeral convoy approach Ana-Beyit to find that it has been fenced off with barbed wire because the cemetery is about to be destroyed to make space for a new township, in another dimension the Earth itself is cut off from all external impulse and influence.

It appears that modern man is determined to sever links not only with his past and his roots, but also with any existing potential for evolution and development. Yedigey finally buries his friend outside the grounds of the cemetery and, as the book concludes, sets off to plead with the authorities for the preservation of Ana-Beyit and the memory of his people.

The Day Lasts More than 100 Years warns of a danger that the human race may lose both its past and its future, and settle into a limbo where it will eventually simply dry up and wither away. From the religious angle, the interest of the novel lies particularly in the references and images taken from the pre-Islamic Central Asian tradition which add impact and perspective to its themes.

The Soviet anthropologist, S. M. Abramzon, has commented on the eclectic quality of the Kirghiz tradition, and on the fusion of a range of cults reflected in it.[23] He mentions particularly the cult of the earth and sky, the mother cult and the totemic animal cult — all of which feature in this novel.

The rite of burial, which is thematically at the centre of the work, plays an essential part in the cult of dead ancestors, whose spirits continue to affect the lives of the living and demand constant attention. Burial must take place on land where the ancestor was born and where he lived. Until as late as the nineteenth century it was quite common practice for the leader of a Kirghiz tribe to be carried a great distance for such burial to be possible,[24] much in the way Aitmatov describes it here.

It needs to be said, however, that Yedigey's motivation in arranging the burial is shown to reach considerably beyond a straightforward tendency to cling to traditions of the ancient past. His actions are dictated and justified by the quality of his contemplative reasoning which indicates that he sees in religious tradition a way to improved psychological balance, a fuller life, and an enhancement of the best of man's potential. He acts as his conscience and the will of his old friend have decreed for, he believes death must be given its due if human life itself is not to be devalued.[25] The ritual acknowledgement of the transition from life to death must be enacted for the benefit of the living as much if not more than for the dead.[26] To Yedigey, religious rite and prayer — whether Islamic[27] or more ancient in form — is a means of bridging the conceptual gap between life and death, and of elevating the mind to a state in which an acceptance of the transience of individual human existence is possible. He repeats half-forgotten prayers to prepare himself for the burial: to organise in his mind the correct sequence of thoughts, the appeals to God — for only He, the unknown and unseen, could reconcile the unreconcilable in a man's consciousness of the beginning and end of life and of death. . . . [28] Prayer is a technique by which a balanced psychological stance towards the rationally inexplicable can be achieved, and it is also the means by which man may reach the essence of his own being which *is* the Deity. 'I want to believe that you exist,' Yedigey says to his God, 'and that You are in my thoughts. And when I turn to You in my prayers, in fact I turn through You to myself, and then I am given the gift of thinking as the Creator Himself would think. In that lies the heart of the matter! . . . If a man cannot imagine himself in secret as a god fighting for others, as you would have to fight for people, then You, God, would also cease to exist . . .'.[29] Unless man touches the quality within himself which he calls God, and unless he has learnt the technique by which to do it, the Deity Himself will cease to be. In other words, if God is not remembered, then He will be lost.

Yedigey's interpretation of religion in the end comes down to an idiosyncratic cult of his own: a cult of remembrance evolved from a combination of the cult of the earth, the ancestor cult, the mother cult and totemism, as I will try to show.

The earth is the very stuff of memory, it is the only remaining tangible bond with lives which have made unwritten history. 'The Sarozek land is a forgotten history book',[30] Yelizarov, a geologist, says in the novel. The ritual act of burial which acknowledges man's link with the past through the earth is, in Yedigey's view, an expression of the very nature of things, and to deny its value is a gesture against the inborn urge to recollect and reaffirm the state of human bondage.[31] Remembrance is expressed in the form of tradition passed from generation to generation, reflected in ritual or in song and legend which likewise remind one of the links between man and man at all times — past, present and future.[32] The spirit of men gone to earth can be resurrected through the songs they sang and the stories they told, which are their heritage and their teaching. For, as Yedigey's friend, Abutalip, believes, the song is one way in which the experience of one may become the property of many and the rebirth of a life lived: 'He said that there were certain happenings, events, certain stories which became the property of many because their value was so great; that the story contained in itself so much that although it was experienced by one person originally, it could, as it were, be distributed to and shared by all living at that time, even to those who came long afterwards . . .'.[33] Through song and legend, the memory of the people is preserved and, Aitmatov implies, the importance of that memory lies in its function as the very quality of the mind which makes man human and allows for the growth, development, and perhaps also for a kind of immortality.

The thematic centrepoint of the novel is the legendary history of the ancient cemetery, Ana-Beyit (meaning 'the resting place of the mother'). According to this, Ana-Beyit is the burial place of Nayman-Ana, the mother who in times of old, went out in search of her son who had been enslaved by a nomadic Mongolian tribe: the Zhuan' zhuan. Nayman-Ana found her son, but he killed her because his masters had transformed him into a *mankurt*, a slave whose absolute loyalty was guaranteed because he had been deprived of his memory and his identity. 'The nomadic Zhuan' zhuan encroached on the sacred being of man,' Aitmatov writes, 'for they had discovered the means of removing from slaves their living memory, in this way causing to a human being the most dreadful of all imaginable or unimaginable evils.'[34] Yet, the legend continues, as the *mankurt* shot the fatal arrow at his mother, and as she fell dying from her camel, the kerchief from her head dropped and was transformed into a white bird which henceforth haunted the area crying the name of the *mankurt*'s father.

According to Abramzon, the mother cult was particularly widely practised in the ancient Turkic, Uzbek and Kirghiz traditions in the form of the cult of Umay-Ana (the mother Umay). The Kirghiz word *umay* refers to a fantastic bird which nests in the air, and Abramzon goes on to trace its etymology to the Persian word *hūma* meaning the great eagle-like bird of good omen which inhabits the World-Tree.[35] He continues to give evidence that in Kirghizia the Mother Umay was often associated with the bird motif, widespread in many ancient cultures. In one Khorezmic legend he writes, Ambar-ona, a mother in search of her son, is also represented as a bird.[36]

The story of Nayman-Ana evidently has its roots in a legend deeply ingrained in the Central Asian tradition, and may also be associated with the totemic cult of the bird. In the Turco-Mongolian religious system, the bird is the mediator between earth and sky, as well as the form taken by souls of the dead.[37] In Kirghizia it is also the emblem (*tamga*) of a number of tribes, and indeed Yu. A. Zuev has argued that the ethnonym *kirgiz* should be understood as meaning the 'gryphon people', from the Indo-Iranian *karkasa, karkus* meaning eagle.[38]

In Aitmatov's legend of Nayman-Ana, the sacrifice of the mother for her son made to preserve his memory and his identity releases the bird image which is associated specifically with Kirghiz tribal identity. Through her death, the mother figure is transformed into a totem of the people — the syumbol of a common ancestry.

The bird image in fact recurs a number of times in the novel. The burial of Kazangap is watched over by a white-tailed kite circling overhead, and in his prayer over the grave Yedigey expresses a desire to be reincarnated in that form.[39] Later, as he runs from the noise of the defence rocket which is taking off to orbit the earth and isolate it from the cosmos, he senses a white bird beside him and knows that it is the one which had once formed from Nayman-Ana's white kerchief. The bird cries in his ear: 'Whose son are you? What is your name? Remember your name! . . .'[40]

Yedigey is associated, thus, with the bird symbol, which is a symbol of tribal and national consciousness and therefore appropriate to his function in the novel as the preserver of the memory of his people. In addition to this, he appears often in the company of two other animals which possess specific cult associations for the Kirghiz — the camel and the dog. In some areas, Abramzon observes, the camel is venerated as a spirit of holy places, and it is also the protector spirit of shamans.[41] Yedigey's prize camel, Karanar, is born of the stock of Nayman-Ana's white camel, Akmaya. Karanar and Yedigey are in fact like brothers with a shared totemic ancestry, since both were nourished by the milk of Karanar's mother.[42]

The introduction of the dog image is also not without significance, since the red dog (Aitmatov's dog is 'rusty coloured') is an animal ancestor in one legend of the creation of the Kirghiz people. Yedigey is accompanied in the fulfillment of his task — which is, like Nayman-Ana's, to restore lost memory and identity — by a beast of almost supernatural strength,[43] his camel, who is like a brother and a descendant of the white camel which bore Nayman-Ana herself, and also by his most ancient ancestor, the dog.

Finally, a brief comment must be made on the sky cult. In the Turco-Mongolian religious tradition, a correct relationship between earth and sky was essential to the maintenance of the cosmic order. Tragedy or disaster on earth was seen as the result of a tip in the balance between the two.[44] The sky was of course identified with the Supreme God, *Tengri*, and Soviet anthropologists have noted that as Kirghizia was Islamised, so the notions of the Sky God and Allah fused.[45] This is worth bearing in mind as one reads in *The Day Lasts More than 100 Years* that, just as man has learnt to sever his links with memory, the past and the earth, so he now seeks to sever his links with the sky. By cordoning off his planet, man is performing an act which must precipitate the apocalyptic destruction of the universe which in ancient Central Asian tales was foretold in terms of the separation between the sky and the earth.[46] According to the oldest of traditions then, this is an act of supreme sacrilege, and there is nothing in this profoundly pessimistic work to suggest that Yedigey's heroic efforts to preserve his bond with the earth can do anything to persuade humanity to re-establish its bond with the sky.

Aitmatov's recent and highly controversial novel *Scaffold*[47] published in *Novyy mir* in 1986, touches upon some of the themes common to earlier works such as the intrinsic innocence of the natural world and the human capacity for corruption and destructive action. However, his treatment of religion here reflects a new and considerably more explicit approach. The Russian Christian tradition is brought to the fore, never previously having featured in his writing, with a suggestion that the rediscovery of religious culture and faith may be more than psychologically, morally or aesthetically enriching, but that it could also serve as a guiding force in the development of modern society. In an interview published in *Literaturnaya gazeta* (13 August 1986), Aitmatov indicated that in his view Christianity bears a universal moral message which his hero, Avdy Kallistratov, carries to the world:

> Avdy is Russian, but I see him in a broader way — as a Christian . . . In this case I have tried to let religion lead me to man. Not to God, but to man! . . . Christianity offers a very powerful example through the figure of Jesus Christ. The Islamic religion, with which I am associated by origin, does not have a similar figure. Mohammed is not a martyr . . . He may have suffered, but he was never crucified for an idea nor did he forgive men for this for all time. Jesus Christ gives me reason to reveal a hidden truth to modern man. . . .[48]

Nevertheless, in *Scaffold*, Aitmatov appears to give two contradictory illustrations of the religious experience: one which suggests that it is a primitive means of psychological self-protection in the face of the incomprehensibility of the world (which rather reflects Lenin's understanding of religion as a reflection of undeveloped man's helplessness in the battle with nature), and another which indicates that today a religious world-view can give impetus to confront and perhaps overcome social evils; that it can motivate the individual to positive action and give him the courage to face discomfort, pain, and even death for the sake of an elevated vision of reality.

I shall begin by briefly examining the first view, and then go on to look more closely at the second Christian or neo-Christian aspect, its possible roots, purpose and implications.

Scaffold begins and ends with the theme of man's persecution of the natural world, and of the retribution he brings upon himself through it. The Christian element introduced in the story of Avdy Kallistratov appears like an extended *entr'acte*, breaking up the main plot a third of the way through part 1, and abruptly concluding at the end of part 2. It seems to have little connection with the rest of the novel. The following is a short summary of the principal story:

> Tashchaynar and Akbara are a pair of wolves whose seasonal existence of hunting and cub-rearing is repeatedly

and cruelly broken by human intervention. In part 1, they are chance victims of a helicopter attack on a herd of antelopes. They lose their cubs in the slaughter. In part 3, a man steals their second litter. The wolves instinctively set out to wreak revenge on the human race. Tashchaynar is shot in the process. Akbara later steals a human child by way of retribution. The child's father shoots her and kills his own son doing so.

The interesting point about this story from the religious angle is that according to the Turco-Mongolian view of the world, the animal kingdom exists as a parallel society, similar and indeed superior to human society. Animals are not necessarily gods, but all animals are closer to the gods than men because their very form is a direct expression of the soul, and is reflected in all the attributes they possess, which the anthropomorphic form is denied.[49] The animal is more in tune with the essential unity of things, and closer to the source of life. If he is an ancestor and protector of a human tribe, then he plays the role of a mediator between men and the source of things. The wolf is one such animal.

In a number of Turkic legends, the she-wolf appears as the mother or surrogate mother to a human tribe, and in medicinal traditions of the Central Asian area, the wolf is treated as an animal with magical healing properties who can counteract possession by evil spirits. In *Scaffold*, mankind's attack on the wolves could therefore be understood as an attack on his most ancient ancestry,[50] on the collective totemic principle, and on a source of healing. And Avdy Kallistratov seems to recognise this. Towards the conclusion of his story, when he is tried by a gang of thugs he has sought to convert to his religious views, he has a vision of wolves wandering the steppes, and murmurs a semi-conscious plea to the she-wolf to save him. Later, as he hangs crucified on a tree, Akbara approaches. He recognises her and it is to her that he seems to commend his spirit: 'You have come,' he says.

Another feature worth mentioning briefly is the introduction of polytheistic and animist elements in part 3 of the novel. The cub-thief, Bazarbay, prays to the pagan gods as he makes off with his prize, for fear of the parent wolves in hot pursuit. Here, prayer is the means by which consciousness looks for comfort in moments of crisis and extreme fear. Akbara also has her own wolf-goddess in the moon, and turns to her in despair when she loses her offspring.

The beginning and the final part of the novel are concerned, then, with the rebellion of man against nature, and by extension against his own nature.[51] At that level, *Scaffold* may be understood as a fable about human rejection of the unity of life, about separation from the natural collective which the environment and the society of man are destined to form, and about the tragedy of the exclusion of the individual element from the social and universal compound. This is the experience described in the final paragraphs of the novel, when Boston — the aspiring private entrepreneur — kills the man who stole the wolf cubs to avenge the death of his child.

And suddenly, Boston understood that there and then he had stepped over a limit and separated himself from others . . . [and] a dreadful truth was revealed to him. Until then the whole world had existed within him, and now that world was at an end. He had been the sky and the earth and the mountains and the she-wolf Akbara, the Great Mother of All Substance, and his ultimate hypostasis, the little boy Kendzhiash, whom he himself had shot, and Bazarbay, whom he had rejected and killed within himself. All that he had seen and experienced in his lifetime had been his universe and had lived in him and for him. And he saw that even though all this would continue to be as it had always been, the world would be different, and his own irreplaceable, unrenewable world had been [forever] darkened and would never be reborn in anyone or in anything. And this was his great tragedy. This was the end of his world.[52]

These lines, which are perhaps some of the finest in the work, reflect the bitter fruits of man's abuse of the collective totemic principle, personified in the wolf, and the inevitable retribution it must bring.

The central section of the novel, which deals with the fate of Avdy Kallistratov, lends an unprecedentedly prescriptive dimension to Aitmatov's writing. It introduces the notion of religion as a reflection of human creative potential, rather than a result of fear in the face of an incomprehensible universe, or indeed a method of reaffirming the essential unity of things. Aitmatov draws attention to the potential social value of religious faith in the battle against corruption, materialism, drink, drugs and all the false gods which man has created. The military arsenal is also given a mention here: 'A powerful new religion is moving in on us,' Aitmatov writes. 'It is the religion of military supremacy. . . . Who are the gods now if not the men who hold these weapons . . . .'[53] It is perhaps worth drawing attention to the fact that these are all the most promoted issues of Gorbachev's era.

Avdy Kallistratov is introduced as the son of an Orthodox deacon, and a seminarian expelled from the Church for his idiosyncratic theological views. He becomes a journalist, only to be exploited by his paper and made to write anti-Church propaganda. Finally, he turns his attention to ways of saving Soviet society from the corrupting influences of the drug racket.

Aitmatov calls Avdy a latter-day 'god-seeker', but he evidently aspires to be more than just that. Teaching and prophecy are more in his line and, although he performs no miracles, his message takes him to the scaffold, just as it took Christ to Golgotha. Avdy wants to resurrect the *idea* of God in modern society in order to improve the quality of living. His message is less about the imminent presence of a transcendent Deity than about a definition of the nature of god-consciousness, and of the ways this can assist man to live correctly and well in a post-industrial era. His vocation is the development of a notion of God which will fall in line with the historical progress of man 'razvitiye vo vremeni kategorii Boga v zavisimosti ot istoricheskogo razvitiya chelovechestva'.[54] The religious dogma once formulated for the benefit of the nascent consciousness of the masses can now no longer be taken seriously, he argues.[55] God is a feature of human consciousness ('vne soznaniya Boga net'),[56] and — like consciousness — He is destined to develop in history. God-consciousness is a reflection of an awareness of the best and most elevated elements in the human personality as it aspires to affirm its freedom from social repression.[57] Once the new concept of the Deity has been acknowledged by the mind, it must be reflected in will and in action, and have a revolutionary effect on the world.

For it is through a personal rebirth and a personal internal revolution that social evils will be overcome.[58]

Avdy identifies himself with Christ in so far as He was a propagator of 'the purest ideas and inspirations of the spirit',[59] and at a climactic moment in the story, after being thrown off a moving train, he has a vision of the conversation between Christ and Pilate on the eve of the crucifixion.

The immediately striking thing about this scene is its similarity to the confrontation between Ieshua Ga-Nostri and Pilate in Bulgakov's *The Master and Marguerita*. Aitmatov has confirmed that there is a connection, while continuing to emphasise that his version was written specifically to draw attention to problems facing the contemporary world.[60]

In both interpretations of the meeting, the conversation works around a challenge to temporal power and authority, which Pilate represents. In *Scaffold* Christ puts forward the notion of an Empire of Justice as an alternative, in *The Master and Marguerita*, Ga-Nostri stands rather by the notion of an Empire of Truth.[61] However, Bulgakov's timid, anonymous Ieshua, whose strength lies above all in his capacity to perceive and put things right in the here and now, has little in common with Aitmatov's more verbose and historically aware Christ, who offers a cogent treatise on the nature of the deity, of retribution, the Last Judgement and the purpose of human existence. Through Christ's explanation, the essence of Avdy's thinking is clarified, and the potential social implications of his religious world-view are revealed.

The purpose of human life, Christ says, is the perfectability of the human spirit. History records the way in which man is coping with the divine gift of Mind, determined ultimately to evolve into an ascent of man to Christhood. And this will be the Second Coming. 'I shall return unto myself in men through my sufferings,' he explains, 'I shall return to men in men . . . I shall be your future . . . The purpose of the Most High is to elevate man to his proper vocation, the vocation of goodness and beauty . . .'.[62]

Christ's suffering will be an example. It will raise up the consciousness of humanity and thus resurrect the Deity within it. Man and God are to be identified. All men, collectively, are the image of God on earth, and this hypostasis of the deity, Christ says, is 'the God of Tomorrow, the God of Eternity'.

Within Himself He holds the sum-total of human actions and aspirations, and His nature, whether He is to be fair or foul, depends entirely on man. ('Bog-Zavtra i est' dukh beskonechnosti, a v tselom — v nem vsya sut', vsya sovokupnost deyanii i ustremlenii chelovecheskikh, a potomu, kakim byt Bogu-Zavtra — prekrasnym ili durnym, dobroserdechnym ili karayushchim — zavisit ot samykh lyudyey'.)[63] So it follows that every man is a particle of the God of Tomorrow, and the creator and judge of every day in history.

The notion of the Deity as a reflection of the quality of individual and collective human consciousness bears a considerable resemblance to Maxim Gorky's idea that man is 'a depository of the living God'[64] who 'exists in the reason of man, though not in the Church'.[65] Avdy too declares that he is his own Church ('moya tserkov eto ya sam').[66] His vocation as a prophet is to awaken in men the realisation that God is the highest element within them. Gorky's vocation as a writer was not all that far removed from this. His aim was, he wrote in 1898, 'to help man understand himself, raise his faith in himself, wage war against vulgarity in men . . . make them noble and strong, make them capable of suffusing their life with the holy spirit of beauty.'[67] It was, in other words, to elevate the mind of man to its full dignity and potential — to the Godhead. And that, of course, is also the aim of Avdy and of his Christ. The religion Avdy offers is a faith in man striving to be a perfect being through the development of his faculties and his awareness — which is the way Gorky expressed it in the Mercure de France in 1907.[68]

The notion of the perfectability of man and of the resurrection of the Godhead in human consciousness as the means to the improvement and perfectability of the material world and society can be traced back to Gorky's pre-revolutionary god-building theory, which is given its fullest exposition in the novel Confession (Ispoved'). God-building is about inspiring man's faith in his own creative potential as an individual, and above all as a particle of the collective. It is about promoting the fusion of creative social energy, and the incarnation of a living Deity through that fusion, which social repression has thus far prevented. 'God existed when, in a single spirit, men created him out of the fibre of their thoughts in order to bring light to the darkness of life,' the revolutionary worker, Pyotr,

says in *Confession*. 'When the people tore apart their thought
and free will — God died.'[69] He died because He existed only
in the awareness of a spiritual kinship between men. 'In unity
you will find immortality; in isolation there is only inevitable
slavery, darkness, comfortless longing and death!' Mikhail,
another worker in the novel, declares.[70]

Aitmatov's God of Tomorrow, the spirit of collective hope,
aspiration and achievement, seems to echo this. The sheer
physical power of the collective spirit, which Gorky emphasises in his work, is also evoked in *Scaffold* during a scene in
which Avdy listens to the singing of a church choir. The fusion
of voices appears to reflect the spirit of mankind striving
towards the heights of his own being. It seems to absorb
and dissolve individual identity and awaken in the listener a
yearning to be part of that common cry of a humanity longing
to affirm itself and calling to the heavens for help. 'Oh vast
delusion', Avdy reflects, 'How great is man's yearning to be
heard above . . . how painfully was man's humanity born
within him.'[71]

According to Anatoly Lunacharsky, the 'enthusiasm' and
motivation to creative activity which religion could generate
were valuable, if not essential, to the effective realisation of
the social ideal. An understanding of religious principles could,
he felt, help to resolve the psychological tension between individualism and collectivism. 'I am,' he wrote 'of the opinion
that the singling out and understanding of these ideals, as
realistic religious principles within proletarian socialism must
powerfully facilitate the development among the proletariat
of the mighty rudiments of psychological collectivism.'[72] The
instinctive human drive to triumph over the finality of death
could, he believed, be satisfied by the mergence of the individual personality with the collective, and in a sharing in the
great and heroic deeds of humanity as a whole. God was not
in the world, Lunacharsky maintained, but He could be. 'It is
necessary to give him to the world . . . The path of the struggle
for socialism, that is the triumph of man in nature, that is
bogo-stroitel' stvo.'[73]

Avdy Kallistratov also seeks to give God to the world. He
fits in well with Lunacharsky's notion of a prophet as one who
demands a re-examination of man's covenant with God, and
therefore — as Lunacharsky believed — of social relations.

Avdy may not, appear to be a social reformer; he wants only to be a moral reformer, but, as a priest in the novel tells him, his views are bound to upset the social status quo. God-seeking may be a crime against the Church, he says, but it is regarded as such to a no lesser degree by society.[74]

In a violent attack on god-building and god-seeking made in a letter to Gorky, Lenin declared that the two were virtually synonymous. 'God-seeking differs from god-building no more than a yellow devil from a blue one . . . Every religious idea, every idea of any little god, even every bit of coquettishness with a little god is unutterable vileness,' he wrote.[75] An article criticising religious themes in recent Soviet literature, published in *Komsomolyskaya pravda* in July, 1986, made reference to Lenin's letter while reproving Aitmatov for introducing a god-seeking character into his writing and for suggesting that a religious vision can have a positive effect on social ethics.[76] In December, a letter from Yevgeny Yevtushenko was published, defending Aitmatov on the grounds that his novel suggests that it is culture (and that of course includes religious culture) which determines the moral and ethical standards of society.[77] As a work of literature, *Scaffold* was deemed a disappointment by V. Lakshin writing in *Izvestiya*,[78] but received a more positive review in *Pravda* which emphasised its appeal to cultural memory and acknowledged that it sought to tackle an unusually difficult theme.[79]

If the novel has not received an over-enthusiastic response from the Soviet press, it has at least been made very widely known. It is unlikely that Aitmatov's reputation as a Soviet writer will suffer as a result. The work does appeal, after all, primarily to the collective spirit, whether through illustrative references to the totemic cult or through an indirect re-exposition of the god-building theory. The two are by no means incompatible: both aim to preserve, protect and promote the strength and cohesion of society.

To conclude, I would like to refer briefly to an interview with Aitmatov, published in *Pravda* in February 1987, under the headline 'I believe in Man' (*Veryu v cheloveka*).[80] In it, Aitmatov emphasised that Soviet society's greatest potential investment was its moral capital. It is in this area, he suggested, that work must be done to overcome social and economic problems. He spoke of the importance of conscience, emphasising that a reawakening of moral instinct and of a sense of social responsibility, was the means by which to consolidate the collective. First, it is necessary to build the individual, he said, by applying new, more sophisticated methods of ideological and moral education.

This is where Aitmatov now stands. If, in the early 1970s, with the publication of *The White Steamship*, he seemed to be emerging as a defender of values associated with spiritual individualism, more recently — both as a writer and as a public figure in the Soviet Union — he appears to have taken up the role of spokesman for the ethical renewal currently being promoted by the Soviet media in tandem with the notions of 'open publicity' (*glasnost'*) and 'reconstruction' (*perestroika*). Aitmatov's main themes are now the new social conscience and the new moral rearmament — a far cry from the painful tension between the personalist religious urge and the tendency to refer to the values of the collective which *The White Steamship* depicted.

In this paper I have tried to indicate the direction Aitmatov's writing appears to have taken over the years between 1970 and 1986, and to show the way this has been reflected in his handling of religious subject matter. *The White Steamship* demonstrated the incompatibility of a child's animist perceptions with a totemic world-view which puts the survival and glory of the social group in the position of a Supreme Absolute. In *The Day Lasts More than 100 Years* Aitmatov drew on elements from a range of ancient Central Asian cults associated with the natural world, and so emphasised the need to look to a real collective tradition acknowledging the interdependence of man, his physical environment and his historical roots. The novel suggested, even, that this is essential to the maintenance of a fully human personality. Aitmatov's most recent work, *Scaffold*, also refers to the totemic tradition, but gives it unprecedented prescriptive weight, while also tentatively advancing a neo-religious solution to the ills of the modern world. This solution proposes the elevation of the future of the collective to the position of a godhead, closely reflecting the thinking of a group of early twentieth-century intellectuals, including Gorky and Lunacharsky. Over the sixteen years covered by the works studied here, the thrust of Aitmatov's writing appears to have shifted markedly from the examination and expression of a spontaneous and unspoilt experience of life's variety, towards the formulation of possible solutions to contemporary social problems in the Soviet Union.

Notes

1 Bronislaw Malinowski, *Magic, Science and Religion*. London 1974, pp. 17–22.
2 Ibid., p. 21.
3 Ibid., p. 22; *Encyclopaedia of Religion and Ethics*, vol. 12. London 1908, pp. 394, 406; G Jobes, *Dictionary of Mythology, Folklore and Symbols*,
4 Mircea Eliade, *Shamanism*. New York 1964, p. xx.
5 Ref. Joseph Campbell, *The Masks of God: Primitive Mythology*. London 1960, pp. 231–75; Jean-Paul Roux, *La Réligion des Turcs et des Mongols*. Paris 1984, p. 65.
6 Roux, *Réligion des Turcs*, p. 58.
7 See G Gachev, *Chingiz Aitmatov i mirovaya literatura*. Kirgizstan 1982, p. 211.
8 Aitmatov, *Belyy parokhod* in *Sobranie sochinenii v trekh tomakh*, vol. 2. Moscow 1983. Translation: Tatyana and George Feifer, *The White Steamship*. London 1972.
9 The word *bugu* is Kirghiz for deer.
10 Feifer trans., *The White Steamship*, p. 164.
11 In the Central Asian tradition, water is manifest purity, and the element which reflects the sky and therefore the Sky God. See Roux, *Réligion des Turcs*, p. 137.
12 Ded Momun makes the following observation: 'The prophet himself does not know that he is a prophet. He is a simple man. Only a rascal knows himself to be what he is'. *Belyy parokhod*, p. 31. (my translation, I. J.).
13 Campbell, *Primitive Mythology*, p. 230.
14 Ibid., p. 266.
15 Eliade, *Shamanism*, p. 466.
16 Ibid., pp. 15–35.
17 Campbell, *Primitive Mythology*, p. 252.
18 Eliade, *Shamanism*, p. 474.
19 Feifer trans., *The White Steamship*, see 'Afterwood', p. 179.
20 Gachev, *Aitmatov i mirovaya literatura*.
21 Ibid., p. 218.
22 Aitmatov, *I dol' she veka dlitsya den'* in *Sobranie sochinenii v trekh tomakh*, vol. 2. Moscow 1983. Translation: John French, *The Day Lasts More than 100 Years*. London and Sydney 1984.
23 S M Abramzon, *Kirgizy i ikh etnogeneticheskiye i istoriko kul'turnye svyazi*. Leningrad, 1971. p. 273.
24 Ibid., pp. 319 and 325–6.
25 French trans., 'If death is nothing . . . then it follows that life also has no value', p. 34.

26 French, trans., 'It's not right to leave a man in an empty house'. ('How can he know if he's alone or not?'). 'We know . . . it's a man who's died — not some beast', p. 21.
27 The cite of burial which Yedigey performs is Islamic in form, although the emphasis on place reflects pre-Islamic beliefs, as do some of his philosophical musings.
28 French, trans., p. 97.
29 French's translation has been adapted to fall more closely in line with the original Russian text. See Aitmatov, *I dol' she veka* . . . , p. 480, and French, trans., p. 342.
30 I dol' she veka . . . , p. 233. My trans.
31 French, trans., 'Don't go against man's customs, don't go against nature.' p. 335.
32 Abramzon notes the particular importance of the oral tradition for the Kirghiz. See *Kirgizy* . . . , p. 340.
33 French, trans., p. 265.
34 Ibid., p. 127.
35 Abramzon, *Kirgizy* . . . , p. 277. In the shamanistic cosmic order, the World Tree or the Cosmic Tree unites the three cosmic zones. Its roots are in the underworld, its trunk is the axis of the universe, and its branches touch the firmament.
36 Ibid., p. 278.
37 Roux, *Religion des Turcs*, pp. 105, 158.
38 Abramzon, *Kirgizy*, p. 289.
39 French, trans., p. 342.
40 Ibid., p. 351.
41 Abramzon, *Kirgizy*, p. 289.
42 French, trans., 'We're like two brothers, fed with the same milk', p. 85.
43 Aitmatov refers to Karanar as *verblyud syrttan*, a 'wondercamel'. French, trans., p. 89.
44 Roux, *La Religion des Turcs*, p. 103.
45 Abramzon, *Kirgizy*, p. 291.
46 Roux, *La Religion des Turcs*, p. 109.
47 Aitmatov, Plakha, *Novyy mir*, 6, 8, 9. Moscow 1986.
48 *Liternaturnaya Gazeta*, 13 August 1986. My translation.
49 Roux, *La Religion des Turcs*, p. 207.
50 Aitmatov refers to Akbara as the 'Great Mother of All Substance' (velikaya mat' vsego sushchego), *Plakha*, part 3, NM 9, p. 63.
51 Describing the slaughter of the antelopes Aitmatov uses Dostoyevsky's term 'mangod': 'lyudi, lyudi-chelovekobogi'. *Plakha*, pt 1, NM 6, p. 11.
52 Plakha, pt 3, NM 9, p. 63.
53 Ibid., pt 1, NM 6, p. 121.
54 Ibid., p. 26.
55 Ibid., p. 47.
56 Ibid., p. 50.
57 Ibid., p. 52.
58 Ibid., p. 47.

59 Ibid., p. 47.
60 *Lit* ——
61 Bulgakov M, *Master i Margarita*. Frankfurt 1969, p. 41.
62 *Plakha*, pt 2, NM 8, p. 113.
63 Ibid., p. 114.
64 Gorky's letter to Tolstoy. As quoted in B D Wolfe, *The Bridge and the Abyss*. Connecticut 1983, p. 37.
65 Gorky, *Mother*. As quoted Ibid., pp. 40–1.
66 *Plakha*, pt 1, p. 53.
67 Gorky, *Dialogue between Writer and Reader*. In Wolfe, p. 36.
68 *Mercure de France*, 'Enquête', 15 April 1907. Ibid., pp. 42–3.
69 Gorky, *Ispoved'*, Ladyschnikow Verlag, Berlin, pp. 163–4 (My translation).
70 Ibid., p. 166.
71 *Plakha*, pt 1, p. 38.
72 In C Read, *Religion, Revolution and the Russian Intelligentsia, 1900–1912*. London/Basingstoke, 1979, p. 85.
73 In T E O'Connor, *The Politics of Soviet Culture*, Ann Arbor, 1983, p. 112.
74 *Plakha*, pt 1, p. 48.
75 In Wolfe, *Bridge and Abyss*, p. 50.
76 Article by I Kryvelev, *Komsomslskaya pravda*, 30 July 1986.
77 Yevgeny Yevtushenko, *Istochnik nravstvennosti — kultura, Komsomolskaya pravda*, 10 December 1986.
78 V Lakshin, *Po pravde govorya . . .* , *Izvestiya*, 3/4 December 1986.
79 Ye Surkov, *Tragediya v Moyunkumakh*, *Pravda*, 22 December 1986.
80 Interview with Aitmatov. *Veryu v cheloveka*, *Pravda*, 14 February, 1987.

References

Works by Chingiz Aitmatov

'Belyy parokhod', in *Sobranie sochinenii v trekh tomakh*, vol. 2. Moscow 1983
'I dol'she veka dlitsya den'', in *Sobranie sochinenii v trekh tomakh*, vol. 2. Moscow 1983
'Plakha', *Novyy mir*, nos. 6, 8, 9. Moscow 1986

Translations

Tatyana and George Feifer, *The White Steamship*. London 1972
John French, *The Day Lasts More than 100 Years*. London and Sydney 1984

Other works in Russian

S M Abramzon, *Kirgizy i ikh etnogeneticheskiye i istoriko-kulturnye svyazi*. Leningrad 1971
M Bulgakov, *Master i Margarita*, Frankfurt 1969
G Gachev, *Chingiz Aitmatov i mirovaya literatura*, Kirgiztan 1982.

M. Gorky, *Ispoved'*, J. Ladyschnikow Verlag, Berlin

Other works in English

J Campbell, *The Masks of God: Primitive Mythology*, London 1960
M Eliade, *Shamanism*. New York 1964.
B Malinowski, *Magic, Science and Religion*. London 1974
T E O'Connor, *The Politics of Soviet Culture*. Ann Arbor 1983.
C Read, *Religion, Revolution and the Russian Intelligentsia*, London/Basingstoke 1979
B D Wolfe, *The Bridge and the Abyss*. Connecticut 1983.

Work in French

J-P Roux, *La Religion des Turcs et des Mongols*. Paris 1984.

Articles in Russian

Interview with Ch Aitmatov. *Literaturnaya Gazeta* 13 August 1986.
I. Kryvelev, 'Koketnichaya s bozhenkoy', *Komsomolskaya pravda* 30 July 1986.
V Lakshin, 'Po pravde govorya' . . . , *Izvestiya* 3/4 December 1986.
Ye Surkov, 'Tragediya v Moyunkumakh', *Pravda* 22 December 1986.
Ye Yevtushenko, 'Istochnik nravstvennosti — kultura', *Komsomolskaya pravda* 10 December 1986
Interview with Ch Aitmatov, *Veryu v cheloveka*, *Pravda* 14 February 1987.

5

SCRIPT CHANGES IN XINJIANG

Ildikó Bellér-Hann

In this paper I will focus on the regional capital, Urumqi, for two reasons: firstly, this is where my own observations were carried out, secondly, this is where linguistic and cultural policies are most clearly manifested.

To a foreigner the most obvious signs of regional bilingualism are bilingual inscriptions on government offices, public buildings, shops etc. Chinese characters are followed by an Uighur translation rendered in the Arabic script. The juxtaposition of these seems natural: the Uighurs like some other Turkic minorities of Xinjiang have been Muslims for several hundred years, and following in the footsteps of other converts to Islam they adopted the Arabic script.

However, this seemingly straightforward historical explanation of the official use of the Arabic script among the Uighurs, the Kazakh and the Kirghiz is misleading: it is in fact a recent phenomenon dating from 1982.

The presence of Turkic-speaking peoples, including the old Uighurs, in the vast area which is known as Xinjiang today dates from the tenth to twelfth centuries. As one author puts it 'by the end of the eleventh at the latest, the Turkic language had by and large spread through the entire Tarim Basin as a lingua franca' (Geng Shimin 1984, p. 10). The emergence of what can be called the modern Uighur nationality can be dated from around the turn of the fifteenth and sixteenth centuries (Geng Shimin: 1984, p. 13). Linguistic unification involved the adoption of the Arabic script which followed their conversion to Islam. At approximately the same time the Chagatai literary language emerged, which strongly influenced the development of other Turkic literary languages for centuries onwards. It

71

also affected the formation of modern Central Asian Turkic languages, with modern Uighur and Uzbek among them.

So it is easy to understand why Uighur intellectuals today regard the outstanding literary achievements of the Middle-Turkic period as well as the Arabic script as their own cultural heritage.[1]

This strong identification of modern Uighurs (who acquired this name again only after a group of Uighur migrants to the USSR officially adopted it in 1921, see Silde-Karklins 1975, p. 343) with both Islamic and Turkic traditions is reflected in their attitude towards the script changes which took place in Xinjiang in recent times. It appears that in view of the Uighurs' strong adherence to their cultural heritage, these changes were inevitable in an increasingly non-Muslim and non-Turkic environment, either Russian or Chinese.

At issue here is the role played by script changes in a peoples' history. It may appear of minor importance at first sight. However, a change in the means of written communication has a strong significance for both the individual and for the political nation. Before elaborating these aspects, let us review the history of actual and attempted script changes among the Turkic speaking groups of Xinjiang.

The History of Script Changes

The well-known fact that the rich vowel system of Turkic languages cannot be appropriately rendered by the Arabic script became the main slogan of reformers in Turkey and in Soviet Central Asia.[2] Although this is an undeniable fact, in the case of the Uighurs this popular argument seems to have been refuted, as will be shown later.

To the best of my knowledge, the need to reform their script was overtly expressed by Uighur intellectuals in the 1920s (Emiloğlu: 1973, p. 128). These attempts roughly coincided with the actual implementation of script changes in Turkey and the Soviet Union. That minority intellectuals were aware of the cultural changes which were taking place amongst related people is indicated by the fact that both the main fractions of the Uighur intelligentsia tried to follow the example of reform movements abroad.[3] However, these efforts did not result in any tangible changes. Officially, the Uighurs kept on using the

Arabic script up until the 1950s. The scarce material available on the subject indicates that even before 1956 the example of Turkic-speaking peoples living in the Soviet Union was having certain practical though sporadic effects in Xinjiang, in spite of the overall failure of the reform movement. Apparently, when the Soviet Uighurs, who had used the Arabic script until 1930, changed to the Latin alphabet (in use from 1930 to 1946), the same script was introduced in some places in Xinjiang. The same thing happened to the modified Cyrillic script which the Soviet Uighurs finally adopted in 1946 (Silde-Karklins 1975, p. 355).[4]

The history of official script changes among the Turkic minorities in Xinjiang goes back to the 1950s. In response to the Uighurs' own wish to reform and also to Soviet encouragement in 1956 a decision to change to the modified Cyrillic script was taken (Jarring 1981, p. 230). From personal contacts I have learnt that in certain schools the teaching of the Cyrillic script began virtually at once, on an experimental basis.[5] However, this decision was soon changed. In 1958 the introduction of a modified Latin script based on the Chinese pin-yin system was put forward (Jarring 1981, pp. 230–1). Apparently the very idea of changing the Arabic alphabet, whether to Cyrillic or Latin script, provoked violent reactions on several occasions (Alptekin 1978, p. 161). If this source can be taken seriously at all, it would seem that those opposing the script changes were conservatives who would not constitute more than a fraction of the Uighur intelligentsia. Alternatively, if the suggested changes were opposed by the entire nationalist intelligentsia, it would seem that, while a reform movement carried out by the Uighurs themselves might in principle stand a good chance of success, changes initiated by the Chinese authorities were unacceptable. The cultural line followed in Xinjiang in the 1950s was part of a large scale reform programme which concerned all the minorities living in China. In the mid-fifties Chinese linguists from Beijing were sent to minority regions, including Xinjiang. Their task was to study minority languages and to help these groups carry out changes deemed necessary by the experts. Several minorities without a writing system of their own were given a script based on the Chinese system, while others with a history of literacy were advised to carry out changes (*Til wä Tärdźimä* 1986, 1, pp. 2–3).

The above-mentioned decisions concerning script changes in Sinkiang were obviously motivated by political factors. The suggestion to adopt the Cyrillic script by the Turks of Xinjiang was influenced by cordial contacts with the Soviet Union. The Soviets tried to encourage the official adoption of the Cyrillic alphabet in Xinjiang by practical means such as printing and sending Uighur language books and dictionaries in the Arabic script as well as in Cyrillic, even though the former was no longer in official use in the USSR (Silde-Karklins 1975, pp. 356–7). The decision in 1958 to introduce a pin-yin based Latin alphabet reflected the worsening state of Sino-Soviet relations. Besides, recognition of the threat posed by allowing the same script to be used by the Turkic peoples on the two sides of the border may also have been important.

In spite of the obvious political connotations of these changes we must also remember that after 1949 the PRC's minority policy can hardly be deemed crudely oppressive. After that time the use of minority languages was positively encouraged and the linguistic and cultural programme of the 1950s aimed to expand literacy rates amongst minorities. One must not forget either that the idea to reform the Arabic script came from the Uighurs themselves originally, which made it possible for the Chinese to pose as the benign realisers of indigenous dreams.

The 1958 decision to introduce the pin-yin based Latin script was followed by an experimental period between 1960 and 1964. Later, as a direct result of the Cultural Revolution its use spread slowly. In this process the official introduction of the new script in 1965 made little difference. Its large-scale use started in 1974 (Jarring 1981, p. 232). As a result, a generation of Uighur intellectuals now in their twenties and early thirties was brought up with this script only. In these circumstances it is easy to see how Jarring reached the conclusion in 1981 that 'It has to be anticipated that the introduction of of the new Romanised script for the Uighurs of Xinjiang will have the same long-term effects as the change to the Latin alphabet had in Turkey' (Jarring 1981, p. 234). This prediction, however, did not come true. In 1982 another script reform covering the Uighur, Kazakh and Kirghiz peoples in Xinjiang was introduced (*Ujghur yezighinin* 1983, pp. 1–2). This reform reintroduced the Arabic script as it had been amended in the 1950s, with a few additional modifications.[6] The fact that very little is publicly known about how this latest decision was brought about and realised suggests that the whole reform was deliberately played down by the authorities.[7] The change is widely regarded as a victory of the Uighur people. It has been suggested by my Uighur contacts that this is what all Uighurs wanted, and also that this change was somehow (never explained how) initiated by the Uighurs themselves. Naturally, many Uighurs feel that this latest reform is a positive development in their national position. However, the change was not welcomed by all the Uighurs. The generation referred to above which was brought up with the pin-yin based Latin script and with no knowledge of the Arabic script are discontented.[8] When the latest script change was introduced short courses teaching them the Arabic script were organised at work places and universities to bridge this cultural gap. School children faced with a second script seem to be able to cope very well. Young adults, however, are reluctant to give up the script they were brought up with, and even those who successfully finished the Arabic script course avoid using it. This presents itself as a generation gap with such awkward manifestations as young Uighurs writing to their parents in Chinese since this is the only mutually understood script (Scharlipp 1984, p. 8). This, however, may easily gain more significance. Although the older generation is quite happy with their newly regained old script, and therefore they cannot see any grounds for yet another change, some younger intellectuals anticipate and would indeed welcome the reintroduction of the Latin script.

Comparison

The script reforms in Xinjiang invite comparison with similar reforms among other Turkic groups. For various reasons I will mainly concentrate on the changes which took place in modern Turkey. The script and language reforms of Soviet Central Asia are equally interesting and important. However, a comparison with Turkey seems more revealing because of the relative absence of direct communication between two regions which nevertheless shared similar religious, cultural and linguistic characteristics.

The script reform of modern Turkey, dating from 1928,

which abolished the Arabic script and replaced it with a modified Latin script was a prelude to the large-scale language reform which was itself part of Atatürk's overall programme to modernise, westernise, secularise and democratise the new state. Discussion of such linguistic changes can be traced as far as the *Türk-i-Basit* movement (Köprülü 1966, pp. 272–82) and acquired a more definite shape during the reform movements of the nineteenth century (Levend 1949). One sees in this history the extent to which Turkic script and language reforms were bound up with a conscious search for the national identity. The use of elegant Persian by the educated upper classes and Arabic by the conservative-religious elements was intolerable to young nationalists who sought to emulate European patterns. The Arabic script came to be regarded as the representative of a conservative and declining culture as well as a serious impediment to mass education. The introduction of the Latin script was considered the only way to achieve higher literacy (Hütterman 1978, p. 63). At the same time the virtually unlimited use of Arabic and Persian words hindered the development of a unified national language. By purifying the language of large numbers of foreign elements the reformers tried to decrease and finally eliminate the gap between the language of the highly educated elite and that of the common people.[9]

It seems that there was no comparable history of planned cultural reform in Xinjiang. But the traditional Arabic script was here, too, seen as an obstacle to raising literacy rates.[10] Besides, the Xinjiang reform movement was also motivated by nationalist sentiments. However, in contrast to Ottoman Turkish, which, at the time of the script and language reform showed considerable differences between the literary language and the vernacular, no such gap could be traced in the Uighur language at the time of the script reforms here. Religion also played different roles in the two regions. In Turkey the script reform formed part of a larger programme of secularisation, thus it enjoyed the full support of the progressive nationalists. In Xinjiang, in the context of a large non-Muslim population, to defend the old Arabic script against the Latin alphabet seemed an important task to all nationalist sympathisers, including conservatives. Finally, the script reform in Turkey ushered in a large-scale language reform, which, on a reduced scale, continues today. In contrast, no comparable language reform has accompanied the script reforms in Xinjiang. From personal interviews I have learnt that Arabic and Persian loan-words are felt by Uighur native speakers as an integral part of their language. It is true that Uighur has preserved more lexical as well as grammatical archaisms than its western Turkic counterparts and its vocabulary never deviated from the original Turkic structure to the same extent as Ottoman Turkish. But the number of Arabic and Persian loans in modern Uighur is not negligible (Nadzhip 1971, pp. 30–6). The reason for the complete lack of enthusiasm on the part of the Uighur intellectuals to purify their language from its Arabic and Persian elements must be the more direct threat represented by other languages with completely different structures to that of Turkic, namely Chinese and Russian. We know that Arabic and Persian were just as alien to Turkic as Chinese and Russian. However, in the course of time Arabic and Persian loans have become integrated into spoken Uighur. This was, of course facilitated by the religion these cultures shared. Such words have been used within the framework of Turkic grammatical structures for centuries. Arabic and Persian loanwords had also been integrated into Ottoman Turkish in exactly the same way, and these were accepted and preserved by the moderates of the Turkish language reform movement.

As for Chinese words, they began to penetrate the old Uighur language a long time ago, but these borrowings had become completely integrated into Uighur. Besides, their number is relatively small (Nadzhip 1971, p. 37).

The situation in Xinjiang today is one in which the importance of Chinese in daily life, especially in urban areas, creates favourable grounds for the adoption of Chinese terms. This is particularly so in the case of new scientific and technical concepts. Since most minority students studying for a higher degree in Xinjiang must use Chinese textbooks, the penetration of increasing numbers of Chinese terms is more easily understood.

However, it has also to be emphasised that there have been voices demanding the purification of modern Uighur from its numerous Arabic and Persian lexical elements, as well as to prevent new borrowings of this kind. The means by which this trend gains ground are more subtle than the measures taken by Ataturk's reformers. In modern Turkey the Turkish Linguistic Society was appointed to carry out the language reform (Heyd 1954, pp. 25–6). The work of the Society was strictly controlled by the state. The public was also directly involved in this work, e.g., they could suggest new words etc. (Heyd 1954, p. 29). There is no sign of such populist initiatives from the Language Committee that was founded in the 1950s in Xinjiang (Yang Bingyi 1985, pp. 5, 7). As for the creation of new Uighur words, this committee seems to have been barely able to carry out such a task (Abit 1985, p. 16). The appointment of another committee with this task, with reference to all the minority languages spoken in Xinjiang has recently been suggested (Abit 1985, p. 17). So far most of the newly-formed Uighur words have been the creation of the media only. A definite programme has recently been published about modernising Uighur and other minority languages of the region. The main principles expressed here have a lot in common with the Turkish language reform. These include the widening the meaning of existing words, reviving archaic Turkic lexical elements, borrowing from dialects and the vernacular as well as from related languages (cf. Heyd 1954, pp. 88–91; Abit 1985, pp. 14–16).

Following the example set by the Turkish reformers, the Uighurs are also ready to accept or at least tolerate loan words from non-related languages, but they also warn against the acceptance of large numbers of such borrowings.[11]

This new proposal concerning language reform in Xinjiang reflects a moderate attitude. This was the eventual path followed by Turkish reformers, too. Had it not been thus, the Turkish language reform probably would not have done as well as it has. Such pragmatic policies accept into Uighur those Chinese words which have already become fully integrated (Abit 1985, p. 15). New technical terms, however, should be based on Uighur words as much as possible.[12] This limited acceptance of loan words made the creation of a standardised orthography necessary both in Turkey and in Xinjiang. In fact, it would appear that the latest script change in Xinjiang has been treated as merely a revision of orthography (it is true that some new graphic signs have been added to the Arabic script for such sounds as *ö, ü*) rather than a significant cultural change. This is perhaps because a change of orthography is in less obvious need of ideological explanation.

Despite the prevailing moderate line there are some linguists who would ideally favour a more drastic purification of the Uighur language from its Persian and Arabic elements.[13]

Similar development can be seen among the Turkic-speaking peoples of Soviet Central Asia too, where some nationalists were equally opposed to the Cyrillic as well as to the Latin alphabet, and pressed for preserving the old Arabic script and later a modified version of the same. There were also attempts to alter the respective Turkic languages themselves along the lines of the Turkish reforms (*The Turkic Peoples of the USSR* 1953 pp. 2–4).[14]

Concluding Remarks

Although a detailed comparison of language and script reforms in Turkey, the USSR and Xinjiang is beyond the scope of the present paper, it is possible to suggest the lines along which such a comparison would have to proceed.

The most obvious difference between Turkey and Xinjiang is that modern Turkey has developed as an independent national state with Turkish as its official national language. In the absence of any direct threat to the dominant language, Turkey was able to follow without disruption a path of modernisation which involved a radical break with such decisive symbols of the past as religion, and a script which was strongly connected to that religion and foreign borrowings in the language which had widened the gap between the ruling elite and the common people. In Xinjiang Uighur nationalist aspirations could develop only within the constraints of powerful alien (Russian and Chinese) cultures. In these circumstances national identity could only be asserted and maintained through preservation of all that could be in some way associated with a 'national heritage': religion, Arabic script, and, to some extent, lexical elements that can be regarded as the legacy of a Muslim past.

The Turkic peoples of the USSR seem to occupy an intermediate position between these extremes. They may enjoy more autonomy than the minorities of Xinjiang, if only by virtue of their numerical concentration in Soviet Central Asia, but they are not as independent as the Turks of modern Turkey. This position is reflected in linguistic changes which have taken place there. After brief experiments with modified Latin, and in some places, modified Arabic scripts, the Turks of the USSR have apparently been reconciled to the use of the Cyrillic script that is standard throughout most of the Soviet Union. This was not their choice and it was not their script. But at least it did not threaten their basic identity as the imposition of the pin-yin based Latin script was perceived to threaten the numerically smaller and therefore more exposed Uighur nation in China.

How should the latest script reform, i.e., the reintroduction of the modified Arabic script, be evaluated? The major disadvantage of the pin-yin based Latin script was usually seen in the fact that the sound value of many letters is different from that of the same signs in Western languages, a state of affairs which may cause confusion. The minor modifications introduced in the 1950s and 1980s have created an Arabic script which is at least as well suited to rendering Uighur as the modified Cyrillic scripts are suited to rendering the Turkic languages of the USSR, or the modified Latin alphabet to modern Turkish.[15] Its reintroduction in Xinjiang combined with the possibilities for Uighurs themselves to supervise changes in their language reflect the improving political atmosphere for ethnic minorities in the region. Since the Uighurs and other groups involved in the latest script change consider it important in maintaining their national identity, this script reform must be regarded as a positive change. But we must remember that it also adds to the cultural separation of the Turkic-speaking peoples which now have three fundamentally different writing systems. Furthermore, the frequent changes in the region in the last thirty years have created confusion (*Til wä tärdžimä* 1986, 1, p. 8) and a cultural gap between generations.

Script changes in Xinjiang naturally reflect changes in cultural policy towards ethnic minorities.[16] Although most authors avoid tackling the question of the script changes, all seem to admit readily that mistakes were made during the Cultural Revolution (Azizi 1986, p. 3; Ämät 1982, p. 1; Yang Bingyi 1985, p. 14). Occasionally we also find explicit criticism of the alphabet reform of the late fifties. In a recent article it is argued that the obligatory introduction of the pin-yin based Latin alphabet 'made it more difficult for the minority peoples to learn how to read and write, caused more confusion in their developing their language.' (*Til wä tärdžimä* 1986, 1, p. 8). This is scarcely consistent with the assumption that one of the basic aims of the reform was to decrease illiteracy among minorities.

To sum up, the recent reinstatement of the Arabic script is definitely regarded by many Uighurs as the manifestation of a more democratic era that started in 1979. It is hoped that the recently enacted Law of Regional Autonomy for Ethnic Minorities will guarantee the continuation of these trends in the future (cf. Äzizi 1986, pp. 1–6).

Notes

1 This is ironic. Although the old Uighur script was widely used all over Central Asia and even became the official script of the Golden Horde, modern Uighurs rarely express claim on this tradition. The obvious reason for this must be the unifying impact of Islam.

2 Although it is true that the Arabic alphabet obscured dialectal differences in Turkic languages this cannot be regarded as a positive feature, as some authors claim (Henze 1956, p. 30).

3 While the Ili intellectuals supported the Turkish and Central Asian models (Latin script), the so-called Tarbagatai group advocated the example of the Turks living in the Volga-Ural region (modified Arabic). (cf. Emiloğlu 1973, p. 128).

4 The so-called *Orta Imla* used by some in Xinjiang as a result of Soviet influence is not exactly clear to me. Regardless of whether this was a modified Latin or Cyrillic script, its use was certainly not widespread or officially recognised (Emiloğlu 1973, p. 129).

5 This also suggests that there must have been some precedents for teaching such a script in Xinjiang.

6 In the fifties this included the acceptance of some Persian letters, the abolition of some Arabic characters deemed unnecessary for Uighur, and the introduction of six letters to denote eight vowels (Sabit A 1986, pp. 2, 6; Yang Bingyi 1985, pp. 8–9). In 1982 the most important change was the addition of two letters to render the vowels *ö* and *ü*.

7 It seems that the change was not so sudden as the presently available Uighur language publications suggest: while in Xinjiang I learnt that Uighur books printed in the Arabic script were reappearing in book shops from 1981.

8 According to one source, however, half of the total Uighur population had to learn the Latin alphabet (Dilger 1976, p. 32).

9 On the Turkish alphabet and language reform see Heyd 1954; Levend 1949; Korkmaz, Z, *Türk dilinin tarihi akisi icinde Atatürk ve*

dil devrimi, Ankara, 1963; Steuerwald, K, *Untersuchungen zur türkischen Sprache der Gegenwart*, 3. vols., Berlin 1963–66, etc.

10 This can be illustrated by the fact that in January 1965, on the verge of the official introduction of the Latin script, a new campaign was launched simultaneously to increase literacy rates among the minorities of Xinjiang (Dilger 1976, p. 29).

11 It is interesting to see how an Uighur author may cite the example of modern Chinese, which often makes use of classical Chinese words to avoid foreign borrowings, to support an argument in favour of reviving old Turkic words rather than replacing them with Chinese or Russian ones (Ghopuri 1985, p. 13).

12 This principle is often contradicted in practice. For example, Uighur doctors practising Western medicine tend to use large numbers of western words which are unintelligible to their patients, with whom they have to use ordinary Uighur expressions.

13 For a minor attack on modern poets who use such loans when Uighur equivalents are available see Tursun, D (1985).

14 For script and language reforms among the Turks of the USSR see for example, Bacon 1966, especially chapter VII, pp. 189–201; Wurm, S (1954) *The Turkic Peoples of the USSR*, Central Asian Research Centre, Oxford, and Baskakov, N. A. (1960), *The Turkic Languages of Central Asia*, translated by Wurm S, London.

15 Another example when a Turkic group adopted and successfully used a modified Arabic script was that of the Volga Tatars. They started to use such an alphabet in the early 1920s. Because it was successful and popular it was particularly difficult to make them adopt the Latin script instead in 1929 (Henze 1956, p. 49).

16 For an overall picture of minority policies in China see Dreyer 1976, pp. 261–76.

References

Abit, E. (1985) Söz-atalghularnin geliplašturuš toghrisida pikir, in *Til wä Tärdžimä*, 8. pp. 10–17.

Alptekin, E (1978) *Uygur Türkleri*, Istanbul.

Ämät, I (1982) 'Tädžrililerni jägunläp, ittipaqliqni kučäjtip, milli tiljeziq xizmiti wä tärdžimä xizmitini jänimu jaxši išläjli', in *Til wä Tärdžimä*, Urumqi, 1, pp. 1–2.

Äzizi, S (1986) 'Millätlär özlirinin til jeziqini qolliniš wä täräqqi qilduruš ärkinlikigä igä', in *Šindžan dašü ilmi žurnili*, Urumqi, 2, pp. 1–6.

Bacon, E (1966) *Central Asians under Russian Rule: A Study in Cultural Change*, Ithaca, New York.

Batirqan (1985), 'Milli teritorijilik aptonomijä qanunini jaxši üginip, milli til- jeziqnin rolini toluq džari qildurajli', in *Til wä Tärdžimä*, 1, pp. 4–9, Urumqi.

Dilger, B (1976) 'Die Uiguren und ihr gegenwärtiges Bildungswesen' in *Materialia Turcica*, 2, Bochum, pp. 28–37.

Dreyer, J T (1976), *China's Forty Millions* Harvard Univ. Press Cambridge (Mass.)- London.

Emiloğlu, A T (1973) 'Changes in the Uighur Script during the Past 50 Years', in *Central Asiatic Journal*, XVII, No. 2–4, Wiesbaden, pp. 128–129.

Geng Shimin (1984), 'On the Fusion of Nationalities in the Tarim Basin and the Formation of the Modern Uighur Nationality' in *Central Asian Survey*, Vol. 3, No. 4, pp. 1–14.

Ghopuri, G (1985) 'Qädimqidin bugünki üčün pajdiliniš' in *Til wä Tärdžimä*, Urumqi, 6, pp. 6–14.

Henze, P B (1956) 'Politics and Alphabets in Inner Asia' in *Journal of the Royal Central Asian Society*, Vol. XLIII, Jan., pp. 29–51.

Heyd, U (1954), 'Language Reform in Modern Turkey', in *Oriental Notes and Studies*, published by the Israel Oriental Society No. 5, Jerusalem.

Hüttemann, K (1978), 'Zum 50. Jahrestag der Schriftreform in der Türkei', in *Materialia Turcica* 4. Bochum, pp. 55–64.

Jarring, G (1981) 'The New Romanized Alphabet for Uighur and Kazakh and Some Observations on the Uighur Dialect of Kashgar' in *Central Asiatic Journal*, XXV, 3–4, pp. 230–245.

Köprülü, M. Fuad (1966) 'Millî edebiyat cereyaninin ilk mübes s̀irleri', in *Edebiyat Araştirmalari* (Türk Dil Kurumu) Ankara, pp. 271–315.

Levend, A S (1949) *Türk dilinde geliş'me ve sadeleş'me safhalarî*, Ankara.

Nadzhip, E N (1971) *Modern Uighur*. Nauka Publishing House, Moscow.

Osmanow- Sabit- Džappar *et al* (eds) (1985), *Hazirqi zaman ujghur ädäbi tilinin imla lughiti*, Urumqi.

Sabit, A (1985), 'Ujghur tilinin imla qaidiliri wä imla lughatlirinin išliniši häqqidä qisqiča tonušturuš', in *Til wä Tärdžimä*, Urumqi, 2, pp. 1–9.

Scharlipp, W -E (1984), *Auxiliarfunktionen von Hauptverben nach Konverb in der neuuigurischen Schriftsprache von Sinkiang*, Berlin.

Šilde-Karklins, R (1975) 'The Uighurs Between China and the USSR' in *Canadian Slavonic Papers*, Ottawa, vol. 17, 2–3, pp. 341–365. *Til wä Tärdžimä* (1986), pp. 1–10, 'Gülläp-jašnawatqan Šindžan millätlirin tiljeziq išliri'.

'The Turkic Peoples of the USSR: The Development of Their Languages and Writing' in *Central Asian Review* (1953), No. 1, pp. 1–8.

Tursun, D (1985), 'Hazirqi zaman ujghur šeirijitidä äräp-pars sözlirinin qolliniliši häqqidä qisqičä mulahizä', in *Til wä Tärdžimä*, 8, pp. 21–25. *Ujghur jezighinin elipbäsi wä ujghur ädäbi tilinin imla quaidisi* (Aptonom Rajonluq Millätlär Til-Jeziq Xizmiti Komiteti), Urumchi (1983).

Yang Bingyi (1985) 'Partijinin millätlär til-jeziq xizmitidä tirišip jeni wäzijät jaritajli', in *Til wä Tärdžimä*, 2, pp. 1–19, Urumqi.

6

CENSUS AND SOCIOLOGY: EVALUATING THE LANGUAGE SITUATION IN SOVIET CENTRAL ASIA

Simon Crisp

Recent decades in the Soviet Union have seen a rise in the role of Russian and an increase in the measures taken to maintain this which may be described as little short of dramatic. Even the barest summary of the census figures speaks clearly enough: between 1926 and 1959 the number of non-Russians claiming Russian as their native language increased by 3.3 million, between 1959 and 1970 (11 as against 33 years) by 2.8 million — and between 1970 and 1979 by a further 3.3 million. At the same time, according to the census of 1979, the proportion of the non-Russian population of the Soviet Union speaking Russian as second language or claiming it as mother tongue has reached 62.2% (as against 48.7% in 1970). Furthermore, since the end of the period of what might be termed 'positive discrimination' in favour of the national languages (which may be said to have come with the school reforms of the late 1950s) a whole string of measures has been enacted specifically to strengthen the position and improve the command of Russian among the non-Russian population: the use and teaching of Russian at all educational levels — from university to kindergarten — has been debated at length and copiously legislated, the role of Russian in the Soviet armed forces has been discussed openly and in detail for the first time, and the ideology of supra-national or supra-ethnic consciousness has been developed in great detail and some complexity as writing on nationality questions has been dominated by the concept of the 'Soviet people'.

Of course, the results of such measures and other similar

developments have been uneven, differing from area to area according to a variety of factors: notably size of people, administrative status, demographic situation (in terms of compactness of settlement, etc.) and strength of cultural tradition. This paper will focus on the titular nationalities of the Turcophone Central Asian Republics together with the two largest of the other Soviet peoples (the Azerbaidzhanis and the Tatars), but will also make use for comparative purposes of material drawn from other parts of the Soviet Union. The aim will be to consider in some detail the extent and scope of national-Russian bilingualism in these areas. There are of course a number of other types of bilingualism found among these peoples by virtue of their long history of contact and migration (for Central Asia a good account is given by Vinnikov 1980), but it is bilingualism with Russian which undoubtedly carries the greatest social and political significance in the contemporary USSR. There is no need here to argue in detail the hypothesis that the aim of the authorities is to make every inhabitant of the country fluent in Russian (see Solchanyk 1982 for a clear presentation of the relevant material; for the Central Asian Republics, a convenient recent survey may be found in Ivanov *et al*. 1980), but it is perhaps not inappropriate to note the marked increase in the amount of popular and semi-popular writing devoted to the Russian language, from newspaper articles defending government language policy against foreign critics (Orusbaev 1985) to a collection of panegyrics to Russian by writers from all over the Soviet Union, which includes such well-known names as Aibek (Ojbek), Mirmukhsin and Abai Kunanbaev (Mikhajlovskaja 1986).

Of more interest however are claims that all this activity has indeed led to a radical transformation in the language behaviour of the non-Russians. The following statement, for example, is found in one of the most serious and detailed studies of the language situation in the USSR to appear in recent years:

Study of the actual linguistic competence of the [non-Russian] peoples shows that exactly in the 1970s a boundary was crossed, after which it has become possible to speak of bilingualism not only of an individual or an isolated group, but of bilingualism of a whole people (Guboglo 1984, p. 121).

The principal source for testing the validity of such claims is of course the results of the various All-Union censuses. For the study of bilingualism however we are limited to the two most recent censuses, those of 1970 and 1979, because the question which was asked about command of a second language was introduced for the first time only in 1970. Since the results of the 1979 census have yet to be published in full, this does impose limitations on the number and detail of comparisons which can be made. Table 1 gives the simplest comparison, between the percentages claiming command of their native language, Russian and other languages in 1970 and 1979, for the largest Soviet Turkic peoples.

Table 1 *Census figures on language*

	% claiming national language as mother tongue		% claiming command of Russian		% claiming command of other language	
	1970	1979	1970	1979	1970	1979
Uzbek	98.6	98.5	14.5	49.3	3.3	2.8
Kazakh	98.0	97.5	41.8	52.3	1.8	2.1
Tatar	89.2	85.9	62.5	68.9	3.5	4.9
Azerbaidzhani	98.2	97.9	16.6	29.5	2.5	2.0
Turkmen	98.9	98.7	15.4	25.4	1.3	1.6
Kirghiz	98.8	97.9	19.1	29.4	3.3	4.1

Sources: Zakiev 1982, p. 31, Kozlov 1982, p. 232

There are two ways of approaching this data, which we may characterise respectively as internal and external. One internal method would be to apply to the census data mathematical or statistical operations, with a view to refining the figures on bilingualism. A method of this mind was proposed by Silver (1975), who used simple arithmetical relationships between the figures given in the census reports of 1970 (numbers claiming national language, Russian or other language(s) as first or second language) to give an index of bilingualism with Russian and a four-point scale of linguistic russification. Table 2 gives the indexes of bilingualism for 1970 and 1979 for the same six Turkic peoples. These should be compared with the percent

Table 2 *Index of bilingualism (%) according to Silver 1975*

	1970	1979
Uzbek	12.9	52.7
Kazakh	42.0	50.9
Tatar	55.4	66.6
Azerbaidzhani	15.3	28.3
Turkmen	15.0	24.3
Kirghiz	19.8	28.5

Calculated from: Natsional'nyj Sostav 1973, pp. 144, 202, 223, 263, 284, 306; Chislennost' 1984, pp. 80–81, 110–111, 116–117, 126–127, 130–131, 134–135

ages claiming command of Russian in Table 1, the differences being due in part to the greater accuracy of Silver's technique, which takes into account all the census information on language claiming, and in part to the fact that while the figures in Table 1 refer to the entire population of a given nationality, those in Table 2 are calculated on the basis of that proportion of the population living within the confines of their own titular Republic (SSR for the four Central Asian peoples and for the Azerbaidzhanis, ASSR for the Tatars).[1]

The differences between the two sets of percentages are, not surprisingly, rather small, taking into account as they do the figures for language change and bilingualism with a language other than Russian, both of which are low for the peoples considered here. Moreover, all such re-analysis of the census data (for a much more complicated example see Garipov and Argunova 1980) begs some important assumptions, as Silver 1975, pp. 574–6, admits: firstly that the categories 'native language' and 'second language' are reliable, and secondly that the figures for language claimed correspond in some way to actual language use.[2] Both these assumptions, however, are open to question.

As Lieberson (1966, pp. 139–40) has pointed out, the form of census questions on mother tongue will tend to determine the response of those surveyed. In the various Soviet censuses the wording of this question has changed a number of times (Kozlov 1982, pp. 236–7; Arutjunjan and Susokolov 1983, pp. 15–17), but in both 1970 and 1979 the language claimed as mother tongue by the respondent was registered. In neither case has this procedure been adopted without discussion: before both censuses appeals were made to change the wording of the question on native language (for 1970 see Silver 1975, pp. 574–5; for 1979 see Labutova 1984, p. 13), but in both instances appeal was made to the precedent set in 1959 and the desirability of consistency with this. For the census of 1979, then, the Instruction for census takers enjoins registering the response to the question about native language without asking any questions about actual knowledge or use of the language except in those cases where the respondent has difficulty in answering (*Vsesojuznaja Perepis'* 1978, p. 51). As Karklins has shown in a survey conducted among recent emigrants from the Soviet Union, this means that the answer to this question may reflect many factors other than language use — specifically 'it should be realised that in a considerable number of cases "native tongue" is less an indicator of actual linguistic ability or usage than a psychological measure indicating self-perception'. (Karklins 1980, pp. 418–19). The subjective nature of the census figures on mother tongue has not escaped Soviet scholars either: the authors of the ethnolinguistic survey conducted in the Tatar ASSR in the late 1960s already pointed to the mixture of subjective and objective elements in the concept of 'mother tongue' and the consequences of this (Arutjunjan *et al.* 1973, p. 271), and more recently one of the compilers of a sociolinguistic questionnaire for Belorussia stressed the need to devise an objective means of eliciting the native language, since 'a number of people calling Belorussian their mother tongue have no practical command of it' (Bolotina 1982, p. 134). Reflecting on such material, Guboglo 1984, p. 277, frankly concludes that the concept of 'mother tongue' has become 'an inalienable component part of ethnic self-perception' and that the value of the census data on language may therefore approach the symbolic. That this is so should occasion no surprise: in a detailed study of the responses to language questions in US censuses Joshua Fishman concludes that 'most of those who claim non-English mother tongues no longer currently use these languages' (Fishman 1984, p. 68), yet holds, nevertheless, that despite the subjective status of mother tongue claiming, the resultant figures still have value as indicators of a psychological perception of ethnicity. Of course the connection between immigrant minorities in the US and large indigenous nationalities in the USSR is tenuous; nevertheless, the facts presented here should give us pause when considering and interpreting the extremely high levels of indigenous mother tongue claiming in the Soviet censuses. At the least, they reveal the need for some more objective measure of real linguistic ability and language use.

This becomes even clearer when one turns to the question introduced in the census of 1970 and repeated in 1979: 'Indicate also of which other language of the peoples of the USSR [the respondent] has good command [*svobodno vladeet*], since now we are dealing not just with command of a given language, but also potentially with the relationship between languages as they are used in daily life. Once again, problems of definition and interpretation are by no means unique to Soviet censuses; as Lieberson points out, 'it is particularly with questions about the ability of the respondent to speak one or more languages that we encounter considerable difficulty in present censuses. The key shortcoming for such questions hinges upon the lack of a clear-cut operational definition of ability to speak a given tongue[2] (Lieberson 1966, p. 141; Lieberson 1981). This is certainly so in the Soviet case; the Instruction for the 1979 census once again looks for a subjective response, though it does infer that 'free command' may be expressed as spoken fluency (*Vsesojuznaja Perepis'* 1978, p. 51). As Arutjunjan and Susokolov (1983, p. 17) point out, such an approach will hardly give a reliable indication of command of the language. The same Instruction (also) opens the door for possible distortion of the overall picture of bi- and multilingualism by saying that in the case of respondents speaking more than one language in addition to their mother tongue, only that language they felt they knew best was to be registered. And finally, another possibility of distortion is raised by the fact that the question about command of a second language 'has the aim of obtaining information characterising the process of convergence of peoples which is taking place in our country' (*Vsesojuznaja Perepis'* 1978, p. 30). In other words the census question is not (politically) neutral but is ideologically weighted. There would seem to be no doubt that, as Guboglo (1984, p. 131) recognises, we need some objective means of evaluating national-Russian bilingualism in the Soviet Union.

We are bound to ask, therefore, what other sources are available for study of the command and use of Russian in the Soviet Union as a whole and in Central Asia in particular. We have seen already that Soviet scholars are far from ignoring the kind of difficulties with the census data which we have examined. The language questions have been discussed by those compiling the census forms and accompanying instructions (albeit with few if any tangible changes), and a number of shortcomings have been pointed out by ethnographers and others using the census results. More tangibly, Soviet specialists in the national languages have been trying to get more detailed and reliable information on a whole range of questions, including bilingualism, by means of what have become known as 'concrete ethno-sociological surveys'.

The first step in this direction was taken in 1964, when a group of scholars from the Siberian section of the Academy of Sciences of Novosibirsk initiated an ethnolinguistic survey of the indigenous languages of Siberia. Having constructed a suitable questionnaire they began in 1965–6 by conducting a pilot survey with some 4,000 respondents, and this was subsequently refined and expanded to a full-scale study involving 58,000 respondents who represented almost all the indigenous peoples of Siberia (this information, together with the further details given below about the Siberian language project, is taken in the main from Avrorin 1970 and 1975, pp. 230–56). The project's questionnaire consisted of 37 questions divided into 4 sections, the first two of which were designed to elicit basic demographic data (place and length of residence, age, sex, nationality, profession and so on). The third section contained questions on command and use of native, Russian and other languages in various spheres (domestic, work and informal social settings, speaking, understanding, reading and writing), while the final group of questions asked about the language preferred for various levels of education. The population sampled, for all its large size, was not a true statistical sample, since instead of being spread evenly over the whole area inhabited by a given people it consisted of virtually the entire population of settlements previously chosen as typical for that nationality. The completed questionnaires were analysed by computer in a relatively sophisticated way (Badmaev 1967) and the results were discussed widely, though unfortunately it appears that they were never published in full. (In addition to the summaries published by Avrorin and referred to above, the Tuvin data were published by Serdobov 1968 and the Nanai results by Onenko 1972).

The Siberian language project attracted a good deal of interest and also some criticism, both of its design and of the conclusions drawn from its results. It was pointed out for instance that the design of the questionnaire precluded any objective assessment of the extent of command of any given language (Guboglo 1973, p. 117) — though to be fair, Avrorin had foreseen this charge from the beginning and tried to defend himself against it (1970 p. 36; 1975 p. 251) on the grounds of what was practically possible. It was also alleged that the composition of the survey sample made it unjustifiable to extrapolate from the results obtained to the population as a whole (Fedorov 1982, p. 132). Perhaps most importantly of all, Avrorin's assertion (1970 p. 42) that the survey results flatly contradicted the view frequently found among Soviet sociolinguists that bilingualism with Russian leads to the decline of small languages, has itself been challenged; in a retrospective account of the Siberian language project we find the statement made that 'a consequence of the transition of the small peoples of Siberia to bilingualism has been a contraction in the areas of use of the native language, a narrowing of its functions' (Fedorov 1982 p. 130).

We have considered the Siberian language project in some detail here because of its considerable influence on ethnolinguistic surveys undertaken in other parts of the Soviet Union, including extensive work in the Baltic region (Kholmogorov 1970) and in Tataria (Arutjunjan et al. 1973). Very similar questionnaires have been used in a number of surveys reported since, in the Tuvin ASSR (Anajban 1979, 1983), Chuvashia (Andreev 1969), Daghestan (Madieva 1970) and Karelia (Klement'ev 1971, 1974), among the Siberian Tatars (Tomilov 1978) and in the Khakass Autonomous Region (Krivonogov 1984, Chuprov 1984). Furthermore, the experience of the Siberian researchers attracted the attention of the Institute of Ethnography of the Academy of Sciences in Moscow, which in 1966 created a sector for concrete sociological research into the culture and way of life of the peoples of the USSR (Guboglo 1984, p. 24).[3] This sector in turn established a coordinated programme of research under the rubric 'Optimisation of sociocultural conditions for the development and convergence of nations in the USSR' (Arutjunjan and Drobizheva 1981, p. 69; Drobizheva and Susokolov 1981, p. 17), and has supervised to date some 14 specific research projects in 8 Union and Autonomous Republics in which considerable attention has been paid to linguistic matters. (A convenient survey of these projects from an ethnolinguistic point of view is given in Guboglo 1984, pp. 43–57; a detailed study of their methodology is presented in Arutjunjan et al. 1984).

Before looking in more detail at the light shed by all this work on certain aspects of national-Russian bilingualism in Central Asia, we must first briefly consider and evaluate the methodology of such ethnolinguistic surveys. As Lieberson has pointed out (1980, 1981), while it is perfectly normal practice to use detailed surveys of a limited sample of the population to check on census data, care must be taken to ensure a statistically random sample and to design a set of questions which avoids the subjectivity and ambiguity which tend to characterise censuses and which we have discussed already in the Soviet case. The literature on language surveys is, moreover, quite extensive (Ohanessian et al. 1975; Cooper 1980), and so it is not all that difficult to find a standard against which any given survey can be measured. The crucial questions would appear to be, do Soviet ethnolinguistic surveys constitute by their design a significantly more reliable source than the census reports, and is it justifiable to compare their results directly with those of the census? In an article to which we have already referred, Silver (1975 p. 575, n. 3) affirms that since the samples used in Soviet surveys are not truly random no direct comparison with the census results is possible, and indeed very little use has been made of survey material in Western studies of national-Russian bilingualism in the Soviet Union. The Soviet sources however are replete with such comparisons, and recently a major Western study of ethnic relations in the USSR has argued that despite the undoubted shortcomings of such surveys — notably the selective reporting of results and a failure to quote the exact wording of survey questions — they nevertheless represent an important source which if mined with care can yield valuable results (Karklins 1986, pp. 3, 13–14, 127, 164). It is undoubtedly true that Soviet social scientists are constrained in their work by the political climate in which they operate (for more details see the article referred to in footnote 3), but language surveys undertaken elsewhere in the world are often no less free of political constraints. It is also true that Soviet ethnolinguistic surveys, including those which we shall be considering below, are often frustratingly deficient in their reporting of the exact composition of the research sample, the wording of questions and so on. However, it is equally the case that scholars who undertake language surveys elsewhere frequently 'have had little or no training in social science research methods, particularly in the collection, processing and analysis of mass data' (Cooper 1980, p. 125). It is surely not unworthy of approval that the questions asked in the Siberian language project (see above), which have been so influential in the design of later ethnolinguistic surveys in the USSR, correspond very closely indeed to the schedule of questions proposed by Lieberson (1966, pp. 142–3) as a means of gaining a more accurate picture of language use than that provided by most censuses. We would argue therefore that Soviet ethnolinguistic surveys, for all their drawbacks and shortcomings, represent an important resource.

We shall now take a number of specific aspects of the bilingualism in Central Asia and consider to what extent the material found in the sources we have been discussing helps us in our analysis. To begin with we shall look at what has become something of a *cause célèbre* especially in the West, the figures for Uzbek-Russian bilingualism. It will be recalled from Table 1 that according to the census returns the percentage of Uzbeks having command of Russian as a second language increased from 14.5 in 1970 to 49.3 in 1979. (If we take the index of bilingualism given in Table 2 the discrepancy is still wider, between 12.9% and 52.7%). This is an enormous jump, and it is not matched by the figures for the other Central Asian and Turcophone peoples (Tables 1 and 2). Indeed, the comparison is frequently made between the Uzbek figures and those for Estonia at the other end of the spectrum, where, according to the census, command of Russian actually decreased from 29.0% in 1970 to 24.2% in 1979, with the conclusion drawn that 'what took place was wilful understatement in one instance and boastful overstatement in another, both reducing the reliability of the census data' (Rywkin 1984, p. 81). The evidence of antipathy towards the Russian language on the part of Estonians and subsequent under-reporting of command of it seems clear enough (Karklins 1981, p. 32; Solch-anyk 1982, pp. 34–6), and we will not pursue this here. In the case of Uzbek, Western sources are (almost) universally inclined to cast doubt on the accuracy of the figures. (In addition to Rywkin's statement just quoted, see Rakowska-Harmstone 1982, p. 105; Fierman 1985, p. 221; Karklins 1986, p. 60), and Soviet scholars too are prepared to concede that the reported increase may be due to factors like inadequate understanding of their task by census takers and lack of clarity in the definition of command of a second language (Arutjunjan and Susokolov 1983, p. 20; Guboglo 1984, p. 109). Guboglo also points out, however, in a rather balanced account of the matter (1984, pp. 109–11), that the whole context of sociocultural development in Uzbekistan in the 1970s should be taken into account. Certainly, if we consider the pace and enthusiasm with which the measures to strengthen the role of Russian noted at the beginning of this paper were publicised and enacted in the Uzbek SSR (Rashidov 1981, Shermukhamedov 1981 are good examples of reports by prominent government spokesmen), a marked increase in bilingualism is perhaps less surprising. Further, as Guboglo (1984, pp. 110–11) again points out, similar increases in command of Russian between 1970 and 1979 were reported for other peoples living in the Uzbek SSR.[4] Table 3 gives the figures for the portion of these peoples living in Uzbekistan compared with those for the population of that nationality's titular Republic. A useful comparison is provided by Table 4, which gives the percentage command of Russian in 1970 and 1979 for Uzbeks settled in the other Central Asian Union Republics and in Kazakhstan. So far, therefore, it is clear that the increased level of command of Russian noted in the 1979 census is territorially specific to the Uzbek SSR rather than ethnically specific to any one people, as indeed we might expect if political developments within that Republic have played a significant role. We are now in a position to consider the results of an ethnolinguistic survey carried out in 1974–76 by the Institute of Ethnography as part of the coordinated research programme mentioned above. This survey used a reasonably satisfactory true random sample of 2,500 respondents (Arutjunjan and Mirkhasilov 1979, p. 38) and the results were published briefly in an article by Guboglo (1978), some extra information being given in later works of a more general

Table 3 *Command of Russian among Turkic peoples in Uzbekistan and in their own Republicas (%)*

	Uzbek SSR		Titular Republic	
	1970	1979	1970	1979
Karakalpak	9.6	45.2	–*	–*
Kazakh	16.8	48.6	41.8	52.3
Tatar	62.6	75.0	62.5	68.9
Azerbaidzhani	27.0	48.9	16.6	29.5
Turkmen	8.3	36.3	15.4	25.4
Kirghiz	4.8	36.9	19.1	29.4
Tadzhik	8.4	34.8	15.4	29.6
Ukrainian	40.5	40.4	36.3	49.8

Source: Guboglo 1984, pp. 110–11. Additional calculations according to: Natsional'nyj Sostav 1973, p. 202, Naselenie SSSR 1980, p. 23, Chislennost' 1984, pp. 110–111
* The titular ASSR of the Karakalpaks lies within the Uzbek SSR

Table 4 *Uzbeks in other Central Asian Republics*

	Total Numbers (as % of all Uzbeks)		% having command of Russian	
	1970	1979	1970	1979
Tadzhikistan	665662 (7.2)	873199 (7.0)	12.8	21.6
Kirghizia	332638 (3.6)	426194 (3.4)	22.2	31.5
Kazakhstan	216340 (2.4)	263295 (2.1)	34.6	40.3
Turkmenia	179498 (1.95)	233730 (1.9)	17.7	21.9

Sources: Natsional'nyj Sostav 1973, pp. 222, 284, 295, 306, 321; Chislennost' 1984, pp. 116–117, 130–135, 138

nature (above all, Guboglo 1984). The first topic reported on in the survey was in fact bilingualism with Russian; in his treatment of this Guboglo (1978, p. 13) begins by outlining the shortcomings of the census data on command of Russian, namely, that no information is given either about the extent of that command or about actual use of the language in daily life. In an attempt to overcome the first of these drawbacks the Uzbek respondents were asked to grade their command of Russian on a five-point scale ranging from complete bilingualism (equal command of Uzbek and Russian) to total monolingualism. The replies, even to such a graded question, are of course still subjective, and Guboglo unfortunately fails to give any information about the exact wording of the question, the way it was put or any checks on the validity of the answers. Such provisos need to be borne in mind when considering the results, which are presented by Guboglo (1978, pp. 14–15) according to age and occupational dimensions (unfortunately once again, without at any point giving the total number in each category!), and whose overall totals are given in Table 5.

Table 5 *Command of Russian among Uzbeks, 1974/1976 survey (%)*

Extent of command of Russian	Urban	Rural
Think in Russian	9.0	5.5
Speak fairly fluently	34.0	14.3
Speak with some difficulty	21.0	20.1
Speak with great difficulty	12.4	16.8
Did not speak Russian at all	12.9	32.9
Did not reply	6.8	9.1

Source: Guboglo 1978, p. 15. (NB: No explanation is given of why the totals for the two columns do not add up to 100%)

These figures are difficult to interpret without knowing the proportion of rural to urban respondents in the sample. Guboglo, who we must assume to have had this information, drew the general inference that 76.4% of the urban and rural population have sufficient command of Russian to understand and make themselves understood when speaking to someone of a different nationality (Guboglo 1978, p. 13), and that this was evidence of a 'significant trend' on the part of Uzbeks toward increased knowledge of the language (ibid., p. 15). It is, of course, clear however, that in the absence of any proper objective measure of command of Russian any figures, whether from census or survey, are to a certain extent, arbitrary; yet as we shall see below attempts to provide a truly objective measure, notably by reference to the school curriculum (Desheriev 1976) or by administering graded language tests to the respondents (Kopylenko and Saina 1982, pp. 86–92), are too fragmentary to allow detailed conclusions to be drawn. The figures from the Uzbek ethnolinguistic survey do nevertheless give some indication of the range of levels of command of Russian, and this helps us to understand why such variation should occur when an arbitrary point on the continuum is chosen for the answer to a census question. It seems certain that this point was chosen differently in the censuses of 1970 and 1979, and this is partly to be explained by the context of sociocultural policy referred to earlier. It is possible to present a fuller picture, however, if we consider the available material on actual language use in various spheres.

As we have seen already, one of the major drawbacks of the Soviet censuses is their failure to give any information on language use. In the case of bilingualism with Russian, Guboglo (1984, p. 191) finds it necessary to warn fellow scholars against 'mechanical extrapolation' from the figures on command of a second language to conclusions about the use of such a language in everyday life. This (of course) is an area where ethnolinguistic surveys can be of real help, since it is in principle easier to get an objective answer to questions about which language or languages a respondent uses in a given situation than it is to elicit an objective measure of command of that language. As we have already noted however, the extent to which survey results can be compared with census data depends on how genuinely random the survey sample is and how satisfactory the actual survey techniques are.

We have mentioned already that a large part of the questionnaire for the Siberian language project was devoted to language use, and that the questions used have frequently been repeated in other surveys since that time. Each survey has adopted its own way of presenting results, however, and the reporting is rarely anything like complete, which makes the data difficult to re-analyse and therefore hinders systematic comparisons across surveys. What follows is thus a tentative attempt to look at the available Central Asian material against a background of some of the other surveys referred to above. As our starting-point we shall take a remarkable piece of work by Kopylenko and Saina (a survey unfortunately undated, but published in 1982), who presented detailed material on the use of Russian by a carefully controlled random sample of 4,517 Kazakh speakers in several areas and along numerous dimensions, and compare this with data, first from the other major Turkic languages, and second from surveys conducted elsewhere. Such an approach, while it is fraught with technical problems and unsatisfactory in many respects, nevertheless presents us with an overall picture of considerable interest.

For language use within the family, Kopylenko and Saina's material shows, predictably enough, an overwhelming dominance of the native language among urban Kazakhs (the equivalent rural data are unfortunately lacking). Between spouses, use of Russian is well below 1% for all speakers born before 1940, and among younger Kazakhs approaches 10% only in the ethnically mixed surroundings of Semipalatinsk; the incidence of bilingual behaviour is somewhat higher, reaching almost 50% among Kazakhs born after 1950 and living in Alma-Ata (p. 36). The picture is broadly similar for contact between parents and children, brothers and sisters; from the mass of data provided by Lopylenko and Saina for subgroups defined according to age and place of residence, Tables 6 and 7 provide some crude averages (crude in the sense that the figures for the various subgroups are averaged without reference to the number of respondents in each group). Although it would be unwise to press detailed conclusions from such figures, the general outlines are clear enough: the only real point of interest is the discrepancy between the figures for bilingualism of parents to children (Table 6) and of children to parents (Table 7), which the authors put down to a tendency on the part of Kazakh parents consciously to use Russian in speaking to their children in order to improve their command of that language (p. 37). Such variation as exists, apart from that obtaining between different age groups (which is not shown in Tables 6

Table 6 *Language use in speaking to children, Kazakh families (%)*

	Kazakh	Russian	Both
Kzyl-Orda	89.7	0.9	9.4
Alma-Ata	72.9	3.6	23.5
Kokchetav	68.3	3.6	26.7
Semipalatinsk	68.1	5.9	25.9

Source: Kopylenko and Saina 1982, p. 38

Table 7 *Language use in speaking to parents/siblings, Kazakh families (%)*

	Percentage using both Kazakh and Russian	
	Parents*	Siblings
Kzyl-Orda	1	14.6
Alma-Ata	3	29.1
Kokchetav	5.6	27.3
Semipalatinsk	7	32.9

Source: Kopylenko and Saina 1982, p. 37, 39
* The data for parents are converted to figures from a loosely drawn graph in the source referred to, and therefore give only an extremely general indication

and 7 and which is in any case entirely predictable), is due to the ethnic composition of the place of residence: the more ethnically mixed, the greater the potential role for Russian.[5] This corresponds exactly with the situation found by the 1967 Tatar survey: the figures for language use in the family by Tatar speakers in Kazan' (44.2% Tatar, 15.2% Russian, 33.92% both) show a slightly greater role for Russian than do the equivalent figures for Al'met'evsk (54.2 % Tatar, 12.59% Russian, 29.3% both), whereas in rural areas the figure for bilingual behaviour among Tatars does not exceed 5% (Arutjunjan *et al.* 1973, p. 247; a breakdown of these figures by age group is given on p. 251).

Against the background of these general figures we may consider the results of three surveys undertaken among school-children and students in Central Asia: in a survey of Uzbek children in two schools in different areas of Tashkent the level of bilingual behaviour in the family varied from zero to 48% (see Table 8),[6] among two groups of Kirghiz students (one group from Kirghiz schools, the other from Russian) at the Frunze Pedagogical Institute of Russian Language and Litera-ture the variation was between 30% and 80% (Table 9), and among 100 Kazakh families with school-age children bilingual usage among the children varied between 5.5% and 82.6% (Table 10). The variation in these figures is quite striking, and shows that in addition to the different effect of urban and rural

Table 8 *Survey of language use among Uzbek schoolchildren (%)*

	Native language		Russian		Both	
	A	B	A	B	A	B
Family life	100	52	–	–	–	48
With friends	100	10	–	4	–	86
At school	100	21	–	–	–	79
With neighbours	100	43	–	–	–	57
Radio	97	10	–	6	3	84
Books	100	40	–	–	–	60
Cinema	–	12	–	–	100	88
TV	–	–	–	–	100	100

Source: Mukhamedova 1982, p. 62
Group A: pupils of a school in a predominantly Uzbek area of Tashkent
Group B: pupils of a school in an ethnically mixed area of Tashkent
Note: unfortunately, neither the date of the survey nor the number of those sampled are given in the source quoted

Table 9 *Survey of language use among Kirghiz students (%)*

	Native language		Russian		Both	
	A	B	A	B	A	B
Family life	58	10	18	72	24	18
Informal social contact*	38	2	44	86	24	12
At VUZ	16	2	80	94	4	4
Writing letters	20	20	32	42	48	38
Listening to lectures	24	18	38	50	38	32
Writing reports*	28	20	28	80	34	10
Reading literature	68	28	10	44	22	28
Reading press	54	14	26	56	20	30
Specialised literature	12	2	46	54	42	44
TV	52	12	14	50	34	38
Radio	40	4	24	56	36	40
Theatre/cinema	48	8	20	52	32	40

Source: Nurtumov 1984, pp. 213–17
Group A: 50 students from Kirghiz schools
Group B: 50 students from Russian schools
* The inaccuracies in the percentages for these functions come from the source quoted

Table 10 *Language use at home by Kazakh schoolchildren (%)*

(type of school)	Kazakh	Russian	Both
urban, Kazakh	17.4	22.7	59.9
rural, mixed	84.9	4.7	10.4
rural, Kazakh	94.5	1.3	4.2

Source: Khasanov 1976, p. 124

residence the type and language of schooling plays a significant part. (We shall explore this topic in more detail below, but it certainly shows clearly from all the data presented in Tables 8 and 9). Further, there is a not inconsiderable difference between the figures reported for the various peoples, the figures for Uzbek schoolchildren even in a multi-ethnic area of Tashkent, for example, show much greater use of mother tongue than do those for urban Kazakhs (though it must be said that for the Kazakhs, the differences between Tables 7 and 10 are equally striking). This variation in response for different peoples shows even more clearly when we consider the results of surveys undertaken in other parts of the Soviet Union; Table 11 presents a selection of these, once again averaged out for ease of comparison from more detailed breakdowns.

Table 11 Survey data on language use within the family (% figures)

	Preschoolers			Schoolchildren			Adult relatives		
	Native language	Russian	Both	Native language	Russian	Both	Native language	Russian	Both
1. Yakut	87.8	0.5	2.0	92.9	0.5	2.3	97.2	0.4	1.7
2. Khakass	72.3	6.3	11.2	68.0	8.1	14.4	86.6	4.0	7.4
3. Chukchi	40.4	19.2	26.8	32.4	21.6	28.7	69.0	6.3	16.0
4. Nanai	37.2	18.7	23.0	28.1	21.4	31.7	44.4	17.0	30.2
5. Eskimo	15.4	50.0	19.2	11.7	41.1	18.1	34.0	16.3	24.7
6. Tuvin	99.6	0.2	0.2	99.7	0.0	0.3	not available		
7. Korean	32.9	55.9	5.4	not available			62.2	29.9	4.4
8. Avar	90.0	0.0	10.0	77.4	0.0	22.6	87.7	0.0	12.3

Sources: Avrorin 1975, pp. 134–35 (lines 1–5), Serdobov 1968, p. 85 (line 6), Jugaj 1979, p. 173 (line 7, average figures from breakdown by age), Madieva 1970, pp. 239–41 (line 8).

The picture we have presented of language use within the family, even after somewhat arbitrary simplification of the figures, is quite extraordinarily complex, and we cannot hope to do justice to it in the space available; in reality each individual set of figures would require its own analysis and commentary in order to be understood properly. Nevertheless, a rich picture of variation clearly emerges, not surprisingly in view of all the factors at work behind the bald statement of percentage figures: ethnic composition of the place of residence, traditions of language use by the particular people, the urban-rural divide, language(s) used in education, and so on. In the midst of all this complexity however, it becomes clear that for the majority of the peoples surveyed Russian has some role even in this most conservative sphere of language use. With this in mind we now turn outside the family to areas where the incidence of bilingualism and the role of Russian might be expected to be higher.

For language use in the workplace Kopylenko and Saina provide us with a great deal of information presented along several dimensions and allowing comparison across the urban-rural divide. Among urban Kazakhs, the proportions using Russian in this area were 5.1% among the men and 2.6% among the women sampled; the corresponding rural figures were 4.0% for men and 1.7% for women, with the additional data (lacking for urban Kazakhs) that 59.8% of the men and 65.0% of the women used only the mother tongue, while 36.0% and 33.2% respectively used both languages (pp. 55, 68). When the sample was subdivided by level of education, use of Russian among urban Kazakhs ranged between 4.25% for those with incomplete secondary education and 38% for those with higher education in the natural sciences, while in the rural sample the figures for the same two educational levels were 1.77% and 23.6% (pp. 42, 69). When considered according to duration of urban or rural residence the data showed use of Russian ranging from 17% for those who had lived in town for less than 5 years compared with 20% for those who had lived for a similar length of time in the countryside, to 45.25% and 3% for those whose period of urban or rural residence respectively had exceeded 20 years (pp. 47, 73). The data for urban Kazakhs are also broken down by age groups (p. 34) and by type of employment (p. 53), in both cases giving figures which are reasonably consistent with those already presented, whilst for the rural material overall average figures of 62.8% for native language, 3.3% for Russian and 32.6% for both languages are reported (p. 76). Further, the figure for bilingual usage at work by rural Kazakhs is closely matched by a figure of 32.4% for urban bilingual behaviour at work, given by Saina in a later article (1985, p. 129). The Kazakh data then, for all their incompleteness (figures are not given in every case for the full range of possibilities), do present a rather consistent picture of bilingual usage around the mid 30 per cent mark, noticeably lower than the figures for command of Russian reported in the census (Table 1).

The Tatar survey material presents a much sharper divide between urban and rural respondents. By calculating averages from the tables of breakdown by age group we arrive at the following figures: 5.7% of the urban sample use mainly Tatar at work, 44.8% use mainly Russian and 49.3% use both languages. The corresponding figures from the rural group are 72.4%, 7.7% and 19.3% for men, 72.3%, 6.1% and 12.4% for women. Checks for internal consistency with detailed tables giving breakdowns for type of work show these figures to be substantially reliable (Arutjunjan *et al.* 1973, pp. 253–6). Moreover, they come much closer than do the Kazakh data to the reported command of Russian in the census — indeed it seems that in this case a fairly systematic correlation is possible (ibid., p. 258). As in the case of language use at home then, we find considerable variations in the levels of bilingual behaviour reported for different peoples; and once again this variation is even more striking when we bring into the picture the results of ethnolinguistic surveys carried out elsewhere in the Soviet Union. Some of these are presented in Table 12, which shows, in addition to enormous differences in the figures for individual peoples (Yakuts and Tuvins at one extreme, Karelians at the other), a pronounced urban-rural divide (lines 11–12 and 14–15; unfortunately Guboglo gives no rural equivalents for the Uzbek figures presented in line 1), and also clear evidence of a growth in (the role of) bilingual behaviour and the use of Russian in those cases where surveys were repeated after 10 years (lines 6–7, 8–9). Certainly, as Fedorov stated in his assessment of the Siberian language project (1982, p. 132) there would be considerable value in repeating all such surveys;

Table 12 *Survey data on language use in the workplace (% figures)*

	Native language	Russian	Both
1. Uzbek (urban)	34.8	10.2	22.5
2. Yakut	90.3	1.0	4.1
3. Chukchi	32.3	31.3	26.7
4. Nania	19.2	30.8	30.9
5. Eskimo	7.3	50.6	18.4
6. Khakass (1969)	48.4	9.5	25.8
7. Khakass (1978/79)	13.9	38.3	46.4
8. Tuvin (1967)	93.8	0.5	5.7
9. Tuvin (1978)	77.4	8.5	24.9
10. Chuvash	87.5	1.5	11.0
11. Siberian Tatar (rural)	64.2	42.8	–
12. Siberian Tatar (Tomsk city)	10.3	76.3	–
13. Avar	68.4	–	31.6
14. Karelian (rural)	13.6	45.8	37.0
15. Karelian (urban)	1.2	81.8	16.9

Sources: Guboglo 1978, pp. 21–2 (line 1); Avrorin 1975, p. 236 (lines 2–6), Krivonogov 1984, p. 174 (line 7); Anajban 1983, p. 214 (lines 8 and 9); Andreev 1969, p. 8 (line 10); Tomilov 1978, pp. 109, 165–7 (line 11); ibid. pp. 137, 168 (line 12); Madieva 1970, p. 242 (line 13); Klement'ev 1971, pp. 40–43 (line 14); Klement'ev 1974, pp. 31–2 (line 15)
Note that the figures in lines 7, 11, 12, 14 and 15 have been averaged out from more detailed tables for ease of comparison. Also a number of lines add up to more or less than 100%; in the first case this is because the three categories of mother tongue, Russian and both languages were not kept separate, so that the figures for both native language and Russian will include some bilinguals (cf. e.g. line 11), in the second case the shortfall is due to the percentage not answering the question or else using languages other than mother tongue or Russian (lines 1–6).

even with the material we have, however, it seems rather clear that in most cases, and especially in the countryside, the national languages are maintaining their role as significant means of communication in the workplace.

The material on informal social contact outside the family and the workplace is much more straightforward. Kopylenko and Saina's data show clearly that Russian is used much less for social contact with friends than for professional contact with colleagues (p. 54), but that for urban Kazakhs of long standing the incidence of bilingual behaviour is much higher — an average of 47.5% of those Kazakhs who had lived in town for more than 20 years reported using both Kazakh and Russian in informal social contact (p. 49). This, however, is clearly a special case, since the average overall figures for language use in this function are 86% Kazakh, 4% Russian, 7% both (p. 40). Even the level of potential bilingualism in this function, at 19.2% (Saina 1985, p. 129; see ibid. p. 127 for a breakdown of this figure by occupation and place of residence, and see footnote 5 for an explanation of the sense of 'potential' here) is much lower than the 32.4% figure reported above for bilingual usage at work. In the Tatar survey the data on informal social contact and language use in the family were treated as a single category ('sphere of family and everyday life'), so the figures for comparison here can be found above in the section on language use in the family. And indeed, comparison of the Kazakh figures shows these two functions to give very similar results, as do the few available results from other Soviet surveys summarised in Table 13. The figures reported from Uzbek schoolchildren and Kirghiz students in this function and presented in Tables 8 and 9 show how great is the role played by languages of instruction for these groups, and will be considered below in the light of this.

Table 13 *Survey data on language use in informal social contact (%)*

	Native language	Russian	Both
1. Chuvash	93.5	0.9	5.6
2. Khakass	18.1	23.0	58.9
3. Avar	81.9	–	18.1
4. Siberian Tatars (rural)	88.4	28.6	–
5. Siberian Tatars (Tomsk city)	55.4	72.4	–

Sources: Andreev 1969, p. 8 (line 1), Krivonogov 1984, p. 174 (line 2), Madieva 1970, p. 242 (line 3), Tomilov 1978, pp. 109, 165–67 (line 4), ibid. pp. 137, 168 (line 5)
For an explanation of the Siberian Tatar figures see the note to Table 12

The final area of language use which we will consider is the domain of reading and writing. Here too Kopylenko and Saina present a mass of information; because there are so many different types of both reading and writing it is difficult to make a systematic presentation of the material, so we shall aim instead to give a composite account. We may begin by considering the figures given in Table 14; at first glance it would seem that there is an urban-rural polarisation, with respondents in the towns reading mainly in Kazakh, to some

Table 14 *Use of Russian by Kazakhs for reading (%)*

(Type of literature)	Rural	Urban
Newspapers	0.8 (20.7)	10.7 (8.4)
Political works	8.5 (34.8)	25.6 (10.4)
Technical works	14.9 (33.2)	34.3 (15.3)
Belles-lettres	0.1 (4.8)	5.7 (3.7)

Source: Kopylenko and Saina 1982, pp. 45, 78–9
Note: the figures in parenthesis in the rural column are the percentages using both Kazakh and Russian for reading. The corresponding urban data are taken from Saina 1985, p. 129.

extent in Russian but infrequently in both,[7] while there are very few rural respondents who read any kind of literature mainly in Russian, but sizeable numbers who use the language for reading in addition to their mother tongue. For belles-lettres, as might be expected, the Kazakh language dominates absolutely. For more light on these overall figures, we turn now to the more detailed tables provided by Kopylenko and Saina. Urban reading of Russian newspapers by Kazakhs depends very much on the ethnic make-up of the town; the figures range from 5.6% for Kzyl-Orda to 47% for Semipalatinsk (p. 50). For rural Kazakhs there are small variations according to occupation in the numbers reading in Russian (p. 75; note that it is difficult to make the detailed figures given here fit with the general ones reproduced in Table 14), and there are clear correlations between the language most used for reading and that preferred for making speeches (pp. 80–3). In the case of the urban sample, correlations are made between language use in reading and writing and the extent of command of Russian before migration to the town (pp. 56–62) and (also) before beginning school (pp. 63–5). In the main this information presents few surprises, and we shall devote no more attention to it here.

For active use of written Russian Kopylenko and Saina's data are less extensive; they report that 6.9% of the rural sample could write fluently and 54.1% wrote with difficulty, while 38.6% could not write in Russian at all (p. 77; for detailed breakdowns see pp. 71–2). For the urban sample actual use of written Russian in family and other unofficial correspondence is reported; the figures range from 2.7% for Kzyl-Orda to 8.7% for Kokchetav (pp. 44–5). It is clear that for both reading and

writing in Russian, the figures reported by this extensive
Kazakh survey are extremely low; once again, much lower
than those given in the census for claimed command of the
language, and much lower too than the reported figures for
bilingualism in the areas covered by the survey, which are
39.3–80.7% in the towns and 19.1–34.0% in the countryside
(Kopylenko and Saina 1982, p. 25).

The Tatar survey also reported very low figures for reading
in Russian. In the rural sample 5.8% read literature in Russian,
13.1% used both Tatar and Russian and 33.5% only the mother
tongue (Arutjunjan et al. 1973, p. 259); the remainder rarely or
never read material in either language (ibid., p. 261). These
figures can be correlated with the pattern of literary and per-
iodical publication in the Tatar Republic (ibid., pp. 259–65);
similar correlations are made for the Tuvin ASSR by Anajban
1979, pp. 161–2; 1983, pp. 215–6), and they are also very similar
to those reported by Guboglo (1978, pp. 21–2) in the Uzbek
survey. Among rural Uzbek respondents 53.4% read mainly
in Uzbek, 1.1% mainly in Russian and 6.9% in both languages,
while 38.4% did not reply to the question (and therefore presumably read little or not at all); the corresponding urban
figures are 42.2%, 5.3%, 21.5% and 30.8% respectively. Among
the students and schoolchildren whose usage is reported in
Tables 8 and 9 reading and writing in Russian are predictably
more common; the group of Kirghiz students who had
attended Russian schools used Russian either alone or together
with Kirghiz in proportions ranging from 72% to 86% for the
areas of reading and writing surveyed, and a comparable trend
at least toward bilingual usage may be noted in the group of
Uzbek schoolchildren living in multi-ethnic areas of Tashkent.
The findings of other Soviet surveys (see Tables 15 to 19 for
a selection of these) show considerable variation: the Chuvash,
Tuvin and Avar data indicate a prominent role for the mother
tongue even for smaller peoples and those not settled com-
pactly. The Chuvash figures are particularly interesting in
showing a preference for the native language in reading and
writing even higher than actual use; this shows once again the
correlation between language use, particularly in reading, and
the availability of written/printed material in a given language — which is presumably the explanation too for the
extraordinarily low figures reported for Khakass. The Siberian

Table 15 *Language use for reading and writing among rural Chuvash (%)*

	Chuvash	Russian	Both	No reply
Reading	55.6	11.8	18.3	14.3
Understanding what is read	71.3	5.6	15.0	5.4
Writing letters	64.4	6.6	19.6	9.4
Writing official documents	32.8	40.7	16.7	9.8
Preferred language for writing	67.7	9.0	8.7	14.4

Source: Andreev 1969, pp. 8–9

Table 16 *Language use for reading among rural Tuvins (%)*

	Tuvin	Russian	Both
Reading books and newspapers	76.9	3.0	15.1
Listening to lectures and speeches	82.3	1.5	15.8

Source: Serdobov 1968, pp. 100–103 (overall figures calculated from detailed breakdown)

Table 17 *Language use for reading among rural Khakass (%)*

	Khakass	Russian	Both
Newspapers	3.1	58.6	35.9
Belles-lettres	1.3	30.2	68.5

Source: Krivonogov 1984, p. 175

Table 18 *Language use for reading and writing among Siberian Tatars (%)*

	Rural Data		Urban data (Tomsk city)	
	Tatar	Russian	Tatar	Russian
Newspaper/magazines	32.8 (38.1)	72.7 (85.4)	17.4	79.4
Political literature	1.8 (3.7)	14.0 (30.7)	1.3	29.9
Technical literature	0.8 (1.4)	8.6 (22.3)	0.2	19.9
Pedagogical literature	1.3 (3.3)	11.3 (26.3)	0.6	23.9
Belles-lettres	14.9 (21.2)	45.0 (46.1)	10.8	60.7
Correspondence	41.1 (41.1)	39.7 (40.6)	19.4	52.1

Source: Tomilov 1978, pp. 98, 109, 137, 165–68, 187, 201–203
Note: the fact that these percentages do not add up to 100% reflects the lack of a 'both language' column (in the case of the press) and the fact that a certain proportion do not read certain types of literature (the remaining categories)
Note: for the rural data, the first figure is the overall average according to Tomilov's general tables (pp. 98, 109), the second is calculated from the detailed breakdown by social group (pp. 201–203). It is not clear how the discrepancy between these two sets of figures should be explained.

Table 19 *Language use for reading and writing among Avars (%)*

	Avar	Russian	Both
Reading	56.9	25.4	17.7
Correspondence	73.5	14.4	12.1

Source: Madieva 1970, pp. 243–5

Tatar material, finally, shows a clearly diminished role for the mother tongue among urban respondents, a rather stable role for Russian, and a sizeable proportion of those surveyed not reporting reading in either language.

We may conclude from all these figures that given the availability of sufficient published material in a language, all but the smallest and most dispersed peoples will show a marked preference for reading and writing in their mother tongue. As we have seen therefore throughout this section on language use, the data when taken as a whole — albeit with some exceptions — suggest that actual use of Russian in everyday life is considerably lower than the level of command of the language claimed in the census. This begs the question of the relationship between claimed command of Russian and objective measures of such command, to which we will return shortly in the concluding section of this chapter. Firstly, however, we will look briefly at the information about language use in education presented by Soviet ethnolinguistic surveys.

We have already noted that education is one area where numerous measures have been taken to strengthen the role and improve (the) command of Russian (see also Guboglo 1984, ch. 5; Panachin 1984, chs. 6–8). The survey data we have been considering also reinforce the view of schools as a major diffuser of knowledge of Russian: the language habits of the two groups of Kirghiz students summarised in Table 9 clearly show the (differential) effect of language of school instruction and in the Tatar survey considerable space was devoted to the correlation between language of instruction, language preference and language use (Arutjunjan *et al.* 1973, pp. 235–42). For all the attention devoted to increasing the number of school hours spent on teaching Russian and improving the quality of instruction, however, it is clear that many non-Russians pass right through the school system without acquiring a good command of the language (Karklins 1986,

p. 63) and that, certainly in the Union Republics, the native languages retain a dominant role in education (ibid., pp. 105–106; Solchanyk 1982, p. 26). In the light of this we may remind ourselves that the questionnaire for the Siberian language project devoted one section to language use in education, and that similar questions have been put in a number of other surveys. Since Soviet sources frequently refer to parental pressure for an increased role for Russian in the school it is worth considering this material in a little more detail. At the time of the Uzbek survey reported by Guboglo the situation appears to have been stable; 28.6% of urban respondents and 20% of rural ones were in favour of their children being taught in Russian, which compared well with actual educational statistics showing that 71% of Uzbek children in 1969/70 were being educated in native-language schools (Guboglo 1978, pp. 16, 18; for a comparison with figures from Moldavia, Estonia and Georgia see Karklins 1986, p. 106). In Tataria however (an Autonomous as opposed to a Union Republic) the position according to the survey was much less stable; among the rural sample 47.1% of the children were being educated in Tatar schools, 14.2% in Russian ones and 3.1% in schools which switched from Tatar to Russian for instruction in the older classes — the corresponding figures for parental preference in this regard were respectively 26.6%, 56.1% and 10.8% (Arutjunjan et al. 1973, p. 239; and see p. 242 for a correlation between these figures and level of bilingualism) — though since 35% of parents failed to indicate which type of school their children attended these figures lose something in reliability. For smaller peoples the level of preference for Russian as language of instruction is higher, and moreover increasing; Tables 20 and 21 present the data for Avars and Siberian Tatars, while in Table 22 we see a pronounced change over

Table 20 *Preferred languages of instruction among Avars (%)*

	Avar	Russian	Both
Pre-school classes	50.4	39.5	10.1
First year	43.2	48.4	8.4
Elementary school	30.7	58.5	10.8
Middle school	2.0	98.0	0.0

Source: Madieva 1970, pp. 247–50

Table 21 *Preferred languages of instruction among Siberian Tatars (%)*

| | Tobol-Irtysh Tatars | | Baraba Tatars | |
	Tatar	Russian	Tatar	Russian
Elementary school	9.1	73.5	22.8	73.3
Middle school	7.0	85.6	4.7	91.3

Source: Tomilov 1978, pp. 895, 163–4, 191–2

Table 22 *Preferred languages of instruction in elementary school among Tuvins (%)*

	Tuvins	Russians	Both
1967 survey	83.5	4.2	12.3
1978 survey	3.6	29.6	23.7

Sources: Serdobov 1968, p. 87; Anajban 1983, p. 213
Note: the remainder of the 1978 sample either did not reply to the question (21.4%) or were indifferent (21.7%)

time in the case of the Tuvins. The level of support for all these languages to be taught as school subjects nevertheless remains very high: 94.6% among Avars, from 41.7% to 56.7% among Siberian Tatars, 53.7% among Nanais, 88.4% among Khakass, 88.5% among Yakuts, 89.2% among Eskimos and 90.5% among Chukchi (Madieva 1970, p. 250, Tomilov 1978, pp. 163–4, Chuprov 1984 pp. 189–91, Avrorin 1975, p. 238).

Many of the sources we have examined give quite detailed information on the relationship between extent of bilingualism and level of education; Kopylenko and Saina, for example, use educational level as one of the dimensions in a number of their tables. We are unable to present this complex material here, but shall conclude this section by making one or two remarks of a more general nature. Overall, as one might predict, the picture is of a direct relationship — bilingualism, command and use of Russian increasing with educational level — and a number of authors draw the inference that bilingualism and greater cultural activity are connected in a similar way (see Guboglo 1984, p. 253 for data from the Tatar survey. Drobizheva and Susokolov 1981, p. 17 for Uzbek material). There is nevertheless more than a little support for the conclusion drawn in some Western sources and referred to above, that passage through the school system does not guarantee a good command of Russian. Notably, in what is perhaps the most comprehensive survey of the objective com-

111

mand of the language among non-Russian schoolchildren, A. N. Baskakov found that the actual level of such command among the Azerbaidzhanis he surveyed was always somewhat below that envisaged by the relevant sections of the school curriculum (Desheriev 1976, *passim*, but see especially pp. 330–33). Further study of the material offered by ethnolinguistic surveys would undoubtedly enable us to give a more reliable and objective evaluation of the part played by the schools in diffusing command of Russian and encouraging bilingual behaviour.

We showed earlier that one of the main drawbacks to confident use of the Soviet census data on language was their subjective nature, in that they depend entirely on the claims of respondents. We have also noted that many ethnolinguistic surveys, although they graded their questions on command of both first and second language in order to try and obtain a more accurate picture, still relied (very) heavily on a subjective response — and on occasion, specifically in the case of the Siberian language project, they were criticised for this. In the final section of this chapter, therefore, we shall look at some proposed objective measures of command of Russian, consider the ways in which such measures have been implemented in surveys and evaluate the conclusions which may be drawn from the resulting material. There is quite a sound tradition in Soviet sociolinguists of study of language behaviour, dating from an extensive survey of Russian in the early 1960s (Krysin 1974) and carried out also in certain other areas of the Soviet Union (see, for example, Kopylenko and Akhmetzhanova 1984; Mikhnevich 1985, as well as the work of Desheriev 1976, referred to above); such work is strong on linguistic analysis but weak on the kind of sociological information provided in ethnolinguistic surveys, whereas these in turn tend to lack any strict objective definition of the linguistic categories they use. For command of Russian as a second language however, a number of measures of varying objectivity have been proposed, and we shall now consider these measures for command of Russian as a second language.

As the information presented in Table 5 shows, the scholars conducting the Uzbek ethnolinguistic survey attempted to grade their respondents' command of Russian on a five-point scale. This still relies to a considerable extent on subjective response (the extent to which this is so depends much on the techniques used by the investigators to elicit replies), but it is nevertheless by far the most common method adopted in Soviet surveys. Such gradation of responses varies from the extremely simple — the Avar survey, for example, distinguished only between passive and active command (Madieva 1970, p. 238) — to the more nuanced five-way split worked out by the organisers of the 1967 Tatar survey (complete freedom in speaking and thinking in Russian, comparative fluency in speaking, some difficulty in speaking, great difficulty in speaking, total inability to speak the language) and re-stated more elegantly for the surveys conducted under the aegis of the Institute of Ethnography as postbilingualism, full bilingualism, incomplete bilingualism, prebilingualism and monolingualism (Guboglo 1984, pp. 49, 129). In Table 23 we reproduce a summary of the findings of a number of these latter surveys (the Uzbek data are the same as those given in Table 5). The gradations found in other surveys all reproduce this scheme either in full or in part, and need not be discussed in detail here (Serdobov 1968, pp. 91–100; Tomilov 1978, pp. 159–62; Krivonogov 1984, p. 168); we might however compare with Table 24 the findings of an earlier survey of 100 Kazakh families (360 respondents), of whom 25% spoke Russian 'well' (? full bilingualism), 55% 'satisfactorily' (?incomplete bilingualism), 17.5% 'poorly' (?prebilingualism) and 2.5% 'not at all' (monolingualism) (Khasanov 1976 p. 123).

The value of all such figures of course lies in the uses to which they can be put. Their most obvious application is as a check on the census results, and a number of authors have pointed out that the inclusion in ethnolinguistic surveys of respondents whose command of Russian is poor tends to give figures for bilingualism higher than those suggested by the census (Bruk and Guboglo 1975, p. 20; Guboglo 1984, pp. 124–5; Zinchenko 1984, p. 158). Unfortunately this does not take us very far beyond the initial doubts expressed about the census returns, since if bilingualism is a continuum the isolation of any point on it is somewhat arbitrary; indeed it is arguable that the kind of differentiation in actual language use which we discussed earlier represents the most objective form

Table 23 *Spread of national-Russian bilingualism at various levels (% figures)*

(Level of bilingualism)	Uzbek	Moldavian	Estonian	Uzbek	Moldavian	Estonian	Georgian
Monolingualism	12.9	4.1	8.6	32.9	13.9	15.8	25.5
Prebilingualism	12.4	6.8	14.0	16.8	22.5	22.4	14.9
Incomplete bilingualism	21.0	21.7	35.7	20.1	28.6	37.9	27.7
Full bilingualism	34.0	36.8	21.1	14.3	19.2	13.9	17.1
Postbilingualism	9.0	29.2	16.4	5.5	10.7	8.2	5.9
Total bilinguals including:	76.4	94.5	87.2	56.7	81.0	82.4	65.6
Developing bilingualism	33.4	28.5	49.7	36.9	51.5	60.3	42.6
Developed bilingualism	43.0	66.0	37.6	19.8	29.9	22.1	23.0

Source: Guboglo 1984, p. 129

114

of gradation, since it is more detached from the subjective claims of respondents.

Another approach which has been tried, albeit less frequently, by Soviet investigators is the administering of graded Russian language tests to non-Russian respondents — particularly to schoolchildren and students, for whom the organisation of such tests is practically simpler. The large research project carried out under the supervision of Ju. D. Desheriev in 1969–73 studied the objective command of Russian in large groups of Azerbaidzhani, Lithuanian, Estonian and Buryat young people at all levels of schooling (Desheriev 1976). The results of this exhaustive survey are difficult to interpret properly without taking into consideration the specific demographic and sociocultural factors peculiar to each situation; nevertheless, it is fair to draw an overall conclusion that command of Russian at the end of ten or more years' schooling is rather less than might be expected given the attention devoted to it. Other studies tend to bear this out; a survey conducted in 1968 among first-year Estonian students uncovered 21,142 mistakes in 1,060 written tests, of which 16.6% were lexical, 34.2% morphological, 15.5% syntactic and 33.7% phonetic or orthographical (Rejtsak 1972, p. 322) — while Karklins (1986, p. 75, n. 35) reports a similar test conducted in 1979 in Latvia where 2% of the responses were graded 'excellent', 20% 'good' and 51% 'satisfactory', the remaining 27% being unable to complete the test.

For survey work in Central Asia, Kopylenko and Saina (1982) appear once again to have broken new ground not only by administering a written Russian language test to a subset chosen from their whole sample, but also by publishing the full text of the actual test and a selection of the completed returns together with analysis of the overall responses (pp. 86–92). The test was divided into five brief sections; in the first two respondents were asked to give the plural forms of eight substantives and the comparative degree of six adjectives. The third section listed eight brief sentences with nouns in brackets requiring the addition of prepositions and the relevant case endings, the fourth again tested case endings, this time in four longer and more complex sentences. Finally, respondents were asked to put a given verb in its correct grammatical form in five fairly straightforward sentences. 140 such tests were completed and scored on a 30-point system, with mistakes in sections 1, 4 and 5 counting as one point, mistakes in sections 3 as 2 points and in section 2 as three points. According to this system the results obtained were divided into 3 categories; 1–5 points was considered a good score, 6–15 was reckoned satisfactory and 16–30 deemed unsatisfactory. The overall result was that of the 60 urban respondents tested 32 scored well, 15 satisfactorily and 13 unsatisfactorily; the corresponding figures for the 80 rural respondents were 14, 30 and 36. Kopylenko and Saina looked at these results on the dimensions of age, sex and educational level; the figures resulting from these breakdowns are reproduced in Tables 24 and 25.

We have presented the results of this unusual survey not so much for their intrinsic interest (the breakdowns by age and educational level are quite predictable, though the comparison between men and women is illuminating) as for their relevance to our theme. If we express the overall test results as percentages we get figures of 32.9% for those who performed well, 32.1% for those whose test results were satisfactory and 35% whose score was considered unsatisfactory (the figures for the urban subset were 53.5%, 25% and 21.7%; for the rural sample 17.5%, 37.5% and 45%). Combining the totals for good and satisfactory results gives us a total of 65% (78.3% urban, 55% rural), which compares rather well both with the census figures for command of Russian as a second language (52.3% in 1979) and with the survey quoted earlier, which found that 80% of

Table 24 *Results of Russian language test with Kazakh respondents by age and sex (whole numbers)*

(Urban)	Born before 1920	Born 1921– 1930	Born 1931– 1940	Born 1941– 1950	Born after 1950	Men	Women	Total
Good	1	7	11	8	5	14	18	32
Satisfactory	3	4	3	4	1	8	7	15
Poor	7	3	1	0	2	7	6	13
(Rural)								
Good	0	2	3	6	3	4	10	14
Satisfactory	2	4	6	10	8	9	21	30
Poor	14	8	7	14	3	28	8	36

Source: Kopylenko and Saina 1982, p. 91

Table 25 *Results of Russian language test with Kazakh respondents by educational level (whole numbers)*

(Urban)	Incomplete middle school	Middle School	Intermediate specialised	Incomplete higher	Higher	Total
Good	0	2	7	6	17	32
Satisfactory	3	2	2	4	4	15
Poor*	8	2	0	0	1	13
(Rural)						
Good	0	0	2	5	7	14
Satisfactory	0	4	3	4	19	30
Poor	18	8	6	1	3	36

Source: Kopylenko and Saina p. 92
* The discrepancy in the figures for this category comes from the source quoted

a sample of 360 spoke Russian either well or satisfactorily. For Kazakh, therefore, so far as can be deduced from the somewhat fragmentary and episodic data, the fit between claimed and actual command of Russian is quite good. The material for other languages as we have seen is even less complete, but nevertheless suggests a similar situation. The evidence of actual language use which we considered, however, shows that this command of Russian, whether subjectively claimed or objectively measured, does not translate itself into wide use of Russian or extensive bilingual behaviour in everyday life. The figures we have presented and the discussion of them show that not only large peoples with their own Union Republic, but also many nationalities which are smaller and more dispersed, strongly favour their native tongues for day-to-day communication and normal social intercourse.

Although the Russian language is undoubtedly taking on a more prominent role (a neat summary of seven bases for this assertion is given by Guboglo 1984, p. 285) and bilingualism is spreading, at least among certain groups, from being solely a means of inter-national contacts to becoming a part of intra-national language behaviour (Arutjunjan *et al.* 1973, p. 250), there is little evidence of such developments leading either to changes in ethnic self-perception (as the census figures on mother tongue claiming demonstrate) or to real ethnic rapprochement between the Russians and other peoples (Karklins 1986, pp. 216–18).

In a state-of-the-art report on Soviet ethnolinguistic surveys, Bruk and Guboglo (1975, p. 23) commented that 'we often come up against the opinion that concrete sociological investigations (merely) reaffirm well-known truths'. It is hoped, however, that we have shown the value of such surveys as a resource for studying the language situation in Central Asia. For all their methodological shortcomings, and despite the caution needed in interpreting and extrapolating from them, we would argue that they greatly increase our understanding both of the level of command of Russian among Central Asians and of the extent of its use in everyday life.

Notes

1 This difference is of real significance only in the case of the Tatars. In 1970 only 25.9% of the Tatar population lived in the Tatar ASSR; for the other peoples considered here the figure ranged between 84 and 93 per cent.

2 The kind of techniques proposed by Lieberson (1966) for cross-tabulation of census data on language in order to check for internal consistency appear never to have been tried on the Soviet material.

3 The development of 'concrete sociological research' is usefully set within the context of policy changes in Soviet sociology as a whole by Shalin 1978.

4 As Table 3 shows, but as Guboglo fails to point out, the huge reported increases apply only to non-Slavic Muslim peoples, as the Ukrainian figure makes clear. This provides yet more evidence of a link between the 1979 census figures and a drive in nationality policy in the Uzbek SSR in the 1970s.

5 Since the vast majority of Soviet ethnolinguistic surveys report language use in three categories — 'native language', 'Russian' and 'both languages', the potential use of Russian may be inferred from the sum of the figures in the second two categories. This way of interpreting the survey results was first proposed by Avrorin for the Siberian language project (Avrorin 1970, p. 41). It has since gained wide currency in analyses carried out by Soviet scholars, and I have followed it here.

6 These figures have presumably been rounded up or down by the author to give whole numbers. Given the lack of any proper details about the survey it is impossible to be sure of their accuracy or even authenticity; they are reproduced here without further comment.

7 Saina's figures for bilingual reading are extraordinarily low, especially if her table giving a breakdown of the use of two languages by level of education (1985, p. 128) is compared with Kopy-

lenko and Saina's breakdown of the use of Russian on the same dimension (1982, p. 45). It is not clear what the reason for this discrepancy is or how much doubt it casts on the figures, but it should undoubtedly be borne in mind in interpreting Table 14.

References

Anajban Z V (1979), 'K izucheniju ėtnojazykovykh protsessov v Tuve', *Polevye Issledovanija Instituta Etnografii 1977*, Nauka, Moscow, pp. 156–63.

Anajban Z V (1983) 'Sotsial'no-kulturnye aspekty razvitija tuvinsko-russkogo dvujazychija', in Bojko V I et al eds. *Ocherki sotsial'nogo razvitija Tuvinskoj ASSR*, Novosibirsk, pp. 208–18.

Andreev N A (1969), 'O razmerakh rasprostranenija dvujazychija sredi sel'skogo naselenija Chuvashskoj ASSR', *Uchenye Zapiski Nauchno-Issledovatel'skogo Instituta pri sovete ministrov Chuvashskoj ASSR*, Vol. 46, pp. 3–19.

Arutjunjan Ju V, Drobizheva L M, Shkaratan O I eds (1973), *Sotsial'noe i natsional'noe. Opyt ėtnosotsiologicheskikh issledovanij po materialam Tatarskoj ASSR*, Nauka, Moscow.

Arutjunjan Ju V, Mirkhasilov S M (1979), 'Ėtnosotsiologicheskie issledovanija kul'tury i byta v Uzbekistane', *Obshchestvennye nauki v Uzbekistane*, No. 1, pp. 36–41.

Arutjunjan Ju V, Drobizheva L M (1981), 'Ėtnosotsiologicheskie issledovanija v SSSR', *Sociologicheskie Issledovanija*, No. 3, pp. 64–70.

Arutjunjan Ju V, Susokolov A A (1983), 'Perepisi naselenija SSSR kak istochnik kolichestvennogo analiza ėtnokul'turnykh protsessov', *Sovetskaja Ėtnografija*, No. 5, pp. 13–22.

Arutjunjan Ju V, Drobizheva L M, Kondrat'eva V S, Susokolov A A (1984), *Ėtnosotsiologija: tseli, metody i nekotorye rezul'taty issledovanija*, Nauka, Moscow.

Avrorin V A (1970), 'Opyt izuchenija funktsial'nogo vzaimodejstvija jazykov u narodov Sibiri', *Voprosy Jazykoznanija*, No 1, pp. 33–43.

Avrorin V A (1975), *Problemy izuchenija funktsial'noj storony jazyka*, Nauka, Leningrad.

Badmaev A R (1967), 'Metodika mashinnogo analiza materialov sotsiologo-lingvisticheskogo obsledovanija funktsial'nogo vzaimodejstvija jazykov', in *Issledovanija po jazyku i fol'kloru*, Vyp. 2, Novosibirsk, pp. 3–15.

Bolotina N A (1982), 'K voprosu o kharaktere sotsiolingvisticheskoj ankety dlja izuchenija dvujazychnogo goroda BSSR', *Russkij Jazyk: mezhved. sbornik*, Vol. 2, Minsk, pp. 129–37.

Bruk S I, Guboglo M N (1975), 'Faktory rasprostranenija dvujazychija u narodov SSSR (po materialam ėtnosotsiologicheskikh issledovanij)', *Sovetskaja Ėtnografija*, No. 5, pp. 17–30.

Chislennost' (1984), *Chislennost' i sostav naselenija SSSR. Po dannym Vsesojuznoj perepisi naselenija 1979 goda*, Finansy i statistika, Moscow.

Cooper R L (1980), 'Sociolinguistic surveys: the state of the art', *Applied Linguistics*, Vol. 1 Pt. 2, pp. 113–28.

Chuprov L F (1984), 'Nekotorye sotsial'no-psikhologicheskie aspekty dvujazychija (na materiale anketirovanija roditelej-khakasov g. Abakana)', in Borgojakov M I et al eds, *Voprosy khakasskogo literaturnogo jazyka*, Abakan, pp. 187–92.

Desheriev Ju D ed (1976), *Razvitie natsional'no-russkogo dvujazychija*, Nauka, Moscow.

Drobizheva L M, Susokolov A A (1981), 'Mezhetnicheskie otnoshenija i ėtnokul'turnye protsessy (po materialam ėtnosotsiologicheskikh issledovanij v SSSR)', *Sovetskaja Ėtnografija*, No. 3, pp. 11–22.

Fedorov A I (1982), 'Sovremennaja jazykovaja situatsija v natsional'nykh rajonakh Sibiri i ee izuchenie', *Izvestija Sibirskogo Otdelenija AN SSSR*, Vol. 11, Pt. 3 (serija obshchestvennykh nauk), pp 129–34.

Fierman W (1985), 'Language development in Soviet Uzbekistan', in Kreindler I T ed, *Sociolinguistic perspectives on Soviet national languages: their past, present and future*, Mouton de Gruyter, Berlin etc., pp. 205–33.

Fishman J (1984), 'Mother tongue claiming in the United States since 1960: trends and correlates related to the "revival of ethnicity" ', *International Journal of the Sociology of Language*. Vol. 50, pp. 21–99.

Garipov Ja Z, Argunova K D (1980), 'Analiz faktorov rasprostranenija dvujazychija v SSSR', *Sotsiologicheskie Issledovanija*, No. 3, pp. 52–61.

Guboglo M N (1973), 'Nekotorye voprosy metodiki pri sotsiologicheskom analize funktsional'nogo razvitija jazykov (o sotsiologo-lingvisticheskikh issledovanijakh v Sibiri)', *Sovetskaja Ėtnografija*, No. 2, pp. 113–21.

Guboglo M N (1978), 'Tendentsii razvitija natsional'no-russkogo dvujazychija (na materiale Uzbekskoj SSR)', *Polevye Issledovanija Instituta Ėtnografii 1976*, Nauka, Moscow, pp. 12–23.

Guboglo M N (1984), *Sovremennye ėtnojazykovye protsessy v SSSR: osnovnye faktory i tendentsii razvitija natsional'no-russkogo dvujazychija*, Nauka, Moscow.

Ivanov V V et al eds (1980), *Russkij jazyk v natsional'nykh respublikakh Sovetskogo Sojuza*, Nauka, Moscow.

Jugaj I G (1979), 'Ėtnosotsiologicheskoe izuchenie jazykovykh protsessov sredi korejtsev Uzbekskoj SSR', in *Polevye Issledovanija Instituta Ėtnografii 1977*, Nauka, Moscow, pp. 168–74.

Karklins R (1980), 'A note on "nationality" and "native tongue" as census categories in 1979', *Soviet Studies*, Vol 23 Pt 3, pp 415–422

Karklins R (1981), 'Ethnic interaction in the Baltic Republics: interviews with recent emigrants', *Journal of Baltic Studies*, Vol. 12, Pt. 1.

Karklins R (1986), *Ethnic relations in the USSR: the perspective from below*, Allen and Unwin, London.

Klement'ev E I (1971), 'Jazykovye processy v Karelii (po materialam konkretno-sociologicheskogo issledovanija karel'skogo sel'skogo naselenija)', *Sovetskaja Ėtnografija*, No. 6, pp. 38–44.

Klement'ev E I (1974), 'Razvitie jazykovykh protsessov v Karelii (po materialam konkretno-sotsiologicheskogo issledovanija karel'skogo gorodskogo naselenija)', *Sovetskaja Ètnografija*, No. 4, pp. 26–36.

Kopylenko M M, Saina S T (1982), *Funktsionirovanie russkogo jazyka v razlichnykh slojakh kazakhskogo naselenija*, Nauka, Alma-Ata.

Kopylenko M M, Akyhmetzhanova Z K (1984), *Foneticheskaja interferentsija v russkoj rechi kazakhov*, Nauka, Alma-Ata.

Kozlov V I (1982), *Natsional'nosti SSSR: ètnodemograficheskij obzor*, Finansy i statistika, Moscow.

Krivonogov V P (1984), 'Vlijanie natsional'noj sredi na jazykovye protsessy u khakasov', in Borgojakov M I et al eds, *Voprosy khakasskogo literaturnogo jazyka*, Abakan, pp. 162–86.

Krysin L P ed (1974), *Russkij jazyk po dannym massovogo obsledovanija: opyt sotsial'no-lingivisticheskogo izuchenija*, Nauka, Moscow.

Labutova T S (1984), 'Programma perepisi i metodologicheskie osnovy ee provedenija', in Isupov A A, Shvartser N Z eds, *Vsesojuznaja perepis' naselenija 1979 goda: sbornik statej*, Finansy i Statistika, Moscow, pp. 5–25.

Lieberson S (1966), 'Language questions in censuses', *Indiana University Research Center in Anthropology, Folklore and Linguistics*, Publication 44, pp. 134–51.

Lieberson S (1980), 'Procedures for improving sociolinguistic surveys of language maintenance and language shift', *International Journal of the Sociology of Language*, Vol. 25, pp. 11–27.

Lieberson S (1981), 'How can we describe and measure the incidence and distribution of bilingualism?', in Lieberson S. *Language diversity and language contact* (ed. A S Dil), Stanford (paper originally published in 1969).

Madieva P B (1970), 'K voprosu o sotsiologo-lingvisticheskom izuchenii vzaimodejstvija jazykjov v Dagestane (konkretno-sotsiologicheskoe issledovanie avarsko-russkogo dvujazychija)', in *Dagestanskij Filial AN SSSR. Sotsiologicheskij Sbornik*, Vol. 1, pp. 233–51.

Mikhajlovskaja N G (1986), *Put' k russkomu slovu*, Nauka, Moscow.

Mikhnevich A E ed (1985), *Russkij jazyk v Belorussii*, Nauka i Tekhnika, Minsk.

Mukhamedova M R (1982), 'Èkstralingvisticheskie uslovija razvitija uzbeksko-russkogo bilingvizma i leksicheskaja interferentsija', in Ivanov V V, Kuchkartaev I eds, *Problemy izuchenija russkogo jazyka v Uzbekistane*, Fan, Tashkent, pp. 56–77.

Natsional'nyj Sostav (1973), *Natsional'nyj sostav naselenija SSSR, sojuznykh i avtonomnykh respublik, kraev, oblastej i natsional'nykh okrugov* (Itogi Vsesojuznoj perepisi naselenija 1970 goda, Vol. 4), Statistika, Moscow.

Naselenie SSSR (1980), *Naselenie SSSR po dannym Vsesojuznoj perepisi naselenija 1979 goda*, Politizdat, Moscow.

Nurtumov M A (1984), 'Nekotorye aspekty izuchenija funktsionirovanija kirgizskogo i russkogo jazykov', in Orusbaev A O, Shejman L A eds, *Russkoe slovo v jazykovoj zhizni Kirgizii*, Mektep, Frunze.

Ohanessian S, Ferguson C A, Polomé E C eds (1975), *Language surveys in developing nations: papers and reports on sociolinguistic surveys*, Center for Applied Linguistics, Washington.

Onenko S N (1972), 'Kharakteristika dvujazychija u nanajtsev (po dannym anketnogo obsledovanija v ijule-avguste 1967 g.)', in Azimov P A, Desheriev Ju D, Filin F P eds, *Problemy dvujazychija i mnogojazychija*, Nauka, Moscow, pp. 208–13.

Orusbaev A (1985), 'O chem umalchivajut sovetologi', *Sovetskaja Kirgizija*, 13 January, p. 3.

Panachin F G ed (1984), *Sovetskaja mnogonatsional'naja shkola v uslovijakh razvitogo sotsializma*, Pedagogika, Moscow.

Rakowska-Harmstone T (1982), 'A political perspective' in Kreindler I T ed, *The changing status of Russian in the Soviet Union* (International Journal of the Sociology of Language, Vol. 33), pp. 101–11.

Rashidov S R (1981), 'Jazyk nashego edinstva i bratstva', in Panachin F G et al eds, *Russkij jazyk — jazyk druzhby i sotrudnichestva narodov SSSR (materialy Vsesojuznoj nauchnoteoreticheskoj konferentsii)*, Nauka, Moscow, pp. 15–47.

Rejtsak A K (1972), 'Dvujazychie kak sotsiolingvisticheskaja problema (k voprosu o metodologii i metodike izuchenija bilingvizma)', in Azimov P A, Desheriev Ju D, Filin F P eds, *Problemy dvujazychija i mnogojazychija*, Nauka, Moscow, pp. 318–24.

Rywkin M (1984), 'The impact of socio-economic change and demographic growth on national identity and socialisation', *Central Asian Survey*, Vol. 3, Pt. 3, pp. 79–98.

Saina S T (1985), 'Vlijanie obrazovanija na ispol'zovanie kazakhskogo i russkogo jazykov bilingvami gorodov Kazakhstana', in Kajdarov A T ed, *Voprosy tjurkskogo jazykoznanija: materialy Pervoj mezhrespublikanskoj konferentsii molodykh lingvistov-tjurkologov*, Nauka, Alma-Ata.

Serdobov N A (1968), 'K voprosu o nekotorykh sotsiologolingvisticheskikh protsessakh v natsional'noj konsolidatsii tuvincev, *Uchenye Zapiski Tuvinskogo Nauchno-Issledovatel'skogo Instituta Jazyka, Literatury i Istorii*, Vol. 13, pp. 78–109.

Shermukhamedov S Sh (1981), 'Moguchij jazyk velikogo naroda', in Panachin F G et al eds, *Russkij jazyk — jazyk druzhby i sotrudnichestva narodov SSSR (materialy Vsesojuznoj nauchno-teoreticheskoj konferentsii)*, Nauka, Moscow, pp. 121–7.

Shalin D M (1978), 'The development of Soviet sociology 1956–1976', *Annual Review of Sociology*, Vol. 4, pp. 171–91.

Silver B D (1975), 'Methods of deriving data on bilingualism from the 1970 Soviet census', *Soviet Studies*, Vol. 27, Pt. 4, pp. 574–97.

Solchanyk R (1982), 'Russian language and Soviet politics', *Soviet Studies*, Vol. 34, Pt. 1, pp. 23–42.

Tomilov N A (1978), *Sovremennye ètnicheskie protsessy sredi sibirskikh tatar*, University Press, Tomsk.

Vinnikov Ja R (1980), 'Natsional'nye i ètnograficheskie gruppy Srednej Azii po dannym ètnicheskoj statistiki', in Dzharylgasinova R S, Tolstova L S eds, *Ètnicheskie processy u natsional'nykh grupp Srednej Azii i Kazakhstana*, Nauka, Moscow.

Vsesojuznaja Perepis' (1978), *Vsesojuznaja perepis' naselenija — vsenarodnoe delo*, Statistika, Moscow.

Khasanov B (1976), *Jazyki narodov Kazakhstana i ikh vzaimodejstvie*, Nauka, Alma-Ata.

Kholmogorov A I (1980), *Internatsional'nye cherty sovetskikh natsij (na materialakh konkretno-sotsiologicheskikh issledovanij v Pribaltike)*, Mysl', Moscow.

Zakiev M Z (1982), 'Tjurkskie jazyki v sem'e edinoj', *Voprosy Jazykoznanija*, No 6, pp. 28–38.

Zinchenko I P (1984), 'Natsional'nyj sostav naselenija SSSR', in Isupov A A, Shvarcer N Z eds, *Vsesojuznaja perepis' naselenija 1979 goda: sbornik statej*, Finansy i Statistika, Moscow, pp. 150–62.

7

RUSSIAN LANGUAGE TEACHING POLICY IN SOVIET CENTRAL ASIA 1958–86

J. M. Kirkwood

Accounts of various parts of the topic to be discussed in this paper already exist (Shorish 1976, Bilinsky, Pennar 1981, Solchanyk 1983, Glyn Lewis, Mitter 1986). The perspective of this paper, however, differs in two ways. In the first place, more attention is devoted to theoretical issues in the field of language acquisition which have influenced developments in Russian language teaching in the Soviet Union. In the second place, the mode of analysis which is adopted in this paper is pragmatic. The present writer has been learning Russian for 28 years, teaching it for over 16 years (Kirkwood 1972, 1973a, 1973b, 1975, 1976, 1978, 1989). The conclusion to which he has come is that the influence of language learning theory on language teaching practice in the last twenty years has done more harm than good and that practical language learning in the classroom has been hindered thereby rather than helped.

It will be argued in this paper that the problems of Russian language teaching in Central Asia are endemic, that increased central control of research and development is likely to be counter-productive and that little progress is to be expected where Russian is taught as a subject where it does not exist to any extent as a language medium (for instance in outlying village schools where the language medium is not Russian). Moreover, in areas where Russian is the medium of instruction (for instance in boarding schools catering for a range of different nationalities) and where it is supposed to act as a lingua franca, any gain in communicative ability by pupils is likely to be offset by slower learning rates in individual school subjects.

Indeed, in many cases children are exposed to Russian before they have acquired their own mother tongue, with the result that they do not acquire native speaker proficiency in any language (Garunov 1975, p. 33). It will be suggested, further, that Soviet attempts to raise the level of Russian language acquisition are hampered on two counts. In the first place, Russian language theory in the Soviet Union has arguably reflected developments in language teaching theory in the West over the last twenty years, developments, moreover, which have their origins in countries, the citizens of which are not noted for their ability to learn foreign languages. The second factor which inhibits progress is the overriding require-ment on the part of teachers and textbook writers to demon-strate ideological commitment. This requirement vitiates the already low effect of language teaching theory on language learning practice.

Recent Developments in Language Teaching Theory

In the last thirty years language learning theory has been dominated by two important influences. During the 1950s and 1960s the prevailing view of how best to teach foreign lan-guages derived from Skinnerian behaviourism and structural linguistics in the West and contrastive linguistics in the case of the Soviet Union. Skinnerian behaviourism was rejected by Soviet scholars. What was common to both was the belief that the spoken language was paramount and that the skills of listening and speaking should precede those of reading and writing. The latter skills were deemed to be of less importance. Noam Chomsky's early work on transformational grammar (Chomsky 1959, 1965) and his distinction between linguistic *competence* and *performance* (a distinction which was widely mis-interpreted at the time) led to the formulation by another scholar of the distinction between 'communicative' competence and performance (Dell Hymes 1972). Essentially the point is this: Chomsky argued that the native speaker of a language has an internalised language acquisition device which allows the speaker/hearer to encode and decode an infinite number of well-formed sentences of that language. In real life, how-ever, the speaker/hearer's competence might be affected by various factors resulting in the formation of defective sentences, marked by such features as repetition of a word or phrase, syntactic anomaly, hesitation phenomena of various types, and so on. Such 'defects' characterised a speaker's linguistic 'performance'. Other scholars argued that the speaker of a natural language possessed a competence over and beyond his ability to produce well-formed utterances. The speaker had the equally important competence to know what utterances were appropriate in particular circumstances. This important qualification led rapidly (such is the speed by which research proceeds when whole armies are involved) to the development of the approach to language teaching associated with the term 'communicative competence'. Advocates of this approach stressed the communicataive side of language and argued that the acquisition of the linguistic system of the target language was insufficient. Learners must also acquire a system of rules which would enable them to produce communicatively acceptable utterances. This approach dominated the 1970s and continues to influence theory and practice in the 1980s. It was developed largely by American and British scholars and it is now the official approach in the Soviet Union.

It is worth drawing attention to the consequences of these two movements. Pre-Chomsky Skinnerian behaviourism and structural linguistics were very much the engines of the introduction and widespread use of language laboratories. The need to use such expensive equipment had a great influence on the design of materials, which were in turn expensive to produce. It is generally accepted that the approach to language teaching associated with behaviourism and structural linguistics did more harm than good. Three things were wrong. The most favoured learning method was the repetition of non-communicative dialogues and sentence patterns which would, so the argument went, become over-learned to the point where learners could use them 'automatically'. No such outcome ever took place. Secondly, as Chomsky pointed out in his famous review of Skinner's *Verbal Behaviour*, such an approach was an incredibly inefficient way of learning a language. Finally, the communicative aspect of language learning was entirely absent. Whole armies of teachers were aware of these drawbacks at the time, but they were regarded as old-fashioned and elitist — especially by researchers.

The approach associated with the aim of teaching communicative competence did much to undo the damage just described. A cornerstone of the new theory was that language learning should be associated with the solving of problems, whether social, intellecutal or communicative. The cardinal question for syllabus designers and textbook writers was: what should the learner be able to do with a given piece of language? Generally speaking, this orientation towards problem-solving aspects of language acquisition has been a great improvement. A great deal of socio-linguistic research has been carried out to establish precisely how people use language in real life. New syllabuses and course books have been produced based on a much clearer understanding of how language is actually used. What this approach has failed to do, however, is to give sufficient weight to the importance of the written language as a means of communication in the technologically developed parts of the world. Whereas it has tried to overcome problems of lack of motivation by teaching the spoken language through a wide range of communicatively oriented activities, the teaching of reading and writing skills continues to lag behind (Kirkwood 1976).

If the present writer has queried the usefulness of much research into language acquisition, he is aware that, subject to fashion as research very often is, at least in the West it is free of ideological constraint in the political sense of the term. Whereas in the West researchers are not required to demonstrate ideological commitment, Soviet researchers are. For instance, it is axiomatic in the Soviet Union that the state education system exists not only to educate in the sense of the word *obrazovanie*, but equally (indeed, in the view of the present writer, primarily) to educate in the sense of 'bring up' (*vospitanie*). This concept of 'upbringing' is built into the syllabus of every subject, including Russian. The way in which this upbringing is to be achieved is tightly prescribed, and researchers are required to demonstrate their awareness of the importance of this aspect of their work in their published research. Such a requirement leads (and has done for decades) to the production of a tremendous amount of pedagogical nonsense. It is, for instance difficult to restrain a smile when reading the solemn pronouncements of a highly placed official in the Ministry of Enlightenment (the Minister himself, no less!) on how to adapt for classroom work (in every class from class I to X) that unimpeachable source of ethical teaching, the works of Leonid Il'ich Brezhnev (Prokof'ev 1982).

Ideological aims take precedence over subject-based aims and objectives, and the latter are subject to the former. All pupils must be raised in a spirit of communist morality, internationalism and Soviet patriotism. They must be ready to defend their Soviet Motherland (i.e., the USSR, as opposed to any single member republic). Teaching materials reflecting these aims are an absolute requirement at all stages from pre-school to tertiary levels of the educational system. In the case of Russian as a school subject all materials exemplifying Russian must conform to these objectives as must all training and practice in the language. In addition, all children must be taught to appreciate the unique significance of Russian as the language of inter-ethnic communication (*mezhnatsional'noe obshchenie*) within the Soviet Union and increasingly as a language of international communication (*mezhdunarodnoe obshchenie*) within the membership of the East Bloc countries, Cuba, Vietnam, and in the 1980s Afghanistan. Moreover, the role of Russian as the language by means of which the best of world culture is transmitted to the non-Russian peoples of the Soviet Union, its role as the main language in the world for the promotion of socialism, the 'progressive' ideas of mankind, etc., is increasingly stressed.

The ideological 'magnetic field' within which Russian language teaching research is conducted is never switched off. Indeed, over the years it as been intensified and secured by a steady process of centralisation of curriculum planning processes, the production of teaching materials and the training of teachers. A survey of mainstream research in the last twenty years reveals that the requirements of ideology have a serious effect on the quality of research, principally because of the questions which are deemed to be in urgent need of further research and the requirement to demonstrate ideological commitment. This is not to suggest that *all* Soviet research has an ideological bias. Phonology, morphology, syntax can be studied largely outside a marxist-leninist framework. There are real ideological constraints, however, in areas of research which concern the uses to which language may be put, the type of language which should be studied, the selection of topics to be studied, the role of literature, to list only a few.

These remarks on the relative value of language teaching research and its effect on teaching have been included principally to sound a note of caution against taking too seriously educational events which are deemed to be of outstanding importance. There has been quite a large amount of comment among Western researchers, for instance, about the importance of the Tashkent conferences of 1975 and 1979 (Bilinsky, Pennar 1981, Kreindler 1982, Solchanyk 1983). There is no doubt that these events were hailed by the Soviet political and educational establishments as events of national importance, nor is there any doubt that they reveal much about official anxiety as regards the success of Russian language teaching in the schools. An analysis of their recommendations however, makes it fairly clear that there is little justification for anticipating radically improved results. This is not to deny that these conferences did not lead to quantitative change, nor to deny that the status of Russian was further enhanced relative to other languages. It is to deny, however, that many non-Russians started to learn Russian more successfully than before.

At this point it will be useful to highlight factors which are likely to assist the learner in his attempt to acquire communicative competence in Russian. Perhaps the most important of all is whether Russian is the language medium to the environment in which the learner finds himself. The requirement to *use* a language is a most powerful motivating force if that requirement is understood by the learner as a perceived need to use it. To the extent that Russian is not the language medium of the environment that perceived need wanes. In an outlying village in, say, Turkmenistan where Russian is never spoken in ordinary day-to-day contexts by ordinary villagers, the perceived need to communicate in Russian will be very low, if it exists at all. Another important factor has to do with linguistic kinship. Ukrainian and Byelorussian are closely related to Russian. All three are Slavonic languages, their territories are contiguous and there is a great deal of Russian penetration in the Ukraine and Byelorussia. It is not surprising that Ukrainians and Byelorussians are likely to speak better Russian than Uzbeks or Tadzhiks, whose languages belong to another family.

The consequences of this last point are perhaps worth taking a little further. How does one measure kinship between languages? One common method is to compare two language systems along certain parameters and measure the extent to which they differ. It is often argued that the extent to which systems and sub-systems differ is a measure of the consequent difficulties to be encountered by native speakers of one who attempt to acquire the other. It is predictable, for instance, that native-speakers of Russian, a language with no definite or indefinite article will have difficulty knowing when to use words like 'the' and 'a' in Engish and when to omit them. A speaker of a language which does not distinguish between the sounds /l/ and /r/ will predictably have difficulty distinguishing between 'lorry', and 'lolly', 'rolly' and 'rorry'. Althought the two last sounds do not occur as words in English, the learner in question does not know that. Consequently, if he wants to utter the word for a particular type of transport vehicle (lorry), he has one chance in four of succeeding. Such a learner will have difficulty in learning many English vocabulary items and will have to contend with major problems of pronunciation. Similar problems arise for the Uzbek, Tadzhik, Turkmen, Kirghiz learner of Russian.

One might have expected, given these difficulties, that a policy with respect to norms of acceptibility for Turkic learners of Russian might reflect a pragmatic requirement of intelligibility, rather than the normative requirement to attain the standards of the Russian 'literary language' (the Soviet equivalent of Standard British English). After all, one of the tenets of 'communicative competence' theory is that 'communicative well-formedness' takes precedence over grammatical well-formedness. Yet this is not the case. It is official policy that the norms of standard Russian (*literaturnyi yazyk*) are those which non-Russian learners must seek to acquire (Ivanov, Mikhailovskaya 1982, Desheriev 1982).

The reasons for this policy have little to do with any kind of supposed Russian elitism. The fact is that the Russian which non-Russian learners are expected to acquire is not the Russian language as a whole, but only a variety of it, namely that variety which is destined to fulfil the role of the language of inter-ethnic communication. As has been noted already, the role of this language is to be a medium for the communist upbringing of the learner, a medium for the transmission of culture. To these we may now add the no less important role of Russian as the language of many professional occupations and the sole language of use in the Soviet armed forces. Implicit in the various roles is the high importance of the written language. As has already been suggested, the written form of a language is much harder to acquire, even by mother tongue speakers. However, not only is a standardised form of literary Russian the norm, it is inevitable that a pronounciation norm be established as well, given the need for the representatives of many different linguistic backgrounds to communicate with each other in highly complex situations (military, professional, educational).

The setting and assessing of standards in the context of language acquisition is notoriously difficult. Quite apart from the complexities involved in establishing a generally accepted system for evaluating the extent to which a learner may be said to have 'acquired' a given language and to what degree of proficiency (basically: 'how many things can he say and how well does he say them?'), there are insuperable difficulties of instruction and the learner's acquired proficiency. This is particularly true with respect to Russian language teaching policy in the republics of Central Asia. That is to say, one can point to considerable quantitative change in the provision of resources, both manpower and material, during the period under review, but it will be difficult to argue that there has been an overall improvement in the linguistic proficiency of the learner. This is not to say that there has been no improvement but that any improvement is likely to have had more to do with patterns of migration, Government policy with respect to the development of multinational construction teams, the provision of schools with an international clientèle where Russian is the language of communication and instruction, and the language teaching ability of the Soviet armed forces. What is clear is that over the last twenty years significantly greater proportions of the indigenous populations claim to have 'mastered' Russian as a second language. What is equally clear is that there continue to be many problems connected with the production of effective teaching materials and good teachers.

In the remainder of this paper we shall be tracing developments in Russian language teaching policy with reference to the republics of Uzbekistan, Turkmenistan, Tadzhikistan and Kirghizia. The constraints of space prevent discussion of other

Islamic strongholds. As will become clear, however, much of what has taken place in the above-named republics is part of a development which has All-Union significance.

DEVELOPMENTS BETWEEN 1958 AND 1969

1. Census Data

In 1959 the percentage of the eponymous population claiming the eponymous language as their native language was as follows:

Uzbeks	98.4
Tadzhiks	98.1
Turmen	98.9
Kirghiz	98.7.

Soviet citizens were not asked for that census whether they had command of Russian as a second language. Evidence of Russification of the indigenous populations related to patterns of urbanisation and migration suggests that, although Russification is likely to be much greater among the urban population than the rural population, overall the levels for the named republics are very small (Glyn Lewis 1971, Silver 1974a).

2. Government Policy

Political landmarks during the decade under review and to which language teaching policy was tied are undoubtedly the educational reforms of 1958–59, the Programme of the Communist Party, the claim that Russian had become in practice the language of inter-ethnic communication (*Kommunist*, 16, 1961, p. 86), the role of the 'Great Russian People' (Azizyan 1961, p. 47) and the claim that there would be a 'fusion' of all the nationalities in which national differences would be submerged (*Kommunist* 18, 1962; p. 42, *Kommunist* 9, 1963, p. 20).

The implications of Khrushchev's reforms and their reception in the various republics have been discussed elsewhere (Bilinsky 1962, Kreindler 1982) and need not be rehearsed here. The main thrust of the reforms as far as the Russian language is concerned was to enhance its status relative to other languages and to give parents the right to choose the language in which their children should be educated. This right, together with the promotion of Russian as the language of interethnic communication, had an important influence on the development of language teaching policy.

3. Language Teaching Policy

Russian could only serve as a language of interethnic communication if everyone had a practical mastery of it. How to teach pupils and students to acquire that mastery has been the goal of Russian language teaching ever since. In the early 1960s the debate on how best to teach a foreign language reflected debate in the West. The most prevalent method in the 1940s and 1950s had been the so-called 'grammar/translation' method. It was intellectually demanding and was not obviously designed to teach people to *speak* the foreign language. Growing dissatisfaction with this method stimulated a demand for a method which would more obviously teach practical linguistic skills. By the early 1960s the grammar/translation method was in retreat, both in Western schools and in the Soviet Union. It was replaced by the least efficient and most time-consuming method of learning a language that our educational systems have so far devised. A thorough knowledge of the grammatical system of a language allows the learner to encode and decode utterances *accurately*. The process is slow at the beginning but improves with practice. The encoding/decoding process operates via the use of rules to generate utterances. It is much faster to teach a pupil a rule and invite him to apply it than to teach him to learn off by heart hundreds of sentence patterns and invite him to create others 'by analogy'. Moreover, since the grammatical system of a language applies *par excellence* to the written language, learners have a good chance of acquiring literacy in the target language. It is very hard to teach literacy via the spoken languge only.

At the Second Inter-republican Conference on improving the teaching of Russian in Tashkent (28 May to 1 June 1962) such issues were very much to the fore. The grammar/translation method was attacked (Reshetov 1962, p. 8), attention was drawn to the achievements of structural and contrastive linguistics (RYANSh 4, 1962, p. 19), the slowest way possible of teaching the meaning of words (namely by semanticisation rather than translation) was advocated. In addition there was a very interesting debate on the teaching of literature, opinion being equally divided between teaching literature via a reading of excerpts and reading aloud on the one hand, and teaching literature via study of the history of literature on the other.

Teaching a foreign language by the grammar/translation method does not actually require the teacher to be able to speak that language fluently. Teaching it by any direct method does. Since one effect of Khrushchev's reforms was to extend the teaching of Russian and since a switch away from a grammar/translation method entails a high level of teacher proficiency in the spoken domain, it is not surprising that one of the major problems facing planners has been the supply of properly qualified teachers. This was particularly true in the 1960s in the Central Asian republics. At the 1962 Tashkent conference it was reported that Uzbekistan needed another thousand teachers, especially for deployment in village schools (RYANSh 4, 1962, p. 17). Pedagogical institutes and universities were accused of turning out poorly trained teachers and that there was inadequate provision of in-service training (RYANSh 5, 1962, p. 8). At a teachers' conference in Khorezm in 1964 it was reported that there was a shortage of teachers and that a significant number of primary school teachers had a poor knowledge of Russian (RYANSh 4, 1964, p. 81). In a report on the situation in Tadzhik schools (RYANSh, 3 1965, p. 82) it was stressed that many school leavers were deficient in their knowledge of Russian, especially if they wanted to go on to higher education and that the problem was particularly chronic in rural areas. Many teachers did not know the mother-tongue of the learners. This last complaint reflects the fact that the issue of the role of the use of the mother tongue of the learner in the process of teaching Russian continued to be the focus of debate even after the tide had swung away from grammar and translation as the primary teaching method.

Although many teachers continued to teach by the old methods, the trend towards more 'practical' methods was too powerful to resist. In this respect the recommendations of the Tashkent Conference are worth noting. Its first recommendation was that all planning and coordination of research work in the republics of Central Asia, Kazakhstan and Azerbaidzhan (i.e., the republics represented at the Conference) should be carried out by the Institute of National Schools of the Academy of Pedagogical Sciences of the RSFSR (RYANSh 5, 1965, p. 10). Others concerned the need to improve teacher training, to develop 'stable' methodological principles for the teaching of Russian, and especially to study the feasibility of contrastive analysis of the mother tongue of the learner with Russian as a basis for the production of teaching materials. An important recommendation, reflecting developments in the West, was that individual textbooks should be replaced by course complexes consisting of a basic course book plus a range of supplementary practice material for help with pronunciation, reading, listening and speaking in the form of books of exercise material and associated audio and visual material such as tapes and slides (RYANSh 5, 1965, p. 9). Another important recommendation, which did not reflect developments in the West and which, in the view of this writer, is the single most important contribution of Soviet second language pedagogy in the last twenty-five years, was the replacement of a linear approach to the teaching of Russian by a concentric approach. In other words, topics were to be taught in cycles, each new cycle teaching the same or similar topic in greater depth. The great advantage of such an approach is that the linguistic treatment of a topic can be linked much more closely with the maturational level of the learner, different tasks can be carried out at different levels of proficiency, and so on. An advantage claimed for this approach by Soviet advocates at the Conference was that it allowed for a substantial reduction in the amount of theoretical material to be learned by the pupil, with a consequent increase in the time available for practice. The conference was unable to decide whether literature should be taught via excerpts or whether works should be read in the original. By this time the study of literature in foreign language classrooms in the West was very much on the wane, since reading literature required a large vocabulary, which ran counter to behaviourist theory which dictated that pupils should learn only a few hundred words and 'practise' them to the point of 'automaticity'.

By the end of the 1960s there were points of comparison between the dominant Western and Soviet approaches, but also points of contrast. Both approaches downgraded the importance of grammar and the study of literature by focusing on the need to teach 'the spoken language'. Both advocated the production of sets of materials which replaced the study of formal rules by the practice of sentence patterns. But whereas behaviorism excluded the cognitive factor in language learning, the Soviet approach retained, at least theoretically, the need for cognition. Both approaches advocated the use of structural and comparative linguistics as a basis for the development of materials (Kirkwood 1973, p. 47).

DEVELOPMENTS BETWEEN 1970 AND 1979

1. Census Data

The 1970 census produced data for the first time, not only for citizens claiming to speak their own national language as their mother tongue, but also for those who claimed to have mastered Russian as a second language. Those data are reproduced as percentages of the nationalities with which we are concerned, together with the data already produced for 1959:

Nationality	National language as L1		Russian as L2
	1959	1970	1970
Uzbek	98.4	98.6	14.5
Tadzhik	98.1	98.5	15.4
Turkmen	98.9	98.9	15.4
Kirghiz	98.7	98.8	19.1

(Based on Zinchenko 1976)

It is clear form an analysis of the L1 data that the percentages of those citizens claiming their national language as their mother-tongue are either the same in 1970 as they were in 1959, or greater. As we have already noted, there is no L2 data for 1959, consequently any comment about the inter-censal period must be speculative. Hélène Carrère d' Encausse uses the 1970 L2 data to argue that Russian in the Central Asian republics is only progressing 'at a snail's pace' (Carrère d'Encausse 1980, p. 174). Glyn Lewis argues, on the other hand, that migration patterns during the 1960s intensified (Glyn Lewis 1971, p. 156) and Silver adduces some fascinating data to show that adoption of Russian as an L2 by the indigenous population correlates well with contact with Russians. What is particularly interesting is that the pattern is the same for urban *and* rural areas (Silver 1976, p. 414). There is thus some reason to suppose that increased in-migration plus the effect of an extension and intensification of the teaching of Russian since 1959 will have had a stimulating effect on the incidence of the choice of Russian as an L2. As the figures below indicate, with the exception of Tadzhiks, the numbers claiming Russian as an L2 are much higher than for all the other languages combined:

Nationality	L2	
	Russian	Other languages
Uzbek	1,330,865	281,075
Tadzhik	328,773	249,652
Turkmen	234,698	16,572
Kirghiz	277,104	44,440

(Vsesoyuznoye perepis' naseleniya, 1970, p. 20)

Finally, although he does not give figures for individual union republics, Zinchenko calculates that the percentage of young people between 20 and 29 claiming an L2 (not necessarily Russian) ranges from 34.8 to 80.1 (Zinchenko 1976 p. 210). Even the lower figure is very much higher than the figures given for Russian L2 acquisition at republican level and must surely reflect the influence of the educational system as well as of the armed forces.

2. Government Policy

Policy with respect to the nationalities and the Russian language under Brezhnev reflects consolidation and steady development rather than radical change. At the 24th Party Congress the leading role of the Russian people is officially proclaimed (Kreindler 1982, p. 17). The official emphasis on 'fusion of the peoples' (*sliyanie*) is toned down, however, and disappears entirely from all speeches at the 25th Party Congress in 1976 (Carrère d'Encausse, 1978, p. 57). The official view that a new, supra-national entity, namely 'the Soviet people' has emerged; first promulgated in 1963 (Rogachev and Sverdlin 1963, but see Pavlov 1962, p. 46) is incorporated in the preamble to the new Constitution of 1977 (Shtromas 1978, p. 267). The role of the Russian language as the language of inter-ethnic communication continued to be emphasised, in the context, however, of a language policy which had begun to promote the goal of a specific type of bilingualism for Soviet citizens, namely command of the mother tongue plus Russian as a second language for the non-Russian nationalities (Desheriev and Protchenko 1976, Desheriev 1978). In 1978 there was a decree of the USSR Council of Ministers 'Concerning Measures for the Further Improvement of the Study and Teaching of Russian in the Union Republics' (RYANSh 5, 1979, pp. 2–5, Bilinsky 1981, p. 323, Pennar 1981, p. 7). Developments arising out of that decree ocurred in 1979 and will be discussed in the next section of this chapter.

3. Language Teaching Policy

Developments during the period under review in this section can best be examined under three headings: (a) conferences;(b) linguodidactic trends; (c) developments in the republics. In this connection an event of major importance was the establishment in 1969 of the extremely influential Research Institute for the Teaching of Russian in the National Schools of the Academy of Pedagogical Sciences of the USSR (henceforth NII PRYANSh) under the direction of N. M. Shanskii. Since its foundation it has exerted an increasing influence on the development of virtually every aspect of Russian language teaching from the specification of vocabulary items to the training of teachers.

(a) Conferences

Four All-Union conferences which acted as fora for the establishment of new trends were held in Moldavia in 1972 (RYANSh 1, 1973), Moscow in 1974 (RYANSh 2, 1975, pp. 80–83), Tashkent in 1975 (RYANSh 5, 1976; Solchanyk 1985, pp. 81–83), Tallin in 1977 (RYANSh 2, 1978, pp. 86–91). They are associated with key issues, namely the production of centralised 'model' programmes (Moldavia, Moscow Tashkent), the extension of Russian in the the school curriculum and its introduction into kindergartens (Tashkent), the intensification of communist education and its reflection in teaching materials (Tallin).

The Moldavia conference established a list of research tasks which had to have priority. There was the question of what, exactly, should be taught. There was still no 'scientific' linguistic description of Russian as a subject in the national school curriculum. There was a pressing need for research to establish the grammatical and lexical minima which could serve as the basis for a pedagogical grammar. At the same conference there is the first mention of the need to take as one's starting point the 'communicative character' of teaching (Shanskii 1973, p. 11). It was also necessary to find out the current state of language teaching in the republics, to establish 'objective' levels of acquisition and learning and a unified programme of literature. These tasks were specified mainly by Shanskii and were reflected in the conference's recommendations to teachers, scholars and research institutes. The influence of NII PRYANSh is quite clear, as are the signs of the future centralisation of teaching policy and curriculum design.

The importance of the 1975 Tashkent conference is reflected by the presence of it at important Government and Party officials as well as eminent scholars. They included Rashidov, who at that time was a non-voting member of the Politburo of the CPSU and the First Secretary of the Uzbekistan CP, Prokofiev, Minister of Enlightenment, Filin, the Director of the prestigious Academy of Sciences' Institute of Russian Language, Desheriev, one of the Soviet Union's leading sociolinguists. Among the recommendations of this conference to the Ministry of Enlightenment of the USSR and the Ministry of Higher and Secondary Specialist Education of the USSR were the following:

1. Improve and extend the training of primary school teachers;

2. Extend the provision of Russian as an optional subject in all higher and secondary educational establishments;

3. Produce 'model' text books and materials for use in primary, secondary and higher education;

4. Produce 'model' syllabuses for programmes of 'intensified Russian instruction' (*uglublyennoye izuchenie russkogo yazyka*) in national schools;

5. To organise by the end of the first quarter of 1976 measures for the organisation of Russian language teaching in national kindergartens of the Union republics;

6. Begin the teaching of Russian in the first class in the national schools of those republics where it was still being taught only from the second year onwards;

7. Request school supply authorities to launch a programe of equipping schools with language laboratories and A/V centres (*'kabinety russkogo yazyka'*);

8. Produce 'model' teacher training programmes with the joint participation of the Administration of cadres and NII PRYANSh;

9. Pay particular attention to the training needs of primary and secondary school teachers in rural areas;

10. Increase the extra-mural use of Russian;

11. Increase the number of schools offering 'intensified Russian instruction'.

(RYANSh 5, 1976, pp. 81–3)

These recommendations have been reproduced in some detail because many of them became official policy in the years that followed. The centralising tendency of many of them is quite obvious.

The 1974 Moscow conference represents a transitional stage between the Moldavia conference and the Tashkent conference, concentrating as it did on the question of textbook and materials construction. Although there were still voices raised in the defence of grammatical rules (RYANSh 2, 1975, p. 82), the trend away from grammar books towards multi-media language courses was confirmed. This conference also heard proposals that there should be an agreed format for the production of textbooks and materials based on a 'miniaturised' grammar. The requirement that materials should be selected primarily with the aims of communist education in mind was also stated.

The object of the Tallin conference was to discuss the ways in which Russian language teaching could be used for the purposes of intensifying communist education (*kommunisticheskoye vospitanie*). It was the first conference of All-Union significance to discuss the principles of selection of literary works and course content from the specific point of view of enhancing the morally educative (*vospitatel'ny*) function of literature. There were also demands that every lecture, lesson, extra-mural activity should reflect the 'heroics' (*geroika*) of everyday Soviet life so that the study of Russian should become a 'festival of learning' about the achievements of the whole people. (RYANSh, 2, 1978, p. 87). Barannikov, Deputy director of NII PRYANSh, emphasised the advantages of educating children morally at an age when they most receptive and advocated an increase in the ideological content of language instruction for the very young (RYANSh 2, 1978, p. 88). The recommendations of this conference were less specific than those of the other one, no doubt partly because of the vagueness of the term 'communist education'. However, there were calls for a general intensification of ideological work, increased awareness of the moral educative role of Russian and a specific recommendation from the Tadzhik Minister of Education Dadaboyev that all teacher-training courses should have a compulsory special subject on the communist education of learners via the medium of Russian langauge and literature.

(b) Linguodidactic Trends

During the decade under review there were strong centralising trends emanating from Moscow and embracing developments in every aspect of the Russian language teaching process. Some of these trends have been alluded to above. On the level of descriptive linguistics there is little doubt that the central task of the 1970s was the development of miniaturised and standardised grammars and vocabularies which were to form the 'scientific' basis for syllabus content selection. This was also the decade which saw the production of course complexes, rather than individual textbooks, based, however, on the theories of the 1960s.

The gradual influence of the 'communicative competence' approach to language learning can be detected in the pronouncements of people in the vanguard of theoretical innovation (RYANSh 5, 1976, p. 3; Barannikov 1977, p. 10; Andrionova 1987, p. 20). It should be noted that principles of minimisation, simplification and standardisation are counter to the principles of 'communicative competence'. Soviet work of the 1970s in the areas of minimisation and simplification took the language system (i.e. the grammatical system) as its starting point. The 'communicative' approach takes as its starting point language *in use*. It begins by asking what learners need to be able to 'do' with the language and then selects ways of 'doing' it. It aims at variety, individualisation, the development of ranges of communicative strategies for use in varying situations. Learners should encounter language which is partly beyond the level at which they command it, they should have practice, not in carrying out mechanical, repetitive exercises, but in problem solving which entails the use of language.

The decade under discussion also saw the development of the 'model' programme (*tipovaya programma*). As we have seen, questions of the standardisation of textbooks, language courses and literature courses have been discussed at All-Union conference level. They have also been the subject of innumerable articles and monographs. The desire for centralisation on the part of the authorities is doubtless partly (mainly?) political, but there are pedagocial reasons as well. We have noted above that official policy specifies a single variety of Russian in its role as language of interethnic communication. Such a variety has to be described and defined in terms of particular grammatical constructions and lexical sets with reference to centrally determined aims and objectives. Given the widely differing standards of teacher competence, it is desirable that the methodology also be centrally determined, so that all teachers are aware exactly of what they are supposed to do. There are, of course, great drawbacks about such an approach. Centralising processes are difficult to reverse. The educational system reacts slowly to change. Teaching methods which become discredited take longer to change. Developments in the 1970s provide a good example of an inexorable and *standardised* approach to language learning which, in itself, cannot achieve the aims of the Government, especially in the area of higher education, professional and military activity.

Finally, during the decade there was a steady increase in the extent to which Russian infiltrated the curriculum of the national schools, in the form of 'optional courses' in the field of higher education, in the growth of the number of preparatory classes, Russian language classes in kindergartens, schools with Russian as the language of instruction and schools' offering 'intensified Russian language instruction'.

(c) Developments in the Republics

The adoption of new programmes requiring a high degree of proficiency on the part of the teacher together with the extension and intensification of Russian language instruction, especially in the aftermath of the Tashkent conference, imposed great strains on the supply of teachers. A recurring refrain in the pronouncements of republican ministers and educators throughout the period is for the requirement of more and better qualified teachers. The shortage is particularly acute in rural areas (Shamsutdinov 1975, p. 6; Dadaboyev 1975, p. 18). According to Shamsutdinov, in 1975, 70% of teachers had higher education, and Russian was taught in all schools wth Uzbek or Karakalpak as the language of instruction. On the other hand, many children had a poor vocabulary, an insufficient knowledge of grammar, poor prounciation, poor writing ability, an inability to express their thoughts crisply and clearly in Russian, read with ease or consciously apply their knowledge. To remedy this state of affairs it was proposed to set up area kindergartens (*bazovye detskie sady*) to teach Russian to non-Russian children. In 1978, however, together with the announcement that the republic had adopted new programmes and associated materials, attention was drawn to the inability of call-up recruits to the armed forces to use their knowledge of Russian, and a call was issued for more material on 'military-patriotic themes' (Saubanova 1978, p. 85).

In a major report on the situation in Uzbekistan, Shermukhamedov outlined the tasks and achievements of the republic since the Tashkent conference. The Uzbekistan Communist Party and the Uzbekistan Ministry of Enlightenment, in a decree of 12 November 1975 vowed to improve radically Russian language teaching in the pre-school sector; establish in all regional centres boarding schools (*shkoly-internaty*) with intensified Russian language instruction and to develop a network of comprehensive schools offering the same type of intensive instruction; set up well-equipped audiovisual materials workshops for Russian (*kabinety*). In 1976 the results were as follows: 216 kindergartens had Russian language instruction in the preparatory year; a new curriculum was being introduced starting in 1976, for all years from class I to X in which 48 hours per week would be devoted to Russian language and literature;

there were 560 mixed schools with Russian as one of the languages of instruction; there was a 20% increase in the number of classes with 25 pupils which had been split into two groups; 81.6% of teachers had higher education; all 8-year schools had audiovisual rooms, and the use of Russian in institutions such as Houses of Pioneers had increased. There had likewise been an increase in the role of radio and television in the propagandising and teaching of Russian.

Post-Tashkent developments in Kirghizia are reported by Tashmatova and Sheiman (Tashmatova 1978, Sheiman 1978). According to these reports there had been an increase in preparatory classes with Russian language instruction from 110 in 1966 to 440 in 1976 with a more than threefold increase in the number of children taught (rising from 3,000 in 1966 to 11,000 in 1976). Important research work had been done in the preparatory school field and the experience of Kirghizia had been taken into account by NII RPRYANSh and incorporated into the All-Union programme for preparatory classes with a multilingual audience published in 1977. There was a need, however, for more and better training of teachers for the preschool sector and there was a need likewise for a scientific and theoretically sound foundation for the organisation of the educational process in these classes.

The situation is similar with respect to Tadzhikistan and Turkmenistan. Dadaboyev reports in 1975 (Dadaboyev 1975, pp. 15–18)) that there has been a consolidation of schools of mixed nationality with two or three languages of instruction, of which one is Russian. One major problem concerns the supply of permanent teachers to outlying village schools. Another one he sees as the need to maximise the use of materials in the interests of communist education.

In Turkmenistan Russian in the early 1970s had been taught from the second year of school in the national school. From 1976 it was to be introduced from the first class. The number of hours devoted to Russian had been increased in classes VIII to X. New programmes were being introduced (Berdyyev 1975, pp. 18–20).

DEVELOPMENTS BETWEEN 1979 AND 1983

1. Census Data

Data from the 1979 census returns on the numbers of people who claimed their national language as their mother-tongue and who claimed mastery of Russian as a second language are presented in the following table in percentage form together with data from previous censuses:

Nationality	National language as L1			Russian as L2	
	1959	1970	1979	1970	1979
Uzbek	98.4	98.6	98.5	14.5	49.2
Tadzhik	98.1	98.5	97.8	15.4	29.5
Turkmen	98.9	98.9	98.6	15.4	25.3
Kirghiz	98.7	98.8	97.8	19.1	29.3

As can be seen from these figures, retention of the mother tongue continues to be very high. Given the stable migration patterns of the nationalities concerned, i.e., little migration beyond the Central Asian republics, although there is migration among the republics (Rapawy 1985, p. 76, Zemtsov 1985, p. 16, Glyn Lewis 1976, p. 76), it is difficult to account for the increase in the numbers claiming Russian as their L2 other than by considering them to be a consequence of Russian language teaching policy as outlined so far in this chapter. As far as this writer is aware, no figures are available giving a breakdown of the population according to age which correlate with knowledge of Russian as an L2. The increase in the number of Uzbeks claiming mastery of Russian as an L2 is frankly staggering, if not literally incredible.

2. Government Policy

The main policy change in the short period under review in this section is associated with Andropov's mistrust of the nationalities and his attempts to increase still further the international 'mix' in each republic (Zemtsov, 1985). As we shall see in the next sub-section, this policy had its parallel in the extension of the network of schools with Russian as one of the languages of instruction, the growth in the number of schools with intensive Russian language instruction, and an

145

increase in the number of schools (secondary) with Russian as the sole language of instruction for many subjects in the curriculum.

3. Language Teaching Policy

In 1979, in response to the recommendations of the 1975 Tashkent Conference and the 1977 Tallin Conference, the Ministry of Englightenment of the USSR and NII PRYANSh published jointly a 'Model Programme of Russian Language for the Secondary National School' (RYANSh 1, 1979, pp. 72–80; RYANSh 2, 1979, pp. 788–94). This was a detailed blueprint outlining aims, objectives, methods, content, skills, themes for discussion, etc., for every school year from I to X. Textbooks and materials were expected to incorporate the details of these programmes. It was clearly specified what was to be learned in any particular year in a specific number of areas, including phonetics, morphology, syntax, word-formation, the skills of speaking, listening, reading, writing. Each of the language skills was further sub-categorised and there were recommendations on how to teach these skills and the levels of proficiency which were to be achieved. The themes were carefully specified for each year. It is worth listing them here to give an idea of the type of subject matter which would be discussed in the national school and which pupils were supposed to assimilate via their acquisition of Russian:

Year I

School, Family, Home.

Year II

School, Family, Home, Seasons of the Year (general development of these themes).

Year III

The range is greatly extended: School, Family, the Work of Grown-ups, Life on the Sovkhoz/Kolkhoz, On the Farm, In the Factory, Nature Conservation, Sport, In the Pioneer Camp,

The Life and Work of Townspeople/Country People, A Trip to Town/into the Country, The Capital of my Republic, The Capital of our Motherland (*rodina*) is Moscow, The Soviet Army, Victory Day.

Year IV

Summer, Summer Holidays, At School, My Day, The Family, Helping my Parents, The Young Pioneers, Good Deeds of Pioneers, Who Works Where, Winter, Nature in Winter, The New Year, My Comrades, The Village, Work and Leisure in the Village, The Town, Work and Leisure in the Town, Physical Education and Sport, Animals are our Friends, Moscow is the Capital of our Motherland, The Childhood Years of V. I. Lenin, Summer is Coming.

Year V

In the Pioneer Camp, Work Rest and Play, Autumn, Nature, Getting the Harvest in, Our School, My Friends and Comrades, The October Holiday, What am I going to be?, Work and Leisure in the Town, Our Great Motherland, Health and Sport, The Soviet Army, Work and Leisure in the Village, Our Cosmonauts, Nature and Work (*trud*), Work in the School Vegetable Garden, Life in the Pioneers.

Year VI

The Pioneer Organisation, Pioneer Laws and Insignia, The Russian Language, its Lexical Riches, Our Motherland, The Horizons of our Motherland are Wide, The Friendship of the Peoples of the USSR, The Pupil and the Collective, Meeting Interesting People, In the Museums of Our Country, Beloved Nature, The Plant and Animal Kingdoms, During the Great Patriotic War, City Life (transport, trade, health-care), Technology Around Us, The Life of Children Abroad, Sport in Summer and Winter.

Year VII

Nature, Natural Phenomena, Nature Conservation, Pupils and Their Hobbies and Pastimes, School Study Groups, Komsomol Heroes, The Selfless Toil of Soviet People, Our Motherland, The Struggle for Peace, In Fraternal Socialist Countries, We Are Studying Russian, What's New in Science and Technology, The Theatrical and Cinematic Arts, Health and Sport, Soviet People in Space, Our Country's Calendar of Memorable Events (*Zvezdnyi kalendar'*), The Media (press, radio, television), Journeys and Excursions in the USSR.

Year VIII

Beloved Nature, The Beautiful in Nature, Our Motherland, The Moral Stature and Humanism of the Soviet People, Lenin — the Worker's Leader and Teacher, Our Country's Heroic Past, Social Contrast in the Lands of Capitalism, The Importance of Russian in the Lives of Peoples of the USSR, In the World of Science and Technology, Art and Music, Sports Contests, From the History of Sport, Komosomol Life, The Komsomol in our School, Socially Useful Labour in the Life of Soviet Man.

Years IX and X

Consolidation of the above.

As is clear from an analysis of those themes, many of them recur from year to year. This is not surprising for several reasons, not least because a cyclical approach has a reinforcing effect in psychological terms (although perhaps not the one desired by the authorities) and it allows pupils (at least in theory) to become linguistically increasingly sophisticated in their treatment of these themes.

Not only were these themes standard for all programmes in all national schools, but much of the linguistic material was selected centrally as well. In 1980 there was a report in RYANSh (No. 1, 1980) of the immediate plans of the Soviet Academy of Pedagogical Sciences leading research institute (i.e. NII PRYANSh). It contained statements by Shanskii and

148

Barannikov on the outlook for subsequent years and other staff provided details of work being done in preparing standardised textbooks and materials for use in the national schools. Teams of authors had been selected with teachers from a given Republic national school under the leadership of a staff member of the Institute to produce materials based on the Programme. Work was also being done on minimising the amount of grammar and lexis necessary for the goals set by the Programme. The approach is signficant, since for the first time the role of the native language of the learner is downgraded. In practice this meant that Russian language materials would no longer be based on a contrastive analysys of the native language of the learner and the structure of Russian. What was required was a standardised form of the language which would be taught to everyone, irrespective of linguistic background (Shanskii 1982, Filin 1979, Ivanov and Mikhailovska 1982).

Another important event in 1979 was the Second Tashkent Conference, held under the title of 'Russian — the Language of Friendship and Cooperation among the Peoples of the USSR'. It was seen as having at least as much political significance as the Tashkent conference of 1975. Brezhnev saw fit to send a message of greeting to the participants, who included Rashidov, Prokofiev (USSR Minister of Enlightenment), Academicians Khrapchenko and Filin from the Academy Department of Russian Language and Literature and the Institute of Russian Language respectively, and many others. The political significance of this conference has been assessed elsewhere (Pennar 1981, Bilinsky 1981, Kreindler 1982, Solchanyk 1983). Here it is worth reproducing a summary of its recommendations, which applied to every sector of the educational system:

Pre-School

More activities were to be organised in which Russian was to be the medium of communication, including everyday routines such as walks, sporting events, assemblies, etc. Links between the pre-school establishment and the family were to be strengthened, parents were to receive more help in teaching their children to converse in Russian and their native language at home.

149

Comprehensive School (Obshcheobrazovatel'naya shkola)

The use of Russian was to be greatly extended via the Pioneer and Komsomol organisations; schools and classes of intensified Russian language instruction should be organised and developed; Russian language groups should be created both within and outside school to help learners improve their command of the language; all schools should be equipped with special Russian language rooms (*kabinety russkogo yazyka*) which should be properly equipped with audio and visual aids.

Professional Technical Schools (Proftekhuchilishcha)

As for comprehensive schools, with a corresponding emphasis on Russian for technical purposes; the extra-mural use of Russian to be greatly increased.

Institutions of Higher and Further Education (VUZy, etc.)

The practice of the Kirghiz, Uzbek and other Union republican institutions of higher education should be followed concerning the teaching of social sciences, general subjects and certain disciplines in Russian in the Second Year and upwards; the requirement should be introduced that Russian should be the language in which all course work and diploma work should be written; there should be more research into language teaching practice, collective volumes of research findings should be produced; there should be more resources for equipment, the policy should be to appoint teachers wherever possible with higher education.

Teacher Training

There was a pressing requirement to improve the training of teachers to meet the requirements of 'modern science'. In particular much more attention should be paid to the improvement of the teacher's practical command of Russian, their commitment to and interest in the subject, their level of pedagogical 'mastery'.

Finally, there was a list of recommendations concerning the need for greater efficiency on the part of various ministries and coordinating bodies, local municipal and district authorities (RYANSh 5, 1979, pp. 30–33).

When one takes the 1979 Programme and juxtaposes it with the recommendations of the 1979 Tashkent Conference it is difficult to escape the vision of a great juggernaut lumbering into motion and setting off down the wrong road. If you extend the use of Russian at both ends of the educational spectrum, you need many more teachers. If you insist that Russian be spoken by non-Russians in an environment where Russian is not the language medium, to the extent that it is spoken there will be a process of creolisation set in motion. If you insist that students who speak bad Russian, if they speak it at all, then pursue their higher education in that language and *write their dissertations* in that language, you are effectively depriving these students of higher education. And, of course, if the approach is 'communicative', not only do you need more teachers, but these teachers have to be trained to a very high standard, not only of pedagogic skill, but actual proficiency in Russian. In the context of the Central Asian Republics the policy is almost guaranteed to fail in those environments where there are few Russians, Russian is hardly spoken and the teacher has had to learn Russian as a second language. Notice, again, that it is most likely to fail at the level where the Government most wants success, namely in the professional, military and educational spheres.

By the end of the 1970s, however, the 'communicative approach' (*kommunikativnyi podkhod*) is well established (Shamsutdinov 1979, p. 37, Kotok 1982, RYANSh 6, 1984, p. 85). Barannikov in 1979 was of the opinion that the most 'promising' (*perspektivnyi*) solution was likely to be the multilingual classroom with Russian as the language of instruction.

DEVELOPMENTS IN THE REPUBLICS

In 1979 Shamsutdinov reported that, whereas things were improving in certain Union republics as far as Russian language acquisition was concerned (Shamsutdinov 1979, p. 37), the same could not be said for national village schools in a number of other republics, including those of Central Asia. The writer draws attention to a wide range of predictable problems. Learners had very limited vocabularies, could not

151

form complex sentences, had poor pronunciation, made many grammatical mistakes. Interestingly, the cause is diagnosed as being due to a shortage of gaps in teacher-training (p. 37). It is confirmed in this article that the course has been set towards a uniform Russian language programme for the national school and a uniform approach to the teaching of it (p. 38).

In the same year Prokofiev was drawing attention to a major difficulty inherent in the centralised approach to Russian language teaching in the national school, namely, the different rates at which learners progressed and the different levels of proficiency attained. Nationals from different republics would be expected to use Russian as the langugae of interethnic communication and it was important therefore that they be taught the same material. In the same article he announced plans for the retraining of all Russian teachers between 1979 and 1985, drawing attention, however, to the poor fulfilment rates of a previous attempt to raise teachers' qualifications. Whereas between 1976 and 1978 the completion rate for Georgia had been 50%, in the case of Kirghizia it was as low as 30% (Prokofiev 1979, p. 8).

The sixtieth anniversary of the formation of the Soviet Union provided an opportunity for up-to-date reports from the individual republics (RYANSh 6, 1982, pp. 32–37, 68–73, 74–76, 83–88). Clearly the authors wish to highlight the achievements of their republics. Thus we are told that 96% of teachers in Uzbekistan have higher education and that it was in Uzbekistan that schools with intensive instruction in Russian were first introduced, a practice which had now spread to many other republics. Andrianova's paper gives quite a lot of detail about how these classes are conducted (Andrionova 1982, pp. 33–7). Kirghizia, on the other hand, has much more experience with preparatory classes in Russian for six-year-olds preparing to go to school. These began in 1966 with different languages of instruction, Russian becoming the most common (Tashmatova 1982, pp. 69–73). Karimova, writing about Tadzhikistan, lays stress on that republic's new improved programmes based on 'All-Union model programmes', and the greatly increased use of Russian in extra-mural activities. She draws attention, however, to the need for more attention to be paid to ways of working with six-year-olds and to improving the methodology of teaching in intensive Russian classes (Karimova 1982, pp.

75–6). Writing about Turkmenistan, Azimov and Ershova describe the role played by the University of Turkmenistan in the support and development of Russian teaching in the republic. An account is given of work in progress on 'model programmes' and on the production of textbooks and materials. One immediate problem relates to the need to train teachers with a philological background (i.e., who learned Russian by the grammar/translation method) to perfect their practical skills. There was also a grave shortage of teachers to teach Russian to six-year-olds in kindergartens (Azimov and Ershova 1982, pp. 84–8).

As a counterpoint to the data just presented we may end our review of the period 1979–83 by drawing attention to yet another conference, held this time in Samarkand (20–21 May 1983) under the title 'Russian is the language of our students and future warriors' (RYANSh 5, 1983, p. 89–90). Among the participants were First Secretary Rashidov, the Uzbekistan Minister of Enlightenment Shermukhamedov and generals of the Turkestan Military District. The aim of the conference was to discuss ways of improving Russian language instruction given to young men about to be called up. What is interesting, however, is that the conference had five sections, each one addressing problems in a particular sector of the educational system, starting with the pre-school sector (!) This is perhaps not so surprising, however, when we remember the stage at which the Soviet Army is introduced as a theme in the Russian language classroom.

The 1984 School Reform

In April 1984 The Central Committee of the CPSU and the Supreme Soviet of the USSR approved new measures for the reform of the comprehensive (*obschcheobrazovatel'naya*) and vocational (*professional'naya*) school. It was heralded as the most important reform of the school system since the 1920s (RYANSh, 4, 1984, p. 26). The measures proposed were first published in January under the title of 'Guidelines for the Reform of the General Education School and the Vocational School' (Tomiak 1986, p. 13). The full text of the reforms is published in RYANSh 4, 1984, pp. 3–25. Here we shall only reproduce the main points of the reform and consider the implications for Russian language teaching policy. The main points are these:

— The ten-year school is to become the eleven-year school, with children starting school at six years of age;
— There is to be a unified programme for six-year-olds in schools and kindergartens;
— The tenth and eleventh classes will be devoted to providing vocational preparation and some 'on the job' experience;
— Fluency in Russian is to become the norm for all school-leavers;
— There will be much more emphasis on ideology to combat a range of negative attitudes such as lack of commitment, banality, low intellectual endeavour.

These measures are to be carried out between 1984 and 1990.

The implications for Russian language teaching are clear. On the one hand Russian is to be taught from the first year in every school. On the other, every school leaver is supposed to have a fluent command of Russian. Moreover, a fluent command in relation to technical and scientific occupations. Given the growth rates in the indigenous populations of the Central Asian republics there will be a continuing need for more teachers. Given the goals of instruction these teachers will need to be better trained. This is foreseen in the reform measures: henceforth teacher-training programmes for Russian language teachers will last a full five years (RYANSh 4, 1984, p. 14). There will also be a need for a large and increasing programme of teacher retraining.

That teachers will increasingly be trained to use the 'communicative approach' is clear. New programmes for introduction in 'faculties for the improvement of teachers' qualifications' (*fakul'tety povysheniya kvalifikatsii (PVK)*) are completely oriented towards this approach (see, for example, RYANSh 6, 1984, pp. 85–90).

What must be remembered is that the 'communicative approach' to language teaching requires teachers who are highly competent in the target language. It is not a matter merely of being able to pronounce the language correctly and to repeat a few phrases for use in the classroom. They must be able to *use* the language fluently and, hopefully, accurately to 'get things done' in Russian. Not only must teachers be well trained, teaching materials need to be much more sophisticated if the aim is to stimulate genuine communicative activity. This is particularly true at the level of higher education. The 1984 reforms will stretch educational resources to the limit, and possibly beyond. It is highly doubtful that the intended goals will be achieved in many schools and institutes in Central Asia.

Conclusion

We have seen that, over the last thirty years or so, there has been a steady expansion of the teaching of Russian throughout the school system. This expansion has put a continuing strain on available manpower and material resources. There has been and continues to be a shortage of suitably qualified teachers, which in certain areas borders on the chronic. We have seen also that this expansion has increasingly been coordinated and centralised. This centralisation has led to a high degree of standardisation of course content, materials production and teacher training. A particular variety of Russian is being defined as the 'language of interethnic communication' which is different from the Russian language as spoken by Russians. This variety is being defined in terms of vocabulary, pronunciation norms, syntactic patterns. It is to be taught to every non-Russian learner, in the same way.

What are the chances of success? A communicative approach works best in the language medium. People learn to speak best by speaking. In schools and other environments in Central Asia where Russian is widely used and contact with mother-tongue Russian speakers is high, one may expect quite a large degree of success in operational terms. This does not mean, however, that non-native speakers will speak fluent *correct* Russian. They will speak fluent, *incorrect* Russian. In other words, the more non-Russian speakers who learn Russian as a second language use it for communicative purposes, the more they subject Russian to a process of creolisation. Moreover, fluent inaccurate Russian is an impediment to the acquisition of the grammatical system which is indispensable for access to the written language, since learners are inclined to think that they 'know it all already'.

In environments where Russian is not used as a genuine language medium, a communicative approach is unlikely to achieve much. The teaching of French in the primary school in Great Britain was a failure largely for that reason.

If one can raise doubts about the likely success rates of Russian language teaching in the Central Asian republics in terms of learner proficiency, there can be little doubt that the teaching of Russian has been built solidly into the school system and is gradually encroaching on life outside the school as well. The 1979 census showed a clear increase in the number of Central Asians who claimed to have mastered Russian. 'Mastery' is no doubt not the correct word to describe the level of proficiency attained by many. One can predict, however, that the numbers will continue to increase. On the other hand, the fact that Russian has penetrated the school system at the kindergarten stage, coupled with the increasing tendency for Russian to be used as the language of instruction, must raise a question about the intellectual development of many Central Asian children.

Our final word should concern the use of Russian in the spheres of higher education, the military and the professions. It is the written language which is used for the communication of highly complex issues. The processing of complex texts requires a highly sophisticated grasp of grammatical relations between various parts of speech in a sentence and the relation of these to equally complex semantic and pragmatic issues. The ability to read complex texts in Russian does not presuppose the ability to speak Russian. It does presuppose a study of the grammatical system. The difference between 'literacy' and 'illiteracy' is a long list of 'near-misses'. Study of the grammatical system of a language requires a lot of effort and application and an ability to know when not to apply a rule. A 'play-school' approach is unlikely to succeed. The acquisition of literacy is a difficult intellectual task for a mother-tongue speaker of a language. The acquisition of literacy in a second language is even more difficult. As is well known, many do not succeed.

References

RYANSh: *Russkii yazyk v natsional'noi shkole*

NII PRYANSh (APN SSSR): (*Nauchno-issledovatel'skii institut pri Akademii pedagogicheskikh nauk SSSR*) (Research Institute for the Teaching of Russian in the National School of the Academy of Pedagogical Sciences of the USSR).

Andrionovna V I (1978) 'Na glavnom napravlenii', *RYANSh* 1, pp. 19–21.

Andrionovna V I (1982), 'Uglublennoe izuchenie russkogo yazyka i literatury', *RYANSh* 6, pp. 33–7.

Azimov P A & Ershova E N (1982), 'Turkmenskomy gosudarstvennomu universitetu — 50 let', *RYANSh* 6, pp. 84–8.

Azizyan A (1961) 'Stroitels'tvo kommunizma i razvitie natsional'nykh otnoshenii', *Kommunist* 16.

Azrael J R (ed) 1978, *Soviet Nationality Policies and Practices*, Praeger.

Barannikov I V (1977), 'Kommunisticheskoe vospitanie v protsesse prepodavaniya russkogo yazyka i literatury', *RYANSh* 1, pp. 9–13.

Barannikov I V (1979), 'Podgotovka k obucheniyu russkomu yazyku v natsional'noi shkole', *Sovetskaya pedagogika* 11, pp. 60–63.

Berdyyev R D (1975), 'Vedushcii faktor kul'turnogo sotrudnichestva narodov', *RYANSh* 5, pp. 18–20.

Bilinsky Y (1962), The Soviet Education Laws of 1958–9 and Soviet Nationality Policy, *Soviet Studies* (Oct), pp. 138–57.

Bilinsky Y (1981), 'Expanding the Use of Russian or Russification?' *Russian Review* 3, pp. 317–32.

Carrère d'Encausse H (1978), Determinants and Parameters of Soviet National Policy, in Azrael J R, *Soviet Nationality Policies and Practices*, Praeger 1978, pp. 39–59.

Carrère d'Encausse H (1980) *Decline of an Empire*, Newsweek Books, New York, pp. 165–88.

Chomsky N (1959), Review of *Verbal Behaviour* by B. F. Skinner, *Language* 1, pp. 26–58.

Chomsky N (1964) *Syntactic Structures*, Mouton, The Hague

Chomsky N (1965) *Aspects of a Theory of Syntax*, M. I. T., Ma.

Dadaboev R D (1975) 'Zadacha gosudarstvennoi vazhnosti', *RYANSh* 5, pp. 15–18.

Desheriev Yu D (1982) 'Yazykovye problemy mnogonatsional'nogo sovetskogo obshchestva', *Voprosy yazykoznaniya* 6, pp. 14–27.

Desheriev Yu D and Protchenko (1976), 'Perspektivy razvitiya dvuyazychiya v natsional'nykh shkolakh SSSR', *Sovetskaya pedagogika* 8, pp. 18–23.

Filin F P (1979), 'Reshayushchee uslovie garmonnogo dvuyazychiya', RYANSh 4, pp. 33–5.

Garunov E G (1975), 'Nekotorye problemy shkol s mnogonatsional'ym sostavom uchashchikhsya i russkim yazykom obucheniya', *Sovetskaya pedagogika* 11, pp. 31–6.

Glyn Lewis E (1971), 'Migration and Language in the USSR', *International Migration Review* 5, pp. 147–77.

Glyn Lewis E (1976), 'The Present Language Situation in the Soviet Union', Paper presented at the McMaster Conference on The Languages and Literatures of the Non-Russian Peoples of the Soviet Union, McMaster University, Hamilton, Ontario, October 22 and 23, pp. 155–87.

Glyn Lewis E (1986), 'Bilingualism as Language Planning in the Soviet Union', in Tomiak J J, *Western Perspectives of Soviet education in the 1980s*, Macmillan, London, pp. 75–95.

Hymes D (1972), *Towards Communicative Competence*, University of Philadelphia Press, Philadelphia.

Ivanov V V & Mikhailovskaya N G (1982), 'Russkii yazyk kak sredstvo mezhnatsional'nogo obshcheniya: aktual'nye aspekty i problemy', *Voprosy yazykoznaiya* 6, pp. 3–13.

Karimova O B (1982), 'Po usovershenstvovannym programmam', *RYANSh* 4, pp. 75–6.

Kirkwood J M (1973), 'Towards an Integrated Programme for Advanced Students of Russian', *Audio Visual Language Journal* 3, pp. 370–85.

Kirkwood J M (1973b), 'The Influence of Linguistics on Language Teaching with Reference to Russian', *Journal of Russian Studies* 25, pp. 39–54.

Kirkwood J M (with Candlin C N & Moore H E) (1975), 'Developing Study Skills in English', *English for Academic Study*, British Council ELT Information Centre.

Kirkwood J M (with Candlin C N & Moore H E) (1978) 'Study Skills in English: Theoretical Issues and Practical Problems', in Mackay R & Mountford A, *English for Specific Purposes*, Longman, London, pp. 190–219.

Kirkwood J M (1976) Reading and Writing in Russian: the Neglected Skills?, Journal of Russian Studies 32, pp. 13–23.

Kirkwood J M (1980), 'Ovladenie umeniyami v oblasti chteniya i pis'ma primenitel'no k uskorrenomu kursu russkogo yazyka v universitete, *Russkii yazyk za rubezhom* 1, pp. 56–64.

Kommunist 16, 1961; 18, 1962; 9, 1963.

Kotok E V (1982) 'Kommunikativnaya napravlennost' uroka', *RYANSh*, pp. 28–31.

Mitter W (1986), 'Bilingual and Intercultural Education in Soviet Schools', in Tomiak J J, *Western Perspectives on Soviet Education in the 1980s*, Macmillan, London, pp. 97–121.

Pavlov G (1962), 'Rastsvet i sblizhenie sotsialisticheskikh natsii', *Kommunist* 18.

Pennar J (1981), Current Soviet Nationality Policy, *Journal of Baltic Studies* 1, pp. 5–15.

Prokof'ev M A (1979), 'Put' dal'neishego uluchsheniya izucheniya i prepodavaniya russkogo yazyka v soyuznykh respublikakh', *Narodnoe obrazovanie* 9, pp. 5–9.

Prokof'ev M A (1982), 'Ob izuchenii v obshcheobrazovatel'nykh shkolakh knigi General'nogo sekretarya TsK KPSS, Predsedatelya Prezidiuma Verkhovnogo Soveta SSSR tovarishcha L I Brezhneva "Vospominaniya",' *RYANSh* 2, pp. 86–7.

Rapawy S (1985), 'Nationality Composition of the Soviet Population', *Nationalities Papers* 13, pp. 70–83.

Reshetov V (1962) 'Zadachi prepodavaniya russkogo yazyka v natsional'noi shkole v svete reshenii XXII s"ezda KPSS', *RYANSh* 4, pp. 3–16.

Rogachev P & Sverdlin M, 'Sovetskii narod — novaya istoricheskaya obshchnost' lyudei', *Kommunist* 9. p. 11–20.

Saubanova F L (1978), 'Chtoby svobodno vladet' russkoi rech'yu', *RYANSh* 4, pp. 34–35.

Shamsutdinov S S (1975), *RYANSh* 5, pp. 5–9.

Shamsutdinov S S (1979), 'Russkii yazyk v natsional'noi shkole', *Sovetskaya pedagogika* 4, pp. 35–8.

Shanskii N M (1973), 'Sostoyanie i zadachi issledovaniya problem prepodavaniya, russkogo yazyka i literatury v shkolakh soyuznykh respublik, *RYANSh* 1, pp. 5–15.

Shanskii N M (1982), 'Metodika prepodavaniya russkogo yazyka: dostizheniya i problemy', RYANSh 6, pp. 4–8.

Sheiman L (1978), 'Nauka — praktike', *RYANSh* 2, pp. 21–3.

Shorish M M (1976), 'The Pedagogical, Linguistic, and Logistical Problems of Teaching Russian to the Local Soviet Central Asians', *Slavic Review* 3, pp. 443–62.

Shtromas A (1978), 'The Legal Position of Soviet Nationalities and Their Territorial Units According to the 1977 Constitution of the USSR', *The Russian Review* 3, pp. 265–72.

Silver B D (1974), 'The Impact of Urbanisation and Geographical Dispersion on the Linguistic Russification of Soviet Nationalities', *Demography* 11, pp. 89–103.

Silver B D (1976b), 'The Status of National Minority Languages in Soviet Education: An Assessment of Recent Changes', *Soviet Studies* 26, 1974, pp. 28–40.

Silver B D (1976), 'Bilingualism and Maintenance of the Mother Tongue in Soviet Central Asia', *Slavic Review* 3, pp. 406–24.

Sol'chanyk R (1983), 'Russkii yazyk i sovetskaya politika', *Forum* 5, pp. 76–98.

Tashmatova K A (1978), 'Malvshi govoryat po-russki', *RYANSh* 2, pp. 15–17.

Tashmatova K A (1982), 'V podgotovitel'nykh klassakh', *RYANSh* 6, pp. 69–73.

Tomiak J J (1986), 'Introduction: the Dilemmas of Soviet Education in the 1980s', in Tomiak J J, *Western Perspectives on Soviet Education in the 1980s*, Macmillan, London, pp. 1–17.

Zemtsov I (1985), 'Andropov and the Non-Russian Nationalities: Attitudes and Policies', *Nationalities Papers* 1, pp. 5–23.

Zinchenko I P (1976), 'Natsiona'nyi sostav i yazyki naseleniya SSSR', in Maksimov G M, *Vsesoyuznaya perepis' naseleniya 1970 goda*, Statistika, Moskva, pp. 193–210.

8

RITUALISM OF FAMILY LIFE IN SOVIET CENTRAL ASIA: THE *SUNNAT* (CIRCUMCISION)

Ewa A. Chylinski

Introduction

Although the Soviet Union has created a uniform social and political system for all its citizens, the USSR's multinational and multicultural character is clearly represented at subnational level. The All-Union level, being a supra-national ideological ideal, is only to some degree visible at the national level. Local modes either adapt themselves to the symbols of Soviet identity or parallel them. Thus, generalised Soviet symbolism and ritual is particularly concerned with the political-ideological sphere, work morality and social morality. These are instruments by which Soviet society seeks to integrate all its citizens. In contrast, rituals of life cycle, family and community are elements of subnational expression.

Ethnicity and ethnic culture function as autonomous forces moulding the supranational elements to local conditions. Culture and folk culture are the spheres where supranational and subnational spheres interact and clash, such that new feasts and rituals are assimilated according to the traditional scheme. Some rituals like *Pakhta bairam* (cotton harvest festival) or *Navruz* (spring festival) have entered the common official national sphere in altered form.

Differences in observing rituals and adhering to local customs reflect Soviet reality, which one might call 'diversity in unity'. This is because the Soviet system does not integrate the specific character of ethnic, linguistic or religious affiliation at the supranational level. For example, common Soviet rites related to the October Revolution or first of May holidays begin the same way all over the Soviet Union. Following the official part of the celebration (army parade, demonstrations, etc.) the local/national elements come to predominate, particularly in the form of national sports and games.

For the Central Asian republics and their populations, national consciousness is based on ethnicity, common cultural traits and the religion of Islam. Since the late 1930s, when separate republics were created, national development ocurred along consciously republican lines. Nowadays, ethnicity plays a major role in cultural identity in Central Asia, especially in relation to the past. The historical organisation of Central Asian societies — as nomads and sedentary peoples — is still visible in many aspects of social relations. Applying this to today's ethnic divisions one can contrast the Tajiks with the rest of Central Asian indigenous population. This division into pastoralists and agriculturalists continues to operate at the cultural level. It has now acquired symbolic value in that ancestry plays an important role, for example in establishing family relations (marriage among Kazakhs and Kirghiz) attesting to the conservatism and traditionalism of family life.

In general, family ritualism has a special importance in Central Asian societies. For all Muslims and those raised according to Islamic cultural tradition, the family is a central social unit. Practically no one can exist outside family. It creates a framework for men and women to function socially and sexually, with the primary goal of reproduction. Continuity of family line is very important, so that all children, especially male, are welcome. Children are a gift from Allah, and many children bear witness to a family's prosperity. Hence, rituals of infancy and youth are aimed at ensuring for the child a proper position within the community, while at the same time involving the child in community affairs. In this way children can count on the community's help and protection. At the same time they learn to subordinate themselves to communal decisions and to pay due respect as a reward for the community's attention. Therefore all family celebrations are not the concern of one family alone but involve whole community. Perhaps this is why the introduction of Soviet rituals to replace traditional ones has proceeded so slowly. The changes in economic and cultural values during the Soviet period have not had great influence on family rituals. In many instances modernisation has even strengthened some rituals so that tradition becomes more visible. Many newly created Soviet rituals entered the private sphere because of their legal force and because additional opportunities for celebration have been created. Typically, we find a co-existence of Soviet and traditional ceremonies such as birth registration/namegiving, marriage and burial. However, there are still some which have no parallel in common Soviet ritualism. One of them is *Sunnat (khatna, ugil)* — circumcision. This ritual is practised by almost 100% of Central Asia's male population, whether or not they practise other Islamic rituals. Observing *Sunnat* has today a strong social connotation, while the religious perception of the rite is less obvious for some segments of the population. As a symbol of common cultural heritage, however, Islam is manifested both as a religious element and as a social tradition, particularly with respect to community relations.

The *Sunnat* is celebrated differently in different regions of Central Asia, and Soviet literature has registered several local variants (see references). Generally it has concentrated on ethnographic descriptions, seeking the most traditional variations still present in villages. The urban *Sunnat* of different social groups has not yet attracted the attention of Soviet ethnographers nor that of Western scholars, although it reflects some very interesting traits in the general perception of the rite.

This chapter is based on material collected during the author's field research in Uzbekistan, including personal observations in the suburbs of Tashkent in 1985.

SUNNAT AND THE HOLY QUR'AN

In the system of Islamic rituals, circumcision is not mentioned in the Holy Qur'an. Historically, it developed in the pre-islamic period in the Semitic area, and through close contact with Arab conquerors the subordinate people took it over and adapted it to their own cultural conditions. Variations in the ceremony, the age of boys undergoing circumcision in different Muslim groups, point to the late canonisation of *Sunnat* within Islamic ritualism. Islamic law, Shari'a, sanctions *Sunnat* often according to local custom — *adat*; for example, boys in the Arabic area are circumcised from seven days after birth to three years of age; Kurds perform it between three and seven years; Afghans by seven years; Persians even up to fifteen years. The Qur'an says nothing about the duty of circumcising boys or girls (as in some parts of Africa), but for the overwhelming majority of Muslims, the *Sunnat* is regarded as compulsory. With the spread of Islam, circumcision became a symbol of membership in the Muslim community. As such, it is also recognised even by superficially islamicised groups, such as Kazakhs.

According to the Shari'a, the duty to perform *Sunnat* rests upon the boy's parents, in particular the father (or grandfather) and upon close relatives and the community, until he reaches adulthood, when he is able to make independent decisions. In Central Asia, the latter case is in fact only possible for boys being brought up outside their original community, for example, orphans living in orphanages or children placed in children's homes. Those institutions are managed by the state, and implement official policy in religious matters. If the boy is growing up in the community, the person organising the *Sunnat* for him (often together with his own sons) is treated with great respect both by the boy and the community.

The importance of *Sunnat* for Muslims is of a highly ritual character. The rite is regarded as an act of purification, 'to purify the boy's hands'. In some Muslim communities (Indonesia, Tajikistan) uncircumcised boys are considered dangerous to one's health; thus, for example, one should not drink water given by a boy who has not undergone circumcision.

Central Asians consider that every family has a duty to perform *Sunnat* on their boys, but the perception of the rite has changed.

Sunnat in Central Asia

For Central Asia in general, the age of circumcision may vary from one to thirteen years. For Uzbeks the age is between seven and nine years, among some groups observing an uneven number of years. If the boy is circumcised later without any plausible reason, the family would be condemned by the community.

Tajiks usually perform circumcision before children start at school, i.e., up to the age of seven years. The interesting element here is the observance of the cycles of life based on

12-year intervals, combined with animal signs. According to this tradition, circumcision has to be made within the first cycle (Pisarchik 1949, pp. 173–91).

As the majority of Central Asians work in agriculture, the *Sunnat* and other celebrations are postponed till autumn or winter, when the work burden is reduced. Even in urban areas this principle is rather generally observed, as many families have relations residing in villages.

Preparations for the celebration start with a discussion of which family is going to organise a *toi* (feast) and when this will be, so that celebrations do not overlap. The village elder — *aksakal* — or the leader of *mahalla* (town district) is responsible for planning the celebrations. When the date is agreed upon, different functions are divided among close relatives, neighbours and, usually, members of the host's men's association — *dzhura*. (*Dzhura* membership is based either on the same age principle and close social relations, or men of different age from the same community.) One person is chosen as cook; preparation of pilaff and some other dishes are the domain of men. Another one has to take care of tea supplies, another takes charge of other supplies, or organises the reception of guests etc. In urban areas this part of the festivities is relatively simple. Foodstuffs are delivered directly from the store or bazaar to the home, and the rituals associated with receiving them, especially the rice for pilaff, are of symbolic character, if performed at all. Sometimes the driver who delivers supplies is given some money if he helps to unload, or perhaps just a small gift. With the extensive social networks of Central Asians, a family member always knows someone in a food store who can help procure good quality products. Often the 'connection' is a member of the host's *dzhura*. (One might wonder how much influence the *dzhura* has on the choice of the member's profession and his subsequent placement in different spheres of social and public activity.)

Women from the family and neighbourhood are involved in preparation of other dishes, sometimes baking bread. Most purchase bread from a good bakery, where it is baked in a traditional clay oven. Festivities take place at the end of the week, with the first guests arriving on Friday. Close family members are accommodated at the home of hosts (grand-parents, father's brother's family, etc.), while other relatives and community members lodge at the homes of neighbours and friends. In rural areas this problem is easy to solve, as every village has a guest house, and there are often guest rooms in the homes of better-off families. In these houses the guests are completely provided for by their hosts for three days.

On Saturday afternoon everything is ready. Women gather for the preliminary celebrations together with the younger children. The boy or boys for whom the celebration is being held will have been circumcised a few days beforehand, to allow for recovery in time for the approaching festivities. Only boys up to the ages of 10 to 11 years gather with their mothers. Those above this age belong to the men's group and must wait till the next day. Early on Sunday morning the tables are arranged for the men in the courtyard, and the cook starts preparing pilaff in an outdoor kitchen. Residents of the compound with common courtyard collect money (about 20 rb. per family) in order to purchase the necessary equipment for large celebrations. A roof must be built to protect against sun, rain or snow; kitchen facilities and storage must be provided, as well as tea bowls, teapots, soup bowls, plates, large plates for pilaff, spoons, kazans for pilaff, European tables and chairs, or local-style couches and low tables. For the majority of compounds, European tables and chairs were preferred as they were easier to store in the rather small basement.

In a ceremony that I personally observed, the men, according to tradition, were placed outside in the courtyard, while the women occupied several rooms in the host's and host's sister's apartment. The separation of the sexes was very rigid, and priority in serving warm dishes was given to the men. As a stranger, I was able to circulate among both male and female groups, being warmly received by the women, and with distance by the men, who did not converse with each other in my presence. Guests came and stayed for the time it took to eat a portion of all the available dishes. In the courtyard men were placed together according to age — and for the younger generation more than just tea was served in the teapots! The host himself circulated between the courtyard and the family's finest room, furnished with best Russian furniture, where I, the honoured guest, together with the host's close friend, was placed; the hostess took care of the other women guests.

In this blockhouse the typical family network was built up — all five siblings were living there with their families. Although the parents had died, it was not an unusual situation. Parents would rather see all their children living in close proximity to each other so that they can support and help each other. Though the youngest son and his family are expected to remain in the parental home, this can cause problems for maintaining tradition. This is because the modernisation of large cities is progressing rapidly, and young people are interested in acquiring their own apartments.

The family's sitting-room was arranged for special guests. As the host and his wife were educated, as were also his sisters and brother, the notion of European elegance was concentrated on furniture, green plants etc. After I had paid my respects to the families of the circumcised boys by giving them gifts (money was firmly refused, although all the other guests contributed cash), and had congratulated them on the occasion, the food was served, along with strong encouragement to imbibe alcoholic beverages — brandy and vodka. The final dish, the pilaff, is meant to be diluted only with hot tea, and only if absolutely necessary. On festive occasions pilaff is prepared with extra fat. It was a trying experiment because one may not stop eating until the host gives the sign by cleaning his hands. Even in very modern families this ritual is strictly observed, notwithstanding ritualised celebrations. Neither of the host couple were with us during the meal. The hostess came in with dishes and disappeared again, to join the women in the other rooms. The host came in just for a moment to down a symbolic glass of vodka. When asked why he was drinking, he answered by saying that he was respecting the European tradition which I was representing. The hostess did not touch alcohol, and neither did the other women. After a final bowl of tea we were ready to leave, the social duty of host and guest having been satisfactorily fulfilled.

In the late afternoon the party slowly dissolved. By evening close friends and members of the host's *dzhura* had begun to appear with their wives, and a new party with modern music and dance had begun.

Between Faith and Social Duty

Until 1917, and for some time after, the life-cycle rituals — birth, marriage and burial — were connected with religious ideology. Religion was an inseparable part of the complex of rites. Today, their religious significance has weakened substantially, but remains very powerful as social tradition. Changes which Central Asian societies have undergone because of social mobilisation and modernisation have affected family ritual life. Some rites became more simplified; others have disappeared; still others have retained only symbolic value.

Today, the *Sunnat* is one such rite. Its religious, Muslim connotation, as an expression of true faith, is no longer obvious for all social groups. Even non-religious parents regard *Sunnat* as their duty. Few of the young, urban, educated population look upon *Sunnat* as a strictly religious act to be performed as a demonstration of their Muslim affiliation. For the vast majority it is a social ethnic tradition, a symbol of respect paid to the family and community. The party given by the parents also has a symbolic value, especially as it is a community affair. All preparations for the festivities are divided among members of village or town district (*mahalla*). The economic burden of housing and feeding the many guests invited to the ceremony is also a communal task, although all expenses are covered by the host. One of the official criticisms is that too much money is spent on *Sunnat-toi* (and other *tois* as well). However, these expenses are usually covered by contributions made by participants in cash or other gifts, and symbolically also in the form of *dostarkhan* (as a rule it is bread and fruits), offered by the guests and returned by the host at the end of *toi*. Besides, arrangements of this kind are frequent in any community, so that givers and recipients are on equal terms. In case of insufficient accumulation of products and other items (gifts for the guests), material help is required from the next of kin, or even the *dzhura*. This is decided by the *toi*-comission (*kengash/tui-komisiasi*) (Snesarev 1971, p. 258).

Entertainment is sometimes provided at large *tois*. The most popular is the fight of *palvans* — the wrestlers. This kind of entertainment is often seen in *kolkhozes*, while city dwellers in new quarters either have no common show or organise modern dance and music when the more official, traditional party is over.

The social connotation of *Sunnat* is so strong that persons who do not perform it, i.e., do not give a party, are condemned and excluded from the local community's social network. Such a situation is unthinkable not only in relation to neighbours, friends, *dzhura* and kin, but also for the boy or boys who were not circumcised. They would become outsiders for the rest of their lives, and could even have difficulties finding a wife, as families are very suspicious about giving their daughters to persons who are not circumcised (Khamidzhanova 1981, p. 105). It would mean that the man's father has not respected his own family and the tradition, implying that he may not respect his wife nor her family. Even those attempts to individualise *toi*, to restrict community involvement, were condemned in the form of boycott — *bir-uily* (Snesarev 1960, p. 135). Such 'innovators' risk refusal of help and exclusion from participation in other *tois* and in other community affairs. As recent research in Uzbekistan has shown, even the youngest group of Uzbeks (aged 18 to 19 years) are overwhelmingly in favour of *Sunnat (Socyalno-kulturnyj* . . . 1986, p. 274) This is certainly not only because of its ethnoreligious meaning, but also because of the social consequences of not performing it.

The force of this social communal tradition can be illustrated by an example of a German director of a *kolkhoz* who married his daughter to an Estonian engineer and who gave a party according to local tradition. Although he was neither a Central Asian native nor a Muslim, he paid respect to the community he was working with. He told me that he could not expect people to respect him or his family, or successfully perform his work, if he did not behave according to local custom.

In this system, the act of circumcision itself seems to be of secondary importance. Nonetheless it is often performed after the *toi* in the presence of close family (Snesarev 1971, p. 261; Khamidzhanova 1981, p. 101), or, as I observed, before the *toi*; the latter seems to be the case in urban areas.

Sunnat in the System of Life-Cycle Rituals: Prospects for the Future

Since the victory of the October revolution, Soviet authorities have worked intensively on imparting new life-cycle and family rituals free of any religious connotations, and in accordance with the new ideology. The separation of church and state in 1918 gave civil ceremonies legal authority, while religious acts remained of a private character. Revolutionary ritualism was in many instances very radical in relation to age-old customs and their perception of decency. This was especially true of the Christian religion, while Islam was able to retain its legal power until 1928, paralleled by civil revolutionary ritual. In the early 1930s, however, Islamic law — *Shari'a* was abolished — and civil rites formally took over. Soviet authorities tried to work out a set of new customs and rites to accompany ceremonies like marriage, name-giving or burial, making them identical for all Soviet cultures. However, it proved to be a difficult task, as people were reluctant to accept them. Ethnographers were involved in this programme, and they suggested reintroducing some elements of previous rites, concentrating on folk tradition and eliminating religious elements.

Today's life-cycle rituals are a mixture of Soviet and traditional elements, often paralleled by religious ceremonies; in most cases these conform to people's perceptions of social duty in relation to family and community. In spite of this complementarity and parallelism, *Sunnat* has a special position. Being a Muslim is a religious and a cultural phenomenon; it has no Soviet counterpart. At the same time, its strong social connotation makes it very difficult to eradicate, despite the authorities' propaganda against such customs. As a physical expression of *Shahada*, it emphasises a person's Muslim affiliation as different from Christian or that of any other group. In addition, it confirms organic ties with the local community.

Hence, attempts to depart from, or even abolish *Sunnat* have little chance of success. It would require fundamental changes not only in people's relation to religious ceremony, which is deeply rooted in both Orthodox and popular Islam. Moreover, such efforts would require a psychological, social and cultural reorganisation of Central Asian societies. That seems to be rather a question of time, if Central Asia is going to proceed along the present direction of development, than of conscious ideological action.

References

Khamidzhanova M A (1981), 'Tui khatna: obrezanie u tadzhikov Verkhnego Zeravshana', in: Pisarchik A. K (ed.) *Istoria i etnografia narodov Srednei Azii. Sbornik statei*, Dushanbe, pp. 90–105.

Kerimov G M (1978), *Shariat i ego socyalnaya sushchnost*, Moscow, pp. 87–92.

Pisarchik A K (1949), 'Tablicy dvenadtsatiletnego zhivotnogo cikla s privedeniem sootvetstvuyushchikh im godov sovremennogo letoischislenya', in *Materialy Yuzhno-Turkmenskoi kompleksnoi ekspedicii*, Ashkhabad, pp. 173–81.

Snesarev G P (1960) 'Materialy o pervobytnoobshchinnykh perezhitkakh v obychaiakh i obriadakh uzbekov Khorezma', MKHE, vol. 4, p. 135.

Snesarev G P (1971), 'K voprosu o proiskhozhdenii prazdnestva Sunnat-toi v ego sredneaziatskom variante', in *Zaniatia i byt narodov Srednei Azii. Sredneaziatskij etnograficheskij sbornik III*, Leningrad, pp. 256–72.

9

PROFESSIONAL BELIEFS AND RITUALS AMONG CRAFTSMEN IN CENTRAL ASIA: GENETIC AND FUNCTIONAL INTERPRETATION

Z. Jasiewicz

The subject of this chapter is the beliefs and rituals which are accepted and practised among the craftsmen in the part of Central Asia where I carried out my research. I shall present some theories about the genesis of these beliefs and rituals and also about their social functions. I shall concentrate mainly on metal crafts, particularly on smithery — smiths were, at one point, my interest also in Poland — though I shall make use of materials about other crafts as well. The area which interests me is Uzbekistan, Tadzhikistan and northern Afghanistan, which even in the nineteenth century still formed a more or less uniform historical-cultural region, inhabited mainly by various groups of Tadzhiks and Uzbeks. The period of interest begins at the close of the nineteenth century and continues into the twentieth, and my researches date from this period. Material has been collected and published by Soviet ethnographers as well as from my own observations and from field studies in Uzbekistan, Tadzhikistan and Afghanistan. I visited the Soviet territories in Central Asia twice, once in 1963 and then again in 1974, for several months on each occasion; the first visit was connected with the Uzbek SSR Academy of Sciences and the second with the University of Tashkent. I also spent four months in Afghanistan in 1976 with the Ethnological Expedition of the Institute of Ethnology, Poznań University. The aim of this chapter is to present the different mechanisms and directions of change in the beliefs and rituals of craftsmen in two regions which differ from each other politically, economically and ideologically: in the Central Asian republics of the Soviet Union and in Afghanistan. I would also like to present differences in the beliefs and practices which exist within the separate categories of crafts which can be distinguished according to their organisation and their place within the socio-cultural system.

The problems of the area of Central Asia which I covered in my research are highly absorbing for various reasons. The first is the long existence in these territories of ancient city centres like Tashkent, Samarkand, Bukhara, Khiva, Balkh, Mazare-Sharif. The development of crafts in these and many towns in this region was connected not only with supplying the demands of the agrarian communities but also with production for the nomad shepherds. The second reason is the present-day differentiation of this territory, which used to be uniform, but which found itself within the borders of various countries from the second half of the nineteenth and the twentieth century and, hence, was subjected to the influence of several different cultural systems. The third reason is the appearance in these territories of a variety of categories of craftsmen which can be distinguished according to the organisation and the place of craftsmen in socio-economic life, as follows:

1. Craftsmen organised into guilds which appeared in the past in every larger town in this region, embracing a part of the craftsmen who inhabit the villages on the outskirts of these towns. Craft guilds still exist in Afghanistan providing the craftsmen, on the one hand, with a self-government, and on the other, with a body for controlling the country's administration of crafts. However, in Uzbekistan and Tadzhikistan, guilds disappeared in the period following the October revolution and craftsmen were regrouped to form the cooperatives. In the late fifties, the craft cooperatives were reorganised into the State industry system (Jasiewicz 1977, p. 117).

2. Craftsmen existing in groups as 'non-food-producing nomads' as A. Rao calls them, and whose character is well described by the concept of marginality and symbiosis (Rao 1982, pp. 115–33). This type of group

embraces smiths, sieve-makers, craftsmen working with wood, and barbers. Some of these groups, having found favourable conditions, would sometimes settle near large towns. One of these groups is the Haydarihā — an endogamic group of smiths with a low social status inhabiting the area around Qaysār in the northern province of Fāryab in Afghanistan, where I carried out some preliminary research in 1976. The settlement of this group was connected with its subordination to the Qipchaqs according to principles reminiscent of the domestic slavery practised some years ago and transformed into patron-client type relations.

3. Craftsmen who are scattered and who work in small towns and villages as well as among the nomad-shepherds. Their social status took, and still takes, a variety of forms: domestic slavery; work as craftsmen serving the local community and using tools and a workshop belonging to the community and being paid in farm produce (both these forms existed in the past); craftsmen working for money; craftsmen working in a *kolkhoz* or a *sovkhoz*.

4. Craftswomen who work in towns as well as in villages. In situations where a larger number of craftswomen worked in towns or in villages, a certain form of organisation, ceremonies and beliefs arose in connection with their profession. Of particular interest in these territories was the craft of the women — potters of the high mountain region of Tadzhikistan who practised pottery without the use of a potter's wheel or a kiln for firing the pots.

The professional beliefs and rituals of Central Asia developed from a group of religious-cum-magical practices and was most widely followed within the guilds. The isolation of guilds created a demand for an ideology which, on the one hand, could integrate the craftsmen and provide them with a sense of the value of their own work and, on the other, present the craftsmen in a favourable light to the other social groups. These functions were performed by the cult of patron saints of crafts, noted by Russian ethnographers as thriving within the guild organisation on the territory of Uzbekistan and Tadzhikistan before the changes brought about by the Russian

revolution. Some recent manifestations of this cult I have recorded during my field research in northern Afghanistan in
1976.

This cult depend on the selection, by individual guilds or
by groups of craftsmen, of one saint worshipped throughout
the Muslim world or within one region, and declaring him to
be the founder and patron of a craft (pir). The patrons of
crafts were not only figures exclusively connected with Islam
(Khazrati Ali — the patron of textile craftsmen who gave the
final shine to materials, for example, silk, or Fatima — the
patron of women-potters) but biblical figures too (David-
Doud — the patron of smiths and all metal crafts, including
the embroiderers of Bukhara who worked with gold thread;
Noe-Nukh — the patron of wood crafts; Eve — the patron of
many of the women's crafts) as well as special representatives
of sufism and local saints. Patrons of crafts who do not orig-
inate from Muslim circles arouse special interest: the patron of
butchers from Khoresm — Dzhonmardi-Kassob who is linked
with Zoroastrianism, Khazrati Burkh — the patron of all the
khalfa-hired masters, as well as the patrons of the female
professions — various great-grandmothers (*momokho*). Apart
from this, the amelioration of every craft, however small, was
assigned also to Satan. An analysis of the names of the patron
saints of the crafts, of both the important and the less important ones, enables an attempt to be made at reconstructing
their succesion in time. It is accepted that the holy patrons
associated with Islam gradually ousted the patrons who origna-
ted in the religious systems which preceded Islam (Sukhareva
1960, pp. 197–8).

Patron saints have assigned to them not only the initiation
of the skills used in the crafts which were received by them
from God and which they communicated to the people, but
also their betterment. Linking innovation in a craft with the
name of a saint, provided religious sanction for the breaking
of a tradition and marked the reintroduction of the principle
by which productive practices were subordinated to religious
convictions (Sukhareva 1960, p. 203). This principle also motivated the creation of patrons for newly-formed crafts and
guilds (Sukhareva 1962, p. 180).

Legends about the patron saints of crafts were transmitted
orally and in written form. These legends were propagated

through booklets called *risola* which were handwritten or, at
the beginning of the twentieth century, lithographed. Apart
from legends about the patron saints of a craft, *risola* contain
prayers and verses from the Koran which should be read while
performing productive activities, as well as other principles of
behaviour for the craftsmen. *Risola* were most common in the
Persian language, though the development of a printing press
in Tashkent at the end of the nineteenth and the beginning of
the twentieth century led to the dissemination of *risola* in
Uzbek (Andrew 1928, p. 117). The *risola* of crafts in Central
Asia have long been the subject of research by Russian and
Soviet historians and ethnographers. At first, they were compared with the statutes of European guilds. However O. A.
Sukhareva is correct in treating *risola* rather as a prayer book
and an amulet (Sukhareva 1960, p. 201). This was the role
played by the lithographed *risola* from Tashkent which I came
across in northern Afghanistan, which frequently were carefully wrapped in a shawl and kept in the workshop, or were
worn by the craftsman.

The cult of patron saints, together with other elements of
their faith, played an important role for craftsmen during their
craft-meetings and in their rituals. A general meeting of the
guild, at which an elder guildsman was elected (*kalantar, okso-
kol*), was devoted to the patron saint of the craft and was
called *piravi* (Dzhabbarov 1959a, p. 380). Another ritual, which
was also devoted by the guild to its patron's care, was the
ritual of initiation for apprentices, who then were bound over
to their masters. This ritual, called in Khoresm *patiya-piravi*
(Dzhabbarov 1959b, p. 84), also marked the acceptance of the
apprentice into the ranks of both living and dead masters —
members of the whole structure of the guild (Peshchereva
1955, p. 280). Apart from reading the *risola*, this ritual involved
putting a belt on the apprentice and the pronouncement, by
the master, of the words of blessing and of the release of the
apprentice into independent practice of his trade called *fotikha*
(Ershov 1966, p. 209). This ritual was accompanied by a feast
which, depending on the material wealth of the apprentice,
gathered a greater or a smaller number of guests. The ritual
of binding the apprentice over to his master, or of releasing
him, was not compulsory when he was the son of a master;

in these cases, only a blessing was enough (Tursunov 1972, p. 112).

Ceremonies which took place on Thursday evenings were also linked with the patron saints of guilds. On these occasions, lamps were lit at the forges in the workshops of smiths in honour of the souls of masters who had died, and special dishes were prepared, whose smells were pleasant to the souls (Peshchereva 1955, p. 280; Sukhareva and others 1962, p. 244). The joining of some rituals connected with the patron saints of the crafts with the cult of the dead led to the formulation of the hypothesis that they are genetically linked (Basilov 1970, p. 70). Patron saints of crafts were also addressed during the performance of difficult productive activities such as the casting of metal products, the making of, or repairs of, anvils or the firing of ceramic pots. When pots were being fired by women potters in Karategin in Tadzhikistan, two puppets were placed by the fire which were meant to represent the patrons of the craft (Ershov 1966, p. 242). When difficult tasks were being performed in guild crafts, a *mullo* was invited who read the *risola* or relevant passages from the Koran. *Risola* and the Koran were also read while tools were being prepared for a newly-released master-smith, an activity which gathered together several experienced craftsmen and which was connected with a feast at the forge. Feasts organised by several persons or by individuals were regarded as offerings — the sharing of the profit with the patron saint of the craft. An offering made to the prophet David by smelters who melted iron ore in the Wanch region of Tadzhikistan, was registered. It depended on giving away part of the iron which was obtained for the first smith to appear (Sukhareva 1960, p. 199).

The cult practices connected with the patron saint of a craft took place in various spots — in workshops, in the homes of craftsmen, in meeting places of the guildsmen, which sometimes were caravansaries. However, the special places for this cult were the graves of saints. In Bukhara, meetings of the guild of embroiderers who worked with gold were held by the graveside of Boboy-Paradus — one of the patrons of this craft who was also the patron of the shoemakers' guild (Peshchereva 1955, p. 280; Sukhareva 1960, p. 197). In the course of my field study at Davlatābād in northern Afghanistan, I learned about the grave of the prophet David at a place called Keshendeh in the province of Balkh, which was visited by metal craftsmen, frequently coming from distant places. This grave is not mentioned in the interesting article by L. Dupree, 'Saint Cults in Afghanistan' (1976). Moreover, this author makes no mention of the function of some saints as protectors of crafts. Unfortunately I did not manage to visit Keshendah.

The cult of patron saints of crafts and the cult of ancestors which appears amongst craftsmen was, in some forms, close to the beliefs and practices of magic. There were, too, beliefs connected with crafts which were magical and had nothing to do with the cults as, for example, belief in the power of the evil eye or lucky or unlucky days for productive activities (Ershov, 1955, p. 259).

I am not familiar with the beliefs and rituals of craftsmen in contemporary Uzbekistan and Tadzhikistan. I did not come across any in conversations with craftsmen, nor do Soviet ethnographers make any mention of them in their works. The abolition of guilds and the new forms of organising craft activities as well as the secularisation of public life resulted in their decrease. It is highly likely that they come to be incorporated into family life and have been retained by small groups of craftsmen.

However, I did manage to record some of the beliefs and rituals of contemporary craftsmen during research at Davlatā-bād in the province of Balkh of Afghanistan, in 1976. There is a small town which has a bazaar which, having developed over the last few years, has a few guilds functioning in it, among them a smiths' guild. Meetings of smiths, in spite of the fact that they have their own *kalantar*, are rare — each of the craftsmen is, as I was told, occupied with his own work. One occasion on which they can meet is the binding over and the release of an apprentice. Guests at the feast which inevitably accompanies the ceremony of the apprentice's release, include the apprentice, his master, the *kalantar* and several other invited guests. The master — *khalfa* — recites the prayer: 'May the prophet Doud (David) gird you with the belt', but the act of girding is not performed. The apprentice, in order to show his gratitude to his master, dresses him in ceremonial dress, called a *chapan*. The master in return presents him with a kit of tools and, sometimes, a handwritten *risola* copied out by the master himself or by a *mullo*. The *risola* contains, among other things, a chronological list of masters of a craft starting with the newly named master and leading right up to the prophet David. However, not all craftsmen possess a *risola*.

Another occasion for meetings is the repair of anvils. Several masters gather together and their work is accompanied by a feast and by readings from a *risola*. Craftsmen also gather at the weddings and funerals of members of a guild. A special occasion is the pilgrimage to the grave of the prophet David in Keshendeh. This pilgrimage takes place in the month of Amal and members of the smiths' guild buy a sheep or a goat, rice and fat and then hire a car, paid for by communal funds. By the graveside of the prophet David, under the supervision of a *kalantar*, the pilgrims read the Koran and *risola*, feast, sing and go for a walk. Their stay in Keshendeh lasts one week and is of a religious and recreational nature. Only the richer craftsmen travel to Keshendeh. According to my informant *usto* Jacob there are many who do not visit the grave of the prophet and these are people whom he holds in low esteem.

The data from Davlatābād indicate that the rituals connected with crafts have deteriorated (for example, the belt is no longer tied around the apprentice) whereas a few are no longer regarded as compulsory. I did not have the chance to determine whether the image recorded at Davlatābād is typical for the northern territories of Afghanistan. The limitation of beliefs and rituals in this town my be the result of the fact that Davlatābād is a relatively new crafts and market centre.

A few of the beliefs and rituals connected with crafts were spoken about by Haydarihā — members of the endogamic and with low social position group of blacksmiths. They have not adopted the organisation of guilds, nor do they travel to the grave of the prophet David in Keshendeh and only recently have some of them bought a *risola*. However, according to what they relate, the ritual of releasing the apprentices as a master is compulsory, though, of course, only in cases where the apprentice is not the son of a master (Jasiewicz 1987, pp. 37–8). The lack of smiths as relatives, also among the Haydarihā, demands an exceptionally strong bond under the care of sacrum and the group of craftsmen, which is unnecessary in the case of descendants of masters. They also meet in groups, made up of several members in order to produce tools for a new master and to repair anvils. This communal work is accompanied by readings from the Koran and by a feast. I presume that craftsmen from these non-food-producing groups which are separate ethnically and are not connected with the past of the settled urban craftsmen, have only recently accepted the beliefs and rituals connected with guild crafts. They regard the acceptance of these elements as one of the possible ways of advancing socially and thus discarding the low social position which they had occupied. I cannot provide an answer to the question whether beliefs and rituals, unique to these groups, existed separately from those encountered in craft guilds.

The beliefs and rituals of craftsmen from the part of Central Asia which has been discussed in this chapter, present, I think, a syncretic religious-cum-magical configuration which has been subjected to the long-lasting influence of Islam and developed within the bounds of the guild organisation. This influence was transferred from the towns to groups of craftsmen in the country as well as to wandering groups. It is likely that in Soviet Central Asia part of these beliefs and rituals were transferred from the former guilds to family life and to the existence of small groups of craftsmen. In Afghanistan, however, changes in these beliefs and practices depended on their reduction and on the weakening of social control over their acceptance and realisation. The most important function of the beliefs and rituals which have been discussed is, it seems, the symbolic expression of their group value: their aim being to integrate the group, which is treated as a community of both living and dead members of the guild, as well as gaining approval for the work performed, by sanctifying it. Thanks to the beliefs and rituals, the existence of the group is ensured as well as a suitable place for it in the structure of society. The second important function of these beliefs and practices is the presentation and preservation of patterns of behaviour which would facilitate the organisation of work and provide a sense of control over the technological processes within a craft.

This chapter is only a preliminary discussion of problems requiring much more additional data and consolidation.

References

Andreev M (1928), 'Poezdka letom 1928 g. v Kasanskiy rayon', *Izvestiya Obshchestva dlya Izucheniya Tadzhikistana i Iranskikh Narodnostey za ego Predelami*, Vol 1 pp 109–131

Basilov V N (1970), *Kult svyatykh v islame*, Izdatelstvo Mysl, Moscow

Dupree L (1976) 'Saint cults in Afghanistan', *American Universities' Field Staff Reports*, South Asia Series, Vol 20 no 1 pp 1–26

Dzhabbarov I (1959a), 'Novye materialy k istorii goncharnego remesla Khoresma', in Tolstov S P, *Trudy Khoresmskoy Archeologichesko-etnograficeskoy Ekspedicii*, Izdatelstvo Akademii Nauk SSSR, Moscow, Vol 4 pp 379–396

Dzhabbarov I (1959b), 'Ob uchenichestve v remeslennykh cekhakh Sredney Azii v konce XIX i nachale XX v.', in Tolstov S P, *Materialy II Soveshchaniya Archeologov i Etnografov Sredney Azii*, Izdatel' stvo Akademii Nauk SSSR, Moscow, pp. 81–88

Ershov N N (1966), 'Domashnie promysly i remesla', in Kislyakov N A, Pisarchik A K, *Tadzhiki Karategina i Darvaza*, Izdatel'stvo Donish, Dyshanbe, Vol 1 pp 195–290

Jasiewicz Z (1977), 'Traditional Handicraft of Uzbekistan in the process of culture changes in the II half of 19-th and in 20-th centuries', *Ethnologia Polona*, Vol 3 pp 103–119

Jasiewicz Z (1978), 'The Haydarihā. An Afghanistan community of blacksmiths. An attempt to change the ethnic situation and social position', in Burszta J, *Poland at the X International Congress of Anthropological and Ethnological Sciences*, Ossolineum, Wroclaw, pp 35–42

Peshchereva E M. (1955), 'Bukharskie zolotoshvey', *Sbornik Muzeya Anthropologii i Etnografii*, Vol 16 pp 265–282

Rao A (1982), 'Non-food-producing nomads and the problem of their classification: the case of the Ghorbat of Afghanistan', *The Eastern Anthropologist*, Vol 35 no 2 pp 115–134

Sukhareva O A (1960), 'K voprosu o genezise professionalnykh kultov u Tadzhikov i Uzbekov', in Kislyakov N A, Pisarchik A K, *Pamyati M. S. Andreeva*, Izdatel'stvo Akademii Nauk Tadzhikskoy SSR, Stalinabad, pp 195–207

Sukhareva O A (1962), *Podznefeodalny gorod Bukhara konca XIX — nachala XX v.*, Izdatelstvo Akademii Nauk Uzbekskoy SSR, Tashkent

Sukhareva O A and others (1962), 'Uzbeki', in Tolstov S P, Zhdanko T A, *Narody Mira, Srednaya Aziya i Kazakhstan*, Izdatel'stvo Akademii Nauk SSSR, Moscow, Vol 1 pp 165–407

Tursunov N (1972), 'Iz istorii remeslennych cekhov Sredney Azii. Na Materialakh tkackikh promyslov Khodzhenta konca XIX — nachala XX v.', *Sovetskaya Etnografiya* no 1 pp 110–118

10

WOMEN AND POWER: A PERSPECTIVE ON MARRIAGE AMONG DURRANI PASHTUNS OF AFGHAN TURKISTAN

Nancy Tapper

Discussions of Muslim women, particularly those in rural areas, commonly describe the disabilities suffered by women compared with men: women may have the jural status of minors, and, like children, have little responsibility for their actions and little control over their sexuality, labour and property. The position of women vis-à-vis men can be viewed in this way; but such a perspective is limited. It focuses attention on explicit constructions of sex and gender and formal positions of authority in the society and leads to underestimation of the informal power exercised by women and the relation between this power and the values to which both women and men subscribe.

Ortner and Whitehead have suggested that 'the structures of greatest import for the cultural construction of gender in any given society are the structures of prestige' and that 'the cultural construction of sex and gender tends everywhere to be stamped by the prestige considerations of socially dominant male actors' (1981, p. 12). A corollary of their argument (Strathern 1981; Brandes 1981) is that where male prestige is heavily dependent on women, whether in terms of female productive or reproductive labour or on women's general comportment, women have a capacity to undermine male ambitions and damage male prestige (Ortner and Whitehead 1981, pp. 20, 21).

This paper is a preliminary attempt to examine the dominant model of gender asymmetry and consider its relation to the

181

conflicting demands of social goals and private interests of men and women. Material drawn from anthropological fieldwork among the Durrani Pashtuns of northwestern Afghanistan is used to suggest the outlines of the system which links the covert or 'muted' (see E. Ardener 1972, 1975; S. Ardener 1975) women's models which include women's experience of spirit possession, with their involvement in illicit sexual activities, and those much rarer occasions when women openly defy the notions of female subordination and passivity implicit in the ideology of honour and shame and express their interests in unilateral actions often of a most drastic kind.

The fact that individual women may have private interests which differ from those of the men and women of the household in which they live casts doubt on the basic premises of Durrani social organisation and structure. Expressions of such women's interests are either dismissed in terms of spirit possessing, or they are construed as subversive by both men and women of a local community. Nonetheless, they demonstrate both the degree of women's power implicit in the logic of the gender categories themselves and in the idiom of honour and shame, and the limits of women's willingness to accept the constraints on personal identity and autonomy defined by these ideologies.

The Asymmetry of the Sexes

An assumption of the basic inequality of the sexes and the superiority of men over women is fundamental to Durrani Pashtun thinking. Thus, men and women are held to differ in their relation to the supreme human faculty of 'reason' (*'aql*) — which refers to the self-control and discipline needed to make rational, sensible decisions. As elsewhere in the Muslim world, Durrani men too are thought to have greater 'reason' than women. Consequently, it is said, they are genuine (*asl*) and have more privileges and more responsibilities, than women who are, conversely, held to be only poor imitations or copies of men (*badal; kamasil*) and expected to be less able to control themselves and their bodies. The grounds for this construction are ultimately religious and serve to exclude women from public worship. The inferior status of women also keeps them apart from the formal decision-making processes in the community, nor can women exercise any overt control over economic resources of any kind.

However the ideology of gender encompasses other kinds of relation between men and women. For instance, the complexity of ideas of the self and the person makes it possible for Durrani to accept and accommodate the idiosyncracies of individual men and women while preserving the system of gender stereotypes: thus, though in general men are thought to be wiser than women, all men are not equally responsible, nor all women equally feckless, and some individual women may be considered wiser than many men.

Equally, the ambiguities contained within the system of gender stereotypes admit areas in which women as a category are important to Durrani identity, as is the case with certain theories of procreation which define the roles of men and women as complementary and both of positive value. Thus, for instance, the blood (*wina*) a child is believed to inherit from both its parents is crucial to its identity in terms of lineage and descent while the blood of childbirth is linked with the key Pashtun notion of homeland (*watan*) round which concepts of Durrani identity focus (see N. Tapper and R. Tapper 1982, and forthcoming).

The Ideology of Honour and Shame

Among Durrani, gender distinctions are particularly elaborate where they are associated with the idiom of honour and shame. Within Durrani communities the notions of honour and shame constitute the principal idiom through which prestige, status and virtually all social activities are managed and understood. It is the conceptual basis of the ideology of control of resources of all kinds, whether people, land, animals or other property.

As elsewhere, among Durrani, concepts of honour and shame are elaborated in an extensive vocabulary, but most often the ideas are subsumed under a few key notions. *Num* (reputation, literally name) is the big name or good name of a big man; *Pashto* a synonym for all or any facet or honour. The latter term suggests explicitly the intimate connection between honour and personal and tribal identity. The same intimate association is implicit in the concept of *namus* which is that aspect of a man's honour as it derives from the morality of his womenfolk.

Also, as elsewhere, any particular activity may be differently interpreted by different people: by some as for the general good of the community, and thus honourable, and by others as serving personal interests to the detriment of the wider society, and thus asocial, antisocial or shameless. Achieving a balance between the areas of social good and private interest is the fundamental, if implicit, goal of all Durrani social activities.

Durrani social identity is based on a conflict. On the one hand, Durrani insist they form an ethnic group superior to all others and they insist that they have a collective responsbility for maintaining this superiority through endogamy and united political action. On the other, they strongly subscribe to an ideal of the equality of all Durrani and the autonomy of each Durrani household which must compete with others for the control of resources of all kinds.

North-central Afghanistan is an area of considerable ethnic and linguistic complexity, in which Durrani Pashtuns can claim political superiority because of their tribal associations with the rulers of the country (R. Tapper 1984). In practice, however, the ordinary Durrani occupy no distinct geographical or economic niche, but are in continuous competition for economic resources with members of many other ethnic groups. In their struggle to maintain and improve what productive resources they control, they stress their ethnic identity, through patrilineal descent and endogamy.

Women's relation to property and productive resources is of direct relevance to these issues. Women have no right to dispose of any produce or capital goods of the household in which they are living, including items from their trousseaux. A woman's right in Islamic law to inherit as a daughter and a wife is acknowledged, but women do not exercise their right, nor do the men (normally brothers or sons) who inherit in their place feel any debt to them. In effect women cannot directly alienate resources from their families of either birth or marriage. And yet Durrani are well aware that this is contrary to the religious precepts accepted by rival ethnic groups and upheld in local courts.

This situation constitues both an ideological and a practical dilemma for which no logical resolution is possible. But, by defining the ethnic boundary in terms of the control of women, Durrani partly resolve the problem. The existence and rare use of severe collective sanctions, and the frequent and emphatic insistence by both men and women that Durrani never give daughters or sisters to men of other ethnic groups, make literally unthinkable the fact that if Durrani women did marry such men then their husbands could gain control of property legally due to the women.

Within the Durrani group the constant competition between households of kin and neighbours focuses on the control of women, both as objects of exchange and as reproductive resources. The success or failure of a household is most characteristically and most frequently and dramatically expressed in terms of the marriages its members make (see N. Tapper 1981). Just as household heads have sole responsibility for their own economic and political affairs, they also control the marriages of all members of the household, and further, have sole responsibility for controlling the household women, over whom they have, in effect, the power of life and death.

The reputation of a household is an active element in determining its future. For a household to be successful, it must not only manage its affairs to ensure economic survival, but must also create a belief in its ability to defend itself and its resources against encroachment by other households. Pooling resources within a household is an ideal which is often realised in practice, for internal dissension is liable to weaken seriously the household's ability to compete and protect itself. Household unity, *entepak* (see N. Tapper 1979, pp. 184, 283) is among the most valued of Durrani ideals, while one of the commonest, and most offensive, opprobrious epithets relates to the ruin of the household (*kor-spera*).

Thus the Durrani ethnic group as a whole and Durrani households are both defined explicitly in terms of marriage and the control of women. It follows then that these areas are central to the construction of Durrani identity and society. Women, who have so little autonomy or control over their lives of the resources of the household in which they live, nonetheless have considerable power to subvert the social order.

The Household and Domestic Roles

Young men, like young girls, have little say in the marriages arranged for them by their parents. And, once the wedding rituals have been completed, the couple can expect to live together for the rest of their lives; among Durrani there is virtually no divorce. In this respect, a man and his wife share a common identity and are mutually dependent whether as a conjugal unit within a large, joint household or as the male and female heads of their own; together they must seek prosperity and success or face failure and destitution. Their close cooperation, support and companionship is in fact usual.

All adult Durrani are expected to be humane and well-mannered. But men are expected to be more serious or mature and display courage in the measured defence of right against wrong. Such expectations focus crucially on the men's obligation to protect the weaker members of their households and household resources against all threats.

Women's domestic authority is accepted and valued as part of their status as adults who are dependent on men and, as a number of local aphorisms imply, a household may stand or fall according to the character of its women. However, a woman's key responsibilities concern childbearing and raising children and these nurturing roles are held to require a minimum of 'reason', courage and piety. Indeed, both men and women are liable to express the opinion that by far the greater burden falls on men who must act in a wide range of public contexts.

Gender stereotypes emphasise ultimate male dominance of the domestic sphere and the essential and complementary but ultimately subordinate status of women. In this respect, the only exception is that of widows with male children who may refuse to remarry and choose to form a separate household on their own. Such women may achieve a considerable degree of independence from men; they are, in effect, the only Durrani who elude the strictures of the male dominance of women in the domestic sphere. (Widowers, by contrast, are felt to be helpless and economically and politically vulnerable without a wife to manage their households and almost invariably seek to remarry).

The relative independence of such widows is little known:

partly because they often head relatively poor households which pose no threat to others in the community, and partly because they are often seen as ideally feminine, accepting personal privation to protect their children from the possible tyranny of an uncaring stepfather who might usurp their inheritance. However, some widows are particularly successful as the heads of independent households. One such woman was known, jokingly, as the women's headman (*qariadar*) and played an active, if formally unrecognised role in certain political negotiations (see N. Tapper and R. Tapper 1982, pp. 173 ff.).

A strong woman may be said to behave 'like a man' and may be referred to by a term which translates as 'man-woman' (*nar-shedza*). This term belies the categorical gender differences and premises on which Durrani social order is founded. It is notable that it is only rarely used of even successful, independent widows by either men or women.

Women's Non-conformity and Irresponsibility

In spite of the importance of women's domestic roles, there is virtually no explicit recognition of the fact that women of a household have certain minimal expectations and rights which men must meet if they are to remain honourable and the household viable. The issues of women's conjugal rights is almost entirely hidden both by the ideology of honour and shame, on the one hand, and by the system of beliefs and practices associated with spirit possession on the other.

The idiom of honour and shame is a male-dominated discourse and affords men many opportunities to expound a point of view which defines their interests as honourable and in accord with those of the wider community. Indeed, there is far greater scope of men to define their interests as honourable — even when these diverge from the social norms which define key groups and identities — than there is for women to do so. Honourable women are those who passively accept roles defined in terms of their dependence on men. It is virtually impossible for a woman to justify, in terms which others would accept as honourable, any perception that she might have legitimate personal experiences or interests which diverge from those of the household with which she is associated.

187

Only people who are recognised as socially competent, independent individuals can be labelled either honourable or dishonourable; those who are not full participants in the Durrani community are dismissed in quite other terms. In the case of men, social failure is most often construed, like men's 'honour', as active and part of the public domain, while among women, social failure is usually consonant with women's 'honour' as passive and domestic. The inability of men and women to fulfill their social and moral responsibilities is explained, typically, in the case of men, in terms of 'insanity' (*lewantop*) and, in the case of women, in terms of possession by *jinn* spirits. 'Insanity' in men refers to a lack of 'reason', the main quality necessary for performing the male responsibility of providing for a household and defending its resources; *jinn*-possession in women is particularly associated with illness and difficulties in performing female reproductive responsibilities.

Though victims of *jinn*-possession are considered non-culpable, it is nonetheless the case that if a woman's ill-health persists, or if, over time she fails to produce surviving children, her roles as wife and mistress of a household may well be usurped by a cowife or some other woman of the household and her status and domestic power diminished significantly. Women greatly fear and dread such a fate, which strikes randomly and serves to isolate individuals who, like 'insane' men, are rendered socially invisible. The fundamental difference between the afflictions of 'insanity' and '*jinn*-possession' is the attribution of responsbility for the former and not the latter. Women are defined as passive in the face of their misfortunes; men are not (see R. Tapper and N. Tapper, n.d., for a more detailed account of these issues).

In many respects, *jinn*-possession among the Durrani shares many of the characteristics of the analytical category of what Lewis has called 'peripheral possessions' (1971). Peripheral possession offers an explanation of misfortune in which amoral spirits possess people, particularly women, who have a marginal relation to the centres of power and authority in a society. However, Durrani ideas of spirit possession differ from other examples of the system Lewis describes in the way they both deny and disguise the relation between spirit possession and social grievance.

In many if not most social contexts a woman's first responsibility as an adult is successful reproduction. By focusing on physiological difficulties, *jinn*-possession relieves Durrani of the need to consider further what are otherwise the quite obvious social concomitants of a women's distress and helplessness in the face of circumstances which define her as a failure as wife, mother and household manager.

Some thirty per-cent of women in the community of some seventy households can expect to experience *jinn*-possession at some time during their lives. Possession is usually diagnosed after a woman's illness during or after childbirth or when her children become ill or die. Possession fits or trances, in which an afflicted woman experiences a state of mental dissociation, are less frequent; fewer than half of the women said to be possessed by *jinn* spirits are likely to experience possession fits. It is notable that *jinn*-possession in general is a diagnosis which may be applied to women of any household of the community, whereas those women who have experienced possession fits are almost invariably associated with large, often wealthy, paternal or fraternal joint households.

Durrani women always affirm the authenticity of *jinn*-possession and possession fits in other women. *Jinn*-possession offers women an implicit explanation for failure and the possibility of catharsis. There may also be a distinct element of self-acclaim in women's spirit possession (cf. Galt 1982). Moreover, both spirit possession and possession fits allow Durrani women to define themselves in terms other than those which concern reproductive activities and their domestic roles.

Unlike the women, Durrani men are particularly interested in the authenticity of women's possession experiences. Though questions of the authenticity are never raised by men unless a possession fit has occurred, within the group of women who had *jinn* fits, men labelled some experiences genuine (*asl*) and others fake (*badal*). These labels not only excuse men from responsbility for reproductive success or failure, but they also direct attention away from the social implications of defining female gender roles in narrow terms.

Of the fifteen women we knew who had experienced *jinn*-possession fits, the twelve whose experiences were accepted as genuine were all strong-willed, intelligent women. They were all women who, unusually, had fought openly and cogently to have their place in the household reassessed. These women may have had only limited success in this respect, but in doing so, each woman had actively promoted herself for a position to which she had no ascribed right: three of them were known to dominate their husbands, eight others challenged the rightful authority of the household headwoman, while the last was in a household where the women were unusually strictly segregated, which she resented.

By contrast, three remaining women were said by men to have faked their experience of possession fits. They explained that this was evidently so because they were women who, as they put it, 'were angry with the men of their household'. To us, as outsiders, the salient difference between the two groups was certainly not the degree to which the fifteen women expressed their domestic distress in anger, but that the second group, whom men considered frauds, were women whom, for whatever personal or structural reasons, were ineffectual and unable to influence their husbands or to convert other members of their household to their point of view.

By labelling their fits 'authentic', women's emotions and personal interests and ambitions may be ignored or dismissed as the work of *jinn*. Thus, the ideology of possession, like that of honour and shame, leaves little room for social action by women. The category of 'authenticially' possessed women certainly included active, articulate domestic rebels. But because they are 'known' to be possessed, the social significance of their rebellion is in effect publicly denied. The extenuating circumstances of possession provide an explanation of their potentially and subversive behaviour, and the principle of female irresponsibility is upheld. In this respect the fits, whether or not consciously faked, seem to reflect these women's recognition of their weakness as women and their inability to redefine female roles in a way acceptable both to them and to society at large.

There are, however, other women who appear deliberately to cause a variety of scandals through blatant sexual irregularity. As the dominant ideology does not allow social responsibility to women, and channels domestic rebellion into behaviour that is attributed to *jinn*, so it lays the moral and social responsbility for women's more public rebellion squarely to the account of men. The ideal (but rarely carried out) action of such men — killing the offending woman — is regarded not as a punishment for moral error, but as a vindication of the man's honour.

Subversive Women

Because of the comprehensive rights which men have in women, it is usually the case that a Durrani woman's own interests are best served by unswerving loyalty to the household in which she is resident. However, the men who so completely control women in this society do have mininal responsbilities towards the women in their households, particularly in terms of maintenance and protection. Only when the men on whom women are dependent signally fail to live up to the expectations associated with the ideals of male dominance, may a woman act in her own self-interest to modify the terms of her dependence or, in some rare cases, to extricate herself entirely from a man's control.

Such action on the part of a woman will of course confirm Durrani stereotypes of women's irresponsible and dangerous nature, but this does not necessarily diminish the far-reaching consequences which such actions may have on men's political and economic status in the wider society.

In spite of the very severe nature of the punishments Durrani feel are proper if the rules governing sexual behaviour are breached, their practical consequences for men and women vary considerably. Though it is impossible to know how women perceive the personal risks they take, it is without doubt the case that on occasion it is women rather than men who either initiate or willingly agree to an illicit liaison. The reasons why this should be so are clearly revealed in the most extreme cases. These cases also suggest that in many, less dramatic ways, the practical aspects of the ideology of honour and shame allow women to threaten or force men into a degree of conformity, and hard work, to support the household.

In a household where a woman has access to a modicum of material goods and where her domestic status is duly respected, she will have little cause to jeopardise her own and the household's honour through sexual misconduct. Moreover, a household economically and politically strong enough to meet the women's needs is also likely to be a household strong enough to punish severely any public betrayal of its standards.

Rather, illicit liaisons seem to occur when the household with which a woman is associated is weak in the first place. Thus, a common pattern is one where a woman, having decided that the men of the household to which she belongs are inadequate providers or defenders of household resources and honour, attempts to escape the household via a romantic liaison. Whether the woman literally flees the household or not, the liaison will, if it becomes known, shame the men of the household and threaten the viability of the unit as a whole.

In such circumstances there are more options available to unmarried women than there are to married women, but, conversely, the risks the unmarried woman run are in many ways greater.

An unmarried woman may extricate herself from her guardian's household through the institution of 'calling out' (nara kawel) (see N. Tapper 1979, p. 418). Thus, if a young unmarried girl considers her guardian (whether her father or brother) is behaving in a way which is likely to ruin her chances of a good marriage, she may shame him by publicly 'calling out' for a certain man who becomes obligated to marry her.

If an unmarried woman's guardian realises she is considering 'calling out' for a man, he will try and forestall her at all costs. Ideally he can keep the whole business quiet and marry her off immediately, but he may judge that her life is not worth the dishonour she will bring him and kill her.

However, the value of a woman's life depends on the circumstances of the household in which she lives. For example, one local man was said to have murdered his unmarried daughter when she refused to agree to an engagement he had planned for her and sought to 'call out' for another youth; her father killed her before her lover could react (assuming he had intended to do so). Ironically, in this case, though the father's drastic action conformed with ideals of honourable behaviour, other Durrani consider the man a fool who was too poor to afford such a gesture. In effect, people said he had cut off his nose to spite his face: he had lost his daughter and her brides-price and had gained precious little in return. The case is an exception which proves the rule that women normally only take drastic steps to influence their lives when the men of the household with which they are associated are too weak, politically, economically or in personal character, to take effective action against them.

In two other cases an unmarried woman and her lover successfully eloped, but the cases were very different in other respects and show clearly that a woman's worth to others in her household or in the community as a whole depends on the strength of the household with which she is associated.

In the first, the couple came from impoverished client households whose dependent and precarious economic and political status within the local community was hardly affected by the scandal the girl's father experienced. Indeed, as one of the men of the wealthier households of the community commented when the girl's father pleaded with him to help recover her, 'It will cost more than 50,000 Afghanis in time and trouble (and bribes) to get her back. You would not have received that much in brideprice for her, so let her go. It is not important.'

In the second case, Kaftar, a woman from a weathy household, forsook her Durrani identity and eloped with a Shiite Hazara youth (see N. Tapper 1979, pp. 91, 161, 415; N. Tapper and R. Tapper forthcoming). The dishonour of Kaftar's elopement, which in this case was shared by all members of the local community, lay in the relation between her status as a member of one of the more important households in the community and her betrayal of the most basic rule of Durrani ethnicity, that a Durrani woman should never marry or have sexual relations with a non-Durrani man. The scandal confirmed all the Durrani's worst fears about both the nature of women and about the Hazara, the most despised of ethnic groups. The reaction of the local community was as swift and forceful as they could make it. Search parties were organised to recover Kaftar and later vast sums of money were collected to negotiate government action to secure her return. When we left the area at the end of our fieldwork with the Durrani, Kafter had not been caught, but ultimately, the Durrani said, they would get her back. When they did so, they said, they would make an example of her and shoot her in front of all the women of the community.

Though no one will ever know for certain, the Maduzai speculated on the various grievances that had precipitated what they saw to be Kaftar's extraordinary act. Her father had

193

been involved over a number of years in quarrels with his closest relations and in particular with his own half-brother. These disputes had been very costly and shaming and it seemed unlikely that an attractive suitor would come for Kaftar whose contemporaries were now married women with young families.

In spite of the severe sanctions for sexual misbehaviour, these are not uniformly applied. In the ten other local cases involving unmarried girls I learned of, a variety of things occurred: either the girl and her lover eloped, or they were married in the conventional way; or her guardian turned a blind eye to the liaison while seeking a suitable spouse for the girl from elsewhere (often enlisting the help of her mother's kin (*mamakhel*) to do so; or, if the girl had 'called out' for a man, the very fact that her action was labelled this way, meant that the man in question had accepted the political challenge to marry and protect her.

A public scandal precipitated by a woman may well gain her material and emotional security. In several cases, unmarried women who had broken the rules of sexual morality were eventually married to non-Durrani men. Durrani men hushed this up, or if that was impossible, they rationalised such marriages by suggesting that breaking the rule against exogamous marriage was less terrible than keeping a 'bad' woman within the group. However, from the woman's point of view, though she had abandoned Durrani status, she had gained a degree of control over her life and some recognition of her individual worth.

The absence of divorce among Durrani and the fact that the children of a marriage will always remain with their father's household means that the remedies open to a married woman are unlikely to lead to her escape from her marital household. They may, however, offer her personal consolation and support while involving little risk.

Women unhappy with their situation within a large, successful household headed by men of character are most unlikely to risk involvement in an illicit liaison which might threaten the honour of the household, quite simply because the men of such a household can and will respond in the most severe terms. They can afford to punish and replace women who besmirch their honour and they will be expected to do so.

Ironically, it is married women associated with successful households who have the fewest alternative means of personal expression. As we have seen it is the lively women of strong households who may experience possession fits, and this is the situation of some fifteen per cent of married women in the community.

By contrast, a woman unhappy with her situation in a weak, impoverished household, whose menfolk are ineffectual and fail to support household women and children, may take a lover or even engage in covert prostitution for money and presents which she can dispose of as she wishes. Meanwhile, her husband cannot punish her with impunity. Should he act as the code of honour suggests and kill his wife, he will find himself helpless to run his household alone and, and unless he leaves the community altogether, he is unlikely to find another woman to marry. Perhaps five to ten per cent of married women in the community were involved in illicit liaisons of this kind.

Conclusions

Women are expected to fulfill reproductive and productive roles while remaining passive, circumspect and accepting of the ultimate authority and control of men in all areas of their lives. However, there are certain minimal duties of maintenance and protection which women can expect of the men in whose households they live. However, women have few remedies to ensure that these expectations are met and limited compensations, in spirit possession or romantic liaisons, if they are not.

I know of only one other alternative open to a woman. It is perhaps not surprising that only when events in the wider society themselves threaten a Durrani community and its domestic institutions, that a 'man-woman' may come to the fore. There were reports in the nineteenth century of Pashtun women fighting against the British. Another unusual example of an Ishaqzai Durrani woman who adopted a man's role is worth recording. In July 1923 it was reported in a British agent's diary that,

a young woman, locally known as 'Dukhtar-i-Ishakzai'

whose husband was executed the year before by the Kandahar authorities for robbery, has collected round herself a band of some 50 young men and occupied the passes north of Kandahar. She has told the Governor that she has established an independent government there. She already calls herself the 'Sardar Badshah' (or Lord King) and she has earned a reputation as a daring raider (L/P & S/10, 860/1923).

Her rebellion did not last long and later than summer conflicting reports were received: her brother was later executed in Kandahar, but of Dukhtar-i Ishakzai we learn no more than that she may have been assassinated, or she may have fled to Pakistan.

Though there is too little information to be sure, it may be that the execution of her husband was associated with the destruction of the woman's household, and it was only after this that the woman reversed all ordinary conventions. With this in mind, we need to ask, 'What roles do women play among the Pashtuns in Afghanistan today?'

References

Ardener E (1972) 'Belief and the problem of women' in La Fontaine, J.S., ed., *The Interpretation of Ritual: Essays in Honour of A.I. Richards,* Tavistock, London. (Reprinted in Ardener, S. 1975).

Ardener E (1975), 'The "problem" revisited' in Ardener, S. 1975.

Ardener S (1975), 'Introduction' in Ardener, S., ed., *Perceiving Women,* Dent, London.

Brandes S (1981), 'Like Wounded Stags: Male Sexual Ideology in an Andalusian Town' in Ortner, S.B. & H. Whitehead, eds.

Galt A (1982), 'The Evil Eye as Synthetic Image and its Meaning on the Island of Pantellena, Italy', *American Ethnologist,* Vol,9, no,4, pp. 664–681.

Lewis M (1971), *Ecstatic Religion* Penguin, Harmondsworth.

L/P & S/10 – 869/1923: 2882, 3141, 4835. India Office Library, London.

Ortner S and Whitehead, H (eds) (1981), *Sexual Meanings,* Cambridge U.P., Cambridge.

Strathern M (1981), 'Self-interest and the Social Good: some Implications of Hagen Gender Imagery' in Ortner, S. & H. Whitehead, eds.

Tapper N (1979), *Marriages and Social Organisation among Durrani Pashtuns in Northern Afghanistan,* Unpub. Ph.D. thesis, University of London.

Tapper N (1981) 'Direct Exchange and Brideprice: Alternative Forms in a Complex Marriage System', *Man*, Vol 16 no.3, pp. 387–407.

Tapper, N and Tapper R (1982), 'Marriage Preferences and Ethnic Relations among Durrani Pashtuns of Afghan Turkestan', *Folk*, Vol. 24, pp. 157–177.

Tapper N (forthcoming), 'Concepts of Disorder and Responsbility among Durrani Pashtuns in Northern Afghanistan' in Jansson, E. & B. Utas, eds., *Afghanistan — A Threatened Culture*, Croom Helm: London.

Tapper, R and Tapper N (n.d.), 'Possession, Insanity and Responsibility in Northern Afghanistan', Unpub. ms.

Tapper, R (1984), 'Ethnicity and Class: Dimensions of Intergroup Conflict in North-Central Afghanistan' in Shahrani, N. & R. Canflied, eds., *Revolutions & Rebellions in Afghanistan*, Univ. of California: Berkeley.

Note: My data are drawn from fieldwork carried out by Richard Tapper and myself in the summer of 1968, and over a year between 1970 and 1972. The research was done jointly as a Social Science Research Council (U.K.) project. Many of the ideas and arguments of the paper were formed in discussions with Richard Tapper, both during and after fieldwork. The ethnographic present refers to the fieldwork period. The data relates particularly to one hamlet of 70 households associated with a tribal community numbering some 200 households, though I feel certain that much of what I describe characterises the situation of women in many other rural Durrani Pashtun groups in Afghan Turkistan.

11

GOLDEN TENT-PEGS: SETTLEMENT AND CHANGE AMONG NOMADS IN AFGHAN TURKISTAN

Richard Tapper

Introduction

Pastoral nomadism, the tending of livestock by communities living in portable tents or huts, is the traditional occupation of a variety of peoples in the drier parts of Asia and Africa. Typically, the nomads are scattered thinly over vast stretches of steppe and mountain so arid that they cannot be exploited by any form of agriculture unless as seasonal pasturage for livestock.

During the twentieth century, nomadism as a way of life has fast receded in most of these areas, mainly as a result of government policies: for example the closure of frontiers to migrations across them, sometimes direct military action to stop nomads from moving, sometimes the provision of settled bases for pastoralism. Meanwhile, an improved agricultural technology has allowed the expansion of cultivation into former nomadic pasturelands.

In Afghanistan until 1978, nomadism did not decline in the same way as in many other countries — largely because of a *de facto* liberal government policy. It is likely indeed that the numbers of nomads increased rather than declined. This alone, apart from any practical objections to nomadism, constituted a problem for a country intent on a programme of modernisation. In conformity with other states, Afghanistan had long determined on the solution of settlement, though it was recognised that such an aim could not be achieved overnight, and must take account of the diversity in character, and situation of the various nomadic elements in the country. What was not widely recognised, however, was the degree to which the nomads in many areas have for long been settling of their own accord, with only indirect help from government.

In this chapter I argue that it is better to understand Afghan nomads as they see themselves: as 'pastoralists', whose interest in nomadism is mainly economic and ecological rather than cultural, ideological or psychological. They recognise farmland as a more secure resource — a 'golden tent-peg' — and may be tempted by cultivation when it is also shown to be as profitable as stock-raising. Apart from their economic commitment to pastoralism, Afghan nomads identify ethnically and tribally with their settled fellows. Settlement and the acquisition of land of themselves involve no major change of identity, rather, it is only when population growth, pressure on resources and the concentration of wealth in the hands of the few bring political inequality and conflict into the tribal community (nomad or settled) that ethnicity and tribalism begin to shift towards class awareness. These processes are examined through the case of a particular group of Durrani Pashtun nomads in the course of settlement.

The tragic circumstances of the past ten years or so have pushed the question of nomad settlement far into the background, but it is not a problem that will be solved automatically by any conceivable conclusion to the current struggle between the resistance movement and the Soviet-backed Afghan regime. Although my remarks here derive from field research in the early 1970s, (to which my 'ethnographic present tense' refers), and although I do not belive the outcome of the war will be any sort of return to a *status quo ante* (whatever that might have been), the issues and processes I describe retain considerable relevance for the future of Afghan rural society.

Nomadism in Afghanistan

Who are the nomads in Afghanistan? The term evokes images of steppes and mountains, caravans of camels, black tents, flocks of sheep and goats, tribally organised society. But the variety of forms of nomadism is considerable. There are pastoralists who have neither tribal organisation nor tents and do not nomadise; there are both tent-dwelling nomads and settled tribal groups who have no pastoral interests at all; and among the tent-dwelling, tribally organised pastoralists there are those who migrate many hundreds of miles during the year with the aid of camels, and those who move only a mile or so with donkeys to carry their dwellings.

Estimates of the numbers of nomads vary widely, and rarely specify which kinds of nomads are included. There are perhaps 2 to 3 million Afghan citizens who, for at least part of the year, live in tents tending their flocks. With a narrower definition — people who have no fixed dwellings at all and no other occupation than pastoralism — the numbers would not exceed a few hundred thousand. By either definition, the majority of nomads are Pashto-speakers of a variety of tribal groups, mainly Durrani and related groups in the southwestern parts, and Ghiljai and others in the east. But nomads by the broader definition include members of almost all the other linguistic and cultural groups in Afghanistan: Baluch, Brahui, Moghol, Kirghiz, Turkmen, Uzbek, Arab, Aymaq, Tajik, Hazara. It should be remembered that though these are not usually seen as part of the 'nomad problem' (which concerns the Pashtuns), they are likely to be affected by any measures taken to deal with it.

In the 1970s it was reckoned that two-thirds of the country could, in the foreseeable future, be used only for seasonal grazing by mobile pastoralists; that is, in present-day Afghanistan, the nomads will continue to fill an important ecological niche, by using pastures that are not otherwise accessible to exploitation, particularly in arid, uncultivable lowland regions and high mountain ranges, far from settlement.

Thus, although villagers in the mountains can raise flocks with a high milk yield, they depend on the provision of winter fodder, and in their necessarily restricted cultivation they must maintain a balance between growing fodder for the animals and other crops for human consumption. With this winter limitation on their growth, local flocks are large enough to exploit only small areas of nearby mountain pastures in summer, and vast ranges are left for seasonal visitors — the nomads. In the same way, in the lowlands, villagers are limited in the size of flocks they can maintain throughout the year in the arid steppe and desert country of the vicinity. In both lowland and highland contexts, the nomads exploit the pastures left over, by seasonal movements between them. Their flocks are closely adapted to such conditions.

But there is a sensitive and fluid frontier between the grazing of the nomads' flocks and that of the local flocks; and another between the nomads' flocks and the farmland of the villagers. So long as each side remains behind its frontier, good relations prevail, and useful exchanges of produce can take place. Moreover, in more isolated regions, the nomads bring in not only goods but information from 'the outside world'. Historically, such mutually beneficial exchanges have on many occasions alternated with periods in which one side — usually the nomads — has dominated and exploited the other.

In terms of their role in the national economy, the evidence is not clear, and there are strongly opposed points of view: some see nomads as unproductive consumers of valuable grain supplies; others, more reliably in my view, estimate that the nomads' livestock (over half the nation's total) make a considerable contribution of wool, meat and skins to the economy.[1]

In what way are the nomads different from anybody else? Is there any justification for the notion that in Afghanistan the nomads live in a world apart, have customs, traditions and attitudes that distinguish them from the rest of the population, that they are implacable enemies of settled society and would die rather than abandon their tents, their flocks and their migrations? This seems to be a popular view, and it has been perpetuated by Louis Dupree in his authoratative book on Afghanistan, when he writes:

Show me a nomad who wants to settle down, and I'll show you a man who is psychologically ill . . . Many Afghan officials believe that nomads genuinely desire to settle down if given the opportunity. Nomads, however, look on themselves as superior beings, envied and feared by the villagers. Any nomad desiring to settle down would be considered psychopathic by his peers (1973: 168). The nomad continues to look on the farmer with contempt. Even after he becomes semi-nomadic, semi-sedentary, and eventually fully sedentary, his pride of nomadic ancestry makes him feel superior to his agelong farmer neighbours (1973: 179).

I believe these remarks to be unfounded for most if not all the nomads in Afghanistan. As Klaus Ferdinand, the main authority on the nomads, has pointed out, the very word for 'nomad' used in most of the country makes no clear distinction between nomad and villager. In south, west and north, the standard term is *maldar*, literally 'flock-owner', but the term can also apply to fully settled pastoralists. More specific to nomads is *powinda*, but this too appears to refer to their pastoral activities rather than to movement. Pashtuns, whether nomads or settled, are commonly called simply 'Afghan'. In other words, the identity of the nomads, as of other people, is marked most clearly by either occupational or ethnic criteria, without reference to movement or tents. It is true that in eastern parts of the country the Pashto term *kuchey* (Persian *kuchi*) is widely used by and of the Pashtun nomads (and has been adopted into the vocabulary of Kabul-based foreigners), but here too tribal or local identity is more important than the easily changed status of nomad or villager. There are undoubtedly some countries (e.g., Iran) where tents and a mobile way of life are of crucial ideological and symbolic importance to the nomads — but the historical and cultural background of nomadism is very different there from Afghanistan, where this is not the case (R. Tapper 1984a).

However the nomads are defined, whether simply the comparatively small numbers of fully nomadic pastoralists or in the wider terms I have suggested, and whether they include only the Pashto-speaking majority of all the different groups with tents and pastoral interests, it is difficult to find any basic differences of custom and social life that distinguish them *as nomads* from the rest of the population; certainly not on the scale of the differences of custom, tradition, language and so forth that distinguish one ethnic group from another. For the majority of nomads, those of the Durrani and Ghiljai Pashtuns, the only differences between them and their settled fellow-tribespeople are related directly to their pastoral occupation and their mobility, and they share with them other features such as language, customs and traditions.

In other words, neither from the perspective of popular discourse, nor in terms of objective criteria, is it possible to find any reality that corresponds with the conventional — and official — notion of 'nomad'. Moreover, nomads, particularly

Durrani, have always been liable to settlement in various ways and for various reasons. In spite of high infant mortality, nomadic populations increase naturally and often at a faster rate than settled village populations. Overgrazing of the pasture occurs and its effects may well have been worsened by a gradual climatic dessication in many nomadic areas, such as the southwest. In all, there is great pressure on the nomads to shed surplus members into settled non-pastoral society. Usually it is the richer and the poorer nomads who settle first: the rich find that the risk of keeping too many animals with the chance of climatic disasters is too great, so they invest in trade or farmland, sooner or later build a house, and 'retire' from the nomadic scene, leaving their flocks to supervisors. As for the poor, when their flocks fall below a certain minimum they cannot support a family and may have to seek outside employment, probably as labourers in village or town.

Nomads prefer to acquire land already under cultivation, but in the 1960s and 1970s, with government encouraging farmers to open up new lands, the nomads too, particularly in the north, took to ploughing and sowing crops on their pastures before someone else could do so and thereby claim rights to the land. As landowners, they avoid working the land themselves and instead employ settled peasants. In so far as nomads do have a characteristic view of village life, it springs largely from this process: as pastoralists, they scorn, farming unless they can be landowners and employers. None the less, nomads throughout the country see the virtues of mixed farming, of combining pastoralism with cultivation from a settled base, even if they do not farm themselves. As I was told by nomads in the north, *zamin mikh-i zarin*, land is a golden tent-peg.

Many village communities include both settled households occupied with cultivation and others who pursue a nomadic life in tents, spending only the autumn and winter with their relatives in the village. Families often divide into two parts for this purpose, one specialising in pastoralism, the other in cultivation — on the pattern of Cain and Abel. Occasionally members of such a family take it in turns to accompany the flocks to the mountains — 'nomads' for a season.

Afghan nomads are not isolated, primitive tribes. On the contrary, they are one of the most dynamic elements in the population, open to innovation, investment, enterprise. They are, and always have been, closely bound up with the rest of the nation in economic, political, social and cultural relations. Many of them are too highly specialised, vulnerable to years of drought and disaster like 1970–2. They pose undoubted problems for administration and welfare to a government which has limited resources for controlling a large country with a formidable terrain. But the nomads are far from inveterate opponents of the idea of settlement: it is a process familiar to them and they are generally eager to welcome it — on their own terms.

Durrani Nomads and Settlement in Afghan Turkistan

Towards the end of last century, northern Afghanistan was considerably underpopulated. There were rich pastures, used only by a small number of Arab and Turkmen nomads, while settled Uzbek and Tajik farmers barely kept going the irrigation systems along the river valleys. As the area came under the control of Kabul, there was a massive influx of population, from the east, south and west, encouraged and promoted by government, which had also opened up the central mountain regions of Ghor and the Hazarajat for summer grazing by the nomads. Among the immigrants to the north around 1900 were many groups of Pashtun nomads, especially Durrani from the southwest, spurred by arid conditions in their homeland and by a Durrani government keen to have its northern frontiers repopulated and defended by loyal tribespeople (N. Tapper 1983, Kakar 1979).

In the early 1900s, these newcomers thrived in the lush pastoral conditions. In summer they migrated to the central mountains, where they sold their surplus stock, traded and brought back cloth to the north. In Afghan Turkistan (the area between Badakhshan in the east and Faryab in the west), much of the best and most convenient irrigated land, cultivated by local villagers, came into the ownership of the Pashtun nomad leaders, who quickly settled down to live in comfort on the income from their lands. They became khans, dominating economic and political life in most parts of Turkistan. Other farmlands, of great potential, remained for some time uncultivated, the extensive irrigation networks temporarily out of use, but many of these lands too were gradually acquired by other Pashtun nomads.

In the 1920s and 1930s, further developments occurred. Turkmens introduced the karakul breed of sheep, and many of the Pashtuns took this up too. The nomads had formerly gone to the mountains to market their main produce — live-stock — but the valuable karakul lambskins were sold in Turki-stan to dealers who took them to Kabul by road, so now the nomads had less reason to visit the mountains.

Meanwhile, population expanded rapidly. By the 1950s, the pastures were filling up, and all the irrigable land was coming back into cultivation. Gradually those nomads who owned farmland saw profits from it coming in with greater regularity and less hardship than from their flocks. Wherever possible they built houses and adopted a fully mixed economy. Large numbers of pastoral nomads in the north have not managed to acquire farmland — but they are experimenting, not very successfully as yet — with dry farming in the steppes. The other main trend is that wealthy settled pastoralists are increas-ingly sending their flocks out to seasonal pastures accompanied only by hired herdsmen and supervisors in white canvas tents.

In the Saripul region of Jouzjan province, where Nancy Tapper and I did field research in 1968, 1971 and 1972, most Pashtun nomads belong to the Ishaqzai, one of the major Durrani tribes. In the region at that time, out of a population of about 150,000, there were 30–40,000 Pashtuns, of whom 15,000 were Durrani, mainly of the Ishaqzai tribe. The rest of the population were Uzbeks and Turkmens (about 60,000), Aymaqs and Tajiks (about 30,000), Arabs and Sayyids (5–10,000) and Hazaras (15–20,000).

The Saripul region is dominated economically and politically by members of the Nazarzai subtribe of the Ishaqzai, leading members of which — the khans — are near descendants of the leaders of the Durrani migration to the region at the turn of the century. Nazarzai khans conduct extensive pastoral activities but base their power partly on control of immense areas of farmland and partly on privileges granted them by successive Afghan governments. The head of the khan family lives in Saripul town, and other branches of the family live on and supervise their estates, scattered throughout the region.

The fourteen subtribes of the Saripul Ishaqzai vary widely in situation and character, falling into three main categories. The largest, with 5–6,000 people from seven subtribes, comprises pastoralists with winter tent-villages in the dry hill-steppes west of the Saripul river valley. They are comparatively isolated from other ethnic groups and from adminstrative controls: only during their summer transhumance to the central mountains do they have individual economic contacts with Aymaqs and Tajiks.

In the second category are a few thosand tent-dwelling pastoralists from four subtribes, who camp most of the year beside the fertile Saripul valley. They have greater contact with local Uzbeks, Hazaras, Arabs and Aymaqs, both in the valley and during the transhumance to the mountains. Few of them own any valley farmlands, though they often dry-farm the neighbouring pastures.

The third category comprises about 5,000 people from five subtribes, including the Nazarzai. These groups are semi-settled, having villages in or on the edge of the valley where they own lands and have mostly built mud houses; half or less of the population make the summer transhumance to the mountains, though all are in regular contact with members of a whole range of other ethnic groups.

The Madozai of Saripul

One such subtribe is the Madozai. In the early years of the century, severe droughts in the southwest of the country drove some farmers off the land and some nomads to seek new pastures; one group that came north in about 1915 comprised about 65–70 families led by Hajji Afzal of the Madozai. The group was heterogeneous in composition, a bare majority being from the Madozai themselves; some had owned land, but all came north as pastoral nomads; none of them were wealthy, and no one exercised authority over any but his immediate relatives; in the years after their arrival, many families left and others joined. In 1920 they numbered about 70 familes (500 people), of which 14 belonged to three core lineages and the rest were from a variety of Durrani tribal groups and others.

After their arrival in their present habitat (about 1917) the

Madozai prospered. The area was underpopulated, and land, water and food were plentiful. Moreover the leaders of the two main lineages were offered very cheaply some 2,850 jeribs (570 hectares) of irrigated valley land. Initially there was little interest in this offer; the Madozai leaders were disillusioned with farming after the disasters in the southwest and were content with the easy life pastoralism offered in the north; but the land was bought, and was divided, together with the associated water rights, into equal shares among the five leading men of the two main Madozai lineages; eventually the shares were further divided and distributed among all 41 households of the three core lineages.

The two decades following the Madozai arrival in Saripul were relatively uneventful for them (apart from a brief inter-ethnic war in 1929, at the time of the Bacha-Saqao revolt). They learned karakul sheep husbandry and in general their pastoral enterprises thrived in the abundant grazing. Meanwhile, and at a pace that coincided with the increase in population in the region, the Madozai began to farm their rich valley lands and to learn the techniques of intensive irrigated agriculture. In the early 1930s the first dwellings were built in their winter settlements.

Despite the initial lack of interest in the purchase, and the fact that the land for many years lay underexploited, the land distribution was a crucial factor in defining relations within the subtribe. In essence, there emerged a sharp division between the landowners and the rest who became, to a greater or lesser extent, their clients (*hamsaya*). Incipient cleavages, both between and within the main lineages, were reified. The first major conflict was the outbreak, in 1936–7, of a feud between the two main lineages, resulting in men killed and wounded on both sides. Peace was made with difficulty by the Ishaqzai khan, who arranged the customary exchange marriages between the sides; but the hostility, with its roots in events and relations in the southwest, continues today between the two lineages, whose settlements are distinct and whose camps rarely move together to the mountains.

The Madozai Economy

The Madozai subtribe today (1972) comprises about 1900 people in 272 households, occupying two villages and several hamlets and tent-camps. Over 75 per cent have mud dwellings, though this in itself is no index of sedentarisation. The Madozai speak of themselves as *maldar*, pastoral nomads, but acknowledge that the uncertainly of the national and world markets in karakul skins, their main pastoral product, has encouraged them to look elsewhere for economic security.

The three landowning lineages number 162 households, whose heads all descend from the original migrants; another 15, from a closely related Madozai lineage that did not get shares in the original lands, have bought land elsewhere; the remaining 95 households are more or less transient, landless 'clients'. Although many of the 177 households from the landowning lineages have already lost their land, sold or usurped by more powerful relatives, about half the Madozai households own and benefit directly from shares in irrigated lands, totalling over 1,000 hectares; others also farm dry lands nearby. The leader of one lineage, the wealthiest man in the subtribe, is reckoned a 'khan' himself; his main rival in wealth and power is the leader of the other lineage. Both these men inherited substantial shares of land, but managed to buy additional large holdings elsewhere.

In 1970 the Madozai were still heavily involved in pastoralism, owning around 10,000 ewes, and half the households had between twenty and several hundred head of animals. Between September and early May the flocks are kept in the hill-steppe pastures to the east of the valley. From early March until May, while the lambs are born and the spring wool is shorn, about three-quarters of the Madozai go out to camp in their pastures to provide the additional labour required, to supervise the collection of lambskins, and also to get away from the villages and enjoy the festive spring atmosphere and the best season in the pastures. In mid-May usually about a third of the households send tents to accompany the flocks on the 300-km migration to spend the early summer months in the central mountains; the rest return to the villages to supervise or take part in the summer's agricultural activities.

However, 1971 was the second year of a severe drought in

northern Afghanistan, affecting both pastures and crops.[2] Many Madozai suffered sheep losses and many who previously used to accompany the flocks to the mountains did not bother to do so, or sent only an unmarried son to supervise them, living with friends or kin, in a canvas tent or in the open. That year, of the 177 core households of the Madozai, 124 (70%) went (in whole or in part) to the spring pastures (43 camps), and only 35 (21%), accompanied by young supervisors from 9 other households, went on the summer migration to the mountains.

The following winter was very harsh and the flock losses were terrible; by summer 1972 many families had abandoned pastoralism, most of them temporarily, some of them perhaps for good. Few families joined the remaining animals in spring pastures, and none went to the mountains that year.

The Madozai subtribe as a whole operates in a surplus economy, that is, the grain grown on the irrigated valley lands owned by members of the subtribe is usually adequate for the needs of the total population; similarly the wool and meat from the Madozai flocks are on the whole adequate for all the subtribe, while deficiencies in milk products and wheat are far more than made up by proceeds from the sale of lambskins and cash crops such as cotton.

In general and in brief, a flock of 60 ewes could produce milk and meat sufficient for the expected annual consumption of the average family of three adults, and four children, while income from skins (c. 10,000 Afs., £50 at that time) and fleeces (c. 1,000 Afs.) would allow them the bare minimum of bought goods; flour, rice, fat and incidental items. Thus, 60 ewes, allowing a cash income of 11,000 Afs., would seem the breakeven point for the budget of the 'average' pastoral household owning no land. Ownership of 10 jerib (c. 2.5 hectares) of irrigated land would allow for similar consumption patterns in a household with no herds.

In 1972 a day labourer was paid 50 Afs. a day (800 Afs. a month), but employment was very seasonal. A domestic servant or herding assistant was paid 200–500 Afs. a month, as well as food and clothing; even the maximum annual wages of 6,000 Afs. were insufficient to keep a family of two adults and two children, particularly in years of very light grain prices like 1970–71. Such jobs are usually taken by men without dependents, who can save almost the full cash wage. A man with dependents who becomes a servant survives only on charity. A shepherd receives food and clothing and 10 per cent of pastoral produce; his average income is worth probably about 10,000 Afs., though it can range from nothing to more than 20,000 Afs. in a good year. A man who sharecrops in the valley, providing only his own labour, may gain produce worth more than 10,000 Afs., but even if the crop fails completely he is guaranteed around half a ton of wheat, on which a family of four could just live for a year.

Although they had known extreme differences of wealth in the southwest, members of the group that came north — at least the core lineages — were relatively homogeneous in this respect. With the acquisition of irrigated valley lands, their eventual exploitation and most recently their rapid growth in value, wealth differences have once more widened, between those who own several hundred head of animals and a hundred or more jeribs of land, and those who have no such capital at all and depend on selling their labour.

Table 1 shows the distribution of wealth in the 67 households of one of the main lineages.[3] I have grouped them into four quartiles of wealth (based on units of 1000 Afs. = 1 ewe or 1/10/ jerib). The wealthiest quartile owned 65 per cent of all the wealth; all had sheep and went to spring pastures, and their tents and flocks comprised the large majority of those going to the mountains. Most households in the two middle quartiles had sheep (23 out of 34) and went to spring pastures (22), while most in the poorest quartile (11 of 17) went to spring pastures though only 3 had sheep. All in the top two quartiles had land, and so did most of the third (14–17), though none of the fourth did. Altogether 47 of the 67 households had land, and holdings averaging over 20 jerib (4 hectares). 42 households had sheep, flocks averaging 111 head. Fourteen households had no capital at all, though some of them had expectations of inheriting land in due course.

There is a clear correlation of household wealth and size; but it is striking that the top two quartiles have roughly similar average holdings of irrigated land per person, while the top quartile has much larger average flocks. In flock sizes, on the other hand, the second quartile differs little from the third, which has a much lower average land holding. The main impli-

Table 1 *Household wealth and size*

Wealth quartiles	I	II	III	IV	totals
Number of households	16	17	17	17	67
Units of valley land (10 × jeribs)	5895	3180	745	0	9820
	(16)	(17)	(14)		(47)
Ewes	3560	635	414	54	4663
	(16)	(13)	(10	(3)	(42)
Total, land and ewes	9455	3815	1159	54	14483
	(16)	(17)	(17)	(3)	(53)
Household mean	591	224	68	3	216
Percentage of total wealth	65	26	8	0	99
1971 hh. (all or part) in spring pastures	16	12	10	11	49
summer pastures	11	4	1	(1)	16(+1)
Hh. with members employed outside	4	6	15	17	42
Population	217	130	109	84	540
Mean hh. size	13.6	7.7	6.4	4.9	8.1
Land per person	27	24	7	0	18
ewes per person	16	5	4	1	9

cation of this is that large-scale pastoralism is now chiefly an enterprise for the wealthy household with labour in excess of agricultural requirements; indeed, very few Madozai households now depend exclusively, or even predominantly, on pastoralism alone.

On the basis of expected income from capital holdings, households in the two wealthiest quartiles are all fundamentally self-sufficient. Such prosperous households are said to be 'full' (*sir, mor*). They are well-off and secure (*tayar*), while this is certainly not the case for many households in the third quartile and all those of the fourth, who are known as 'hungry'; other terms for households without capital are 'poor' (*khwar, gharib*) and 'light-weight' (*spak*). In fact only 25 households depend entirely on production from their own land and/or flocks, so that 42 gain some or all of their income from various kinds of employment or by engaging in small-scale trading activities.

The Madozai in many ways remain pastoralists at heart, and the pastoral sector of the subtribe economy continues to be of great importance, but it is nonetheless the case that they are basically settled, and most people spend most of the year in winter villages in the river valley. The village communities and the camps form a single arena, and political and economic decisions made in the villages, for example, over agricultural concerns, are likely to have a direct effect on relations in the pastoral arena, and vice versa. At the same time, the dual economy of the Madozai affords them a wider range of solutions to political and economic problems than those available to other local groups which are more exclusively pastoral or agricultural. The Madozai are well aware of this advantage and are likely to continue their dual economy for the foreseeable future.

The Effects of Settlement

Madozai ethnic identity as Durrani is defined principally in terms of descent and a strict ban on giving their women in marriage to non-Durrani. Within the Durrani ethnic group, on the other hand, there is no formal differentiation by descent or marriage rules. A strong egalitarian ethos pervades Durrani social organisation, corresponding with their religious ideals. No intrinsic social differences are admitted among Durranis, who are held to be equal by virtue of common descent.

For Madozai, like many Durrani in Saripul, their ability to approximate these ideals has changed dramatically in recent decades. The growing importance of the control of farmland and the expansion of local government bureaucracy have made economic and political inequality an established fact of life, both within the local communities and between the powerful khans and the ordinary tribespeople. The egalitarian ethic has been transformed into ideals of independence and self-sufficiency, adherence to which is expressed at the local level in a highly competitive form of laissez-faire capitalist political economy.

In the 1930s, when the Madozai feud occurred, the rules of tribal co-responsibility and blood compensation were still in full operation. When talking of those events today, which they do with reluctance, Madozai express a combination of regret and relief that such a succession of killings would be almost impossible now. Violence occurs, but 'there are two things the government will not tolerate now: sheep theft and homicide', and revenge killings are nowadays rare in the Saripul area.

The rights and duties involved in agnatic kinship of itself are nowadays few and rarely invoked in practice. There is a fairly strong ideal that descendants of a common ancestor should be neighbours and politically united, and the strength of this ideal is greater the closer the ancestor, but people continually express regret at the degeneration of the times, such that nowadays even one's agnates cannot be relied on, brother fights brother, father fights son — all moreover regarded as signs of the impending end of the world. It is, of course, impossible to be sure that the Saripul Durranis did not always have this attitude to agnatic relations, but some of the evidence to hand does indicate that in practice the strength of agnatic ties is not what it was.

Some reasons why this might be so have already been suggested. Increased government intervention has reduced the possibility of interethnic warfare and consequent demands for solidarity at that level. Similarly, improved security has lessened the need for migrating nomads to move together in large, lineage-based groups. Settlement, on the other hand, has deprived groups like the Madozai of the flexibility of movement and camp association which they had as nomads, and competition and conflict among close kin have intensified as a result. Finally, individual ownership of, and now pressure on, agricultural land have led to widening inequalities among close agnates and provided them with further grounds for quarrelling. Madozai families are now ruthlessly competitive with each other. The evidence indicates that this was not always so. The particular character this competition now takes among the Madozai is related to the value now set on household independence.

Madozai tribespeople are well aware of all this. They see clearly that when there was an abundance of land and pasture, 'everybody had adequate means, people had means and *qaumi* (tribal solidarity)'. Even more fundamentally, the tribespeople recognise the major difference as having come from the fact

213

of landowning itself. As one man put it, 'In the old days there were no khans and no inequality; such leaders as there were were called *malik* and were *khan bisterkhan'*, literally, khans without tablecloths; that is, wealth and lavish hospitality played no part in the relations between a leader and his followers. 'It was before the people had land,' he explained, 'and a man's opportunities were the same as his father's. Now land enters the question, and inheritance, and power and wealth pass from father to son.'

I have described elsewhere (R. Tapper 1984b) how the Nazarzai khans, having both vast land holdings and support from government, dominated the region, oppressing the local Uzbek and Aymaq population, especially after 1930. This oppression did not go unopposed, meeting a series of revolts throughout the region. Pressure on resources, and the dominant position of the Pashtun khans, focused competition and hostility generally into a common opposition to the Pashtuns on the part of the rest. Confrontations with the khans were perceived as interethnic disputes, evidence of the polarisation of Pashtuns and the rest in local political affairs.

By 1970, however, perceptions were shifting; with increasing population, scarcity of resources and the growth of material inequalities, a fourfold class structure was emerging in the region, comprising an elite, a bourgeoisie, a proletariat and an intelligentsia, which cut across ethnic divisions. The khans had a series of disputes with fellow-Pashtuns, and had been meeting resistance from their own Ishaqzai tribespeople. Violence in such cases may be perceived as part of intra-tribal, factional feuds, but the major regional conflict was increasingly recognised as oppression by Pashtun khans of non-Pashtun peasants; Pashtun peasants and nomads faced a growing contradiction between their ethnic loyalties and their class position, particularly when they found themselves liable to oppression by the khans.

In the early 1970s ethnic and tribal identity (*qaumi*) still provided the basic framework and language of social and political interaction in the region; 'class' (for which there was no term in common speech) was not explicitly recognised except by newly educated urban youth. Among Pashtun nomads and villagers, the term *wolus* (originally a Turkic term for 'people') was in constant use to describe the power of united community effort, especially against the tyranny of both khans and government, and was justified in both religious and tribal terms, in maxims such as *da wolus zur da khuday zur*, the people's power is God's power.

At that time, although neither the concept of class nor the notion of class unity were explicit in discussions of political identity and interest, nonetheless ordinary Pashtun nomads and villages were becoming aware of their economic class interests and weakening in their ethnic and tribal allegiances; class consciousness was particularly evident among those without property, who were used to travelling throughout the region as petty traders and labourers.

Whatever has happened since, or may happen in the future, the story of nomads in northern Afghanistan, particularly in the case of the Madozai, shows how little can be understood about their role in the wider society simply by assuming that their nomadism is central to their culture and identity. More important to them are pastoralism and tribalism. Settlement in villages on the one hand is little more than an alternative economic and ecological strategy of 'adaptation and response' (Salzman 1980); on the other, of itself it involves little cultural and social change, which follow only when settlement is accompanied by population pressure on resources and consequent extreme inequalities of wealth and power.

Notes

1 Studies of nomads in Afghanistan include: Ferdinand (1962, 1969), Kraus (1969), Jentsch (1973), Korgun (1973), R. Tapper (1974), Janata (1975), Glatzer (1977, 1983), Sandford (1977), Shahrani (1979), Barfield (1981), Balland (1982), Tavakolian (1984).

2 On the effect of the drought on nomads elsewhere in Afghanistan see Balland and Kieffer (1979).

3 These households were the major, and more permanent, part of the population of one of the villages; the 'sample' is skewed in favour of the better-off members of the community, in that it does not include the dozen or so transient 'client' households living in the same village and camps; but the village was not that of the 'khan' and his family, the wealthiest in the subtribe, so perhaps the sample does represent the middle range of tribespeople; and it certainly depicts a population in the process of settlement.

References

Balland D. (1982), 'Contraintes écologiques et fluctuations historiques dans l'organisation territoriale des nomades d'Afghanistan.' *Production pastorale et société*, 11, 55–67.

Balland D. and Keiffer C. (1979), 'Nomadisme et sécheresse en Afghanistan.' In Equipe écologie et anthropologie des sociétés nomades (ed.), *Pastoral Production and Society*, Cambridge University Press.

Barfield T. (1981), *The Central Asian Arabs of Afghanistan*. Austin, University of Texas Press.

Dupree L. (1973), *Afghanistan*. Princeton University Press.

Ferdinand K. (1962), 'Nomadic expansion and commerce in central Afghanistan.' *Folk*, 4, 123–59.

— (1969), 'Nomadism in Afghanistan.' In L. Foldes (ed.) *Viehwirtschaft und Hirtenkultur*, Budapest, Akademiai Kiado.

Glatzer B. (1977), *Nomaden von Gharjistan*, Wiesbaden, Steiner.

— (1983), 'Political organisation of Pashtun nomads and the state.' In R. Tapper (ed.) *The Conflict of Tribe and State in Iran and Afghanistan*, London, Croom Helm.

Janata A. (1975), 'Beitrag zur Völkerkunde Afghanistans.' *Archiv für Völkerkunde*, 29, 7–36.

Jentsch C. (1973), *Das Nomadentum in Afghanistan*, Meisenheim am Glan, Hain.

Kakar M. H. (1979), *Government and Society in Afghanistan*, Austin, University of Texas Press.

Korgun V. G. (1973), 'K voprosu o roli kochevnikov v Afganistane novoyshego vremeni', in L. M. Kulagina et al. (ed.), *Arabskie Strany, Turtsiya, Iran, Afghanistan: Istoriya., Ekonomika*, Moscow, Nauka.

Salzman P. C. (1980), 'Introduction: processes of sedentarisation as adaptation and response.' In P. C. Salzman (ed.), *When Nomads Settle*, New York, Praeger.

Sandford S. (1977), *Pastoralism and Development in Afghanistan*, London, Overseas Development Institute, Pastoral Network Paper 4b.

Shahrani M. N. (1979), *The Kirghiz and Wakhi of Afghanistan*, Seattle, Univeristy of Washington Press.

Tapper N. (1983), 'Abd al-Rahman's North-West Frontier: the Pashtun colonisation of Afghan Turkistan,' in R. Tapper (ed.), *The Conflict of Tribe and State in Iran and Afghanistan*, London, Croom Helm.

Tapper R. (1974), 'Nomadism in modern Afghanistan: asset or anachronism?' In L. Dupree and L. Albert (eds), *Afghanistan in the 1970s*, New York, Praeger.

Tapper R. (1983), 'Introduction.' In R. Tapper (ed.) *The Conflict of Tribe and State in Iran and Afghanistan*, London, Croom Helm.

Tapper R. (1984a), 'Holier than thou: Islam in three tribal socieites,' in A. S. Ahmed and D. M. Hart (eds), *Islam in Tribal Societies*, London, Routledge.

Tapper R. (1984b), 'Ethnicity and class: dimensions of inter-group conflict in Afghanistan,' in N. Shahrani and R. Canfield (eds),

Revolutions and Rebellions in Afghanistan, Berkeley, Institute for International Studies.
Tavakolian B. (1984), 'Sheikhanzai nomads and the Afghan state', in N. Shahrani and R. Canfield (eds), *Revolutions and Rebellions in Afghanistan*, Berkeley, Institute of International Studies.

12

ETHNIC GAMES IN XINJIANG: ANTHROPOLOGICAL APPROACHES

C. M. Hann

When the ethnic history of a territory is as complex as that of Xinjiang, any starting point is necessarily arbitrary. Besides, I am not a historian. Rather, my aim in the first part of this chapter is to suggest how recent anthropological discussions of 'ethnicity' might illuminate nationality relations in Xinjiang in the period before its liberation and incorporation into the People's Republic of China. I stress that this part of the chapter is all hypothesis and suggestion, based upon limited acquaintance with a small part of the secondary historical materials available to me, all of them in Western languages. The second part of the paper is based more securely upon an anthropological convention, namely, fieldwork observation. I was in Urumqi, modern capital of Xinjiang, in August 1986 for the duration of the Third National Minority Sports Meeting. This occasion, in the context of five months' continuous residence in Xinjiang, provided a good opportunity of studying a kind of modern ritual in which many anthropologists have been interested, and in particular, to consider how such rituals can help to legitimate the policies pursued towards minority groups in China today.

1. Ethnicity in the Past

Many authors who have written about Xinjiang (or Chinese Turkestan in the older designation) have offered a more or less detailed background historical outline (Lattimore 1950; Chen 1977; Rossabi 1975; Akira 1978, etc.). Since I rely on these same authors for my own understanding of earlier centuries, I shall not attempt to repeat their outlines or to reconcile them where divergences occur. I propose only some differences of interpretations in more recent times. My arbitrary baseline will be the turn of the sixteenth century. The region had come under Chinese political influence long before, but had not remained over any long period an integral part of the Chinese state. It had been influenced by an extraordinary variety of religions, among them Buddhism, Nestorian Christianity and Islam, and by a variety of tribal societies, some of which had given up pastoral nomadism in favour of a sedentary agricultural economy, particularly in the fertile oases of the Tarim Basin. It is possible that a historian might find more order in the ebb and flow of dynasties, both imperial and tribal, if he were to examine this period more closely in terms of models which anthropologists have helped to develop for other Islamic societies; but as far as I know this has not been attempted.

I shall start at the beginning of the sixteenth century because I am impressed by Geng Shimin's claim that from this date onwards we can see the Turkic speaking peoples and the Muslem religion clearly dominating other linguistic and religious identities and creating a new national identity in the Tarim Basin. As he puts it (1984, p. 13):

> By the late fifteenth century and the first half of the sixteenth, because the entire Tarim Basin was unified politically, economically, religiously, culturally and linguistically, the time was ripe for the formation of a new ethnic community, the modern Uighur nationality. At that time, after the Kashgar khanate was established, the Tarim Basin was politically unified (although it was under the feudal system) and in religion Islam had become pre-eminent everywhere south of the Tienshan. In language and script, the previous situation in which two literary languages coexisted (northern literary languages represented in Uighur script and southern literary languages written in Arabic script), gave way to the use of a single written language, modern Uighur, that is what we generally call the Chagatai Literary Language.

This argument raises the fundamental issue of what we mean by 'formation of a new ethnic community'. We may mean any number of things, but what, if anything, does ethnic identity mean to the people themselves? Usually, when we speak of an ethnic community in modern contexts, we assume a more or less strong degree of self-identification. However, in the case of this putative community of Uighurs, there is evidence to suggest that between the sixteenth and twentieth centuries no such self-consciousness existed at national level. The name itself was adopted only in the inter-war period of the twentieth century, via Turkic nationalists in Soviet Central Asia; and it was probably not a term that would receive ready acknowledgement from those to whom nationalists applied it until after 1949. Until the present century the highest level of group identity, apart from religious identity, for most purposes seems to have been a local one. The cultivators of the Tarim Basin identified with their local oasis. Some at least of the officials and landlords to whom they paid taxes were of the same 'ethnic group', and they seem to have maintained their position regardless of what was happening at more elevated levels of the political structure, if and when such levels could be identified. (Incidentally evidence from this region scarcely supports the concept of an Asiatic mode of production. Control over the waterworks essential to oasis economies was in the hands of *local* elites, and there is no evidence to suggest that, even for construction purposes, a well developed state power was a prerequisite (Toru 1978, Warikoo 1985).

Of course the Tarim Basin is not the whole of Xinjiang, and in the mountains and in Dzungaria, Turkic, Mongolian, and other groups practised a pastoral economy. However, in these cases there is perhaps even less cause to speak of emerging national identities. Separate identities clearly were maintained, although the ethnic 'boundaries' were probably permeable, enabling, for example, pastoralists who settled in an oasis to adapt the new local identity, including its speech and other cultural traits. The same might occur in the other direction. Groups thus maintained their 'objective' identities through time in specific territorial niches. This does not imply any 'subjective' loyalty to a collective identity such as we understand by the modern notion of ethnic community. On the contrary, in the oases the identity was circumscribed by the local territorial boundary, and in the mountains it was given by the genealogical structures of the 'tribe', which seldom if ever mobilised at tribal level, but regulated its affairs through comparatively small-scale descent-groups.

When we look at Xingjiang as a whole, the diversity of groups is actually greater than can be contained within any simple pastoral versus sedentary peoples' model. (In this sense the region is more complex even than the other stretches of inner Asian borders examined by Lattimore). Some smaller groups survived in local niches in the Tarim Basin even after the unification which Geng Shimin argues had taken place by the sixteenth century. Other groups appeared fresh on the scene after this date, such as the Manchu and Xibe settlers sent to the Ili Valley as garrison troops by Ching Emperors in the eighteenth century. Of particular interest are those groups which were tied not to specific tracts of territory but to particular roles in the economy. The most significant such group would appear to be the Tungans (Hui), who I would like to consider in a little more detail both because I think their role in the modern history of Xinjiang has been disproportionate to their numbers, and because they raise intriguing questions for all anthropologists concerned with ethnicity.

As far as I am aware there is no adequate modern study, anthropological or other, of China's large Han-speaking but Muslim population. In some respects neither Israeli (1980) nor Dreyer (1982), is much of an advance on Broomhall (1912), and the history of this group is still shrouded in mystery. For the same reasons given above, there must be some doubt as to the period in which it can be claimed that they came to constitute an ethnic community. It is possible that they too have obtained their collective self-consciousness only as a consequence of being treated as an ethnic group in the socialist period. For the socialist authorities, this is perhaps the preferred alternative to recognising the specifically religious aspect of Hui identity: they have sought to evade the problem of religious rights by passing the question off as an 'ethnic' one. At any rate the Hui (or Tungans as they are commonly known still in Xinjiang) clearly do not constitute the same sort of territorially based ethnic community as the Uighurs, either historically or today. They are commonly cited as an example of the power of religion as a determinant of ethnic identities, alongside such well known cases as the Serbo-Croat speaking inhabitants of Yugoslavia, who through affiliating to three distinct religions (Islam, and Orthodox and Catholic Christianity), are now recognised as belonging to three distinct ethnic groups. It has been even harder in China than in Yugoslavia to assign the groups thus demarcated to unique territorial bases. The Hui people have since 1958 had an autonomous region in Ninghsia, but even here they form less than one-third of the population. Their concentration along trading routes and in artisan and commercial occupations suggests that they might be usefully compared with other diaspora communities, for whom ethnicity is, among other things, a functional device to gain and maintain control over certain economic and political goods (Cohen 1969). Now, the expansion of this group in Xinjiang coincides roughly with the relatively stable period of the early and middle Ching when trade with metropolitan China was quite substantial (this is quite distinct from the Silk Road of old, which was already virtually defunct by this period). Later on, as this internal trade declined (to some extent it was replaced by expanded trade with the new Imperial powers of the region, Russia and Great Britain) so did the economic opportunities available to the Tungans. This may be one of the reasons which drove so many of them to seek employment instead in Warlord armies. In many of the oases of the Tarim Basin, where the Tungans had not been prominent as a trading community, they came to prominence in the late Ching and Republican periods when they were perceived as a marauding or occupying Chinese armed force, rather than as Muslim co-religionists.

The role played by these Chinese Muslims in Xinjiang is surely one of the main reasons for the political incoherence of the region in the nineteenth and early twentieth centuries, and for delays in the emergence of an Uighur nationalist movement. Islamic fundamentalism was a powerful force in the successive Khoja rebellions and again in the era of Yakub Beg. But one of the reasons why it did not leave a more profound mark upon either the political or the religious consciousness of the people was the conspicuous military presence of a Muslim group firmly identified with China and Han power.

Religion, then, was sufficient basis for the maintenance of collective identity by a diaspora trading community, in Xinjiang and elsewhere in China. But the very fact that it was the same religion as that espoused by the mass of Turkic speakers, (who were in any case divided by the cleavage between sedentary and pastoral) that prevented religion from serving to promote a territorially based national identity in Xinjiang. For the East-ernmost Turks, Karpat's (1984) stress upon the general primacy of religions identity in Central Asia thus stands in need of qualifications.

There were of course numerous other factors involved and nationalist, separatist rebellions were intermittently effective in the Republican period. The complex political background to the emergence of the Uighurs as a political entity in the twenti-eth century has recently been expertly documented by Forbes (1986), whose monograph brings the story up to 1949. Yet it is possible to suggest that the collective mobilisation of the mass of the sedentary Turkic-speaking population as Uighurs was not actually achieved until after 1949, when full political unification was again restored, anti-socialist opposition routed, and the Peoples' Liberation Army, Chinese officials, and Chi-nese controlled media all firmly established in their current positions. Perhaps only then could the masses of the putative national community of Uighurs gain ethnic self-consciousness. The second baseline might then be determined as the year 1955, when Xinjiang was given the official designation that has survived to the present day: Uighur Autonomous Region.

Let us now pause to consider which theories or types of theory can best account for the development of the Uighur national identity in modern times. Clearly both language and religion were objective features distinguishing the inhabitants of this region from neighbouring imperial powers and other groups, from the sixteenth century onwards. But neither separ-ately nor together could the factors cited by Geng Shimin in themselves create a modern consciousness of ethnic identity. Other theories (e.g., Smith 1986) which emphasise the dif-fusion of nationalist ideas from a homeland in Europe and the Mediterranean, also seem inadequate in the case of the Turkic peoples of Central Asia, who had relatively little contact even with the new nationalist government of Turkey. Karpat (1979) seems justified in stressing the extent to which the national movements of the peoples of Central Asia were *internally* gen-erated. There may, however, be considerable differences within Turkic Central Asia as a region, and in the case of the most easterly of the Turkic peoples, the diffusion of ideas from neighbouring groups to the West, encouraged by Russian and Soviet power, was perhaps decisive after all. The detailed story of how some small intellectual elites constructed a distinct 'Uighur' identity which within a few decades was adopted by the mass of the population of Xinjiang remains untold. There must be numerous individuals still alive today who could shed light on the cultural and intellectual history of the 1930s and 1940s, and there must be abundant documentary materials. However, as far as I know, no such researches have been published to date.

The same Chinese authorities who have until now been reluctant to encourage researches into the construction of the modern Uighur identity can also take much of the credit for the mass dissemination of that same identity. It seems that the power of this identity, like all ethnic identities, is fundamentally relational. The Uighur identity has grown and consolidated itself as the Chinese presence in Xinjiang has been consolidated in the socialist period. Like the minority groups of many multi-ethnic states elsewhere, the Uighurs have found that the Chinese state was concerned to rationalise and to stabilise, but not to homogenise. Such pressures as may encourage upwardly mobile Uighurs to teach their children Chinese and avoid being seen at the mosque are more than balanced by resources newly available to strengthen the collective identity. The most important are the spread of education in minority languages, and the use of those languages by the mass media, especially radio and television. It may well be true that the goal of modernisation and efficient running of the industrial state is best served by a polity in which culture and political entity are exactly congruent, as, for example in Gellner's (1983) theory of nationalism. But this should not blind us to the evidence, abundantly available in other socialist societies, and also in other kinds of social system, that the very factors which Gellner stresses, notably education and communication, may also, where there exists the political will, serve to sustain two or more separate national identities within a single polity.

It follows that my general view of Chinese policies towards ethnic minorities in the socialist period falls between the extreme positions adopted by some other observers. My own experience, admittedly restricted to five months in Urumqi, makes me equally suspicious both of eulogies of socialist policies such as those of Chen (1977) and Myrdal (1980), and of those who understand Chinese policy in terms of 'colonisation' or 'sinicisation', such as Rossabi (1975). One author who manages to avoid these extremes is Helly (1984). But her otherwise persuasive essay tends in the end to see ethnic phenomena as merely a vehicle for the expression of economic frustrations. She is surely correct (Dreyer 1976) to note the correspondence between the fluctuations in ethnic policies and fluctuations in basic political and economic strategy, 'liberal' phases being characteristic in both for much of the 1950s, again in the first half of the 1960s, and continuously since the late 1970s. But Helly does not quite clinch her argument that resistance to certain economic and political policies 'could only have taken the form of a defense of cultural difference'. The issue of *why* ethnic identities should remain important, and how the authorities have sought and continue to seek to influence these identities, raises an interesting set of problems, both in Xinjiang and in other peripheral regions of China; the second part of this paper attempts to address these problems by focusing upon a particular case-study of minorities policy.

2. Ethnicity in the Present

The official framework for the regulation of contemporary ethnic group relations in China is of course modelled substantially on the practice of the Soviet Union and, more remotely, on the writings of Lenin and Stalin. This is notwithstanding the considerable differences between the Soviet and Chinese cases (Bergere 1979). One major difference lies in the relative numerical strength of the dominant ethnic group (about 50% of the inhabitants of the USSR are Russians, compared to about 94% of Han nationality in China). Official policy declares that all ethnic groups have equal rights, which means that the Uighurs must take their position alongside fifty-five other groups in the country as a whole, of whom twelve are present in Xinjiang (they are the Han, the Kazakhs, the Mongols, the Hui, the Kirghiz, the Uzbeks, the Tadjiks, the Xibe, the Manchus, the Russians, the Daur, and the Tatars). The implications of this are obvious, in that major peoples occupying large territories and perhaps with a strong historical identity become equivalents of groups with only a few hundred scattered members and perhaps no significant collective identity at all. To

225

some extent there is an attempt to involve even quite small groups in the politico-administrative structure. Thus within the Uighur Autonomous Region there are Autonomous Counties for most of the other groups, including such small ones as the Xibe, numbering a mere 40,000 in all, and a mere 27 per cent of their own 'autonomous county' near the Soviet border.

In addition to paying careful attention to political representation and economic development, the Chinese authorities have stressed the 'preservation' of cultural identities and sought to achieve this in a variety of ways. Many activities correspond to the encouragement of 'folklore' in other modern states, and they are pursued separately for each minority. Thus the Uighurs, as a large group, have several song and dance ensembles etc. There are also special festivals, held at provincial and national levels, when the minority groups interact with each other.

The specific ethnic festival that I wish to discuss is the Ethnic Games Sports Meeting, which involves all the minority people of China, but not the Han themselves. It does not appear to have any equivalent in the USSR today, although precedents may be sought in the Central Asian Games held in Tashkent in the 1920s (Riordan 1977, pp. 80–1). The first Ethnic Games of the PRC were held not in a minority area but in Tientsin in 1953. They were revived in Hohhot, Inner Mongolia, in 1982, and the Third Games were held in the second week of August 1986 in Urumqi, the finales coinciding with the three-day Islamic holiday, the *Kurban*.

These Games were the subject of very extensive coverage in the Chinese media, and not only in media aimed at the minorities. Publicity in Xinjiang itself in the weeks preceding the Games was massive. This included newspaper articles, posters and elaborate placard displays in the capital city, and daily television programmes during the Games and over the weeks preceding them, giving information about many of the activities actually performed during the festival. The television coverage was rather good, greatly enhanced by the folklore elements present. Thus many of the sportsmen and sports-women wore traditional costumes for their displays, as well as for the opening parades. Particularly picturesque footage was obtained on rest days when the visiting minority representatives were taken on trips to the regional museum, and to mountain ranges in the vicinity of Urumqi. On the latter occasion the minority people were depicted in an appropriately idyllic rural setting, whilst the Chinese officials accompanying them wore the usual urban dress. Minority members were filmed playing traditional musical instruments and singing, while Han people looked on passively.

The Games also had a big impact on the city itself. Apart from public posters and banners, there was a good trade in souvenirs, from T-shirts to badges and commemorative postage stamps. Virtually all tourist accommodation had to be requisitioned, as, apart from the minority representatives, journalists came from all over China, and even from abroad. The regular food supply channels were disrupted, as resources were diverted to cater for the needs of the visitors.

The grand opening ceremony took place on a Sunday morning, Sunday being the day of rest for most workers. Although all tickets to the stadium were carefully allocated in advance, millions could watch at home on television. I was very lucky to obtain a ticket through the good offices of the college to which I was affiliated. This was the most explicitly political occasion of the Games, since it featured welcoming speeches from regional and national level political leaders, in addition to addresses by the organisers and sportsmen. The politicians were brief and did no more than echo the slogans visible in all quarters of the stadium, which I estimated could accommodate about ten thousand spectators. One of the most common was this: 'To develop the sports of the minority peoples is to further the prosperity of the Motherland'. The highlight of the opening ceremony was the march-past by all the representatives of the minorities, officials and sportsmen, the former mostly in cadre attire, and the latter in national costume. All were cheered, especially those who had colourful or unusual costumes, or who did demonstrations as they filed past the main stand. 'Circus' elements were also much to the fore, with acrobats and clowns mingling with the sportsmen. These all paraded according to region of origin, so that every region of the country was represented and groups were *not* formed according to strict ethnic criteria (thus even Beijing and Shanghai could send substantial delegations).

After this parade, horses and camels galloped around the track, and when the track had been cleaned up after this, the minority representatives disappeared to be followed by a mass gymnastics display. This was performed by High School students, both male and female, overwhelmingly Han children from Urumqi schools. It lasted over an hour, and was expertly executed. The discipline of the performance contrasted sharply with the more spontaneous and light-hearted elements of the march past by the minorities. For no obvious reason, small numbers of Chinese soldiers were to be seen goose-stepping up and down the stadium during this phase of the proceedings. However, the attention of most of the audience was focused on the calisthenics and on a linked display of gigantic images and slogans performed by thousands more well drilled children, seated in the stadium directly opposite the main stand which contained the visiting dignitaries and the television cameras. The precise contents of the allegorical scenes represented by the dancers and the accompanying visual images produced by the crowd deserve a separate analysis. Suffice it to say that the theme was vaguely related to the geography and history of the Xinjiang region, that the text of key slogans was given in both Chinese and Uighur, and that the climax featured all the peoples of the region joining hands in friendship. In the closing phases some of the sportsmen who had filed past earlier came back into the stadium and participated in a climactic finale; Hui dancers were particularly prominent in this finale. At the end of it all, hundreds of balloons were released, and thousands of doves swarmed confusedly over the stadium as spectators and participants left.

For ethnographic authenticity, I should perhaps add that that particular Sunday morning was the wettest and coldest of the entire summer, and, partly because I had been obliged to turn up some hours before any of these events began, a certain numbness had set in by the end. The entire opening ceremony was in fact repeated later in the week on a sunny afternoon for the benefit of the television cameras.

Over the next eight days we followed events at the main stadium, at a specially constructed hippodrome, and also every evening on the television round-up. Most of the 'sports' were, contrary to my initial expectations, not competitive sports at all, and there were very few that would be recognised internationally in, say, the modern Olympic programme. Rather, they were for the most part exhibition displays of games or activities unique to particular groups. Some would have seemed more appropriately pursued in the framework of a folk-dancing festival. They were of some aesthetic interest, but it was hard to see how they might qualify as sports. For example, there were Tibetan kite-flyers in action at the hippo-drome; unfortunately, it was a bad week for kites, as the wind was too slight. The 'circus' elements were strongly represented all week, as, for example, in the case of the Uighurs them-selves, who performed tight-rope acts and swung around a sort of maypole with colourful skirts billowing. But at the other extreme there were also many outstanding athletes demon-strating their skills. This applied particularly perhaps to the Mongolian and Uighur wrestlers, but also to some of the jock-eys in action at the hippodrome, and to some of the players of a team game which seemed to resemble rugby in certain aspects, including commitment. However, it should be noted that not even these competitive sports attracted masses of supporters into the stadium, which was sparsely populated throughout the week.

Moreover, it should be stressed how very limited the com-petitive element was. (Apparently in Hohhot in 1982 there were even fewer competitive events, the Games being almost exclusively for exhibition purposes.) Teams were formed along regional rather than ethnic lines, as in the opening march-past. Thus, for example, a Mongolian jockey who lived in Xinjiang would find himself in the Xinjiang team. Teams were recruited by the regional and county level authorities, and I was told that alongside sporting ability, there might well be a deliberate policy to favour individuals belonging to the smaller minorities of a diverse region such as Xinjiang. Although sometimes it was made clear on the occasion that all the jockeys represent-ing the Xinjiang team in a particular race were Kazakhs, or that the best Xinjiang archery squad was in fact entirely Xibe, in general in the competitive sports the emphasis in the report-ing was on the region and not the ethnic group. There was certainly no effort to mobilise ethnic supporters, and no points table was published in the local media. For local people, there-fore, comparative performance could not be assessed. A medals table was, however, published later in the English language press — see *China Sports*, November 1986.

What kind of interpretations might the anthropologist wish

to develop of the Festival thus briefly described? I would see this as a kind of modern ritual, and I believe the kind of communication achieved on such an occasion to be exceedingly complex, and not reducible to any simple intellectual statement. In the words of one anthropologist who has recently attempted to set forward a general theory of ritual communication, all ritual is both *statement* and *action;* it *does* things that a purely intellectual summary of its contents and their meaning cannot fully grasp (Bloch, 1986). In these Games there are important elements of humour and 'circus', of celebration and pageantry, of admiration for physical prowess, and of aesthetic stimulus, all of which has some bearing on what is ultimately communicated about the dignity of minority groups and the legitimacy of current policies towards them. I do not wish to underestimate the importance of these various elements for many of the participants and spectators. Ironically, they may have greater force for those who watched on television, for the Games were, on the whole, skilfully packaged by the media. It seemed to me that the television coverage gave the impression of rather more zest and enthusiasm than was actually evident to live spectators. The pageantry was real enough, but those who were present could see that it was also very well organised, and that even the 'spontaneous' parts were subject to an overall discipline. Therefore I propose to concentrate on the 'message' that the state goes to such trouble to put across on this occasion, and to consider how successfully it is received by one part of the intended audience.

The overriding message would seem to be that the state is doing well by its minority groups, that it is tolerant of cultural differences and, while wishing to *integrate* its minorities into an overall socialist polity, has no intention of *assimilating* them as Hans. It seems clear that the 'integrative' function remains central, as it was in similar festivals in the Soviet Union in the past. Simply through holding such festivals and giving them such publicity, in both minority and metropolitan Han regions, the authorities are showing all concerned that they are pursuing a coherent and apparently liberal set of policies. They have also managed to impress many overseas observers, including the International Olympic Association. For the minorities, their participation is a reminder of the diversity of ethnic groups over the whole country, of their equal status in the socialist

230

polity and of the *small size*, even of the largest groups, when compared to the Han. If these points were not obvious enough through the Festival's mere existence, they are driven home by the political speeches, commentaries in the media and ubiquitous slogans. It is of course extremely difficult to estimate the general effects on participants and spectators; but from conversations with Uighurs in Urumqi, I am inclined to think that these officially initiated rituals have to a significant degree been accepted (Lane 1984, p. 216). All citizens are well aware of the improvement that has taken place since the end of the Cultural Revolution, both as far as minority rights are concerned and in so many other aspects of life. The fact that planning has already begun for the next Minority Games, to be held in Nanning in 1990, encourages people to believe that the present liberal interpretation of minorities policy will not be reversed.

Of course many other states, both socialist and non-socialist, have sought to deal with minority problems by permitting diversity in cultural expression, so long as this does not lead to political nationalism and separatism. And many other states have found that it is in practice extremely difficult to keep these areas firmly apart. Few states have gone further than socialist regimes in their efforts to develop the 'folklore' of ethnic groups, and to concentrate the energies of intellectuals on these matters rather than elsewhere. This has often involved official support for intellectuals who, in the absence of a high culture inherited from the past, had a great deal to do before the essence of a national culture could be distilled from a folk culture. To some extent this was true also for the Uighurs. The details of the search for the 'authentic' national culture varied from place to place, and the extent to which the ethnographers, linguists and others had themselves to influence (or invent) key contents also varied. However, even when the 'folk traditions' made sacred in the new national identity are better recognised as 'fakelore' (Dorson 1976), this does not essentially alter the problem. From an anthropological point of view, the past is *always* more or less imaginatively reinterpreted by the present, and certainly there is no such thing as 'objective authenticity' for the elites who manipulate the identities of modern nations. In China today the authorities, with their monopoly control over the media, over all educational institutions, and all publishing, are in a strong position to do exactly this. For example, apart from the Festival discussed here, they have published long inventories of 'minority games'. Some of these, such as Tibetan kite flying, and Uighur tight-rope walking, might seem 'objectively' to outside observers to have a longer history in Chinese society than in any minority society, yet they are now espoused by many Tibetans and Uighurs themselves as 'national' sports. All this is part of the process of constructing the sort of national identities which the modern socialist polity can contain without difficulty. The authorities must be hoping to *confine* ethnic consciousness to the realm of folklore. They wish to encourage such activities as colourful reminders of a group's history, which do not hinder its integration in the present.

The reasons for concentrating on sports, within the wider field of cultural policy, are of additional interest. As Riordan (1977) has shown, other socialist societies too have stressed the role of sport in modernisation processes, and this is presumably at least part of the import of the slogan quoted earlier. This echoes a slogan current generally in the PRC in recent years, asserting the need to maintain personal physical fitness in order to help to achieve the 'four modernisations'. Certainly the emphasis on mass sports has been very strong. Sport may have been encouraged for this kind of 'disciplinary' reason, as in modernisation movements associated with national sentiment in certain Western countries in the nineteenth century (Germany, Czechoslovakia); or it may have been encouraged as an obviously 'apolitical' activity, to absorb energies that might otherwise have been expended in social conflicts (in a separate paper I have considered some significant changes of emphasis in this field in China in recent years). However, it would appear that the actual physical elements of sport (i.e., fitness) and the degree of competition which enables sport to play its energy-absorbing role in many mass societies, are both largely missing in the case of the Ethnic Games. A nearer parallel might be with the Highland Games in Scotland, although the main national cultural celebration of the Scots also features an individual competitiveness that many Chinese would still consider unhealthy.

I am suggesting that, firstly, many of the activities which take place in the Ethnic Games are products of deliberate official policies to see all minority groups equipped with distinguishing features in specific areas of 'folklore'. Secondly, there are probably particular reasons why socialist states should stress the area of games and sport, even though in this context the Ethnic Games have to be largely divorced from 'sport' proper, i.e., from the development of standardised competitive sports involving individuals, teams and nations in the modern world. Here I think that from the point of view of the authorities, several dangers arise. For some well educated members of the minorities, and possibly for larger numbers, the Ethnic Games may be highlighting the gap between 'traditional' sports and the sporting life of the modern world, in which, as the national media emphasise with their usual efficiency, China is nowadays determined to rank among the best (witness the tremendous interest in the Asian Games, held later in 1986 in South Korea, and the great fear of defeat at the hands of smaller rivals such as South Korea or Hong Kong).

For other minority spectators the Ethnic Games have less value than, say, a concert of folk music at the provincial theatre, in terms of raising the status of the group and its traditional culture. An Eisteddfod is worth more than a non-competitive Highland Games. There is a danger that the Games will emphasise primitiveness, for example, for urban members of a group such as the Kazakhs, whose traditional sports all involve rather dirty animals. There is a further danger that games will trivialise the national identity, as with the 'circus' and 'children's playground' elements.

Above all, however, there is frustration that so few genuine competitive elements are allowed, whereas everybody knows that these dominate sporting events in the modern world. As indicated above, the authorities are careful to prevent the kind of competition that might intensify rivalries between groups, and encourage disruptive 'minority' patriotism; although the number of competitive events has risen steadily, these are decided between regions rather than groups, and the Hans themselves are not present at all. Yet this is the opportunity that several Uighurs told me they would most like to see: pure Uighur teams, rather than Xinjiang teams of multi-ethnic composition and invariably, outside the special Festivals, including Han. These would then take on other ethnic teams, including the Han, and prove by defeating them the worth of their own group. Needless to say, football is nowadays the most popular sport in Xinjiang. It may be reassuring to read in Uighur language inventories of minority sports that soccer was invented in Kashgar around the eleventh century (Chinese sources claim a much older Chinese ancestry, of course; I wonder how many other nations, in addition to the English, believe sincerely that *they* gave this game to the world!). But what the Uighurs would really like, they said, was to be allowed to form their own teams, and, having proved they were the best in China, then go on to represent the whole country in international competitions. They also rejoiced in the fact that the best table-tennis player in Xinjiang was no longer a Han but an Uighur: beating the Chinese at their own traditional game!

Thus some Uighurs are not satisfied with the sort of cultural distinguishing traits that are encouraged at present, but would prefer to see *more* standardisation in this area of culture, and the chance to demonstrate their commitment to their group by supporting it in open competition against all-comers. This would be nearer to collective mobilisation than the Ethnic Games framework permits, but it would still fall far short of political separatism. One wonders if at some stage the tolerance of the authorities might be pushed this far: the experience of the USSR, which has long since gone further in this direction, may again be instructive. In the meantime, I suggest that the Ethnic Games are astutely 'packaged' and will remain effective, both in contributing to the maintenance of minority identities still rather recently acquired, and in convincing most minority group members of the relatively benign intentions of the Han-dominated centre. Having brought minorities such as the Uighurs to full collective self-realisation after 1949, the socialist authorities in China are now, after deviations under Mao that are now explicitly condemned, pursuing integrative rather than assimilationist policies. They are no longer aiming at the elimination of cultural diversity, but it may be in their own interests not to attempt to confine these separate identities too restrictively to the realm of 'folklore. In historical perspective it could be argued that China has come full circle, since the policies of the early imperial dynasties also aimed at a looser sort of 'pluralism' (Dreyer 1976, p. 12). If 'pluralist' trends continue in the contemporary political economy of

China, such that, for example, small groups of Uighurs can travel freely between major cities and form a trading diaspora specialised in the currency Black Market, then familiar anthropological approaches to ethnicity will remain useful.

Bibliography

Akira, Henada (1978), 'Introduction to special issue on Historical Studies on Central Asia in Japan', *Acta Asiatica*, No. 34, pp. 1–21.

Aubin, Francoise (1983), 'Islam et sinocentrisme: La Chine, Terre d'Islam', in *L'Islam de la seconde expansion: Actes du Colloque tenu au College de France a Paris les 27 et 28 mars 1981*, Paris pp. 235–94.

Bergere, Marie-Claire (1979), 'L'influence du modele sovietique sur la politique des minorites nationales en Chine: le cas du Sinkiang (1949–1962)', *Revue Francaise de Science Politique*, Vol. 29, No. 3, pp. 402–25.

Bloch, Maurice (1986), *From Blessing to Violence*, Cambridge University Press.

Broomhall, Marshall (1910), *Islam in China: a Neglected Problem*, London: Morgan Scott.

Chen, Jack (1977) *The Sinkiang Story*, New York: Macmillan.

Cohen, Abner (1969), *Custom and Politics in Urban Africa*, London:

Dorson, Richard M. (1976), *Folklore and Fakelore*, Cambridge Mass.: Harvard University Press.

Dreyer, June Teufel (1976), *China's Fifty Millions. Minority Nationalities and National Integration in the People's Republic of China*, Cambridge Mass.: Harvard University Press.

Dreyer, June Teufel (1982), 'The Islamic Community of China', *Central Asian Survey*, Vol. I, Nos. 2–3, pp. 31–60.

Fletcher, Joseph (1968), 'China and Central Asia', in John K. Fairbank (ed.) *The Chinese World Order* Cambridge, Mass.: Harvard University Press, pp. 206–24.

Forbes, Andrew D. W. (1986), *Warlords and Muslims in Chinese Central Asia. A political history of Republican Xinjiang 1911–1949*, Cambridge University Press.

Gellner, Ernest (1983), *Nations and Nationalism*, Oxford: Blackwell.

Geng Shimin (1984), 'On the Fusion of Nationalities in the Tarim Basin and the Formation of the Modern Uighur Nationality', *Central Asian Survey*, Vol. 3, No. 4, pp. 1–14.

Helly, Denise (1984), 'The Identity and Nationality Problem in Chinese Central Asia', *Central Asian Survey*, Vol. 3, No. 3, pp. 99–108.

Israeli, Raphael (1980), *Muslims in China. A Study in Cultural Confrontation*, London (and Malmo): The Curzon Press.

Karpat, Kemal (1979), 'The Turkic Nationalities: Turkish-Soviet and Turkish-Chinese Relations', in William O. McCagg Jr. and Brian D. Silver (eds.), *Soviet Asian Ethnic Frontiers*, New York: Pergamon Press, pp. 117–144.

Karpat, Kemal (1984), 'Introduction: Opening Remarks' (to special issue Focus on Central Asian Identity), *Central Asian Survey*, Vol 3, No. 3, pp. 3–13.

Lane, Christel (1984), 'Legitimacy and Power in the Soviet Union through Socialist Ritual', *British Journal of Political Science*, Vol. 14, No. pp. 207–217.

Lattimore, Owen (1950), *Pivot of Asia*, Boston: Little, Brown.

Lattimore, Owen (1962), *Studies in Frontier History*, London:

Myrdal, Jan (1980), *The Silk Road: a journey from the High Pamirs and Ili through Sinkiang and Kansu*, London: Gollancz.

Riordan, James (1977), *Sport in Soviet Society*, Cambridge University Press.

Rossabi, Morris(1975), *China and Inner Asia from 1368 to the present day*, London: Thames and Hudson.

Smith, Anthony D. (1986), *The Ethnic Origins of Nations*, Oxford: Blackwell.

Toru, Saguchi (1978), 'Kashgaria' *Acta Asiatica* No. 34, pp. 61–78.

Warikoo, K. B. (1985), 'Chinese Turkestan during the Nineteenth Century: A Socio-Economic Study', *Central Asian Survey*, Vol. 4, No. 3, pp. 75–114.

13

CONTINUITY AND MODERNITY IN THE COSTUME OF THE MUSLIMS OF CENTRAL ASIA

Jennifer M. Scarce

The Oriental only here to be met with in his original purity and peculiarity, is fond of the Tchakhtchukh or rustling tone of the dress. It was always an object of great delight to me to see the seller parading up and down a few paces in the new Tchapan [dress], to ascertain whether it gave out the orthodox tone. All is the produce of home manufacture, and very cheap; consequently it is in the clothes market of Bokhara that 'believers' even from remote parts of Tartary, provide themselves with fashionable attire. Even the Kirghis, Kiptchak and Kalmaks are in the habit of making excursions hither from the desert, and the wild Tartar, with his eyes oblique and chin prominent, laughs for joy when he exchanges his clothes, made of the undressed horse-skins, for a light yetkey [a sort of sommer dress] for it is here that he sees his highest ideal of civilisation. Bokhara is his Paris or his London.[1]

Arminus Vambery travelled to Central Asia in 1863 ostensibly to investigate the relationship of Hungarian with the many languages spoken there. Disguised as a dervish, one of his most rewarding activities was to explore the thriving bazaars of the main cities, which gave him excellent opportunities to observe and assess the attitudes of the people, their relationships with each other, their social habits, their dress and shoppig preferences and the state of local trade. His description quoted here, despite its wayward turn of phrase, both captures the bazaar's atmosphere and the delight of a satisfied customer with his new coat, and also makes it clear how important Bokhara was to a wide shopping area. Here it was continuing its traditional role as a commerical city strategically located with Merv and Samarkand along the Central Asian section of the ancient Silk Road linking the West with China.

Today, while fashions have naturally changed, striking and distinctive clothes are still worn by the indigenous peoples of the five Central Asian Republics of the USSR which, in addition to their physical features, make them readily distinguishable from immigrants of the western Republics. The psychology of costume is complex, requiring constant and patient questioning which may lead to often conflicting answers. Costume is a major contributory factor in a first impression of the wearer's character, in which colour and quality of fabric, style, cut and condition of garments, proportion of accessories and jewellery, and harmony of total appearance, all give valuable information. Pride in maintaining a well-groomed appearance and self-respect are closely linked. Costume may be used as a visible means of demonstrating an individual's role within both family and social group. A Türkmen girl, for example, wears different accessories from those of a married woman. In the official sumptuary regulations authorised by the Manchu Emperor of China, Qianlong, in 1759, instructions are given regarding the colours and decoration of the costumes of the civil and military hierarchies, and of the wives and concubines of the Emperor and princes according to their rank. Wealth may be advertised lavishly through the use of expensive fabrics and jewellery or discreetly through costly yet sober materials. The wearing of a costume associated with ethnic and national identity has overtly political overtones in that it may indicate a desire for independence or at least recognition.[2]

A range of historical and cultural factors makes the area of Central Asia formerly the Russian Turkestan and now corresponding to the five Soviet Socialist Republics of Uzbekistan, Turkmenistan, Tajikistan, Kazakhstan and Kirghizia, rewarding to a costume historian. Geographically the area defies tidy definition as it is an immense land mass of great strategic and commercial importance without precise boundaries except those formed by mountain ranges and deserts. The area is characterised by a bewilderingly complex population mosaic in which settled townspeople intermingle with originally nomadic groups who arrived in successive waves from the eighth century BC onwards. This has resulted in a rich mixture of languages, including Arabic, Turkish, Persian and Mongolian dialects, and of religious traditions such as Christianity, Judaism, Buddhism, Islam and Shamanism. Culturally there are links with North-east Iran, Afghanistan and the area corresponding to Chinese Turkestan, resulting in further enriching influences.

It is clear that an attempt to trace and evaluate the costume traditions of an area of such extent would at best result in shallow generalisation and at worst in inaccuracy. It is therefore more sensible within the confines of the present study to concentrate on one region, and here, for several reasons, that included within the modern Republic of Uzbekistan is a practical choice. The region has a strong historical identity, as it has been successively involved in the mainstream events of both Central Asia, Iran and Russia. The area corresponding to Khawarizm (Khiva) and Transoxiana roughly extends through North-east Iran, Western Afghanistan and Uzbekistan with cities at Herat, Bokhara and Samarkand. It witnessed the rise of major powers. The Samanids (819–1005) ruling from their capital at Bokhara sponsored both traditional Arabic learning and the revival of Persian language and literature. Later the Timurids (1370–1506), who claimed descent from Chingis Khan, made Transoxiana the base of a great steppe empire remarkable for the development of the cities of Herat and Samarkand, where today the splendid tile-decorated mosques, medressehs, and mausolea of the fifteenth century rulers who patronised arts and scholarship may still be seen.

Historical and demographic changes in the fifteenth century are significant because they have determined the present-day ethnic pattern of Uzbekistan. They are also revealing of the complex nature of the movements of peoples across Central Asia resulting from the incursions of Chingis Khan's Mongols in the thirteenth century. After his death his territories were divided among his sons. Here the descendants of his son Jochi, who inherited the region of Transoxiana, established themselves and their followers as Khans in Bokhara and Khiva. Another group of descendants, the Shaybanids or Uzbeks, who became converts to Sunni Islam, settled in the fifteenth century in Khiva and Transoxiana, steadily ousting the Timurids. In 1447 the Uzbek leader Abu'l Khayr took Khiva and by 1500 his grandson Muhammad Shaybani had conquered all of Transoxiana, and had established himself at Bokhara. The Uzbek rulers impinged on the affairs of neighbouring Iran under Safavid control (1501–1732) as they constantly threatened the eastern border cities during the sixteenth and seventeenth centuries. Uzbeks contined to dominate in Khiva and Transoxiana throughout the seventeenth to the nineteenth centuries with three Emirates based at Khiva, Bokhara and Kokand. With the Russian conquest of Tashkent in 1865, Bokhara in 1868 and Kokand in 1876, these territories were absorbed into the General Governorate of Turkestan.

Uzbekistan's historical, commercial and cultural prominence has resulted in the accumulation of a varied and adequately documented repertoire of source materials which may be used for the study of costume. Garments, dating mainly from the nineteenth century onwards, have been preserved either from the wardrobes of the Emirs whose palaces have now been converted into museums, or from ethnological expeditions both Russian and European.[3] On a more modest scale, clothing acquired during visits to Central Asia by civil and military officials of the British Administration in India has also found its way as donations into museum collections.[4] The information provided by examinations of surviving garments is supplemented by pictorial sources. Fresco paintings range in date from the seventh to the ninth centuries from the sites of the city of Panjikent, capital of the Sogdian kingdom, located forty miles east of Samarkand (and now in the Republic of Tajikistan) and of the temples in Chinese Turkestan, enable enlightening parallels to be traced in both type and fabric of garments. An interesting group of later pictorial source material consists of single-figure drawings of Central Asian warriors and prisoners by Iranian artists.[5] These are haphazardly identified as Uzbek, Türkmen and Mongol subjects and are mainly of sixteenth and seventeenth century date. This is significant because the Uzbeks of Transoxiana were a constant menace to the Safavid rulers of Iran during these centuries. Shah Isma'il (1501–24) killed the Uzbek ruler Kochkunju in 1510 and captured the cities of Herat and Merv. This success was temporary, however, as the Uzbeks mounted five assaults during the reign of his son Shah Tahmasp (1524–76) and took

Meshed in 1528 and recaptured Herat. The situation was reversed by Shah Abbass (1588–1629) who took Meshed and Herat again in 1598. During the early seventeenth century, however, Imam Kuli Khan the Uzbek Emir of Bokhara (1611–41) constantly harrassed the Iranians by his raids into their lands. All this contact indicates that the appearance of both Uzbeks and other inhabitants of their territories was familiar enough to be recorded by Iranian artists. By the late nineteenth century the traditional costumes of Uzbekistan were being recorded in photography, which added new dimensions of detail and accuracy. Here one of the most informative collections of photographs are those illustrating the account of Hugues Krafft, who visited Bokhara, Samarkand, Fergana in the last decade of the century. His sepia-tinted photographs of Uzbeks, Tajiks, Sarts and Jews are sensitive compositions full of costume detail.[6] His text is but one in a long tradition of accounts compiled by Europeans who passed through Uzbekistan attracted by the prospects of trade with Bokhara and Samarkand, involved in political intelligence work, and later after the Russian conquest working on scientific and exploratory expeditions. Among the most revealing of social customs and therefore of clothing traditions are the accounts of the Venetian merchant Marco Polo in the thirteenth century, of the Scot, Alexander Burnes, a Political Officer of the East India Company who travelled from India through Afghanistan and Central Asia to the Caspian shores of Iran in 1831 and 1832, of Arminius Vambery in 1863, and of two scientists — the Danish ethnographer Axel Olufsen and the British geographer W. Rickmers who travelled in the 1890s.

The fresco paintings which were recovered from Panjikent and the rock temples of Chinese Turkestan illustrate narrative scenes of rulers and courtiers, and deities of the Nestorian Christian and Buddhist pantheons. While these are clearly not specific to Uzbekistan, the costumes are relevant to this study because they depict certain features of shape, proportion and decoration which may, for example, be traced in the nineteenth century costumes of Bokhara and Samarkand. In one of the frescoes from Panjikent seated women are shown in long-sleeved close-fitting robes and with long hair braided into multiple plaits arrayed over their shoulders and backs — a fashion which has survived among Uzbek girls.[7] A Sogdian mural painting of seventh and ninth-century date recovered from Samarkand portrays the local ruler Vargoman wearing a long full coat boldly patterned with large bird and floral motifs within a curved lattice framework.[8] Comparable treatment of men's and women's costume is seen in the frescoes of Chinese Turkestan. A procession of warriors painted in a cave at Kizil of early seventh-century[9] date shows them wearing loose trousers tucked into high-heeled calf-length boots and knee-length belted coats with tight long sleeves and deep collars. Fabrics used are either plain in a shade of beige and blue, or patterned — for example in dark blue with boldly contrasting circular medalliions in white. All the coats, whether plain or patterned, are edged with deep borders at hem, front and cuffs in contrasting colours figured with a continuous guilloche scroll. The total effect may be compared with that of the rich costumes recorded in the photographs of the Emir of Bokhara and his court at New Year festivals in the nineteenth century. Women's costumes are recorded in a figure of a worshipper from the Nestorian temple at Khocho[10] and in an image of the goddess Hariti[11] from Yarkhoto both of ninth-century date. They wear long robes of ample cut. The worshipper also wears a calf-length pleated robe with long sleeves covering her hands. Her hair is smoothed back from the forehead and twisted into braids which fall over the shoulders and back. Hariti's robe is of red fabric patterned with repeated lozenge motifs in yellow. A red scarf is modestly draped over her head.

The custom of wearing lavish and ostentatious garments continued and is recorded vividly by Marco Polo in the late thirteenth-century during his visit to the court of the Mongol ruler Qubilay Khan at his winter capital of Khan Baliq (Beijing). His account is the more interesting because it provides some information about the occasions on which certain garments were worn, notably at the festivities celebrating the Great Khan's birthday and the beginning of each of the thirteen months of the lunar year.

On his birthday he dons a magnificent robe of beaten gold. And fully 12,000 barons and knights robe themselves with him in a similar colour and style, in cloth of silk and gold, and all with gold belts. These robes are given to them by the Great Khan. And I assure you that the value of some of these robes, reckoning the precious stones and pearls with which they are often adorned, amounts to 10,000 golden bezants. Of such there are not a few. And you must know that the Great Khan gives rich robes to these 12,000 barons and knights thirteen times a year, so that they are all dressed in robes like his own and of great value. You can see for yourselves that this is no light matter, and that there is no other prince in the world besides himself who could bear such an expense.

Next let me tell you that the Great Khan has ordained thirteen feasts, one for each of the thirteen lunar months, which are attended by the 12,000 barons called *Keshikten*, that it to say the henchmen most closely attached to the Khan. To each of these he has given thirteen robes, every one of a different colour. They are splendidly adorned with pearls and gems and other ornaments and are of immense value. He has also given to each of the 12,000 a gold belt of great beauty and price, and shoes of fine leather (called *canaut* or *borgal*) cunningly embroidered with silver thread, which are likewise beautiful and costly. All their attire is so gorgeous and so stately that when they are fully robed any one of them might pass for a king. One of these robes is appointed to be worn at each of the thirteen feasts. The Great Khan himself has thirteen similar robes — similar, that is, in colour, but more splendid and costly and more richly adorned; and he always dresses in the same colour as his barons.[12]

Again the parallel with festivities at the courts of the Muslin Emirs of nineteenth-century Bokhara are significant.

By the sixteenth-century a more functional style of clothing other than the elaborate robes worn for the ceremonies is seen in the drawings by Iranian artists of Uzbeks and Türkmen. They range from subtle portraits of Uzbek rulers and noblemen to spirited and humorous studies of warriors and prisoners taken in the border warfare between the Safavids and Uzbeks of Transoxiana. A late sixteenth-century study of the Shaybanid ruler, Abdallah Khan, painted at Bokhara, who added

243

Balkh, Tashkent and Fergana to his realm, clearly shows the main features of the costume.[13] Abdallah Khan is portrayed as a plump middle-aged man seated eating a melon. He wears red trousers tucked into knee high cuban-heeled leather boots. His ankle length robe is buttoned from a close-fitting collar to the waist and has long sleeves. The clear pink of its plain fabric reveals a taste for strong colour which continues into nineteenth-century costume. A narrow fabric girdle is wound around the waist and knotted at the front. His headdress is distinctive, consisting of a full broad white pleated turban coiled so that it is patterned and protrudes as a fan-shaped cockade. The artist had also clearly interpreted the physical features characteristic of Uzbeks, of narrow eyes under finely arched brows set in a broad face and a scanty moustache and beard barely covering the chin. Another portrait of an Uzbek notable attributed to the artist Shaykh Muhammad and dated to c. 1557, shows costume variations.[14] Here the boots are thrust into cuban-heeled shoes, a feature much commented on by later observers. He also wears two garments, a long-sleeved under-robe and a coat comparable to that of Abdallah Khan, but with short sleeves. Otherwise, accessories such as the fabric girdle and the coiled white turban are similar.

Studies of warriors taken as prisoners usually show them seated dejectedly, often with neck and one hand cramped into a wooden yoke.[15] Their costumes are made up of either a plain coat with exaggeratedly long sleeves which fall in puckered creases around the wrists or a combination of a patterned long-sleeved robe covered by a plain coat with elbow-length sleeves. Long pleated sashes are wound round the waists. Head dresses show a variant of the full wide turban coiled around a quilted cap. Cuban-heeled boots are worn either alone or thrust into overshoes. The evidence for the costumes of Uzbek women at this period is more limited, as, following traditional Muslim social custom, their lives were segregated from public view. They also would not seem to have been among the prisoners taken in Iranian campaigns. The subjects of a few paintings, however, may be identified tentatively as Uzbeks. One example painted by Mahmud in the style of the Bokhara school dated to c. 1550 shows two well-dressed young women.[16] They are short, with compact figures and broad faces. Their costume consists of a series of layered garments beginning with an ankle-length plain dress with long tight sleeves covered by a second knee-length robe with loose short sleeves. Over all is draped a luxurious coat of fur-lined brocade. The main fabric is patterned with a bold repeated floral scroll, while the deep borders of the hem and wide sleeves are in a dark colour ornamented with a continuous band of spiralling motifs. The women's jewellery has interesting parallels with surviving examples of the type worn by Uzbek and Türkmen women. A heavy necklace is conspicuous for a central heart-shaped pendant flanked on each side by three large circular discs — all made of metal. High curved tiaras cover dark hair parted in the centre and pulled back and braided into plaits. Cosmetics are used to emphasise the slanting eyes and wide cheeks, as brows are plucked and drawn into fine arched shapes, and black spots are painted on forehead and chin.

During the nineteenth-century a more fully-developed interpretation of Uzbek costume can be formed. Features which have evolved and survived from the past can be understood in the context of better documented source materials in which written and pictorial evidence is supplemented by surviving garments. One of the most enlightening and well documented accounts for the early nineteenth-century is the report which Alexander Burnes wrote of his visit of 1813–2. Energetic and observant, he noted the costumes at various levels of society. He writes of Uzbek men:

> The stranger beholds in the bazars a portly, fair and well-dressed mass of people, the Mahommedans of Turkestan. A large white turban, and a 'chogha' or pelisse of some dark colour over three or four others of the same description, is the general costume, but the Registan leads to the palace, and the Uzbeks delight to appear before their king in a mottled garment of silk called 'udrus' made of the brightest colours, and which would be intolerable to any but an Uzbek. Some of the highest persons are clothed in brocade, and one may distinguish the gradations of the chiefs since those in favour ride into the citadel and the others dismount at the gate.
>
> A great portion of the people of Bokhara appear on horseback, but whether mounted or on foot, they are

dressed in boots, and the pedestrians strut on high and small heels, in which it was difficult for me to walk or even stand. They are about an inch and a half high, and the pinnacle is not one third the diameter. This is the national dress of the Uzbeks. Some men of rank have a shoe over the boots, which is taken off on entering a room.[17]

He further notes of the Emir's retinue

Most of them were dressed in robes of Russian brocade and wore gold ornamented swords — I should well call them knives — the mark of distinction in this country.[18]

These descriptions reveal several interesting points, namely, the continued wearing of the plain robes, boots and white turbans as observed in sixteenth-century paintings, and of brocaded robes such as were recorded by Marco Polo in the thirteenth-century. Burnes is, however, able to provide valuable information about the range of textiles used, which he further supplements in his notes on the trade and products of Bokhara which was still an important commercial city.

He discusses the silks:

I shall next notice the exports of Bokhara; and these are far from inconsiderable, since it has silk, cotton, and wool. The silk of Bokhara is chiefly produced on the banks of the Oxus, where the mulberry thrives luxuriantly, and nearly all the Toorkmans are engaged in rearing silk-worms during the months of summer. It is exported in considerable quantities to Cabool, and even finds its way to India. At Bokhara it varies in price from nine to ten tillas for eight English lbs. The silk is wound and manufactured at Bokhara into a stuff called 'udrus' of a mottled colour — red, white, green and yellow — which is the most fashionable and expensive kind of dress in Toorkistan. It sells from one half to one and half tillas per piece of eight yards long and a foot broad. It is worn by the Mervees, now settled in Bokhara, but it is not exported.[19]

This is clearly a reference to the silks brilliantly patterned in the warp 'ikat' technique. Here the vertical warp threads are tie-dyed in successive stages in bright colours before they are

246

strung on to the loom. The weaving of the weft threads serves both to create the fabric and consolidate the pattern. In this technique designs are bold, relying on striking combinations of colour and large splashed motifs.

Further notes indicate that a busy textile trade flourished with both Russia and India whose products are used in Uzbek costume:

> The staple commodity of Russian manufacture exported to this country is nankeen; it is seldom of a white colour for they have imitated the patterns of this country, which are striped and dark. The article sells for 1½ tillas per piece of forty yards; it is in general use among the people for their pelisses or 'chupkuns'. I had at first imagined that it was a Chinese import; but it is brought by the Russian caravans and sent as far as Cabool, and even India. I have seen it at Lahore.
>
> Velvet is brought into Bokhara from Russia; it is flowered cotton velvet, and about two feet broad. There is a demand for it, and it is not imported from India.[20]

> The demand for Indian goods in Bokhara is steady. Dacca muslins of the larger sort sell for twenty tillas per score, the smaller being half the price. These are about five hundred pieces of Benares brocade (kincob) imported yearly; that from Guzerat is too expensive. The whole of the natives of Bokhara and Toorkistan wear turbans of white cloth which are imported from the Punjab; they are about thirty yards long and a foot broad; and sell for a tilla each; they are in universal use among both sexes, and might be manufactured in Europe, and sent with advantage into Toorkistan.[21]

He also discusses the import of cotton chintzes, English broadcloth via Russia and dyestuffs such as Russian cochineal and Indian indigo, indicating that Bokhara's markets would be opened more to British trade if a more determined effort was made to increase demand by designing to local taste.

Women's costume continued to be less accessible, especially to a European traveller, but Burnes did his best to describe at least the general appearance.

The ladies of Bokhara stain their teeth quite black, they braid their hair, and allow it to hang in tresses down their shoulders. Their dress differs little from the men; they wear the same pelisses, only that the two sleeves, instead of being used as such, are tucked together and behind. In the house even they dress in huge hessian boots made of velvet and highly ornamented. What a strange taste for those who are ever concealed, to choose to be thus booted as if prepared for a journey. On the head they wear large white turbans, but a veil covers the face, and many a lovely countenance is born to blush unseen. The exhibition of beauty, in which so much of a woman's time is spent in more favoured countries, is here unknown.[22]

The account of Arminius Vambery, who was travelling in Bokhara in 1863 — thirty years after Burnes, is significant for his observations on the fabrics used. In the bazaar at Bokhara, for example, it is clear that among the local textiles are also products of both Russia and Britain, indicating that a successful attempt had been made to penetrate this lucrative market.

I kept close to my companions, casting as I passed glances at the booths, which contain, with a few articles from the other countries in Europe, fancy goods and merchandise, more especially of Russian manufacture. There have no particular intrinsic attractions in themselves for a European traveller to this remote city; but they interest him nevertheless, for each piece of calico, each ticket attached to it, identifying the origin with the name of the manufacturer, makes him feel as if he has met a countryman. Here my heart beat when I read the words 'Manchester' and 'Birmingham', and how apprehensive I was of betraying myself by an imprudent exclamation. There are very few large warehouses or wholesale dealers, and in spite of cotton, calico, and fine muslin being sold, not only in the Restei Tchit Furushi (the place where cotton is exposed for sale) which has 284 shops, but also in many other places in the city, I might boldly affirm that my friends 'Hanhart and Company' in Tabriz, dispose alone of as much of the articles above named as the whole city of Bokhara in spite of the latter being denominated the capital of Central Asia. That department in its bazaar has more interest for the stranger where he sees spread out before him the products of Asiatic soil and native industry; such, for instance, as that cotton stuff named Aladja, which had narrow stripes of two colours, and a fine texture; different sorts of silken manufactures from the fine handkerchief of the consistence of the spider's web to the heavy Atres; but particularly manufactures of leather.[23]

He also makes some interesting points on the giving of lavish robes as presents a custom which had survived since the time of Marco Polo.

I had almost forgotten to mention that the Yasaul led me to the treasurer to receive the sum for my daily board. My claim was soon settled; but this personage was engaged in so singular an occupation that I must not omit to particularise it. He was assorting the Khilat (robes of honour) which were to be sent to the camp, to reward those who had distinguished themselves. They consisted of about four kinds of silken coats with staring colours, and flowers worked in them of gold. I heard them styled four-headed, twelve-headed, twenty-headed and forty-headed coats. As I could see upon them no heads at all in painting or embroidery I demanded the reason of the appellation, and I was told that the most simple coats were a reward for having cut off four heads of enemies and that they were now being forwarded to the camp.[24]

While the reports of Burnes and Vambery established the general form of nineteenth-century Uzbek costume it is the descriptions and illustrations of the late nineteenth-century travellers — Krafft, Rickmers, and Olufsen — which can be firmly linked to surviving textiles and garments. They clearly distinguish between the everyday dress of middle-class townsmen and the elaborate robes worn by the Emirs and their entourages. Both Olufsen and Rickmers agree in their analysis of Uzbek costume as a series of layers which can be varied according to wealth, rank and climate. Rickmers's account clearly summarises this.

What one sees of a man's ordinary dress are his goloshes,

the chapan or gown generally known by the Russian name of khalat (dressing gown), and the chalma or turban. The inner layer consists of a square, sack-like shirt and short pants resembling those worn by athletes, but sufficiently baggy for holding three men in proper training. Over this one usually wears an undress khalat, above which is donned the gaily coloured smart chapan when one goes out. A belt or handkerchief is used to keep the inner khalat together; only officials and officers enjoy the privilege of an outward and visible waist sketched with the help of an ornamental belt. When it is cold one increased the number of top-coats or invests in one lined with fur. Gloves are unnecessary because the sleeves are so long that one can always withdraw one's hands into the inner atmosphere heated by the body. This plan is decidely preferable to gloves, especially fingered ones.

The Bokhariot's pride is his chalma whose stately white bulge forms a pleasing off-set to the vivid pattern of the khalat. Its size and shape are determined by the station and rank of the individual; mallash and ministers having the largest and finest. Neatness of clothes and distinction of manners are a peculiarity of the citizen of Bokhara. Here we find high-bred aristocrats, smart clerks, swells and dudes, everybody trying to look as much as possible. This one would think, cannot be difficult, seeing that nothing but a flaring dressing gown need stand between you and the outerworld. But class distinctions not easily noted by our eyes are expressed by certain rules of dress.[25]

Examples of the chupan have survived and may be seen in museum collections. They could be made of plain or neatly patterned fabric and also in the brilliant 'ikat' dyed silks. Two such coats in the collection of the National Museums of Scotland illustrate fabric, cut and finishing detail.[26] They are both made of heavy warp-faced ribbed silk woven in narrow loom-widths which determine the positioning of seams and treatment of shaping. The tie-dyed warp 'ikat' patterns are in strong colours — fuchsia pink, purple, green, crimson — worked in bold exploding ray motifs and in repeated stylised carnations. The shape of each garment is based on two rectangular loomwidths of fabric, joined at centre back and folded over at the shoulders. The skirt is widened at sides and centre front by the addition of triangular pieces. The overlong sleeves are set straight into the garment from shoulder to waist, each made of several loomwidths to maintain the vertical alignment of the pattern. A chupan is usually lined, here in one example with red printed European cotton fabric. Both garments are bordered at neck, centre front, hem and cuffs with neat edgings of knitted silk braid worked in green and pink and of corded green silk. Such braid edgings are clearly seen in a photograph of young Uzbek boys wearing loose unbelted chupans whose sleeves cover their hands.[27] The patterned silk chupan was normally worn unbelted to show the design effectively. In some cases the chupan could also be worn draped around the shoulders like a cape.[28]

Another of the photographs taken by Krafft at the end of the nineteenth-century shows the total costume.[29] The man is wearing three chupans, two patterned with small floral motifs and vertical stripes respectively. A wide length of cloth — a lungi — is folded and wrapped around the waist. Since the man is about to embark on a journey his third chupan is a long unbelted robe of plain wool. It may be compared with an example in the National Museums of Scotland woven in a firm camel hair fabric and cut according to the same method as that used for patterned silk garments.[30] His costume is completed by high-heeled knee-high black leather boots and a large turban wound around an embroidered cap or kalaposh.

All the sources carefully distinguish the costumes of the Emirs and their officials, which were most prominently displayed at the New Year festivities. Among the photographs recording these occasions one of the most explicit is that taken by Krafft of the police chief of Samarkand resplendent in his robes.[31] He wears loose ankle-length trousers in velvet with borders of scrolling designs embroidered in gold. His robe or khalat is cut on square bulky lines, as it is made of heavy embroidered fabric.[32] Again an example in the National Museums of Scotland illustrates both fabric and construction.[33] A rich purple velvet is lavishly embroidered in gold and silver thread, using couched threads with a design of intertwining flowers, and stems. The cut is simple, based on a wide rectangular piece folded at the shoulders and slashed from neck to hem at centre front, to which long straight sleeves are attached. The garment is lined with 'ikat' silk, patterned with large circular motifs. From pictorial evidence, the khalat was always worn with a woven or embroidered silk belt adorned with heavy metal clasps. While the khalat was usually made of locally embroidered velvet, imported fabrics were used. Burnes in 1831 referred to the import of Russian velvets and brocades. It seems also on certain evidence that after the Russian conquest of Turkestan enterprises were established by Russians to produce textiles for local use. An example of a fabric length in the National Museums of Scotland of gold and red silk brocade patterned with floral motifs has Russian inscriptions woven into the border, recording that it was from the factory of the Trading Company M.V.K.i.D. of the Vishikin Brothers, and was displayed at the Central Asia Exhibition held in Moscow in 1891.[34] Despite the elaboration of the costume, however, turbans of plain white fabric continued to be worn.

The information collected about women's costumes is more detailed for the late nineteenth-century. The Danish ethnographer, Olufsen, was able to collect examples of women's costume which are now in the National Museum of Copenhagen, while Krafft photographed Uzbek and Tajik prostitutes in the entertainment quarters of the cities. Olufsen provides a clear account of the main garments of women's dress.

The women's dress consists of a smock, like the men's shirt low at the neck and adorned with strings of different colours. It reaches to the middle of the thigh and has short sleeves. On the shoulders two triangular cloth cases, tumar, hang in strings in which written copies of prayers are kept or passages from the Koran serving as amulets. The smock is of cotton or silk according to the means of the woman concerned. The smock is stuck into a pair of wide trousers generally blue, red or white cotton. The trousers are narrowed below and very long, hanging in folds around their ankles. They are fastened by cords in tucks round the waist, the cords often end in long woollen and silk tassels. Over the smock a small jacket of coloured cotton or silk is worn which covers the band of the trousers. Within doors the women often wear a common short man's caftan over the jacket, but in the open air the large square black horse-hair's veil (chas-band) is placed before the face and fastened above to a small round kalaposh (cotton with a gay braiding or velvet with gold-brocade) that covers the head. Others fasten the veil to a head-dress which with the more well-to-do is of silk and with an edging of gold-brocade round the forehead. Over which is thrown the long blue cloak, farandje, shaped at the top like a sort of hood for covering the head, and below almost reaching the ground. The feet are covered by a pair of kaush like those of the men or by embroidered leather shoes or gold-brocade shoes with pointed toes, or they wear soft leather stockings like the men which they stick into the galoches, when out of doors.[35]

Krafft's photographs bring this costume vividly to life. His handsome young Uzbek women wear long tight dresses with close-fitting sleeves and crossover fronts covered frequently by a loose striped chupan.[36] Their hair is dressed in the traditional multiple plaits displayed over shoulders and back and covered by an embroidered pillbox cap. Out of doors they wear a farandji resembling a man's chupan of grey or blue silk decorated with black braid. It is pulled up over the head which is enveloped in a black veil.[37]

As the late nineteenth-century sources so eloquently demonstrate, tradition in Uzbek costume was strong enough to absorb such features as the use of imported and factory woven textiles without drastic alteration of its basic forms. The costumes were part of a way of life based on an urban infrastructure of the ruling Emir's court, the Islamic establishment, a bazaar economy and social customs in which men and women were segregated. This infrastructure was to change after the Revolution of 1917 with the implementation of Marxist-Leninist Socialism with its emphasis on an industrialised economy and secular education. The Soviet government's solution to the old Russian Governorate of Turkestan was to divide it into republics based on the dominant ethnic group of a region, with the aim of encouraging a national rather than traditional religious and cultural loyalty. As the Uzbeks formed the majority population of the Emirates of Bokhara, Khiva and Kokand they were formed, together with Samarkand and Tashkent, into the

Soviet Socialist Republic of Uzbekistan in 1924. Tashkent was created the capital in 1931. The Latin script was introduced for the Uzbek language in 1930, to be replaced by Cyrillic in 1940, while the disestablishment of the Islamic institutions discouraged the continuity of Muslim life at an official level. Today the Uzbeks number approximately 16,000,000 and are the largest Turkic group and the third largest nationality in the USSR. Most of them inhabit Uzbekistan. There are also significant minorities in Afghanistan and in the Xinjiang region of China.

The structural changes in Uzbekistan were accompanied by economic reform in that the traditional bazaar system with its craft and retail outlets was replaced by the state factory, cooperative workship and store. Today in such cities as Bokhara the picturesque narrow streets and squares of the bazaar quarter have been restored as a tourist attraction and include small shops selling mainly gift items and some clothing accessories. In the main, people now buy either ready-made clothes, or factory-woven textiles in state shops. While the intrusion of modern working patterns in factories and offices has resulted in a decline in the domestic production of clothing and changes for practical reasons certain features have survived in an adapted form. Men's costume has undergone the most drastic changes. For the most part the brilliantly patterned chupans, high-heeled boots and turbans have given way to the more sober forms and colours of western European shirts, trousers and jackets. Many men, however, wear a neat black quilted skull cap — the kalaposh or duppi — embroidered with stylised floral motifs in white. Although mass-produced they are descended from the quilted caps around which the turban would once have been wound. In cities such as Bokhara and Samarkand it is still possible to see old Uzbek men wearing their traditional dress of striped chupan, swathed girdle and turban. They also wear soft leather boots with upturned toes.

Women's costume is more varied and reveals a mingling of tradition and change. Despite the broadening of women's role encouraged by Socialism, family ties are still strong and most Uzbek girls will expect to marry and raise a large family. The old customs of segregation and seclusion have gradually been eroded and it would now be very rare to see a woman on the streets shrouded in farandji and veil. Such clothing is severely discouraged and would in fact be worn only by old women who do not have an active role in Uzbekistan's modern society. Costumes now vary mainly according to a woman's age and professional status. Here styles are more conservative in historical towns like Bokhara and Samarkand and in the rural areas than in the modern capital of Tashkent. They are also indicative of Uzbek identity in the preference they show for the use of boldly striped and patterned fabrics worked in the 'ikat' tie-dyed technique. Now, however, the fabrics are mass-produced in factories using synthetic fibres as well as silk. In many cases the bright red, yellow, green and black motifs are printed against white. This type of material is worn by all age groups. Young girls, notably in Bokhara and Samarkand, wear a loose knee-length dress with short sleves — *kujlak* — which may be machine-stitched at home or by a local dressmaker from lengths of fabric purchased in the state shops, or selected ready-made from the rails of the clothing section of a department store. Features of European-style tailoring have been incorporated into this type of dress. An example in the collections of the National Museums of Scotland shows a fitted yoke with a turned back collar.[38] Depending on the conservatism of their families girls wear the dress with or without long full trousers — *ishton* — made of red flowered fabric. Footwear may consist of embroidered slippers, *schlujpka* European style sandals or shoes. Some young girls still wear a version of the traditional hairstyle of many long plaits hanging down their backs, occasionally with ornaments attached to them.[39] Where a headdress is worn it consists of a pillbox cap — *duppi* — of velvet elaborately embroidered with floral motifs and scroll-work in coloured silks and gold. Both caps and slippers are still made in a workshop in Bokhara specialising in embroidered work of high quality. Older women married and unmarried, wear more adult versions of this costume. The loose brightly coloured dress may be worn with smart high-heeled shoes. In some cases the fabric is made up into a European-style dress with a fitted waist and pleated skirt. A woman wearing such a style would also alternate her dresses with European skirts and blouses. Hair generally worn long, usually in a range of styles based on coiled plaits wound round the head and chignons. A more traditional married woman who still follows a domestic role will wear the long floral printed trousers with the loose dress, often with discreet wristlength sleeves. She will not wear the pillbox cap which is reserved for unmarried girls, but will instead cover her head with a brightly patterned scarf — *rumol*. The most conservative interpretations of modern Uzbek costume are naturally found in older women who may be seen been walking in the streets or sitting in the doors of their houses in the old quarters of the cities wearing trousers, loose dress with their heads tightly bound with a scarf and covered with a discreet white shawl.

Notes

1 Vambery, Arminius (1864), *Travels in Central Asia*, London, pp. 171–172.
2 For example the Kurds of Sanandaj Iran, were observed in 1977 going about the bazaar in resplendent national dress.
3 The Ark in Bokhara has Emirs' costumes on exhibition. Important collections of Central Asian material are in the Museum of Fine Arts Tashkent, the State Museum of Oriental Art Moscow, the Ethnographical Museum Leningrad and the National Museum Copenhagan.
4 For example the camel wool chupan worn by Lt. Col. F. M. Bailey and given to the National Museums of Scotland, Department of History and Applied Art (reg. no. 1920.684).
5 I am indebted to Basil Robinson, formerly of the Victoria and Albert Museum London, for guiding me to this category of source material.
6 Published in Krafft, Hugues (1902) *A travers le Turkestan Russe*.
7 Azarpay, Guitty (1981) Sogdian painting, University of California Press, Plate 12, Panjikent VI, 41.
8 Azarpay (1981) fig. 51.
9 Berlin, Museum für Indische Kunst, III, 8426, a, b, c.
10 Berlin, III, 6912.
11 Berlin, III, 6302.
12 Latham, Ronald (1958) *The travels of Marco Polo*, London, p. 114, pp. 116–117.
13 London, British Museum, Department of Oriental Antiquities 1948. 12–10.010.
14 Boston, Museum of Fine Arts, Francis Bartlett Donation of 1912 and Picture Fund (14.592).
15 For example the portrait of a seated Mongolian c. 1590–1610, Stockholm, Nationalmuseum NMH 470/1926; Türkmen prisoner c. 1585, Oxford, Bodleian Library MS. Ouseley, Add. 173.f.1.
16 Istanbul, Topkapi Sarayi Kütüphanesi, Revan 1964 (2a).
17 Burnes, Alexander (1834) *Travels into Bokhara*, London, Vol. 1, pp. 274–275.
18 Burnes (1834), vol. 1, p. 292.
19 Burnes (1834), vol. 2, p. 439.

20 Burnes (1834), vol. 2, p. 433.
21 Burnes (1834), vol. 2, pp. 434–435.
22 Burnes (1834), vol. 1, pp. 287–288.
23 Vambery (1864), pp. 171–172.
24 Vambery (1864),p. 140.
25 Rickmers, W. (1913), The Duab of Turkestan, Cambridge University Press, p. 101.
26 Edinburgh, National Museums of Scotland, Department of History and Applied Arts, reg. nos. 1982.810, 1985.283.
27 Krafft (1902) op. cit. 'Jeunes Ouzbeg de Samarkand en Khalat de soie,' p. 147.
28 In 1971 I saw Uzbeks in Mazar-i Sharif, Afghanistan, wearing ikat silk chupans in this manner.
29 Krafft (1902) op.cit. p. 175, 'Un cavalier chaussé de bottes à hauts talons pointus'.
30 Edinbrugh, reg. no. 1920.684.
31 Krafft (1902) op. cit. p. 177, 'Le Starchii Aksakal de Samarkand, en grand costume de cerémonie'.
32 See Sidorenko, A. I., Artykov, A. R., Radjabov, R. R. (1981), Gold embroidery of Bukhara, Tashkent, for a discussion of these garments and fabrics.
33 Edinburgh, reg. no. 1979.36.
34 Edinburgh, reg. no. 1984.373.
35 Olufsen, Axel, (1911), The Emir of Bokhara and his country, London, pp. 479–480.
36 Krafft (1902), op. cit. p. 149, 'Une femme Ouzbeg de Kokan coiffée du topi,' p. 151, Une jeune femme Ouzbeg de Khodjent coiffée d'un topi brodé d'or'.
37 Krafft (1902) op. cit. 'Un femme revêtue de son manteau et de son voile'.
38 Edinburgh, reg. no. 1984.531.
39 I observed a girl in the market place at Samarkand in 1984, with a large diamond-shaped silver pendant attached to the ends of her plaits. She was probably of Türkmen origin.

14

MUSICAL CHANGE IN HERAT DURING THE TWENTIETH CENTURY

John Baily

In the 1930s the urban music of Herat, in western Afghanistan, started to undergo a remarkable change. Whereas in the early part of the century the Persian style was the dominant type of music played in Herat, the 1930s saw the adoption of a quite different form of art music from Kabul which was in turn inspired by the example of North Indian (Hindustani) music.

Music is a social fact, music making a social activity, musical performances a social performance. The relationships between musical structures and social structures are diverse and complex and have yet to be teased out and examined in detail by ethnomusicologists, but it is already clear that music is a highly sensitive indicator of general social and cultural trends. The purpose of this chapter is to describe the musical change that took place in Herat and to consider some of the non-musical social and cultural processes that seem to lie behind it.

Herat in the Early Twentieth Century

In the early part of the twentieth century 'Persian music' was very much in vogue in the city of Herat. It is difficult to date this precisely, but the heyday was probably in the 1920s, during the reign of the progressive monarch Amanullah Khan. Many informants described the old music of the city as Persian (*Pārsi, Irāni*), and its identification as such is corroborated when we compare what remained of this kind of music in Herat with the contemporary art music of Iran. The comparison shows it to have been essentially the same music. Interest was centred on the art of *ghazal* singing, with texts drawn from classical

258

Persian poetry. As far as can be established, the manner of singing was often slow and in free rhythm, unmetred in the musical sense, like the *āvāz* style of Iran, with Iranian vocal technique and ornamentation. The musicians performed in a variety of what they identified as 'Persian' modes with names such as *Shur, Chahārgāh*, and *Homāyun*, and they evidently understood and used the Iranian *dastgāh* principle.

One of the most obvious Persian features of this music was the use of the Iranian *tār*, called *chahārtār* in Herat. A typical urban music group of the 1920s consisted of several singers and *chahārtār* players, accompanied by tabla drums and two types of idiophone: the *sekh*, a rifle barrel suspended by a string and struck with a metal beater, and the *tāl*, a pair of small brass cymbals. The *santur*, another Persian instrument, seems to have sometimes been incorporated into this kind of group. The use of the tabla in this ensemble is certainly remarkable, unheard of in Iran, where the *dombak* is the normal drum of accompanying urban music. Tablas were imported directly from India by tea merchants on their camel caravans and were never manufactured in Herat. The tabla players of the 1920s did not play according to the Indian system of strokes and *tāl*s (rhythmic cycles), which were adopted later.

Information about the melodic modes used for the urban music of this time was gathered from Mohammad Karim, the son of one of the leading singers of the 1920s. From Mohammad Karim performances were rcorded in the following modes: *Chahārgāh, Shur, Homāyun, Bayāt-e Turk, Garayli, Abu-Atā, Māhur, Segāh, Dashti, Nawā, Maqām-e Rāst, Bayāt-e Shirāz, Now Ruz Sabā* and *Hejāz*. These are all the names of modes in the Persian art music system. The Herati versions, as far as could be established from a single but well placed informant, more or less corresponded to the equivalent Persian modes in terms of scale type, but there were rather greater differences with respect to the characteristic melodic formulae of the modes.

The Heratis played according to the *dastgāh* principle, with modulations from the original mode (see Farhat 1965, Caron and Safvate 1966, Zonis 1973). Thus, when Mohammad Karim played some modes, notably *Shur, Chahārgāh* and *Homāyun*, each was divided into several sections (*heseh*), which took a progressively higher tessitura and ended with a modulation back to the original mode. His performances would conclude with a *reng* (dance) followed by a *tasnif* (metred song melody) in the original mode. This kind of piece was called a *dastgāh* in Herat, though it seems the term *dastgāh* was employed more widely than in Iran, and could be used synonymously with *maqām*, an old word for melodic mode. Although the Herati musicians do not seem to have been familiar with Iranian terms such as *radif, gusheh* or *forud* in a musical context, they were using these elements of form in their performances of *dastgāh* music. In a *dastgāh* with several parts (*heseh*), whose finalis (*shahpardeh*, 'king fret') was positioned progressively higher in the pitch range, each *heseh* was called a *gāh* ('place'), and Mohammad Karim told me that the names of modes such as *Dugāh, Segāh, Chahārgāh* and *Panjgāh* referred to the number of 'places' they have on the neck of the *chahārtār*. This is an old explanation for the meaning of these terms in Persian music.

The Political and Social Significance of this Period

A certain amount can be inferred about the social and political context of the Persian music vogue of the 1920s. In the turmoil of the nineteenth century the Shiah merchants of Herat were an oppressed community and it seems unlikely that they would have called attention to such wealth as they had by holding lavish wedding celebrations. By about 1900 Herat was recovering from the chaotic conditions of the preceding epoch, the Shiah merchant class had re-emerged, and it was no longer necessary to take precautions against the expropriation of riches by the authorities. Weddings became lavish displays of wealth, and the venue for sophisticated musical entertainment, as they had no doubt been in earlier times. There was increased patronage of urban music. Furthermore, in 1919 King Amanullah came to the throne of Afghanistan. The ten years of his reign were characterised by strenuous attempts at social reform and modernisation and the 1920s was a time when music acquired a new respectability and popularity in the face of religious censure.

When the patronage of art music in Herat was re-established, the demand thus created was met by adopting msuic from Iran. There are several reasons why Iran should have been the source. Firstly, it was physically close; Mashhad, the nearest Persian city, was only two hundred and twenty five miles from Herat, while Kandahar was three hundred and fifty miles distant. Land communications at that time were slow and difficult. The Shiahs of Herat, who made up the wealthy merchant class, looked to Iran as the source of their 'persian culture', and many visited Iran, especially Mashhad, on pilgrimage. Herat had a long history of shared music culture with Iran, and one might guess that the Heratis simply adopted the current style of Persian music, the *dastgāh* system. In Iran, too, music was undergoing a renaissance, with a surge of renewed interest in music and music making after the Constitution of 1906. Musicians from Herat visited Iran to collect new items of repertory. Phonographs may also have been an important medium for the communication of Persian music, which could even help explain why the Heratis played seemingly rather truncated versions of the *dastgāh*s and were unfamiliar with technical terms such as *gusheh* and *forud*. The popularity of Persian music in Herat at that time might be interpreted as confirming traditional cultural links with Iran.

Musical Change since the 1920s

The 1930s saw the adoption of Kabuli art music in Herat, while the 1950s, once radio broadcasting was well established, witnessed the adoption of a popular music style, based on Pashtun regional music with (usually) Persian song texts, which had been developed at the radio station in Kabul (see Baily 1988 for more details). The musical changes which took place can be summarised as follows:

1 The harmonium, *rubāb* and, later, the fourteen stringed *dutār* replaced the *chahārtār* and *saŋtur* as the predominant instrument of urban music making.

2 Different tonal, modal and rhythmic systems, that is, different principles of musical organisation, came into use with the adoption of Indian *rāg*s (melodic modes) and *tāl*s (rhythmic cycles). These principles were systematised according to a modified form of Hindustani music theory.

3 New musical forms were adopted, notably the Kabuli

261

ghazal (usually a setting for a Persian *ghazal* text), the *naghmeh-ye kashāl* (the extended instrumental piece), and the forms for popular and dance music.

4 There was an increase in the frequency of music making, at wedding festivities, concerts, in the theatres, and at small private parties.

5 There was a decrease in the condemnation of music and musicians by orthodox mullahs, and by the public at large.

6 There was the emergence of the high ranking hereditary professional musician, the *ustād*, or 'master-muscian', a category of musician that had certainly existed in previous epochs (e. g., the Timurid court of Herat) but which fell into abeyance in the nineteenth century.

The analytical notion of *musical change* is highly problematic (see, for example, Blacking 1979). Difficulties arise because a wide range of types of transformation has been described as such. I am using the term in a broad sense, to include not only the adoption of new instruments, principles of musical organisation and musical genres, but changes in the wider socio-cultural context which in some way or other impinged on the structure and/or performance of music. The musical changes listed above (points 1–3) were not so much developments *within* the music itself as the discarding of one system adopted from outside (Iran) and its replacement with another, adopted from somewhere else (Kabul). Certainly the Heratis had made some changes to the new system they had adopted, mixing in certain intervals and modes that derived from the older Persian music they had previously followed. They continued to have an interest in the Persian *ghazal* as a song text, and in Persian popular music, which they adapted for performance in the new Kabuli style. But the most striking feature of this musical transformation is the extent to which the Kabuli style dominated urban music making in Herat.

What is the signifance of these changes in music and music making? Ethnomusicological theory would lead one to expect that they did not occur as isolated phenomena, but were part of more general processes of social and cultural change.

Modernism and Modernisation

A study of the history of Afghanistan at this period reveals certain patterns of social, political and economic change which would seem to intersect with the changes in music making manifested in Herat. They can be understood as facets of the twin process of modernisation and modernism. It is expedient to consider these under three headings: the emergence of Afghan nationalism, the decreasing power of the religious establishment, and the introduction of modern technology.

Afghan Nationalism and National Identity

Music is a potent symbol of ethnic identity; like language, it is one of those aspects of culture which can, when the need to assert 'ethnic identity' arises, most readily serve this purpose. It can serve as an area of shared experience which helps to delineate the boundaries of a social group or nation. Its effectiveness in this respect may be twofold; not only does it act as a ready means for the identification of different ethnic groups, but it has potent emotional connotations and can express ethnic identity in a particularly powerful manner.

'A principal theme in the politcal history of Afghanistan has been the effort to create a unified nation-state' (Poullada 1973). The 'nation-state' is an ethnocentric western concept but may still be usefully applied in this case, for this was the model that Afghan rulers presumably sought to emulate. Two factors hindered this development in the nineteenth century. Firstly, conflicts within and between the dominant Pashtun tribes prevented the emergence of Afghanistan as a state. Secondly, the number of different ethnic groups inhabiting the territory, with different languages and to some extent different cultures, has hindered the development of the people into a single nation. Afghanistan did not begin to emerge as a 'nation-state' until the 1880s, under Amir Abdur Rahman. By building a powerful regular army which could confront the tribes, Abdur Rahman was able to bring the whole of the country under the control of Kabul.

In the 1930s a nationalist trend became clearly discernible. Gregorian in *The Emergence of Modern Afghanistan* gives a fascinating account of the arguments put forward by nationalist writers of the time. They recognised that one of Afghanistan's problems was its ethnic diversity, and the nationalists were preoccupied with establishing a common history, religious background and ethnic origin for all the peoples of Afghanistan, claiming that they were descended from the same Aryan stock. The Pashto language was given great importance in this nationalist ideology, and it was only in this period that Pashto became an official language of the country, along with Dari (Afghan Persian). It was argued that Afghanistan needed the development of a modern national culture.

> Many urged that Afghanistan's folklore and traditional music be collected, and called for the development of a new literature reflecting both the nation's historical legacy and its present social realities, needs and aspirations. Poets and writers were exhorted to see themselves as vehicles of social change and their role as the awakening of the Afghan people.
>
> (Gregorian 1969 p. 348)

If it was the intention of the government to instil in the people a new spirit of nationalism as citizens of Afghanistan and to think of themselves as Afghans irrespective of ethnic origin, then the creation of new genres of urban music — Afghan art music and popular music — in Kabul may have served an important role in this process. We do not know to what extent the creation of a national music was the result of a deliberate policy to foster nationalism, although that was the outcome. Perhaps the adoption of Kabuli art music in Herat in the late 1930s, and of Kabuli popular music in the 1940s to 1950s, expressed a new feeling amongst Heratis of belonging to Afghanistan and of being Afghans. It can be seen as a political statement, an act of allegience, for Heratis outwardly to subscribe to the dominant culture in this way. Certain essential symbols may have been expressed in the instruments used for urban music in Herat. If the *rubāb,* with its strong Pashtun associations, represented the 'Afghanness' of the music, the *dutār,* the Heratis' own instrument, represented the 'voice' of Herat in the urban ensemble, and symbolised the role of Herat as an integral part of Afghanistan.

The Power of the Religious Establishment

By 'power' here I refer to the ability of the *'ulamā* (theologians) to influence central political decisions in Kabul, and to exert control over peoples' lives at the local level through the mullahs. The power of the religious establishment has varied during the period in question, and since in general orthodox Islam in Afghanistan was opposed to music as a an unprofitable and even sinful activity, we may look for a correlation between this and the openness and frequency of public music making. The banning of some kinds of music in Iran under Ayatullah Khomeini is a modern example of the Islamic proscription of music backed by the power of the state.

Although in Afghanistan Abdur Rahman took certain strong measures against the clergy in the 1880s, nationalising all religious endowments and instituting qualifying examinations for mullahs, he also formulated policies that resulted in an increase in their power. He used them to exacerbate the *jihād* movement against the British and they gave, for the first time, religious sanction to the monarchy. In the 1920s the government initiated many social reforms that were opposed by the *'ulamā*, who were unable to influence policy at the centre. The 1920s was a time of musical release from puritanical restraint, both in Kabul and Herat, though with different musical results (in Kabul this period saw the blossoming of Kabuli art music, while in Herat there was a vogue for Persian music). With the fall of Amanullah in 1929 and the return to a more traditional way of life, the clergy enjoyed a greater say in the running of the country, and music was once again subject to puritanical restraint.

Social reform proceeded slowly and cautiously over the next twenty years, but in the 1950s there was a period of rapid modernisation under the prime minister, Mohammad Daud (later the first President of the Republic of Afghanistan). Once again this was a time of conflict between the government and the clergy, with the latter in a weak position, and a period of musical release, during which Radio Afghanistan assumed its role as the centre of musical patronage. As Heratis looked back from the 1970s they saw a great change in the status of music making in recent years, changes which they took to be a product of the process of modernisation. Mullahs might still say that music was sinful, but the opinion of mullahs could now be questioned by those they criticised. More significantly, the general attitude of people had changed.

What we have seen so far is a simple quantitative relationship between the role of the clergy and the amount of musical activity, but there was also a more intimate qualitative relationship between social and musical factors. Mullahs do in fact differentiate between different kinds of music in terms of the amount of sin they incur, and this depends in part upon the intentions of the performers and the purpose of the music. The Iranian music of Herat in the 1920s was at least a serious, grave and melancholic style, with texts drawn from the great tradition of Persian poetry, but since then there had been a change towards exactly those elements that mullahs condemned. The music became faster, rhythmically more exciting; it was altogether more like dance music. Song texts became more overtly romantic.

The eclipse of the mullahs as agents of social control in Herat since about 1950 was the result of political processes, following the gradual assertion of power by the central government and the development of modern institutions. To this extent the musical change can be seen as the passive result of a political process, but there is also the possibility that music played a more active role here. Through operating a policy of popularising music, the government must have been aware that it was placing itself in conflict with the traditional values of the mullahs. When the government set up loudspeaker systems in many towns and cities, including Herat, to relay radio broadcasts, and the streets were filled with the sounds of music, it was perhaps hard to maintain the attitude that music was sinful. It is possible that the government's promotion of listening to music as a normal daily activity was an act of deliberate modernism. Here we may have an interesting case of music not as 'the mirror of society', as popular metaphor puts it, but as a dynamic force that can be used to change society. Music, itself a symbol of modernism, and itself modernised, was a powerful stimulus with which to 'awaken the people'.

266

Music as an Aspect of Modern Technology

The modern European world came to Afghanistan from India, in the nineteenth century. India, under British rule, was the closest site of modernised prototypes for Afghans to emulate and from which to obtain technical assistance. A further factor was the Afghans' natural affiliation with predominantly Sunni Hindustan, and avoidance of contacts with Shiah Iran. While British experts were brought to Kabul by Abdur Rahman (mainly to expand the royal workshops, which provided equipment and supplies for the Afghan army), other technical expertise was provided by Indian Muslims, especially in the field of education. The Muslim culture of North India was undoubtedly one that the people of Afghanistan were likely to 'resonate' with, and historically there has been comparatively free interchange between the two regions. In the context of the general trend it is understandable that music should have been adopted from India, the source of many new ideas at that time. The *ustāds* of the court, brought originally to Kabul from India in the mid-nineteenth century, could be regarded as foreign experts who carried out a 'technical overhaul' of Afghan music in the process of creating a new national music. This was itself a way of modernising the music, and, from the perspective of modernism, of improving it.

Amongst their contributions, the *ustāds* introduced the *'ilm-e musiqi*, the 'science of music', a set of theoretical constructs about the tonal system, scale types, melodic modes and principles of rhythmic organisation which underlay the music they played. This knowledge provided a terminology that allowed these abstract concepts to be discussed, while note names and tabla *bol*s (syllables) could serve as oral or written notation. The musicians accepted that this knowledge derived from Indian music theory, and indeed took considerable pride in this fact. The science of music was in itself a kind of technological knowledge. A further aspect of technical innovation can perhaps be seen in the adoption of the harmonium. The instrument worked acoustically in a totally new way (being a free reed aerophone) and was constructed like a machine, with its leavers, springs and stops.

267

Conclusions

These underlying trends would seem to have predicated (a) the development of a national music, based on the music of the politically dominant ethnic group in Afghanistan, the Pashtuns; (b) The wider patronage of music, which encouraged the recruitment of musicians; (c) The increased technical complexity of music and the adoption of abstract theoretical concepts. The details of how individual musicians translated these trends into specific actions is another story, and is examined in detail in my recent book (Baily 1988); the object of the present paper is to demonstrate a case in which musical change is indicative of much wider procersses of social and cultural change.

References

Baily, J (1988) *Music of Afghanistan: Professional musicians in the city of Herat*, in John Blacking, series editor, *Studies in Ethnomusicology*, with accompanying audio cassette. Cambridge: Cambridge University Press.

Blacking, J (1979), 'Some problems of theory and method in the study of musical change', *Yearbook of the International Folk Music Council*, 9:1–26

Caron, Nelly, and Dariouche Safvate (1966), *Iran. Les Traditions Musicales*. Paris: Buchet/Chastel.

Farhat, Hormoz (1965), *The Dastgah Concept in Persian Music*. Ph.D. dissertation, Univeristy of California, Los Angeles.

Gregorian, Vartan (1969), *The Emergence of Modern Afghanistan*. Stanford: Stanford University Press.

Poullada, Leon B. (1973), *Reform and rebellion in Afghanistan 1919–1929: King Amanulla's failure to modernise a tribal society*. Ithaca: Cornell University Press.

Zonis, Ella (1973), *Classical Persian Music: An Introduction*. Cambridge: Harvard University Press.

Acknowledgements

The fieldwork on which this paper is based was carried out in Herat between 1973 and 1977, when the author was in receipt of a Social Science Research Council Post-Doctoral Research Fellowship, and later a Social Science Research Council 'Conversion' Fellowship, and attached to the Department of Social Anthropology, The Queen's

University of Belfast. An earlier version of this paper was presented at a Symposium on Khorasan held at Uppsala University, November 1982, and the present version was written while the author was a Visiting Research Fellow in the School of African and Asian Studies, University of Sussex.

15

TRADITION AND CHANGE IN CENTRAL ASIAN ARCHITECTURE TODAY

F. Ashrafi

Importance has always been attached to the study and absorption of town-building traditions and architecture with the aim of adapting them to modern architectural requirements. This is, in fact, a problem of progressive and continuous development of our culture, something that retains its value in our time and age of rapid scientific and technological progress and urbanisation.

The viability and survival of traditions depends on the extent to which they conform with modern socio-economic, engineering, architectural and artistic principles. I believe it is essential to explain what we mean by absorbing and utilising the heritage of the past. If we view it as a process of carbon-copying images and forms of past architecture in structures and ensembles of the socialist period, it will mean nothing but deviation from modern principles. In order to retain the individual features of historical cities in the course of reconstruction programmes it is essential to preserve old residential quarters, architectural monuments and elements of landscape art, and adapt them to the new requirements. The creation of material and spiritual values, which is a dynamic and evolutionary process, leads to the development of criteria for a correct social utilisation of tradition.

The present stage in the development of architecture is marked by its growing community with town-building art, by growing interrelationship, by mutual enrichment of national and international elements. There is a growing understanding of the fact that local schools of architecture cannot be divorced from the overall processes inherent in world architecture, that we are all on the threshold of new forms in blending architecture with imitative and plastic art, with the landscape and the infrastructive of cities.

It is from this point of view that I would like to examine the problem of traditions and change in the modern architecture of Uzbekistan. The architecture of Uzbekistan has developed as an integrated part of Soviet architecture on the basis of great social transformations. At all stages of its development Uzbek architecture has striven to borrow from the progressive traditions of the past. The rich cultural traditions of Uzbekistan, enriched by the growing cultural standards of the people, serve as a foundation on which to raise further the aesthetic standards of our towns and villagers. The artistic, typological and microclimatic features of traditional architecture, which have retained their value to this day, stimulate a creative search for modern features of regional architecture. We need the experience of our predecessors in order to attain new professional heights.

Even a brief tour of the old quarters of our cities and acquaintance with the colourful architectural monuments, squares, residential sections and markets leave a lasting impression of beauty. Later, after an analysis of this impression, it may be classified in terms of layout, engineering and microclimatic features. Traditional town-building practice combines the rational and the artistic, imagination and calculation, clarity and refinement. Modern scientific and technological progress has failed to surpass many of the methods practised by ancient architects, for example, the layout of internal courtyards in residential or public buildings, the organisation of space, the scale and proportions of elements.

We can trace continuity of tradition in both new towns and those which have an ancient history. This is particularly true in Tashkent which has gone through a period of revival after the destructive earthquake of 1966. All the national republics of the USSR took part in the rehabilitation of the Uzbek capital, and this manifestation of the spirit of internationalism has left its imprint upon the new architectural ensembles of the city. Meanwhile, Tashkent displays a specific flavour based on the continuity of national traditions. The problem of tradition and change is particularly acute in the sphere of housing construction. Large-scale housing construction architecture is a subject in itself and deserves special discussion. It would be appropriate to point out that in spite of our good knowledge of the national house, the existence of numerous experimental projects by Uzbek architects, and the realisation of a number of recommendations on new types of multi-storeyed apartment blocks, little progress has been made in large-scale housing construction towards improving the layout of apartments, providing outdoor premises, meeting the specific climatic factors and the demographic and everyday life requirements of the people. The use of open-work panels as sun shades, ornaments and coloured facades, diversify the architecture of housing development projects to a certain extent, but fail to introduce any notable changes in the structure and layout of the apartment units.

Concern for preserving architectural monuments and blending them in with modern projects constitutes a priority in the town-building practice in Uzbekistan today. The Uzbek republic boasts not only individual architectural monuments of world renown, but also whole city complexes such as Bukhara, Khiva and Samarkand, whose modernisation calls for a scientific approach and great skill on the part of the architects.

When the architectural heritage is substantial, modern construction must play a subordinate role, as is the case with the historical centre of Bukhara and the Ichan-Kala section in Khiva. There all the historical features must remain undisturbed, perhaps with some slight clearing of later, ramshackle structures.

One of the typical features of Central Asian architecture is the abundance of dominant elements which are very much interdependent. The active role of these dominants (domes, minarets, portals) was always accentuated by bland, unobtrusive structures, as, for instance is the case in the ancient centre of Bukhara. The contrast in terms of the skyline went hand in hand with unity in terms of scale and plasticity. The absence of such a relationship, i.e., any sharp contrast with existing residential structures, makes it difficult to blend new dominants with the texture of the former.

The last few years have seen preference given to sprawling metropolises with a relatively low density of construction. It should be borne in mind, however, that the ancient cities of Central Asia were very compact. It is indeed sad that our modern architecture is losing the charm of proportional scale.

This is ot only an aesthetic but, even more, an economic problem.

It has always been a supreme manifestation of architectural talent to create an ensemble, in which each element is self-expressive and yet, at the same time, constitutes an integral section of the architectural entity. This is the principle to be followed in reconstruction projects of ancient cities. The tactful introduction of new structures into the architectural environment, together with respect for the ancient layout, has always been and remains the basis for creating integrated ensembles.

In recent years, it is often the case that even a well planned and functional structure of the city, coupled with rational methods of construction and high engineering standards of transportation systems, nevertheless produces a bleak appearance because of the failure to ensure an artistic approach to the problem. A blending of the arts is needed to enrich the 'spiritual world' of the city and to provide the organising principle for the territory. The streets and squares are in need of monumental art which would blend harmoniously with the architectural ensembles and accentuate their expressiveness.

The arts of today cherish the humanistic ideals of past generations and borrow from the treasury of national art, while recognising their international aspect. Our approach to the national heritage of the peoples of Central Asia is not limited to mere preferences for a set of artistic forms. This heritage embraces the entire culture of our peoples, everything that has been acquired by generations. That is why the architecture of Uzbekistan today expects artists to adopt a creative approach to the aesthetic appearance of the towns and villages.

Tradition and change are the two fundamental poles in architecture, and it is their relationship within the creative process that accounts for the specific features of architecture and promotes diversification in the course of its development. The degree of change is the main criterion in this process.

Preference is given to those trends in architecture which correspond most to the requirements and potentials of the time, which conform with the demands and principles of the region. Such a search is fertile only when it is divorced from shallow imitation and sentimentalism with regard to past history, when it gets to the heart of the social needs of the people, takes into account their way of life, the specific features of the climate, the outlook of the nation.

Architecture has always been a major factor of human well-being, an integral element of the spiritual and material culture of man. Throughout the ages, the architect has been the indispensable organiser of the human habitat. Today, with the growing human potential in technology, science and the arts, the needs of man are brought to the fore more than ever before. This results, among other things, from the unprecedented scale of human activity in all spheres and the rapid growth of urbanisation which changes substantially the traditional human habitat. All this adds heavily to the responsibility of the architect for the quality of the urbanised environment.

The problems of tradition and change in architecture are inseparable from the concepts of what is national and international. In one way or another national elements are based on traditional features, yet tradition, paradoxically is something that is born anew every day. It is quite possible that the best buildings of our time will be recognised as traditional in the future. What we see as tradition today was once born as innovation. Thus, innovation is a vital tradition in architecture, it is an inherent feature of the architect who looks to the future.

The present level in the social and cultural development of society predetermines and results in profound changes in the way of life, world outlook, concepts and realisation of various life processes. The features of our life today display a blending of past traditions, which have been transformed in the process of evolution, and all the new and progressive things which stem from socialist reality. The genuine roots of tradition in architecture can be traced deep within social life, in all its spheres, and they stimulate the architects in deciding on the logic of organising residential centres, in determining their structure, down to composition of ensembles, individual buildings and interiors.

Many of the cities in Uzbekistan have a lengthy history and their layout clearly displays traces of the social and economic conditions of development. The structural layout, as any other system, is a means of governing the functional processes within the territory of the city, its individual zones, its external contacts, and also governs the entire city organism. Hence, the vital necessity of innovation, of changes of town-building structures, so as to ensure the vitality of the constantly changing and growing organism of the city.

In renovating the environment of our cities we run up against very complicated and acute problems. These concern the preservation or replacement on a qualitatively new level of those elements which traditionally determined the spatial structure of our cities and the appearance of their streets, squares and residential blocks. Grave concern is being expressed over the gradual disappearance of traditional spaces for human communication and the architectural spatial forms which promoted set behavioural patterns.

In the old cities there exists a scale that is proportional to man, whereas in the new development areas this scale is set by the needs of a modern industry and technology, by the automobile boom. In the old cities the streets and squares were focal centres of social life, a place for human contact and recreation. Today, the development of modern transport calls for wider streets, for the creation of squares and parking lots, overpasses and tunnels, all of which divide the city space into parts.

Under these circumstances there appears the problem, and a very acute one at that, of preserving or returning the traditional and proportional elements of the city: the greenery and water spaces, the pedestrian zones which are separated from thoroughfares, the social functions of these pedestrian zones. The architects of Uzbekistan see their priority in the adopting of the traditional approach to the organisation of space, while further developing the principles of structural arrangement of the city organism.

There is a growing demand to boost the role of design in architectural projects. More often than not the smaller forms and decorative sculptures appear spontaneously, without proper deliberation. Nevertheless, this combination of art and architecture holds a promise for a genuinely creative and harmonious combination of the traditional and the modern.

The light and shade, plasticity of details and ornaments can and must play an increasing role as elements of a socially-based architecture and spatially organised plan. We often reprimand our architects for over-indulgence in decorative motifs, but at the same time, fail to get at the root of the problem, prefering instead merely to give advice about restraint and tectonics.

Decoration is a popular form of dialogue between man and architecture, a means of human self-expression. We must master the skill of architectural harmony, something which our forebears brought to a high degree of perfection when they used flexible and logical interpretations of artistic elements which are visually accessible and which impart an atmosphere of authenticity.

The present stage in the development of Soviet architecture is marked by growing emphasis on problems related to the arts and aesthetics, particularly in the sphere of town building. These problems have been brought to the fore as a result of the socio-economic changes in the country, in the course of which we have been able to resolve a number of vital problems which, in their time, served as limiting factors to the aesthetic and artistic solution of architectural and town-building tasks. Both old and new traditions supplement the arsenal of means, methods and even forms of modern construction. National traditions should not be treated as something exotic, representing the 'national flavour'. They constitute a living and changing set of features which are incorporated within the tasks facing the people who are building a new life. The relationship of the old and the new has always constituted a variable value. Tradition and change always find themselves engaged in complicated relations which reflect the advance of architecture. Whenever the objective socio-economic, ideological, technological and other conditions are ripe, the lasting traditions are broken and there appear new regularities, new relationships between change and tradition.

Will national tradition continue to exist in architecture? Beyond any doubt it will, and for a long time to come. It is an organic process which cannot be artificaly retarded or speeded up. The material basis of architecture makes it very different from other forms of art. Nature, the climate, the building material used, the psychology and demography — features such as these will emerge in compositions, in terms of layout and artistic approach, in the treatment of colour, in the approach to the synthesis of the arts, and so forth. Such features are not an end in themselves and it would be futile to seek them out, or, worse still, to create them artificially. The 'national' characteristics may change in superficial ways, but fundamentally there will be continuity.

Bibliography

Babakhanov A B (1960), *Maloetazhnoye stroitel'stvo v Uzbekistane*, Tashkent.

Dmitriev V M (1980), *Voprosy ispol'zovaniya arkhitektury uzbekskogo narodnogo zhilishcha v sovremennoi praktike*, Tashkent.

Kadyrova T F (1987), *Arkhitektura Sovetskogo Uzbekistana*, Moscow.

Nil'sen V A (1988) *U istokov sovremennogo gradostroitel'stva Uzbekistana* (XIX – nachalo XX vekov), Tashkent.

Rempel' L I (1971), *Arkhitekturnyi ornament Uzbekistana*, Tashkent.

16

THE BAHA'I COMMUNITY OF ASHKHABAD; ITS SOCIAL BASIS AND IMPORTANCE IN BAHA'I HISTORY

M. Momen

Introduction

In this chapter I will briefly survey the origin and history of the Baha'i community in Ashkhabad in Turkistan. An analysis will be presented of the social composition of this community. Finally an attempt will be made to assess the importance of the Ashkhabad Baha'i community in terms of the rest of the Baha'i world. The sources for this paper are mainly various Baha'i histories[1] but other corroborating material is presented where available.[2]

The origins of the Baha'i community of Iran lie in the Babi movement which began in 1844. The founder of this latter movement, Sayyid 'Ali Muhammad Shirazi took the title of Bab and eventually claimed to be the Mahdi, the returned Twelfth Imam. The Babi movement suffered a bloody suppression in the years 1848 to 1853 which effectively drove the movement underground. The Bab had, however, prophesied the appearance of another figure whom he called 'He whom God shall manifest'. In the 1870s the movement was to re-emerge under the leadership of Mirza Husayn 'Ali Nuri who took the title Baha'u'llah and who claimed to be 'He whom God shall manifest'. In addition, Baha'u'llah claimed to be the return of the Imam Husayn expected by the Shi'is, the return of Christ anticipated by both Sunnis and Christians, the Messiah or Lord of Hosts prophesied to the Jews and the Shah Bahram Varjavand foretold in Zoroastrian prophecy, and he succeeded in attracting numbers of Jews and Zoroastrians in Iran to the new religion.

The persecutions of the new religion continued however. Although there was not the same intensity that characterised the events of 1848–53, the daily life of many Baha'is was very difficult. Even when specific persecutions which resulted in loss of life were not occurring, the day-to-day harassment and lack of security of property and livelihood made life intolerable. One of the most well-known and well-publicised episodes was the execution in Isfahan of two merchant Sayyid brothers. These two brothers had been among the most wealthy and respected merchants in Isfahan and the Imam-Jum'a owed them a considerable sum. In order to get out of paying his debt, the Imam-Jum'a put himself in league with another prominent religious leader, Aqa Najafi, and denounced the two brothers as adherents of the new religion. They were executed in 1879 and their wealth looted by these two clerics together with the Governor of Isfahan, the Zillu's-Sultan. Such events, catastrophic as they were for the immediate family of the two brothers, were also the cause of pressure upon the other Baha'is of the entire country. For when news of such episodes reached other cities, this would be used by other unscrupulous individuals to harass the Baha'is and extort money from them. And such episodes were a regular occurrence in the 1880s, 1890s and 1900s. Thus it was not surprising that Baha'is should flock in large numbers to anywhere that appeared to promise security for life and property.

Prior to the second half of the nineteenth century, the territories to the east of the Caspian Sea were a vast area in which a handful of stockaded towns nominally controlled vaguely-defined areas. The Russians gradually advanced into this area throughout the years 1840 to 1880. By 1844, they had reached the Aral Sea; Tashkent was captured in 1865; Samarkand in 1868; and Khiva in 1873. By the end of the 1870s, the Russians were poised to move into the lands immediately to the north of the Iran province of Khurasan. In former times this area had been an integral part of Iran and the Iranian government still regarded the area as being under its suzerainty. Despite the protests of Iran, however, Russia pushed into this area. General Lomakin fought a campaign against the Geok Teppe Turkmen in 1879 but was repulsed. In the following year,

General Skobelev returned with a more powerful force, and, after a lengthy campaign, crushed the tribes in 1881. The border with Iran was delineated by agreement in 1881. Thus came into being the Russian province of Transcaspia, which in 1890 was separated from the control of the Government of the Caucasus.

Some six hundred kilometres from the Caspian, they built a new city to be the capital of the new province of Transcaspia. The name of this city was Ashkhabad. According to tradition, the city had been the site of a Turkmen settlement of some 500 tents prior to the Russian invasion. When the Russians decided to make this the site of the capital of Transcaspia, they built a European-style city. In order to bring order to this region and for strategic reasons, the Russians built a railway parallel to the Iranian border from Uzun Ada on the Caspian Sea to Samarkand. Ashkhabad was one of the main stations along this railway, the point at which Iranian trade was able to connect with the railway.

An American Baha'i who visited the city in 1908 describes it thus:

> The city itself lies on the plain a short distance from the mountains, which here are quite rugged and rocky. The town is quite modern in its aspect, being laid off with gardens and broad streets, which meet at right angles. Rows of trees along the sidewalks remind one of a western city, while the buildings and the waterways, which flank the streets and are fed with water coming from the nearby mountains, are strikingly oriental. (Remey 1916, p 153)

The population of Ashkhabad was estimated to be some 4,000 in 1884, 8,000 (of which 4,000 were troops) in 1886, 10,000 in 1888, 19,000 in 1897, 44,000 (of which 10,000 were Russians) in 1910, and 52,000 in 1926, and 127,000 in 1939 (Curzon 1892, vol 1, p. 86n; Boulangier 1888, p. 136; Allworth 1967, p. 98). At first, the Turkmen did not live in the city itself, the population of which was therefore principally composed of troops and government officials from Russia who lived in the European quarter of the city, and others from Iran and the Caucasus as well as a number of Jews and Armenians who lived in the business quarter. The opportunities provided by the newly-opened territories as well as the re-orientation of trade-routes caused by the building of the Transcaspian railway gave the town something of a 'frontier' atmosphere.

The Origins of the Baha'i Community in Ashkhabad

Baha'i's involvement with the new city of Ashkhabad existed from the very start. One of the relatives of the Bab, Hajji Mirza Hasan, known as Afnan-i Kabir, realised the potential of the new city as he was travelling through the area in 1299 (1881–2) on his way to 'Akka.[3] He sent instructions to his son Aqa Sayyid Ahmad Afnan in Yazd that land should be purchased in the new city for him. Aqa Sayyid Ahmad wrote to Hajji Muhammad Kazim Isfahani who was resident in Sabzivar. In 1882, the latter's brother, Hajji 'Abdu'l-Husayn, who lived in Quchan a short distance across the border from Ashkhabad, travelled to that city and purchased land both for the Afnan family[4] and himself.

At about this time, there erupted in Iran a general persecution of the Baha'is that affected most of the country (and in particular, Tehran, Yazd, Isfahan, Sabzivar, Fars and Rasht). According to one account, a plan was conceived among the Baha'is of Isfahan and Yazd that a group of Baha'is should set out for Russia and there implore the protection of the Czar for the Baha'is against the depredations of the State and 'ulama. Permission for this plan was sought from Baha'u'llah in 'Akka but the reply came forbidding this absolutely. However, Baha'u'llah did give approval to Baha'is settling in Ashkhabad (Haydar-'Ali 1980, pp. 98–9).

In about 1884, the first four Baha'is to settle permanently in Ashkhabad arrived there. Two of these arrived from Sabzivar, Aqa 'Abdu'r-Rasul Yazdi and Aqa Muhammad Rida Arbab Isfahani. The story of these two is interesting as it is illustrative of the kind of pressures that caused the Baha'is to go into exile. The first had been driven out of Yazd by persecutions in about 1877; the second was the son of the above-mentioned Hajji Muhammad Kazim Isfahani who had been a Babi and later a Baha'i and had been forced to leave Isfahan in the persecutions that had followed the execution of Mulla Kazim Talkhunchi'i in 1877. Both of these two had come to Sabzivar together with at least a dozen other Baha'is fleeing from both

Yazd and Isfahan at about this time. Quite why all of these chose to come to Sabzivar is not clear, but it may have been the fact that the leading mujtahid of the town, Hajji Mirza Ibrahim Shari'atmadar, was sympathetic to the Baha'is and willing to use his influence to counter the activities of those who wished to stir up trouble against them. However, the influx of a large number of Baha'is must have upset the delicate balance in the town, and a few years later a fierce persecution erupted in Sabzivar as a result of which Aqa 'Abdu'r-Rasul and Aqa Muhammad Rida fled to Ashkhabad. These two set up as traders in tea.

On 3 April 1884, two other Baha'is, arrived, Ustad 'Ali Akbar and Ustad Muhammad Rida, both builders from Yazd. They also had fled Yazd as a result of persecutions there — the former had had several attempts made on his life. They came to Ashkhabad, presumably because the construction of the new town gave rise to plenty of work for skilled builders.

Between 1884 and 1889, there was a steady trickle of Baha'is arriving in Ashkhabad (Table 1). These mostly came from Isfahan, Yazd and Milan in Azerbaidzhan. They were almost all either builders, who could obtain employment in the rapidly expanding city, or merchants, who saw the potential of the new railway line that had reached from the coast to Ashkhabad in 1885 and to Samarkand in 1888. At this time the majority of the Baha'is lived in the area of the Bazaar and their centre was the caravanserai called Sara-yi Rashti, which was owned by the Afnan family. In December 1887 a start was made on the first Baha'i communal buildings in Ashkhabad, a public bath and a meeting-room. By 1889 the Baha'i community in Ashkhabad may have numbered some 400.

Large numbers of Shi'i Iranians had also moved to Ashkhabad and these brought with them their animosity towards the Baha'is. Therefore many of the Baha'is continued the practice which they had followed in Iran of not openly stating that they were Baha'is and also following Islamic practices and rituals in order not to cause offence. To most Baha'is at this time it must therefore have appeared that Ashkhabad was not substantially better than Iran from the point of view of religious freedom.[5]

The Episode of the Murder of Hajji Muhammad Rida Isfahani, 1889

The turning point in the development of the Baha'i community in Ashkhabad came with the episode of the murder of Hajji Muhammad Rida Isfahani on 8th September 1889. Isfahani, as the agent for the Afnan family in Ashkhabad, had been one of the most prominent Baha'is, and he used to openly assert his religious beliefs. The murder took place in the middle of the main bazaar in broad daylight and in full view of a large crowd. In the trial that followed, it emerged that the plan for the murder had been concocted by a number of the leading Iranian merchants, together with 'ulama who had come from Khurasan expressly for this purpose. It had been intended that the murder would be the signal for a general attack on the Baha'is and, for 24 hours, bands of lutis (street ruffians) took to the streets looking for Baha'is to assault. The body of Isfahani lay in the open for most of the day as no-one dared approach it.

Eventually, however, the Governor intervened and began arresting those reponsible. The perpetrators made no effort to conceal their crime. They asserted that it was a purely religious affair between Iranians, and the Russian authorities need not be involved. They assumed that, as in Iran, the mere fact of proving that their victim was a Baha'i would be sufficient to justify their action. When they saw however that the Governor took no notice of this line of argument, those involved in the plot began to flee to Iran. Some seventy persons fled. Nine were arrested and brought to trial. A military tribunal, sent from St Petersburg, tried the case in November 1890. The judges instructed that the different religious communities sit separately in the court-room. This was the first occasion when many who had secretly been Baha'is openly identified themselves by where they sat. It was also the first occasion in Baha'i history when official recognition was given to the Baha'i Faith as a religion independent of Islam. The court found against the perpetrators of the crime. The two who had carried out the murder were sentenced to death, four to imprisonment and exile to Siberia, one to imprisonment and one was found not guilty. Later, after the Baha'is had intervened on behalf of those sentenced, the Czar commuted the death sentences to life imprisonment.[6]

The Baha'is were of course jubilant. It was the first time in the forty-five-year history of the Babi-Baha'i movement that an attack on one of their number had been dealt with justly. Baha'u'llah commended the Russian Government for its action. As the news spread throughout Iran it increased the surge of Baha'i immigrants — particularly since there was a further wave of persecutions in Iran in 1889–91 affecting Isfahan, Yazd, Tihran and Khurasan.

The Growth of the Baha'i Community in Ashkhabad, 1890–1918

The episode of the murder of Hajji Muhammad Rida Isfahani resulted in profound changes. Whereas previously the Baha'is had lived more or less as an integrated part of the Shi'i Iranian social network, there was now a separation between the two communities socially.[7] This had two major effects. Firstly, it meant that conversions from among Ashkhabad's Iranian Shi'is, of which there had been a few during the initial period, now almost entirely ceased. Contacts with native Turkmen tribesmen were minimal because of linguistic and cultural barriers. There was also no attempt made to convert Russians, since Russian law made it a capital offence for a Russian citizen to convert from Christianity, therefore the Baha'i community became rather introverted. The second major consequence was that the Baha'is had to set up their own social institutions and networks. At first these were fairly modest but, as the number of Baha'is in Ashkhabad grew, they became more sophisticated, eventually achieving a high degree of organisation and development. By 1902, there were approximately 1000 Baha'is in Ashkhabad including children (Mazandarani 1975, p. 983).

From the writings of Baha'u'llah and 'Abdu'l-Baha, there emerges a picture of the physical structure and social functioning of an ideal Baha'i community. The centrepiece of the community is the House of Worship (*Mashriqu'l-Adhkār*). This is a building dedicated solely to the worship of God, in which prayers and readings from the Holy Scriptures of any of the world religions may be spoken, chanted or sung *a capello*. Around this building should be buildings for the major social organs of the community: a meeting hall, schools and a university, medical clinics and a hospital, a hospice for the elderly and infirm, an orphanage, a traveller's hospice, etc, ('Abdu'l-Baha 1916, p. 136; Remey 1916, p. 155). The functioning of the community is under the authority of a council, called the Local Spiritual Assembly, elected from among all of the adult Baha'is of the locality. This council appoints committees to carry out the various functions associated with the organisation of the community: a committee to organise meetings and Holy Day celebrations, education committee, women's committee, youth committee, etc.

The Ashkhabad Baha'i community attempted to achieve this ideal pattern. Even before the episode of the murder of Hajji Muhammad Rida Isfahani, they had begun to build a number of communal buildings. A public baths and then a meeting house were built on a piece of land that had been purchased from a man named A'zam. This piece of land, which continued to be called Zamin-i A'zam (meaning both 'A'zam's land' and 'most great land'), was located fairly centrally in the town and became the focus of further Baha'i building. A travellers' hospice was erected on this site as well as a dispensary and hospital. In 1312 (1894–5), a boys' school was founded and a building for it was completed in 1897. A cemetery had also been acquired at an early stage on a separate site. But the plan from the beginning had been to build at the centre of this land a House of Worship, the central institutional building of a Baha'i community. Eventually, in mid-September 1902, Hajji Muhammad Taqi Afnan, Vakilu'd-Dawlih, whose brother Hajji Mirza Muhammad 'Ali Afnan had purchased much of A'zam's land in the first instance, was instructed by 'Abdu'l-Baha to proceed from Yazd (where he had been the Russian Consular Agent) in order to supervise the construction of this building. He spent much of his wealth on the project, and money also came from all over Iran and the rest of the Baha'i world. Construction was begun on 31 October 1902, and in November 1904 there was a ceremony in which the Russian Governor of Ashkhabad, General Subotich, laid the foundation stone. The construction was supervised by Ustad 'Ali Akbar Yazdi and Volkov a Russian engineer (Mazandarani 1975, pp. 995–1002; Whitmore 1975, p. 8; Momen 1981, pp. 442–3).

By 1907 the structure of the building was substantially complete and Hajji Muhammad Taqi left for 'Akka leaving behind his son, Mirza Mahmud, to complete the work. However it was not until 1919 that the building was finally completed, including the external decorative work. An American Baha'i who visited Ashkhabad in 1908 describes it thus:

> The Mashrak-al-Azkar stands in the middle of the city, surrounded by a large garden, which is bounded by four streets. It rises high above the surrounding buildings and trees, its dome being visible for miles, as the traveller approaches the city over the plain. The building in plan is a regular polygon of nine sides. One large doorway and portico, flanked by turrets, facing the direction of the Holy City [Akka], forms the principal motive of the facade, while the dome dominates the whole composition . . . In plan the building is composed of three sections: the central rotunda, the aisle or ambulatory which surrounds it, and the loggia which surrounds the whole building (Remey 1916, p. 153).

It was the most imposing building in Ashkhabad, larger in size than any of the churches or mosques in the city. Over the next few years a number of other buildings were added: a girls' school was founded in 1907, two kindergartens in 1917–18, and a Baha'i Library and Public Reading Room.

The social structure of the Baha'i community proceeded apace with the growth of the physical buildings. Initially, the leadership of the community was vested in those who were its leading members intellectually or in terms of wealth. Among the leading group of merchants were Mirza 'Abdu'l-Karim Ardibili, Mashhadi Yusif Milani, Hajji 'Abdu'r-Rasul Yazdi (Aliov), Aqa Muhammad Rida Arbab Isfahani (Kazemov), Aqa Husayn 'Ali Ahmadov and Mirza Ja'far Rahmani (Hadiov); this group were called by the Russian term 'Khozyain'.[8] Intellectual leadership was provided by some of the leading Iranian Baha'is of the time who came to Ashkhabad. In July 1889, there arrived in Ashkhabad Mirza Abu'l-Fadl Gulpaygani and in the following year Shaykh Muhammad Qa'ini. Both had been prominent 'ulama before becoming Baha'is.

Mirza Abu'l-Fadl arrived just two months before the episode of the murder of Hajji Muhammad Rida Isfahani. He took a leading role in the representations that the Baha'i community made to the Russian authorities during this episode. He remained in Ashkhabad for only nine months before going on to Samarkand and Bukhara where he was to discover the only extant copy of the *Hudūd al-'Ālam* in the library of the Amir. He later returned and spent some time in Ashkhabad. Here Captain Alexander Tumanski met him and obtained much information and many manuscripts which he forwarded to Russia.[9] Mirza Abu'l-Fadl left in 1311 (1893–4) and was replaced by Sayyid Mahdi Gulpaygani, his nephew. Sayyid Mahdi taught the Baha'i children for a time and was editor of a Russian Government magazine in Persian. He remained in Ashkhabad for the rest of his life.[10] and will be referred to again.

Shaykh Muhammad Qa'ini arrived in Ashkhabad in about 1890 and only stayed a short time before journeying to Bukhara where he died in 1892. Accompanying him was his nephew, Shaykh Muhammad 'Ali Qa'ini, who remained a short time in Ashkhabad before returning to Iran. On 'Abdu'l-Baha's instructions, he returned to Ashkhabad in about 1905. He was in charge of the school there until his death in 1924.

These four persons, Mirza Abu'l-Fadl Gulpaygani and his nephew Sayyid Mahdi and Shaykh Muhammad Qa'ini and his nephew, Shaykh Muhammad 'Ali were perhaps the leading Baha'i intellectuals of their generation. With their presence in Ashkhabad, this city became a major centre of learning and intellectual life in the Baha'i world. Mirza Abu'l-Fadl urged the Ashkhabad Baha'is to undertake the publication of a Baha'i magazine. But he did not receive sufficient support and this was a project that was to wait a further twenty years to come to fruition under Sayyid Mahdi.

Despite the presence in Ashkhabad of such eminent Baha'is, authority over the Baha'is of the city did not lie in their hands. Ashkhabad was one of the first places (possibly the first) in which 'Abdu'l-Baha gave instructions for the setting up of an elected Baha'i council. This was set up in 1313 (1895–6) and was called at first the Spiritual Board of Counsel (*Mahfil-i Shawrā Rawhānī*) and later the Spiritual Assembly (*Mahfil-i Rawhānī*).[11] Although prominent Baha'i intellectuals, such as Sayyid Mahdi Gulpaygani and Shaykh Muhammad 'Ali Qa'ini, and leading Baha'i merchants, such as Mashhadi Yusif Milani, were elected to membership of the Assembly, less wealthy individuals such as Ustad 'Ali-Akbar Banna Yazdi were also elected onto this body. 'Abdu'l-Baha always encouraged the Baha'is to regard the Assembly as a whole as the source of authority in the community and not the individual members of it.

The Spiritual Assembly in Ashkhabad appointed a number of committees to which it delegated some of its functions. One of the most active of these committees was the Youth Committee which organised activities for the youth and ran a large youth library; gymnastics, drama and social service were all catered for. There were also a women's committee and various committees responsible for the running of the schools and other social institutions. All of these were under the authority of the Spiritual Assembly.

After the Revolution, 1918–28

The Russian Revolution brought a great deal of turmoil to the region of Turkmenistan. For a time, from 1918 to 1920, there was an autonomous Turkmen democratic government. But in 1920, the Bolsheviks conquered the area. Although a certain amount of political upheaval persisted after this, things gradually began to settle again.

Initially the Revolution was a great boon to the Baha'i community in Ashkhabad. A Baha'i magazine *Khurshīd-i Khāvar* was initiated in 1917 with Sayyid Mahdi Gulpaygani as editor. Youth and educational activities were expanded considerably with the institution of literacy classes, evening adult education classes, and courses for the study of Russian and Esperanto. Acting in concert with other Baha'i communities in the Caucasus, Turkistan and Moscow, publications were brought out in Russian. A Russian Baha'i, Izabella Grinevskaya, had written a play called *The Bab*. This was put on the stage in Ashkhabad by a Russian company in 1922.[12]

Freed from the previous legal restriction of trying to convert Russians, meetings aimed specifically at Russian Christians were established. At first, these meetings were held in the home of an individual Baha'i, Mirza Diya'u'llah Asgharzadih, and some fifty persons attended. Later there were as many as five hundred attending and the meetings had to be held in the main meeting rooms. Sayyid Mahdi Gulpaygani was the principal Baha'i speaker at these meetings.

The Baha'is were vigorous also in defence against the anti-religious propaganda of the state. Government-sponsored speakers toured the provinces attacking all religions. At Ashkhabad, the first such meeting appears to have been held each evening between 8 and 11 June 1921 with some five thousand present in a park.[13] The Government speakers on this occasion were Govsev, Barisov and Sinitsin. On this occasion only Sayyid Mahdi Gulpaygani came forward to defend religion in general and the Baha'is in particular. On 25 and 26 April 1925, Kalinovsky spoke for the Government attacking religion which on this occasion was defended by Yevgeny Kabranov, a Christian priest, as well as Sayyid Mahdi Gulpaygani. At another similar meeting on 19 and 20 October 1925, Arkhangelsky, a former Christian priest, spoke for the Government with the same two defending religion (Sulaymani 1966 pp. 33–36; Mazandarani 1975 pp. 994, 1012).

News of these meetings was reported in the newspapers and increased the attendance. Also through this means news of the Baha'i Faith spread to other Russian cities and small groups of Baha'i converts from Christianity began to be formed in several Russian towns, for example in Oriyol, near Moscow.

The first decade of the Russian Revolution thus marks the apex of the Ashkhabad Baha'i community. The Revolution had given them the opportunity to break out of the social isolation which had characterised the pre-Revolution days. The Baha'i community of Ashkhabad at the time of the Revolution numbered some 4,000, of whom 1,000 were children. The community was, by this time, composed largely of merchants, especially in the tea trade, and shopkeepers, especially of glass products from Russia. A few were craftsmen, such as shoemakers and builders. An increasing number of the younger generation were, however, going on to universities in Russia and were being trained in the professions.

Persecution and Dispersal, 1928–38

Eventually, however, the persecutions that were affecting other religious communities in the Soviet Union began to affect the Baha'is. Indeed the Baha'is were in a particularly vulnerable position. The fact that they had failed to make any great number of converts from among the native Turkmen population and consisted mostly of Iranian nationals made it comparatively easy for the authorities to suppress them. In addition, by this time, a large proportion of them earned their living through wholesale and retail trade, and some were among the wealthiest citizens of Ashkhabad. Thus they were regarded by the communist authorities as archetypal class enemies (see for example comments in the *Great Soviet Encyclopaedia*, vol. 3, p. 10). However, a more compelling reason for the Soviet authorities to try to supress the Baha'i community appears from the following assessment by Walter Kolarz:

> Islam, both in its Shiite and Sunnite form, is attacked by the communists because it is 'reactionary', encourages nationalist narrowmindedness and obstructs the education and emancipation of women. Baha'iism [sic] has incurred communist displeasure for exactly the opposite reasons. It is dangerous to Communism because of its broadmindedness, its tolerance, its international outlook, the attention it pays to women's education and its insistence on the equality of the sexes. All this contradicts the communist thesis about the backwardness of all religions. In the political sphere social reformers appear to the communists more harmful than 'reactionaries', and in the religious field an outlook which is mindful of modern social problems is thought more obnoxious than out-of-date obscurantism. This is perhaps why Baha'iism has attracted the attention of the Soviet communists to a much greater degree than might be warranted by the numerical strength of its supporters (Kolarz 1961, p. 470).

As early as 1922, an article appeared in the official Government press attacking the Baha'is for turning the thoughts of young people away from Bolshevism. But initially, the increased activities of the Baha'i community were not openly opposed. Evidently the authorities were confident that people could be won away from religion through debate and polemic.

From about 1926 onwards, the pressure intensified. At first it was merely a question of a close watch being kept on all Baha'i activities. Then in 1928, as part of a general anti-religious campaign launched under Stalin, the secret police began raiding Baha'i meetings in Ashkhabad, arresting the leading Baha'is, and confiscating books and papers. The Baha'i printing press was confiscated, the Baha'i Assembly was put under severe restrictions and the youth activities disbanded. It was apparently the activities of the Baha'i youth committee that were considered the greatest threat by the communist authorities: 'A Baha'i youth organisation which the communists nicknamed "Bekhamol" was set up in Ashkhabad. On account of its extensive cultural activities and supra-national tendencies it was a serious competitor of the Komsomol.'[14] Not long after the government issued an order that all religious buildings were to become the property of the state. Therefore, the House of Worship, the centre of the Baha'i community in Ashkhabad was expropriated and had to be rented back from the State by the Baha'is on a five-year lease. Later in 1929, the Baha'i schools and kindergartens, which had about 1,000 children in all, were closed.

The Baha'i leadership of all the communities in the Soviet Union tried to make representations to the government, pointing out that the Baha'is did not interfere in political matters and were obedient to their government, but to no avail. The persecutions intensified in 1929 with numerous Baha'is being arrested, some of whom were imprisoned, some exiled to Siberia, some deported to Iran and some died under mysterious circumstances. Baha'i companies were taken over and their employees dismissed. Other Baha'is were turned out of their employment and Baha'i students were expelled from colleges and universities.

From 1930 to 1938, the severe restrictions on the religious activities of the community continued. Individual restrictions were also severe, especially for leading members of the community. Since many of the Baha'is were involved in trade, the general recession following the Revolution had had a severe financial effect on the community as well. By April 1933, it was reported that 40 families were receiving financial assistance from the Spiritual Assembly.

In 1933, the five-year lease on the House of Worship was renewed. Over the next few years there was a degree of relaxation of the strictness of the anti-Baha'i measures. In 1935, under new regulations, the House of Worship was restored to full Baha'i ownership and public meetings were once again held there. Harassment of individual Baha'is also lessened a little but the suspicion of foreigners (most Baha'is in Ashkhabad had retained Iranian citizenship) together with the bleak economic situation of many families, caused an increasing trend of return to Iran.[15]

Shoghi Effendi, the world leader of the Baha'i Faith at this time, discouraged the Baha'is from returning to Iran voluntarily. He even encouraged them, if it would be conducive to their remaining in Ashkhabad, to adopt Russian citizenship. He encouraged them to appeal to the authorities in Ashkhabad and Moscow against these measures taken against them but advised them that, ultimately, if the State's decision went against them, they must submit to this. The following quotation demonstrates his attitude to the measures adopted by the Soviet authorities:

> Faithful to their [the Soviet] policy of expropriating in the interests of the State all edifices and monuments of a religious character, they have a few months ago approached the Baha'i representatives in Turkistan, and after protracted negotiations with them, decided to claim and enforce their right of ownership and control of that most cherished and universally prized Baha'i possession, the Mashriqu'l-Adhkar of 'Ishqabad . . .
>
> To these measures which the State in the free exercise of its legitimate rights, has chosen to enforce, and with which the Baha'is, as befits their position as loyal and law-abiding citizens, have complied, others have followed which though of a different character are none the less grievously affecting our beloved Cause . . .
>
> . . . our sorely-tried brethren in Caucasus and Turkistan have nonetheless, as befits law-abiding citizens resolved, after having exhausted every legitimate means for the alleviation of the restrictions imposed upon them, to definitely uphold and conscientiously carry out the considered judgement of their recognized government (*Baha'i World* 1930, pp. 41–3).

Shoghi Effendi appears to have drawn a distinction between the persecutions of the Baha'is in Iran where the Baha'is were persecuted specifically because they were Baha'is, and the situation in the Soviet Union where the Baha'is were subjected to these measures as a result of a general policy against all religious communities (Rabbani 1969, pp. 313–6).

In 1938 the final blow came. In February of that year, the authorities suddenly arrested every male adult Baha'i in Ashkhabad and even some of the women also. According to one report 'except for a few former members of the Iranian consulate in 'Ishqabad not a single male Baha'i is out of prison (*Baha'i World* 1942, p. 184)'. The women and children were then put across the border into Iran. Some five hundred men were imprisoned and six hundred women and children were deported to Iran. By the end of the year, it was reported that: 'At present only a few Baha'is are left, women, children and old men'. (*Baha'i World* 1942, p. 89).

Of the imprisoned men, most spent at least a year or more in prison. Some were then sentenced to longer terms of imprisonment or exile to Siberia. Many of those who were of Iranian citizenship were expelled across the border to Iran. The House of Worship was then expropriated again and made into an art gallery.[16] Thus ended the Baha'i community of Ashkhabad.

The Social Structure of the Baha'i Community in Ashkhabad in 1900

Ustad 'Ali Akbar Banna Yazdi, who was one of the first Baha'is in Ashkhabad, wrote a history in which he gives an account of the various Baha'is who came to Ashkhabad. The history was begun in 1319 (1901–2) and must have been completed before 1321 (1903) since in that year the author travelled back to his native Yazd and was murdered there in the general anti-Baha'i upheaval of 1903.

Ustad 'Ali Akbar's history is not in fact comprehensive in listing all of the Baha'is that came to Ashkhabad and the matter is further confused by the fact that several of those who are listed had only stayed in Ashkhabad a short time before moving on to somewhere else. Ustad 'Ali Akbar is also not very good at giving details of all of the members of a family that came, but rather concentrates on the male head of the family. Nevertheless, despite these limitations, Ustad 'Ali Akbar gives a good representative sample of the heads of family of the Baha'is who came to Ashkhabad up to about 1900, and the information he gives is corroborated by other sources. Therefore an attempt has been made to analyse in some greater detail the 139 heads of family that have been identified in Ustad 'Ali Akbar's history, together with a further 13 names found in other sources,[17] making a total of 151.

Table 1 *Year of arrival of Baha'i heads of family in Ashkhabad*

Year		Number Arriving
1301 (1883–4)		4
1302 (1884–5)		3
1303 (1885–6)		0
1304 (1886–7)		2
1305 (1887–8)	1308 (1890–1)	42
1309 (1891–2)	1312 (1894–5)	20
1313 (1895–6)	1316 (1898–9)	32
1317 (1899–1900)	1320 (1902–3)	12
	Total	115

Table 1 gives the year of arrival in Ashkhabad of those listed by Ustad 'Ali Akbar. This therefore represents the year of arrival of the heads of family. Not uncommonly, the heads of family would come to Ashkhabad first, and then, once established, would return and bring their families anything up to five years later.

Table 2 *Occupations of Baha'i heads of family arriving in Ashkhabad*

	Number	Per cent
1 'Ulama, a. major	2	1.7
b. minor	10	8.3
2 Notables & government officials	0	0
3 Wholesale merchants (*tujjār*)	18	14.9
c. agents for *tujjār*	3	2.5
c. bankers *sarrāf*	4	3.3
4 Shopkeepers (*kāsib*)	22	18.2
5 Skilled workers (*aṣnāf*)		
a. master builder (*ustād, bannā*)	10	8.3
b. other mastercraftsmen (*ustād*)	21	17.4
c. builder (*bannā*)	4	3.3
d. other skilled workers	24	19.8
6 Unskilled workers	1	0.8
7 Farmers & agricultural workers	2	1.7
Totals	121	99.8

294

Table 2 gives an analysis of the occupations of these heads of family before their arrival in Ashkhabad. The occupations of 121 were identified. Many of these followed the same occupation when they reached Ashkhabad, although a few did change — in particular, in later years, a number who followed different occupations initially became traders and merchants.

By far the largest group was that of the skilled guilded workers (*aṣnāf*), and of these, the majority are specified as builders or masons (*bannā*). Also several of the six who are named *Ustād* but whose exact occupation is not specified and who are therefore listed under 5b, may well have been master-builders. The other *aṣnāf* listed include a wide variety of workers such as : *chīt-sāz* (chintz-maker), *zargar* (goldsmith), *fakhkhār* (lime-burner or kilnsman), *kafsh-dūz* (shoe-maker), *kulāh-dūz* (cap-maker), *dabbāgh* (dyer), *khayyāt* (tailor), etc.

The next largest group was that of tradesmen, shopkeepers and petty commodity producers (*kāsib*, plur. *kasaba*). Here there was no particular pattern at this time and every type of trade was engaged in by the Baha'is.

The third largest grouping is that of the wholesale merchants (*tujjār*). These were merchants that often specialised in the import or export of one particular commodity. In the case of Ashkhabad, many of the Baha'i *tujjār* were involved in the tea trade, importing from India and China and exporting to Russia. In particular, they imported from Shanghai the green tea drunk by the Turkmen. When the First World War closed the Strait of the Dardenelles to shipping that brought the tea via the Suez Canal, the price of tea increased dramatically and several of these merchants became rich.

The last notable group of those who came to Ashkhabad were persons who had been trained as 'ulama. The two major 'ulama listed in Table 2 were:

1. Shaykh Muhammad Qa'ini, known as Nabīl-i Akbar. He was one of the few people who had obtained an *ijāza* (permission to practise *ijtihād*) from Shaykh Murtada Ansari, the foremost *mujtahid* and *marj'a at-taqlīd* of the mid-nineteenth century.[18]

2. Mirza Abu'l-Fadl Gulpaygani, who had studied at Najaf and Karbala, and been head of a religious college, the Madrasa-yi Hakim Hashim (Madrassa-yi Madar-i Shah), in Tihran prior to his becoming a Baha'i.

295

The rest are listed under the category of minor 'ulama. Also in this category is listed Mirza Ibrahim Urumi, a Nestorian Christian priest who had become a Baha'i. Obviously, none of these could continue their former occupation in Ashkhabad, especially after the murder of Hajji Muhammad Rida Isfahani when the Iranian Shi'i and Baha'i communities separated. Several became teachers of the Baha'i children in Ashkhabad. Others used their literacy to work for merchants or as bankers/money-changers (ṣarrāf).

Table 3 shows the geographical origin of the list of persons analysed. It can be seen from this that the largest contingent came from Yazd. Indeed the figures analysed here from Ustad 'Ali Akbar agree closely with the estimate made by another author, 'Azizu'llah Sulaymani, himself an Ashkhabad Baha'i, that one-third of the Ashkhabad Baha'is originated from Yazd (Sulaymani 1966, p. 585). The other large contingents came from Azerbaidzhan and Khurasan.

Table 3 *Places of origin of Baha'i heads of family arriving in Ashkhabad*

	Number	Per cent
Khurasan	26	17.2
Mazandaran	1	0.7
Gilan	4	2.6
Azerbaidzhan, Iranian	32	21.2
Qazvin and Khamsih	4	2.6
Tihran	0	0
Central Provinces (Kashan, Arak, etc)	2	1.3
Isfahan	9	6.0
Fars	3	2.0
Yazd	49	32.5
Kirman	6	4.0
Hamadan	7	4.6
Kurdistan	1	0.7
Caucasus and Russian Azerbaidzhan	6	4.0
Unknown	1	0.7
Total	151	100.1

Table 3 sheds some light on the motives of the Baha'is emigrating to Ashkhabad. If the motivation for emigration had been purely the economic opportunities provided by the 'frontier' territory, then one would have expected that Baha'is would have emigrated there from all zones, with perhaps some preponderance of those from regions geographically close to

Ashkhabad. And yet this is not the pattern that is found. Some geographically close areas such as Mazandaran are poorly represented, while more distant areas have large representations.

The two large contingents from Yazd and Khurasan are understandable in that both are areas in which there were frequent persecutions of the Baha'is, and Khurasan is also geographically adjacent to Ashkhabad. The large proportion from Azerbaidzhan (21%) is a little more difficult to explain, in that there were fewer persecutions of the Baha'is in that province, and also, if the Baha'is from that area had wished to emigrate, then it would seem that the Caucasian provinces of Russia would have been closer both ethnically and geographically. And yet far fewer Baha'is emigrated from Iranian Azerbaidzhan to Baku than to Ashkhabad. Perhaps the reason for this was the greater opportunities presented by the new town of Ashkhabad and the re-alignment of trade routes caused by the Transcaspian Railway.

It is also perhaps rather surprising that more Baha'is did not come to Ashkhabad from Isfahan which was, like Yazd, a focus of persistent persecutions of the Baha'is throughout the whole of this period. Baha'is from Isfahan tended to flee to Tihran. The relative lack of Baha'is from Tihran, Fars and Mazandaran is no surprise, as the Baha'is of these areas were subjected to relatively less persecution. Indeed Tihran was itself a point to which Baha'is from other parts of Iran would flee.

Overall then the pattern of emigration most closely fits the pattern of persecutions in Iran (although Azerbaidzhan remains as an inconsistency in this picture).

A few other facts can be derived from the accounts presented by Ustad 'Ali Akbar. From among Iran's religious minorities, the following were represented among Ashkhabad's Baha'is: 7 Jews, 4 Ahl-i Haqq ('Aliyu'llahis), 3 Christians and 3 Zoroastrians. The vast majority of the wives of the heads of family are described as being already Baha'is at the time of marriage, thus indicating that 'familialisation' of the Baha'i community had proceeded a long way (Smith and Momen 1986, p. 77).

The Achievements of the Ashkhabad Baha'i Community

It would perhaps be appropriate to consider briefly the social and economic achievements of the Ashkhabad Baha'i community. The importance to the Baha'i world of the Baha'i community created in Ashkhabad will be discussed in the next section. Here we will only consider the social and economic achievements of the community.

As has been described, many of those who came to Ashkhabad came as a result of persecutions. Often they had lost everything they possessed as a result of the persecutions, and arrived in Ashkhabad destitute. After their arrival in Ashkhabad, many had to take on occupations that were socially lower than what they had been used to in Iran.[19] However, many of those who came appear to have brought with them skills and experience together with the support engendered by a strong community spirit enabled many to take full advantage of the opportunities presented by the 'frontier' town and to acquire an increasing prosperity through trade and business. The Baha'i merchants acquired a reputation for honesty and fair-dealing. One of them, for example, Mulla 'Ali Khurasani, became the banker (ṣarrāf) for the Kurdish tribes around Quchan (Mazandarani, undated, p. 232). By the time of the Russian Revolution the Baha'is were possibly the wealthiest community in Ashkhabad. The emphasis on education in the community allowed the second generation Baha'is to enter university and produced modern professionals (doctors, teachers, lawyers, etc.).

In the field of education, the Baha'is of Ashkhabad also had significant achievements. The setting up of the boys' and girls' schools in 1312 (1894–5) and 1907 respectively enabled them to provide education for the entire community. These were among the first schools in an Iranian community to be run on modern pedagogic principles. At a time when male literacy in the region must have been less than 15 per cent and female literacy negligible, the Baha'is were able to report full male and female literacy among their youth (Baha'i World 1936, p. 37).

Progress in the field of women's advancement came more slowly. The Baha'i women in Ashkhabad were eager to press forward socially and proposed to discard the veil and chadur, but 'Abdu'l-Baha, the Baha'i leader, advised against this, stating that it would incite the Muslims and give them an excuse to attack the Baha'is. Therefore the Baha'i women remained veiled in public. Other 'Islamic' practices prevailed also, such as the separation of the sexes in the House of Worship, with the men on the ground floor and the women and children on a balcony. Before the Russian Revolution, women did not have a vote and were also not eligible for election to the Spiritual Assembly, but this changed after the Revolution. In private, in each others' houses, however, the Baha'i women put aside the veil and enjoyed considerable freedom. They benefited greatly also from the education provided at the girls' school.

The Significance of the Ashkhabad Baha'i Community to the Baha'i World

Chronologically, Ashkhabad first became important to the Baha'i world as a place of refuge for Baha'is fleeing persecution in Iran. This aspect had already been fully discussed above. It probably played this role most prominently up to about 1910. After this, the role of sanctuary was of less importance, as the persecutions in Iran lessened.

Secondly, Ashkhabad became a staging post for those Baha'is travelling from Khurasan, and as far south as Yazd, to see the Baha'i leaders in the Akka-Haifa area. The greater ease of this route after the opening of the railway line as well as its greater security, offset the disadvantage of the longer journey. Baha'is would travel to Ashkhabad overland and thence to the Caspian by rail, to Baku by steamship, thence to Batum by rail, and finally to Istanbul and Haifa by steamship. Thus Ashkhabad became part of the network of Baha'i communications that enabled the Baha'i leadership exiled in the Akka-Haifa area to maintain contact with the bulk of their followers in Iran. This aspect of the role of Ashkhabad diminished after the First World War with the opening up of better communications directly across Iraq and Syria, and ceased entirely after the Russian Revolution.

Ashkhabad was also of great importance as a centre of Baha'i thought and scholarship. The presence of such persons as Mirza Abu'l-Fadl Gulpaygani for a short time and Sayyid Mihdi Gulpaygani and Shaykh Muhammad 'Ali Qa'ini for longer periods of time meant that Ashkhabad became the equal of Tihran, Haifa-Akka, and later Cairo and Chicago as an intellectual centre for the Baha'i world. The debate with Communists and Christians that developed after the Revolution was also of great importance from the point of view of the development of Baha'i thought. However, it is difficult to assess the true intellectual contribution of the Ashkhabad Baha'i community because its dispersal in the third decade of the twentieth century resulted in its effects being felt over a wide area. A number of important administrators, educationists and other leading Baha'is in the Middle East, Europe and North America up to the present time were products of the Ashkhabad Baha'i community. Ashkhabad was also of importance for the publication of books and periodicals in Persian and Russian.

But the main historical significance of the Ashkhabad Baha'i community for the Baha'i world as a whole must remain the fact that it was the first place where there was a conscious attempt to build up a Baha'i community along the pattern laid down in the Baha'i writings. Here was built the first House of Worship of the Baha'i world as well as the first schools and other welfare institutions. Here also the social institutions of the Baha'i Faith, the Spiritual Assembly and its committees, were first developed. Nowhere else was there both the numbers of Baha'is and the freedom sufficient to do this. In Iran, the numbers existed but not the freedom. Elsewhere in the Middle East, the numbers were not sufficient. Although, there had grown a substantial Baha'i community in Chicago and although these Baha'is did in 1903 decide to build a House of Worship in emulation of the Ashkhabad House of Worship, there was not the same unity and community spirit nor the resources to equal the Ashkhabad achievements.

Paradoxically however, the Ashkhabad Baha'i experience marks both a peak of achievement and a dead end. It was a peak of achievement in that as described it marked the furthest that any community reached in realising the ideal of a Baha'i community. But it was also a dead end in that the manner of expansion that it represented, the concentration of Baha'is in one place and building up numbers and social institutions there, was not to become the manner for the furthest propagation of the Baha'i Faith. Under the leadership of Shoghi

Effendi, the Baha'is were to adopt an alternative strategy. Rather than concentrating on the building up of large communities in a small number of locations and then spreading out slowly from these locations to neighbouring areas, Shoghi Effendi adopted the strategy of diffusing the Baha'i thinly to all parts of the world and then seeking to build up communities in each of these thousands of locations. This was to be the pattern of Baha'i expansion from the 1930s to the present day.

Consequently, it is only comparatively recently, in the last thirty years, that Baha'i communities in other parts of the world have managed to achieve the same degree of development as the Ashkhabad community achieved sixty or seventy years ago. And in some ways, this has still not been achieved even yet, for there is still not any single individual town or city in the world where all of the elements achieved by the Ashkhabad Baha'i community (House of Worship, schools, publications and intellectual life, social institutions, community life) can be said to exist to the same degree of development.

The main importance of the Ashkhabad Baha'i community for the Baha'i world as a whole rests with the fact that it achieved its high degree of social development during the period of Baha'i history when the leadership of the Baha'i community was also the source of authoritative interpretation of the Baha'i scriptures. Authoritative texts in the Baha'i Faith are the writings of the founder Baha'u'llah (1817–93) and the authorised interpretations of his two successors, 'Abdu'l-Baha (1844–1921) and Shoghi Effendi (1897–1957). The writings of these three successive leaders of the Baha'i community are regarded as being authoritative for all Baha'is indefinitely into the future.[21] The Ashkhabad Baha'is were the only Baha'i community to have reached such an advanced stage of development under the guidance of 'Abdu'l-Baha and Shoghi Effendi. Therefore, the statements of instructions and guidance from these two leaders resolving the problems that arose in the course of the evolution of the Ashkhabad Baha'i community to its high degree of social and institutional development will remain for all time as part of the pattern upon which all future Baha'i communities will grow and develop. In this sense, therefore, the Ashkhabad Baha'i experience lives on and will continue to be reflected in the future development of the world Baha'i community.

Notes

1 Unfortunately, due to a lack of knowledge of Turkish and Russian, I have only been able to present the Baha'i view and have not been able to balance this with material from other local sources. Indeed the availability of such material from other sources appears to be severely limited. The sources for the historical survey are: Anthony Lee, manuscript notes of interviews with Mr 'Ali-Akbar Furutan, Mr 'Abbas Parvini, Mr Kazem Kazemzadeh, and Mr Tarazollah Namdar. I am extremely grateful to Mr Lee for communicating these papers to me; 'Ali Akbar, undated; Lee 1977, Mazandarani undated, pp. 993–1002; Mazandarani 1975 pp. 981–1049; Remey 1916; Sulaymani 1966; *Baha'i World* 1928 pp. 30–31, 121–2; *Baha'i World* 1930 pp. 34, 160, 165; *Baha'i World* 1936 pp. 33–43; *Baha'i World* 1937 p. 73; *Baha'i World* 1939 pp. 100–102; *Baha'i World* 1942 pp. 87–90

2 There are brief references to the Baha'is in some European sources but these tend not to be very informative: Christie 1925 p. 26; Kalmykow 1971 pp. 151–3; see also Kolarz 1961 pp. 470–3, who refers to a number of Russian sources; and accounts given in Momen 1981 pp. 296–300, 442–3, 473

3 Baha'u'llah was imprisoned in 'Akka and there was a regular stream of Baha'i pilgrims to that city.

4 The relatives of the Bab are known as the *Afnan*.

5 Mulla 'Ali Khurasani is quoted (in 'Ali Akbar, undated p. 232) as saying: 'I became a Baha'i in 1303 (1885–6). For three years I remained in Mashhad. The entire time I was subject to many taunts and reproaches from my friends and others. Eventually I could not stand it any longer and I came to Ashkhabad. I entered Ashkhabad towards the end of 1306 (1888–9). I found that Ashkhabad to be similar to Mashhad in that the Muslims (*aghyār*) were harassing the Baha'is (*aḥibbā*). I began to wish that I had never come to Ashkhabad.'

6 Details of the murder and trial may be found in several sources: Captain Tumanski, a Russian military officer, wrote details of the episode to Victor Rosen who published these in Rosen 1891 vol 6, pp. 247–8 (trans. Browne 1891 vol 2, pp. 411–12); for a detailed Baha'i account, see Mihrabkhani 1974 pp. 159–198, quoting a lengthy letter from Mirza Abu'l-Fadl Gulpaygani who was in Ashkhabad at the time. For the reaction in Iran, see M. Momen 1981, pp. 298–9, quoting a dispatch from British Legation in Tihran.

7 This phenomenon had also occurred in a few places in Iran in small towns and villages where there was a large Baha'i presence (e.g., Nayriz in Fars) but in most places in Iran there had been no social separation.

8 A term which is difficult to translate but is approximately equivalent to *arbāb* in Persian, 'sahib' in colonial India and 'boss' in the English vernacular

9 Tumanski studied Baha'u'llah's foremost work, the *Kitāb al-Aqdas*

with Mirza Abu'l-Fadl and later produced an edited text with translation in the series *Zapiski Imperatorskoi Academii Nauk S. Petersburg*, 8th series, Vol 3, no 6, 1899.

10 Except for a short sojourn in Merv.

11 The question of where the first Spiritual Assembly in the Baha'i world was established is not yet fully clear. It would appear that following the statement from Baha'u'llah in the *Kitāb al-Aqdas* that a House of Justice should be established in every city, a number of eminent Baha'is in Tihran set up an assembly in 1294 (1877) which was established on a more formal basis in 1297 (1880). However this was an *ad hoc* body and additional members were co-opted onto it (Mihrabkhani 1982). Later 'Abdu'l-Baha, in 1315 (1897–8), instructed a number of prominent Baha'is who had been given the title 'Hand of the Cause' by Baha'u'llah to set up the Central Spiritual Assembly in Tihran. The first Board of Counsel of American Baha'is was established in either Kenosha, Wisconsin or New York City in 1897 or 1898 (Collins 1982, p. 228–9). Therefore it would appear that the Ashkhabad Assembly of 1313 (1895–6) was indeed the first elected Spiritual Assembly in the Baha'i world.

12 For an account of life in Ashkhabad at this time, see Furutan 1984 pp. 8–20

13 Sulaymani 1966, pp. 29, 33, gives both June and July in different places.

14 L. Klimovich, *Sotsialisticheskoe Stroitelstvo na Vostoke i Reliqiya*, quoted in Kolarz 1961, p. 471.

15 Events during these years can be followed in successive volumes of *Baha'i World* — See References.

16 It was severely damaged in the devastating earthquake of 1948 that completely flattened most of the rest of the city. Following this, poor maintenance of the building allowed further damage from the rain and the whole building had to be demolished in 1963 for safety.

17 Since a number of prominent names, such as Ustad 'Abdu'r-Rasul Banna Yazdi and Aqa Muhammad Rida Arbab Isfahani, were not in 'Ali-Akbar's list, the present author made a search of a number of other sources, in particular Mazandarani 1975, pp. 993–1002.

18 Shaykh Murtada Ansari was famed for his extreme caution in his actions lest he err and displease God. One example of this was the fact that he is said to have issued no more than two or three *ijazas* during his entire life.

19 Mazandarani 1974, p. 114 reports, for example, that five of the Baha'is, including one who is designated as 'Ustad', became gatherers and hewers of firewood for the kilnsmen.

20 According to Baha'i teaching, these writings cannot be abrogated and will remain in force until the coming of a future 'Manifestation of God', i.e., a further Divine prophet. Authority in the Baha'i Faith at present rests with the Universal House of Justice. However this elected body can only give pronouncements in areas not already covered by the writings of the three successive leaders.

Furthermore a pronouncement of the Universal House of Justice can be abrogated by a further pronouncement by the same body at a later date.

References

'Abdu'l-Baha (1916), 'Utterances of Abdul-Baha upon the Mashrak-el-Azkar', *Star of the West*, Vol 6 No. 17, pp 133–139

'Ali Akbar Banna Yazdi, Ustad (undated), *Tarikh-i 'Ishqabad*, manuscript

Allworth, Edward (ed.) (1967), *Central Asia, a century of Russian rule*, Columbia University Press, New York and London

Baha'i World (1928), vol. 2 (1926–8), Baha'i Publishing Committee, New York

Baha'i World (1930), vol. 3 (1928–30), Baha'i Publishing Committee, New York

Baha'i World (1936), vol. 5 (1932–34), Baha'i Publishing Trust, Wilmette, Illinois

Baha'i World (1937), vol. 6 (1934–6), Baha'i Publishing Trust, Wilmette, Illinois

Baha'i World (1939), vol. 7 (1936–8), Baha'i Publishing Trust, Wilmette, Illinois

Baha'i World (1942), vol. 8 (1938–40), Baha'i Publishing Trust, Wilmette, Illinois

Boulangier, Edgar (1888), *Voyage à Merv; les Russes dans l'Asie centrale*, Librarie Hachette, Paris

Browne (ed. and trans), Edward G. (1891), *A Traveller's Narrative written to illustrate the episode of the Bab*, vol. 2, Cambridge University Press, Cambridge

Christie, Ella R. (1925), *Through Khiva to Golden Samarkand*, Seeley, Service & Co, London

Collins, William (1982), 'Kenosha, 1893–1912: History of an early Baha'i Community in the United States,' in Momen, M, *Studies in Bābī and Bahā'ī History*, Vol. 1, Kalimat Press, Los Angeles, pp 224–253

Curzon, George N. (1892), *Persia and the Persian Question*, vol. 1, Longmans, London, repr. Frank Cass, London, 1966

Furutan, Ali Akbar (1984), *The Story of my Heart*, George Ronald, Oxford

Haydar-'Ali [Isfahani], Hajji Mirza (1980), *Stories from the Delight of Hearts* (trans. A. Q. Faizi), Kalimat Press, Los Angeles

Kalmykow, Andrew D. (1971), *Memoirs of a Russian Diplomat* (ed Kalmykow, Alexandra), Yale University Press, New Haven and London

Kolarz, Walter (1961), *Religion in the Soviet Union*, Macmillan, London

Lee, Anthony A. (1977), 'The Rise of the Baha'i community in 'Ishqabad', *Bahā'ī Studies*, Vol 5 pp 1–13

Mazandarani, Fadil-i (undated), *Tarikh-i Zuhur al-Haqq*, vol. 6, manuscript

— (1974), *Tarīkh Zuhūr al-Haqq*, vol. 8, pt 1, Mu'assisih Matbu'at Amri, Tehran, 131 *badī'*/1974

— (1975), *Tarīkh Z'uhūr al-H'aqq*, vol. 8, pt 2, Mu'assisih Matbu'at Amri, Tehran, 132 *badī'*/1975, pp. 981–1049

Mihrabkhani, Ruhu'llah (1974), *Sharh-i Ahwal-i Mīrzā Abu'l-Fad'a'īl Gulpaygānī*, Mu'assisih Matbū'āt Amrī, Tehran, 131 *badī'*/1974

— (1982), 'Mahafil-i Shawr dar ahd-i Jamāl-i Aqdas Abhā', *Payām-i Bahā'ī*, No 28, Feb. 1982, pp 9–11; No 29, Mar. 1982, pp 8–9

Momen (ed), Moojan (1981), *The Bābī and Bahā'ī Religions 1844–1944; some contemporary western accounts*, George Ronald, Oxford

Rabbani, Ruhiyyih (1969), *The Priceless Pearl*, Baha'i Publishing Trust, London

Remey, Charles M. (1916), 'The Mashrak-el-Azkar of Ishkhabad', *Star of the West*, Vol 6 No 18, pp 153–155

Rosen, Victor (1891), *Collections Scientifiques de l'Institut des Langues orientales*, Vol 6: Les Manuscrits Arabes, St Petersburg

Smith Peter and Momen M (1986), 'The Babi Movement: a resource mobilisation perspective', in Smith P, *In Iran; Studies in Bābī and Bahā'ī History, vol. 3*, Kalimat Press, Los Angeles, pp 33–93

Sulaymani, 'Azizu'llah (1966), *Maṣābih-i Hidāyat*, vol. 3, Mu'assisih Matbū'āt Amrī, Tehran, 123 *badī'*/1966, pp. 9–62, 549–615

Whitmore, Bruce W. (1975), 'The City of Love', *Bahā'ī News*, July 1975, pp. 6–12

17

ISLAM IN CHINA: WESTERN STUDIES

Jacques Waardenburg

Even a cursory perusal of Jack A. Dables's *History of the Discovery and Exploration of Chinese Turkestan* (1963)[1] makes clear the essential distance separating Western Europe from this heart of Asia, so to speak, beyond Russia and China proper. Our geographical knowledge of the area dates from only a century ago, and it is one of those areas, like Tibet and the Poles, which European explorers were late to penetrate. William Moorcrafts paid for it with his life, while Alexander von Humboldt set out but never reached the region. Famous names in the exploration of it are those of Thomas Thomson, the St Vincentius Fathers Huc and Gabet, the three Schlagintweit brothers, Thomas William Atkinson, Douglas Forsyth, and of course Russian explorers like Semenov, Golubev and Valikhanov, not to mention the indomitable Przhevalski. And of course Sven Hedin also visited this region.

The search for treasures from the past gave rise to various archaeological expeditions by Europeans: those of Mark Aurel Stein from India (1901–1915), the German expeditions to Turfan (1902–1905), the French one under Paul Pelliot (1906/7) and the Italian one under F. de Filippi (1912–1914).

As to knowledge of people and events in the northwestern and southwestern regions of China, this has been scarce among scholars in Europe and almost completely lacking to the broader public. Europeans were hardly aware of the so-called Muslim rebellions of the 1860s and still know very little about Islam and Muslim life in the People's Republic of China. Here we shall pay special attention to the recent history of the Turkic Muslims in Xinjiang and the Chinese Muslims in the rest of China as described in Western studies.[2]

I. SOME HISTORICAL DATA

About the arrival and expansion of Islam in China various theories have been developed.[3] It is fair to say that Muslims entered China from various directions and at different times, so that a number of different groups of Muslims in China can be distinguished:

1. Traders from overseas, in particular Persians, continuing relations of pre-Islamic times;[4] ninth-century Muslim communities are attested in towns like Canton and Hanchow.[5] Muslim traders also travelled overland via the Silk Road.

2. After the battle of Talas (751) in which the Chinese were defeated by the Arabs the latter apparently did not cross the Pamirs to China.[6] There were, however, Muslim military reinforcements who had been sent by the Caliph in 756 and 787 in order to help the Emperor in trouble, and who at least in part settled down in China.

3. Islamised Turkic peoples from Western Turkestan settled and spread Islam in the region of present-day Xinjiang and Mongolia, in particular among the ancient Uighurs who had been influenced by Manichaeism. Insofar as they settled beyond Xinjiang and Mongolia in China proper, they assimilated to Chinese civilisation in the course of time, like the colonies of Muslim traders on the East coast. All these assimilated Muslims were to be called Han-Hui, but physically the types of Mongol Hui, Turkic Hui and Arab-Persian Hui can still be distinguished. As a group they have been called the Han-Hui (Chinese Muslims) since the Ming dynasty (fifteenth and sixteenth centuries) when assimilation took place.

4. A new wave of Muslim immigrants arrived under the Mongol Yuan dynasty (1206–1368),[7] brought by the Mongols from the conquered areas of Turkestan and Iran in order to serve them as administrators, craftsmen, and so on. They settled in particular in the southwestern province of Yunnan, assimilated very much to Chinese civilisation, but keeping Islam as their religion, and have also been called Han-Hui since the Ming dynasty mentioned above.

5. In Xinjiang Islam prevailed, replacing, for instance, Buddhism, thanks to the continued immigration of Turkic tribes from the West which were already Muslim and also through Islamisation on the spot. These Turkic-speaking Xinjiang Mus-

lims were called Ch'an-Hui (literally 'turban-wearing Muslims') as distinct from the Han-Hui (literally 'Chinese Muslims').

Following Donald Leslie's periodisation in his *Islam in Traditional China: A Short History* (1986),[8] the history of Islam in China can be divided into the following periods:

1. *T'ang* period (seventh to ninth century); arrival of Muslim traders and others;

2. *Sung* period (tenth to mid-thirteenth century); success of Muslim traders;

3. *Mongol* period (mid-thirteenth to mid-fourteenth century); immigration of foreign Muslims brought from Iran and Turkestan;

4. *Ming* period (end of fourteenth to mid-seventeenth century); acculturation of the Hui in Chinese society (Han Hui);

5. *Early Ch'ing* period (mid-seventeenth to end of eighteenth century); growing division among Muslims between those who are loyal and who are not with regard to the Chinese government;

6. *Late Ch-ing* period (nineteenth century); millenarist expectations, charismatic and renewal movements among Muslims; a number of rebellions also by Muslims against the central government;

7. *Republican* period (first half of the twentieth century); revival of Muslim learning and closer contact with Muslims elsewhere;

8. *People's Republic*, from 1949 onwards.

II. THE EMPIRE (UNTIL 1911)

1. Xinjiang

Chinese rule over present-day Xinjiang goes back to the second century BC under the Han dynasty.[9] It lapsed thereafter until the Mongol Yuan dynasty (1206–1308) established its authority over the area for some time to come again. It is no wonder that Chinese rule over Xinjiang was not continuous, since the great Takla Mahan desert separates China proper from the region, which is bordered on the other three sides by high mountain ranges. Yet Xinjiang was the gate to the West: influences from Turkic and Iranian cultures penetrated into China by way of traders who travelled along the Silk Road through Xinjiang, mostly passing by Kashgar.[10]

A new conquest of the region took place after the Manchus succeeded in invading China in 1644 and the Chinese Ming dynasty (1368–1644) was replaced by the Manchu Ch'ing dynasty (1644–1911). The Manchus expended much effort on conquering what was at first called Chinese Turkestan. The inhabitants of the northern part of it, the Mongol Dzungarians, were routed in 1757, and those of the southern part, the Uighurs and other Turkic peoples, had to recognise Chinese rule in 1759. This conquest had been decided by the Ch'ing emperor, Ch'ien-lung (reg. 1736–96) especially for strategic reasons, the mountain range West of Xinjiang providing a natural barrier against possible dangers from Russia. From this time on Chinese, including Muslim Chinese immigrants, started to move to these areas as *Han Hui* who spoke Chinese, as distinct from the *Ch'an Hui* inhabitants who spoke Turkic languages. Shortly after the conquest of 1759 the province of Kansu was created between the provinces of Shensi and Chinese Turkestan. The border between Russia and China had been fixed earlier by the Treaties of Nertchinsk (1689) and of Khiakhta (1727).

The basic policy of the Manchu government towards Chinese Turkestan was to hold the natural frontier of China west of this region and govern the region indirectly through the local begs. This kept a balance of power between the various peoples of the region which can be called a colony of the Manchus, since there were no important Chinese officials present. The civil administration was headed by the local chiefs under the control of the Chinese military governor of Ili. A number of Muslim religious leaders had fled from the region to the Khanate of Khokand.[11]

2. The Han Hui

The Han Hui Muslims of different origins were scattered throughout China, speaking Chinese and following a number of Chinese customs. The Muslims in China had no central authority; the *akhonds* and *mullahs* were independent and lived from teaching, support from public and private *wakfs*, and from the benefits of slaughtering animals according to the Muslim ritual. Circumcision apparently was not generally practised and if so, it happened in the boy's seventh year. The dietary laws were rigidly adhered to; wheras pork was a national food for the Chinese, the Muslims did not touch it. The Hui were Sunnis of the Hanafi school, and, since they had a monopoly of the trade along the caravan routes of northern and north-western China and they had their own communications with Western Turkestan, Afghanistan and Iran and further west-ward. The Naqshbandi tarikat which had originated in Western Turkestan had found its way to China where it developed a network of adherents; other orders too, like the Qadiriyya, and branches of the Naqshbandiyya, like the Jahriyya, were known in China. Among the Hui also a growing saints' worship took place.

Marshall Broomhall in his classical but now outdated *Islam in China: A Neglected Problem* (1910) mentions a few character-istics of Chinese Hui Islam as he knew it. The mosques had no minaret, but a small tower, the dome being replaced by a four-sided roof with green tiles. Near the door was the Emperor's tablet. Inside the mosque was a frame of open woodwork for the coffin in which the dead would be brought to the grave but which then would be returned again to the mosque. A mosque had various rooms where guests could be put up, also from outside China. Sometimes there was a col-lege for Islamic teaching.

The dietary rules were observed over against the Chinese whose main meat was pork; *akhonds* shaved their heads and in the mosque worshippers hid their pigtails under a cap which could have various colours. Monogamy was prevalent and divorce scarcely existed; the Hui women were not veiled. Broomhall states that these Chinese Muslims considered them-selves as alien people and superior to the Chinese; this goes back in part to Mongol Yuan times when they held high office. Muslim girls would not be given in marriage to Chinese men, and the Muslims had their own customs at weddings and at burials which distinguished them from the Chinese. Fasting was rigorously observed. Hadjis enjoyed a particular distinc-tion and from time to time Muslims from abroad visited the Muslim communities in China.

Martin Hartmann in his *Zur Geschichte des Islam in China* (1921) adds a few other traits of the Han Hui at the beginning of this century, on the basis of French travel accounts. The Han Hui hardly knew the Shari'a and had no sayyids (descendants from Muhammad); nor were they organised. Some booklets about Islamic religion, containing Quran texts and the main Islamic doctrines and prescriptions, were in circulation.

The women's feet were mutilated like those of the Chinese women; polygamy existed but was rare, and the veil was sometimes worn. Muslims respected their parents and ancestors but stopped short of venerating them.

Chinese Muslims often earned their living through trade or by serving in the army, or by keeping special restaurants. Hartmann also mentions the selfconsciousness of the Muslims in China. Ho-chow in Kansu was according to him the religious centre of Islam in China. Here the so-called New Teaching (*hsin-chiao*) predominated among a largely Turkic Salar population.

3. Old and New Teaching

All authors on eighteenth- and nineteenth-century Islam in China mention and discuss the existence of the *Old Teaching* (*lao-chiao*) of a traditional nature, and its challenger, the *New Teaching (hsin-chiao)*, Islam itself being called *Hui Hui Chiao* (literally Islamic Teaching). Much attention has been given to the origins of the New Teaching, and different theories have been developed about it.[12] According to Jonathan N. Lipman (1984),[13] the New Teaching would have had various origins. The charismatic teacher, Ma Ming-hsin, transmitted the doctrine of the Jahriyya branch of the Yasawiyya Sufi order among the Salars in eighteenth century. This was one 'new teaching'. At the same time tomb-worshipping and a cult of saints arose in Ho-chow and other towns in the South of Kansu. This was another 'new teaching'. Such New Teaching arose in secret in Hsün-hua and Ho-chow, spread and became active in Kansu and Xinjiang. It had its own missionaries and its well-known sheikh and leader Ma Hua-lung (nineteenth century) had charismatic qualities. The New Teaching must have developed over against a certain traditionalism and laxity among the old-established Muslims; it also may have stressed a clear religious stand against Chinese culture and the Chinese authorities. It implied a socio-political resistance to the Han Chinese and must have helped to ferment the rebellions of the nineteenth century. Andrew D. W. Forbes[14] sees in the New Teaching the influence of wider Islamic movements of renewal (*tajdīd*) which reached China overland in the second half of the eighteenth and the first half of the nineteenth century. Such movements of spiritual renewal were apt to lead to revolts and jihāds, and this is exactly which took place in the great Muslim rebellions of the nineteenth century against the central Chinese government.

4. Sino-Muslim Relations; the Muslim Rebellions

Relations between Muslims and Chinese within the country had deteriorated under the Ming and Ch'ing dynasties. From the end of the eighteenth century, which also witnessed the spread of the New Teaching, tensions were increasing. An Islamic renewal was taking place, charismatic leaders appeared, millenarian expectations were arising and the existence of different doctrinal schools caused irritations among the Muslims themselves. Last, but not least, Chinese officials exhibited a haughty attitude to the Hui whom they exploited economically.

Raphael Israeli, in his *Muslims in China* (1979), treats these Sino-Muslim relations at length, interpreting them within a more general framework of majority-minority relations and analysing the options which were open to the majority Chinese as well as to the minority Muslims. He concludes that the cultural change in China between Han and Hui Chinese can be divided into three phases which actually took place in history:

(a) Peaceful, albeit uneasy, coexistence. The Muslim minority outwardly accepts a material acculturation, while inwardly preserving its own way of life and accepting the status quo;

(b) Intensification of outside pressure under the Ch'ing counteracted by an intensification of internal pressure among the Muslims which becomes manifest in new religious expectations;

(c) Rise of a violent antagonism together with an ideological polarisation. Muslims turn to mystic and mahdist doctrines in order to assert their cultural identity, as happened when the Islamic state of Yunnan was established.

Already in the first half of the nineteenth century there were local rebellions in Kansu against the Chinese rulers who found themselves in great difficulty because of the Opium War (1840–2), the T'aip'ing rebellion (1848–64) and the Nien rebellion (1853–68). In these critical years another three massive rebellions took place in the western, Muslim, regions.[15]

In the province of *Yunnan*[16] Sultan Suleiman established an Islamic state which lasted for seventeen years (1856–73). There were serious rebellions in *Shensi* (1862–7) and *Kansu* (1862–73) which were finally put down by the Chinese general Tso-Tsung-t'ang (1812–1885)[17] who had earlier suppressed both the T'aip'ing and Nien rebellions. And thirdly, from 1865 until 1878 an independent sultanate of *Kashgaria*[18] existed in Chinese Turkestan, first under Buzurg Khan and then under Yaqub Beg (c 1820–77)[19] after whose death this region too was reconquered by general Tso Tsung-t'ang. It was on the latter's recommendation that the whole region of Chinese Turkestan was then transformed, by an Emperor's decree of 11 October 1884, into the Chinese province of Xinjiang (literally 'New Border') directly ruled from Beijing. It was divided into four districts, with Urumqi as its capital. Just as somewhat earlier Kazakhstan and Turkestan had been integrated into Russia, Xinjiang was now fully integrated into China. But there were still British and Russian besides Chinese influences in this enormous region of strategic importance.

The times of rebellions, however, was not over. Revolts broke out in Kansu again in 1895/6[20] and in 1928, and in Xinjiang far more frequently. They all aimed at the secession of Muslim areas from China but they never succeeded, even though Urumqi, the capital of Xinjiang, is about 2,500 km from Beijing.

This is not the place to discuss the historical events of these great Muslim rebellions, aptly described by Wen-Djang Chu and other historians. Our primary interest here is in the way in which these rebellions were viewed in the West. A few points may be made in this connection.

First of all, in the eyes of Western contemporaries the nineteenth-century history of Islam in China was largely identified, unfortunately, with rebellions in which Muslims played the main part. What people forgot was that there were rebellions in China everywhere at the time and that the reality at work was not so much religious as political: these were largely national liberation and secessionist movements against the central government and the Han domination. In any case, after the quelling of these rebellions, which made millions of victims, Islam ceased to be a danger to China, as V. P. Vasiliev still viewed it in the 1860s.[21]

Secondly, Western views of the rebellions were largely determined by Western interests in Central Asia and China at the time. Islam was perhaps the most important instrument in the political rivalry between Russia, China and the British. The Indian government, for instance, sent a survey expedition to Yunnan, and the British were quick to recognise the sultanate of Kashgaria under Buzurg Khan. The Russians on their part welcomed any break between the Beijing central government and the northwestern provinces of the empire; they explicitly wanted to counteract British infiltration in Kashgar and Urumqi. They too wanted to see Kashgaria independent from China, but then as a Russian protectorate. The British, on the contrary, wanted an alignment with Kashgaria, and Central Asian Muslims generally as a united front against the Russians.[22]

Thirdly, strong Christian missionary interests existed in Muslim regions of China, with expectations of conversions among the minority Muslims where conversions among the majority Chinese were hardly to be expected. Xinjiang was a particular target for special missionary efforts admitted by the Chinese government. Well-known are the China Inland Mission and the Society of Friends of the Moslems of China. There was also a Swedish Lutheran mission in Xinjiang.

A classic but now outdated description of Islam in China in the period just treated is given by P. D. Gabry de Thiersant in his two-volume work *Le Mahométisme en Chine et dans le Turkestan oriental* (1878).[23] Martin Hartmann, when looking back on the Muslim rebellions in his *Zur Geschichte des Islam in China* (1921), stresses that the sultanate of Kashgaria was a purely political matter in which the Turkic peoples opposed the central government; religion was here used only as a supplementary instrument in the struggle. In Yunnan and Shensi-Kansu, however, there was a religious-political rebellion in which charismatic leaders like Ma Hung-lung in Kansu played an important role and adherents of the New Teraching turned fanatic. It is interesting to see that Hartmann rejects ideas which must have existed in his time in the West, that Muslim-Chinese tensions were beneficial to the West since they would halt the 'yellow peril'. On the contrary, he sees the Muslims as an important factor in the overall development of China and puts his confidence in Muslim reform movements accepting western values.

Apart from the political events just described, the nineteenth century was important for Islam in China also in other respects. In this time Islamic literature began to be produced in Chinese, and no longer in Uighur, Arabic or Persian. Sufi orders further spread through the country[24] and also in other ways communications between Muslims inside and outside China were improved.

III. ISLAM IN THE REPUBLIC (1911–49)

When China became a republic in 1911, the official attitude of the central government towards the Muslims softened. And when Sun Yat-sen took things in hand and founded the Nationalist Party (Kuomintang) in 1912, Muslims in China had good hopes that their situation would improve, after the mounting tensions with the Ch'ing dynasty throughout the nineteenth century. The death of the acting President, Yan Shikai, in 1916, however, meant a collapse of central authority and the following period is rightly called that of the Warlords. In the Muslim regions of Northwestern China the infamous Feng Yu-hsiang waged a campaign of terror in Kansu which led to a Hui rebellion in 1928, repressed with much loss of life, and Ma warlords were continuously at odds with each other, at the expense of the luckless population.[25]

In 1921 the Chinese Communist Party was founded in Shangai. After it had joined forces in a Common Front with the Kuomintang to subdue the warlords in 1926/7, it was increasingly threatened by Chiang Kai Chek, and in 1934 the communists undertook the Long March from the Southeast to the Northwest, where they established their capital in Yenan in Shansi.[26]

315

Soon after the beginning of the Sino-Japanese War (1937–45) the national government of the Kuomintang fell back on the wartime capital, Chungking, in Sichuan. In fact in these years only the Muslims in Yunnan and the other southwestern provinces remained under government control. Xinjiang was very much under Soviet influence, as will be described below. The Hui of the Kansu-Ninghsia border region had already come into direct contact with the Chinese communists in early 1936. In May of that year Mao Tse Tung had appealed to the Muslims of Northwestern China to join him, and the communists had made promises to the Hui, of certain privileges and recognition as a religious as well as an ethnic minority. The Kuomintang had only recognised the Turkic Muslims as a separate ethnic minority called 'Tatars'; it considered the Hui, however, to be a religious and not a national minority, in accord with the ideology of Great Han chauvinism. In fact, the Kuomintang had even arranged for its Muslim protégé, Ma Hung-Kuei, to back the Muslim Modern Teaching (*hsin-hsin chiao*) which advocated a strong acculturation between the Hui and the Han.[27] In other words, the views and practices of the Kuomintang and communists towards the Muslims in China were radically opposed, and it was the communists who recognised the Muslims as an ethnic minority. In the meantime several accounts about Muslim life were written by western observers.[28]

The inter-war period was a very troubled one in Xinjiang, as Andrew D. W. Forbes demonstrates in his book *Warlords and Muslims in Chinese Central Asia* (1986). Under its governors, Yang Zeng Chin (1912–28), Jin Shuren (1928–33) and Sheng Shi-cai (1933–44) Xinjiang succeeded in adopting an increasingly autonomous policy both with regard to the Chinese central government and with regard to the newly established Soviet Union. On one hand, rebellious Muslims had secessionist tendencies; a charismatic figure like Ma Zhong-ying (1909–37), for instance, was striving for an independent status for Xinjiang. On the other hand, British, Russian and Japanese influences tried to use secessionist tendencies in their own interests, and the Soviets, for instance, armed various Muslim separatist movements in Xinjiang.

The Russo-Chinese Peace Treaty of 1924 opened the borders for trade, but also for other influences, and as a result Chiang

Kai Chek soon broke off diplomatic relations with Moscow (1927). In 1924 Mongolia had become a satellite of the USSR, and in 1933 Manchuria was occupied by the Japanese. In the meantime Xinjiang was shaken by successive Muslim revolts which worked in the Russians' favour, and Soviet influence increased in particular after the 1935 agreement between Xinjiang and the USSR which included Russian aid for the reconstruction of Xinjiang. After Japan invaded China on a large scale in 1937, a non-aggression pact was concluded between China and the USSR in 1937 and renewed in 1939. In Xinjiang the Russians were practically in full control during the period 1937–43 but were then obliged to withdraw until the end of the war. In November 1944 the Kazakhs in the Ili Valley, under the leadership of Akhmedjan Kasim, set up what they called the Republic of Eastern Turkestan, in which also Uighurs participated. Its territory comprised Northern Dzungaria. Its Uighur and Kazakh leaders were killed in an aircrash on their way to Beijing in the autumn of 1949, after which the Republic soon came to an end once the People's Republic had been established.

As is well known, after the end of the Second World War in 1945 a civil war between the Chinese communists and the Kuomintang broke out (1945–9), ending in a disaster for the latter. After Chiang Kai Chek's withdrawal to Taiwan Mao Tse Tung proclaimed the People's Republic in Beijing on 23 September 1949.

Various Muslim institutions existed before the transfer of power. First of all there was a network of Sufi orders both in Xinjiang and among the Hui elsewhere in China, most important of them the Naqshbandiyya and in particular its Jahriyya branch. Other orders like the Qadiriyya, however, were active as well.[29] In 1913 the Progressive Chinese Muslim Organisation was founded in Beijing, and in 1926 the Chinese Muslim Cultural Organisation was established in Shanghai. The Union of Islamic Associationshad been founded between the wars, and in 1937 it moved to Kunming. Immediately after the Japanese invasion Hui leaders in Chungking founded the Chinese Islamic Salvation Federation, in order to rally the Chinese Muslims (Hui) to the Kuomintang in the common war effort against the Japanese. Beijing was the seat of the Chen Ta Islamic Academy, and the Chinese Muslim Literary Association and the

Shangai Islamic Normal Academy were established in Shang-hai. None of these institutions survived the advent of the People's Republic; only the Chinese Muslim Association, which also existed before 1949, ensured its survival by moving from mainland China to Taiwan.[30]

At the end of the Republican period four centres of Islamic learning existed in China: in Kashgar (Western Xinjiang), Ho-Chow (at present Lin-hsia, Kansu), Houai-King (Honan) and the Higher Studies Institute in Beijing. There are estimated to have been some 42,000 mosques and tens of thousands of *akhonds* and *mullahs* at the eve of the Republic.[31]

IV. ISLAM IN THE PEOPLE'S REPUBLIC OF CHINA (SINCE 1949)

Given the limited space at our disposal we limit ourselves here to a coherent presentation of some data about the subject. We leave aside speculation and also the international dimension which is obviously present in the Beijing government's treat-ment of its Muslim citizens.

When the People's Republic was formally established in Beij-ing in 1949 one of its first tasks was to establish its authority over the whole of mainland China. During the Civil War there had been clashes between Muslim and Communist armies and in 1948 the Xinjiang League for the Protection of Peace and Democracy had been founded in opposition to Communist rule. Even after its leaders were killed in a mysterious airplane crash, the central government met further resistance in Xinji-ang where the idea of an Islamic Republic of Turkestan had been alive, in particular against the land reform law of 30 June 1950, and it took measures against the local political and religious leaders. There also was a purge of old revolutionaries from the days of the Warlord struggles.

Further to the migration of some 17,000 Kazakhs from Khotan to Turkey during the period 1937–42, another 18,000 Kazakhs tried to escape from Xinjiang in 1949/50 but they were pitilessly persecuted by the new government, and finally only some 350 of them survived, to settle down in Adana in Turkey.

Among the Hui in Northwest China too there was resistance to the new regime, in particular when mosque *wakf* lands were threatened with nationalisation, a policy on which the government had to back down. Muslim leaders were arrested and condemned on suspicion of entertaining ties with the Kuomintang. In Kansu revolts occurred in 1950 and 1952; the Hui of Honan revolted twice in 1953. Here, as in Xinjiang, the government suppressed the resistance which had also taken the form of attacks on Chinese civil servants and communication lines.[32]

In 1953 the new government succeeded in establishing its authority in all the Muslim regions.[33]

1. Official Policies

a. The Census of 1953

The official census held in 1953 provided a number of data both on the Han majority population and on the ethnic minorities or 'nationalities'. Since nationality and not religion served as the primary category for classification, the religious affiliation was not recorded and consequently the census did not provide definite figures of the number of Muslims living in the various provinces. Out of a total population of 573,269,000 in 1953, 35 million — that is to say, 1/16th — were registered as a minority population made up of 45 distinct nationalities. Some ten of these are entirely Muslim, the largest groups being the Hui and the Uighur. Three kinds of groups can be distinguished:

1. *Turkic* nationalities, speaking Turkic languages. They are found especially in the Northwestern provinces. The largest group are the Uighurs, of whom there were 3,640,000 according to the 1953 census. They are followed by the Kazakhs who numbered 470,000 according to the census. Some smaller Turkic ethnic groups are also entirely Muslim (Kirgiz, Uzbek, Tatars, etc.) and some Muslims are also to be found in ethnic groups which have not been Islamicised (Turkic Salars, Hichus and other ethnic groups). An estimate of 1978 mentions 5,480,000 Uighurs and 800,000 Kazakhs at that time. Since 1955 the Uighurs have had their own 'Xinjiang Uighur Autonomous Region'.

2. The Hui (*Han Hui*) or Chinese Muslims, as distinct from Muslims belonging to Turkic and other ethnic non-Han groups in China. Scholarly opinions differ about the Han Hui, some holding that they were Han Chinese who became Muslims

(thus constituting a religious minority). According to the 1953 census directives the Hui Han (Hui Chinese Muslims) had to register as a nationality or ethnic group along with others. Significantly, only 3,560,000 people registered as Hui, and thus, by implication, as Muslims. The 1978 estimate mentions 6.5 million people of the Hui nationality. Those Chinese Muslims who consider themselves not Hui Chinese but Han Chinese by nationality and Muslim by religion are evidently not included. The total number of Hui Chinese Muslims, consequently, is probably much larger than the registered number of Chinese Muslims who consider themselves as belonging to the Hui nationality.

The Hui are spread throughout China but they are to be found in particular in Beijing, T'ientsin and the coastal cities, and in Northwest and Southwest China. They have Chinese names in their relations with Chinese society, and they often have Arab-Persian names in their relations among themselves. Contrary to the Uighur and Kazakhs, no Hui left China after the establishment of the People's Republic. They were granted their own Ninghsia-Hui Autonomous Region according to a decision taken in July 1957 at the National People's Congress, but the decision was only carried out in October 1958 under Hui pressure.

3. A third category includes Muslims who are neither of Turkic or Hui nationality. They are the *Tadzhik* living mainly in Xinjiang, who are of Indo-Iranian descent and are all mainly Shi'ite Muslims, and also Muslims constituting separate groups among other nationalities like the Lolos, Mongols, Sihia, Tibetans, Taosan, etc. According to the 1953 census they totalled 2,330,000. In 1978 their number was estimated to be 4,000,000.

In brief, Muslims of different nationalities are spread over the whole of China but they constitute a majority in Northwestern China — Xinjiang, Qinghai, Kansu and Ninghsia, with Shensi and Szechwan — and in Yunnan in the Southwest. If the three categories are taken together, in 1953 there were some 10 million Muslims in the PRC registered by nationalities, out of a total population of 573 million. As suggested above, there is reason to assume that in fact there were many more Muslims, but they did not register under the typically 'Muslim' nationalities. Their number anyhow will have increased greatly up to 1982, when the total population of China passed a thousand million. For Muslims there is regional autonomy in the two (Uighur and Hui) regions mentioned above, in two prefectures or *zhu* (one of which is an autonomous Hui prefecture in Inner Mongolia, the other the autonomous Kazakh prefecture Ili)[35] in nine counties or *xian* and in 150 townships or *xiang*.

b. Nationality Policies

Government policies with regard to ethnic minorities or 'nationalities' (*min-tsu* meaning 'ethnic group') follow the lines laid down by Lenin and Stalin on the subject. The constitution of the Soviet Republic of Kiangsi, of 1931, still recognised the right of self-determination and of secession for the national minorities in liberated China. From 1950 onward, however, only the right of regional autonomy within the given one-state framework has been recognised, and the real extent of the autonomy enjoyed by the nationalities in the PRC (and in the USSR), politically speaking, is exceedingly limited. With regard to the Muslim nationalities, a strict separation is made between their religious and ethnic aspects, and also between the sociological and religious elements of their communal life, the latter being restricted to the mosque. An interesting detail is that by various means — for instance revision of the script — China's Muslim minorities have been vigorously prevented from entering into direct contact with their counterparts in the USSR.

c. Cultural Policies

The government, generally speaking, is intent on developing the cultural heritage of the ethnic minorities (nationalities) which clearly lag behind the Han Chinese majority. Moreover, their languages have been studied, transcription systems have been devised, and a number of books have been translated from Chinese into the minority languages, including the Muslim ones. In this way the minorities could be reached better by the official state authorities. Likewise, much attention has been given to schooling and, indeed, the number of schools in Xinjiàng has grown tremendously over the last forty years. More specifically, local cadres have been formed and trained so as to develop their societies on the lines desired.

321

Significantly, the traditions, customs and religious beliefs of the national minorities were guaranteed in a formal declaration as early as 1951.[36]

d. Religious Policies

Article 88 of the 1954 Constitution guaranteed the liberty of religious beliefs, and later this was expanded to include the liberty to hold and propagate non-religious beliefs as well.[37] As far as Islam is concerned, it has been observed that the Chinese Communist Party and the government have carried out a rather cautious policy,[38] when compared with policies towards Christianity, discredited by its links with the West, and the Confucian, Taoist and Buddhist religions considered rather as a cultural heritage of the past than as living faiths. Considerations of both foreign and internal policy — the desirability of good contacts with Muslim countries, for instance, in the Middle East,[39] and the repercussions of the Sino-Soviet conflict on the treatment of Muslim minorities living in the border areas — have undoubtedly contributed to make Chinese policies toward Islam more favourable than those towards other religions. These policies during the period 1950 to 1957 could be compared to Soviet policies toward Islam during the years 1920 to 1928. Islam is seen, above all, as a social factor, and is considered to be an ethnic characteristic. Consequently, a Muslim can be a party member in the PRC. A government decree of September 1952 called for Muslim customs to be respected, and in 1954 Islam was declared a protected religion.

Other measures can be summed up as follows: abolition of the Shari'a courts and the office of qādī in 1950; promulgation the same year of the Agrarian Reform Law which protected the rights of mosques to own *waqf* land and stipulated that religious leaders should acquire land if they had no other sources of income; prohibition of the teaching of religion outside the mosque, which at least in the cities applied to Muslim schools (1955). Except for excesses in the Anti-Rightist movement of 1957–8 and the Great Leap Forwards (1958–60), and of course the Cultural Revolution (1966–70) it was not so much Islam as a religion (though there were significant exceptions) but rather reactionary leaders and religious customs and traditions obstructing the production process which were attacked directly.

An effort was made to orientate Muslim cadres toward reform and thus to change Islam from within. Since around 1956 such reform and other activities have been carried out by the United Front Work Department, which has used various strategies and tactics to bring Muslim groups under its sway, through the phases of unification, transformation and annihilation.[40] Some traits of Islam have been considered as particularly negative, notably its ideal of the Islamic state (described as a feudalistic ideology of divine right), its potential danger as a fomentor of rebellion in the form of jihād (described as subversive propaganda), and its international links through pan-Islamism and pan-Turkism (described as reactionary ideologies).

The overall goal of the official religious policy towards Islam was and remains to fit the Muslims living in the PRC into the current state structure. The political and social life of the Muslims is to be reorganised, partly through intense ideological re-education (in particular through the training of cadres from the national Muslim minorities in order to indoctrinate their co-religionists), partly through intense political mobilisation (participation in the political activities all over the nation). On an institutional level autonomous governments drawn from the national minorities and specific organisations provide the framework for the transformation of the Muslim masses of China as envisaged by the party and the government leaders. We shall come back to the new Muslim institutions which have been created since the early 1950s.

2. Two Alternating Approaches: Adversities for Muslims

If the long-term aim of Chinese government policies towards the nationalities in general and the Muslims in particular has constantly been to create a common proletarian culture for all inhabitants of China, and to assimilate the Muslims (and other nationalities) to Chinese socialist and communist society, the short-term policies adopted to attain these long-term aims have oscillated between a conservative approach formulated by moderate pragmatists and a radical approach preached by pure ideologues.[41]

The conservative approach has emphasised the special characteristics of Muslims and advised a cautious, conciliatory policy to realise the long-term aims. It allows a relative tolerance of differences, attacking 'Grand Han' chauvinism as it was current under the Kuomintang of Chiang Kai Chek. This approach has prevailed during the periods 1949–55, ending in the Hundred Flowers Campaign, (1961–64) preceding the Cultural Revolution, and the period from 1977 onwards.

The radical approach, however, has taken class struggle to be the cornerstone of government policy toward the Muslims and all the other nationalities; this class struggle is to lead to the disappearance of all national and ethnic distinctions. No particular customs and religions should be respected; on the contrary, ideologically pure policies should be pursued, coupled with repression. This approach prevailed during the period mid–1957 to 1960. The Anti-Rightist campaign from mid–1957 until the end of 1958 was directed against the Muslim institutions still in existence, special provisions for Muslims, the idea of the unity of Muslims (the unity of the nation being stressed instead), and the religious leaders who were represented as reactionary elements and discredited. The Great Leap Forwards brought the collectivisation of land and animals even in the autonomous regions and zones, the establishment of the people's communes, and an intensification of the movement of migration of non-Muslim Han Chinese from Central China to the Muslim regions in Northwestern China (*hsia-fang*). During it much mosque-owned *waqf* land was confiscated and *akhonds* were obliged to work in the fields, as women were too. The same approach prevailed during the Cultural Revolution, carried out by Red Guard groups of young people supported by radical leaders.

In both these periods general purges throughout the PRC took place, and Muslims in China had no contact with Muslims in the rest of the world. Space prevents us from comparing the Chinese and the Soviet policies towards Muslims and Islam in the periods after an initial 'appeasement', that is, after 1957 and 1927, respectively; this would be an important subject in itself. It may be observed, however, that there is a fundamental difference in the situation of the Muslim population in both countries. Whereas there are no Russian Muslims in the USSR, there are Hui Muslims in China who share language, culture and national affiliation with the Han Chinese. Moreover, the Islamisation of the Russian part of Central Asia has occurred to a great extent through conquest, whereas the Muslims in the Chinese part of Central Asia are mainly the descendants of Muslim immigrants from elsewhere and converts from local populations.

It may be useful to compare the adversities suffered by the Hui and the Uighur Muslims succinctly.

a. The Hui

The Hui Muslims' resistance to measures taken by the central government in the early fifties has already been mentioned. During the period of the Hundred Flowers manifold complaints were made about the treatment of Chinese Muslims by the government and Muslims feeling turned out to be strong. In 1958 the existence of an underground 'Democratic Islamic Party' was discovered, as well as plans to establish an autonomous Muslim Republic of Ninghia which was to be a republic of Hui people.

Then in the Anti-Rightist campaign and the Great Leap Forwards the Muslims in question were attacked on the political level for their separatist ambitions and on the religious level for their superstitious beliefs. Most of the mosques were closed, *ādhān* and public prayers were forbidden, most Islamic teaching was suppressed, *akhonds* were imprisoned and propaganda against Islam intensified. From 1958 onwards the migration of non-Muslim Chinese to Muslim areas greatly increased. The collectivisation of land in the Great Leap Forwards led to widespread famines in which numbers of Muslims perished. Then, after 1961, pressure decreased in those areas with large Hui communities.

The outbreak of the Cultural Revolution by the end of 1966, with its concept of a strictly centralised system into which the minorities were to be incorporated and its concept of one unitarian China as the fatherland, put the Hui Muslims under intense pressure again. Red Guards carried out violent attacks on Muslim institutions and religious leaders; mosques were burned, *akhonds* persecuted and killed, Islamic literature destroyed, Islamic instruction and worship curtailed, Muslim families dispersed. Posters could be seen in Beijing calling for the stamping out of Islam. Red Guards even founded an association, The Revolutionary Struggle Group for the Abolition of Islam. At the great feasts apparently only a few mosques in the country — one each in Beijing, Canton and Kashgar — were open, and then only for foreigners. The Cultural Revolution also enabled the Han to revenge themselves on the Hui for the privileges the latter had enjoyed. In response Muslims rioted in Beijing in February 1967, shouting: 'Muslims of the world, unite!' The worst period was from 1966 until 1969; afterwards there was some relaxation. But still in 1975 the government of Yunnan called on the population to give up the observance of Friday as a religious holiday. The subsequent uprising was quelled by air bombardments of Yunnan villages.

It was only with the purge of the group round Lin Piao, the death of Mao Tse Tung and the purge of the Gang of Four in late 1976 and 1977 that an end was put to a reign of terror of which only scattered testimonies have reached the West and which is reminiscent of Stalin's purges of the thirties.

b. The Uighurs

The picture of the situation of Muslims in Xinjiang is no less gloomy than that just described for the Hui. In the first years Soviet economic, technical and cultural assistance had increased tremendously in the region which embarked on a process of rapid economic development. From 1957 onwards Soviet influence was reduced by the Chinese and tensions between the two countries increased. In 1963 an open break between the PRC and the USSR occurred. Just as Soviet propaganda stressed the oppression the Uighurs in Xinjiang were exposed to, Chinese propaganda directed to the Turkic populations of Soviet Kazakhstan and Central Asia glorified the treatment of the Uighurs in Xinjiang compared with the treatment Muslims received at the other side of the border. In the ideological warfare and in the conflict itself the Muslim minorities were treated simply as pawns in the policies of the opposing countries. In the meantime Xinjiang became a region of major economic and strategic value for the PRC as is clear, for instance, from the fact that in 1964 the first Chinese atomic bomb exploded in Lop Nor in the Takla Mahan desert in Xinjiang. Also Han Chinese have migrated in increasing numbers from the densely populated areas in the east and the centre of China to the steppes of Xinjiang. What happened to the population in these years?

In the first years after the establishment of the PRC in Xinjiang resistance had occurred and its suppression had not been forgotten by the population. During the Hundred Flowers period even Uighur Party cadres had dared to demand the establishment of a federated or even independent republic called Uighuristan or East Turkestan. There was strong opposition to the teaching of the Chinese language everywhere, the new marriage laws imposing monogamy, the introduction of the Latin alphabet for Uighur and Kazakh in 1957/8, and other measures. There were widespread fears that Beijing would pursue a general sinicisation policy after the collapse of Soviet influence in Xinjiang in 1957: sustained immigration by Han Chinese, a strong military presence, the imposition of Chinese as the administrative language, an ever-growing number of Chinese teachers and officials, and last, but not least, a steady promotion of mixed marriages.

The situation indeed deteriorated. In 1958, 35 agents of the central government were assassinated in Urumqi and this was followed by general disorder, which called forth terrible oppression during the Great Leap Forwards. Many Xinjiang Muslims took refuge in the USSR. The collectivisation of the land brought about an economic catastrophe and serious famines. But whatever the cost, in January 1960, 96 per cent of the population of Xinjiang was organised in 451 people's communes. The policies had been imposed by force. Their main elements were differentiation between hard-core 'reactionary' Muslims and Muslims open to reform measures put forward by the party; the destruction of all independent religious institutions and the existing institutional base of religion; the stress on attachment to the ethnic group rather than to the religious faith and community.

The next adversity was the Cultural Revolution. There was strong resistance in Xinjiang to the establishment of Revolutionary Committees, even by the government bodies themselves. From the summer of 1966 onwards a great number of Xinjiang Muslims took refuge in the USSR, when the rebellions were brutally suppressed.[42] Until 1969 Northwestern China was in a state of turbulence brought about by what may be described as a frontal attack on all things Islamic and typically Uighur or Kazakh.

Only the fall of the Gang of Four brought about an improvement in the Muslims' situation. In 1979 and 1980 certain privileges were restored to the Xinjiang Muslims: the imposed limit on the number of children in a family was declared to be valid only for the Han, some right of private property was recognised, taxation was to be reduced, teaching was to take place in the local Turkic dialects, and special provisions were to be made for typically Muslim customs (food, burial, etc.). In November 1979 an appeal was even made to Xinjiang Muslims living abroad to restore contacts with their country of origin.

c. Rehabilitation of Muslims[43]

The first signs of a change in the official attitude toward religion in general, and especially among minority groups, and in particular Muslims, was that in the autumn of 1977 some mosques were reopened for prayer. On 26 February 1978 a meeting took place between the National Committee of the Chinese People's Political Consultative Conference and sixteen religious leaders, and the following month the Fifth National People's Congress pledged to restore minority rights in the PRC. In 1979/80, 158 mosques in the Ninghsia autonomous region were reopened and where necessary restored at the state's expense. In Xinjiang, customs of marriage, burial and circumcision could be observed again and Arabic calligraphy could be employed, while Uighurs and Kazakhs continued to write in Arabic script. People who had been defamed were rehabilitated. Delegations of Muslims were sent abroad to renew contacts with Muslim countries in late 1978. In April 1980 the Chinese Islamic Association again met after a pause of seventeen years. So 1979 and 1980 marked a return to tolerance. In June 1980 official statements declared that ethnic nationality and religion are two different categories, and that freedom of religious belief and the administration of the religions by the state are two aspects of the same reality. In August of that year Ramadan fasting could be observed again everywhere. And the measures the government has taken since 1977 for both Hui and Uighur Muslims have included:

— providing funds for the rebuilding or restoration of mosques damaged during the Cultural Revolution
— the stifling of anti-religious propaganda
— the return of *akhonds* as leaders of Muslim communities
— the end of obstacles being placed in the way of Muslims attending mosque services
— the recognition that mosques could again function as centres for the services Muslim communities
— the publication of a complete edition of the Quran in the Chinese vernacular in 1980
— the restoration of Islamic monuments, attention being given to the 'stone tablets', mentioning their date of origin.

The government has been obliged to accept that Islam, which had shown a remarkable tenaciousness, is a permanent fact. Muslims for their part, have realised that they identify themselves as different, and that they share a common culture distinct from that of the Han Chinese. And, as a logical result of many years of suffering, Muslims are more likely to regard themselves as separate, and where there are stronger Muslim groups the Muslim communities become more cohesive.

3. New Muslim Institutions

With the advent of the People's Republic the different Muslim organisations which had been founded during the Republican period ceased to exist. A new institutional framework, which is basically in force at the present time, was established.

Islam, like other religions, was endowed with a supreme organisation. A conference of Muslims held in Beijing in July 1952 decided to create an organisation for all Muslims in China. Less than a year later, in May 1953, the Chinese Islamic Association was inaugurated, with its office in Beijing; Burhan Shahidi was its president from 1955 until the Cultural Revolution. It held its first congress in November 1955, the second in 1956; a third one took place in the early sixties. It has basically had the same functions as other mass organisations in the PRC, that of an intermediary within the framework of which members can express their opinion to government and Party cadres, and as an instrument of government control and the execution of government policies toward the groups represented by the members. Most important perhaps, it serves to create a bond between the various Muslim groupings in China, which for long suffered from mutual rivalries. The association has local branches and also research institutes on the Muslim minorities, with educational programmes for the minorities in question. It oversees the mosques, decides on printing the Quran and publishing materials on Islam,[44] and supervises the *akhonds* and *mullahs*. The association organises the *hajj* for Chinese pilgrims (for example in 1954, 1955 and 1956), sends delegations abroad and receives foreign missions from Muslim countries. It was apparently abolished during the years of purges, from October 1958 to about 1959, and from 1966 until April 1980. In this connection it is interesting to note that a translation of the Quran into vernacular Chinese by Muhammad Ma Chien was published in part in January 1952 by the Commercial Press, Shanghai; the entire translation appeared in an edition by the Academy of Social Sciences in 1981. It contains an introduction stressing the compatability between Islam and Marxism.[45]

Around 1953 an Islamic College was opened in Beijing, and in April 1955 a Chinese Institute of Islamic Theology was established for the training of modern *imams*. Alongside the Chinese Islamic Association the Chinese Association for the Promotion of Hui People's Culture was also founded in 1953, with Saifuddin as its president. Apparently it closed down in 1958. In the fifties, mosques were ordered by the government to set up Youth Study Clubs which had an ideological function. A Religious Committee for Muslims, which had local branches, was also founded but later disbanded in the Cultural Revolution. In 1964 the Chinese Islamic Institute in Beijing was created to supervise Islamic education, as well as a College of Minority Nationalities which was to grow into a university for students belonging to the minorities. In 1964 a Research Institute on World Religions was created in principle, but it only came into being in 1978, coming under the Academy of Sciences.

In 1953 the Central Institute of Nationalities was created, with the task of supervising and protecting minority cultures, including Muslim cultures. There is a Commission on Nationality Affairs in Beijing which directs policies on the ethnic minorities, whereas a Bureau of Religious Affairs in Beijing directs government policies with regard to the religions. Islam enjoys some privileges, since it is considered to be an ethnic characteristic of specific nationalities; it is not merely identified with 'superstition' as most other religions are.[46]

One of the striking differences between the institutional setting of Islam in the PRC and the USSR is that whereas there are official Spiritual Directorates with their Muftis able to give *fatwā*'s on religious matters in the Soviet Union, in China such an official Islamic authority is absent. Here it is an association which is deemed to represent the Muslims and their interests. In other words, whereas in China the policy on nationalities has in fact determined policies with regard to Islam, in the USSR official Islam has its own structure with an authority formally recognised by the state.[47]

4. Toward an Academic Study of Islam in China

Among the many blank spaces in our knowledge of the history of nineteenth-century Islam there are two that are relevant here: Islam in what became the Tsarist Russian and the Soviet part of Central Asia, and Islam in the Chinese part of Central Asia. This requires knowledge of Islam in the rest of Russia resp. the Soviet Union, and in the rest of China. The whole of our knowledge of nineteenth- and twentieth-century Islam in Tsarist Russia and the USSR, and in the Chinese Empire, Republic and People's Republic is extremely fragmentary. Our concern here, however, is with Central Asia, and in particular Chinese Central Asia. How has Islam in Northwestern and Southwestern China been viewed by the West and by Western scholarship? And how can it better be known in the future?

Three periods can be distinguished for nineteenth- and twentieth-century Islam in China:

1. On Islam in Imperial China after 1800 a few Western works are available as books, chiefly: Vasil'ev (1867, N. 21), Gabry de Thiersant (1878, N. 23), Rocher (1879/80, N. 16), Broomhall (1910), Mission H. M. G. d'Ollone (1911), M. Hartmann (1921), Israeli (1979).
2. On Islam in the Republican period (1911–49) remarkably little has been written and besides three books we can only mention one article: Andrew (1921), Cordier

331

(1927, N. 16), Trippner (1961, N. 29), Forbes (1986, N. 25).

3. As to the third period, it is striking how little scholarly work has been done on Islam in the People's Republic. The available books fall, broadly speaking, into three categories:

  (a) The studies on Xinjiang by Lattimore (1950), Davidson (1957) and Weggel (1985), are interesting but provide little information about Islam in Xinjiang, which evidently was not of much interest to the authors.

  (b) The studies on PRC nationality policies in general, such as those by Dreyer (1976) and Eberhard (1982), hardly go into the Islamic aspects of the Hui, Uighur and some other nationalities.

  (c) The studies by Lee (1973) and McGillen (1979) are basically political science studies.

The books mentioned provide us with scarcely any knowledge about the Muslims themselves and their Islam.

Before mentioning some possible reasons for this startling lack of studies on the subject, I would like first to say something about what I understand here by Islamic studies.

In research on Islam there are three general aspects which are relevant to the study of contemporary Islam, also in the PRC and the USSR.

First we must distinguish between the study of Islam as a religion in a narrow and in a broader sense. First, in the narrow sense, it is the study of Islam strict as the ῾ulamā᾽ understand it, a religion consisting of prescriptions and teachings. It also comprises the study of devotional and spiritual expressions, for instance in mysticism, and folk beliefs and practices. Here we study the history and actual practice of Islam as a religion in the narrow sense.

And secondly, in the broader sense in which I take it, it is the study of ways of life and expressions which Muslims call 'Islamic' and which we may call 'Muslim culture', which is much broader than the religion defined above. Here we study empirical realities which have many aspects and of which the religious ones are not necessarily predominant.

This distinction between a religion in the narrow sense, and broader cultures in the study of Islam is very helpful.

Second, when we study Islam, or for that matter any religion, we are not concerned with Western theories about the causes and nature of religion in general, or with the question whether people should have a religious faith or whether they should be atheists. In our research we are only concerned with data about Muslim communities and individual Muslims in the past or at the present time, which we try to make sense of without imposing a particular philosophy. As far as I am concerned, I want to find out what kind of meaning these data may have, or have had in the past, for the people (societies, communities, individuals) involved, and I search for more general patterns of meaning, trying to understand and explain them. I contend that, besides establishing facts, we should pay much more attention to the qualitative differences of meaning which these facts have for the various people involved. In my view it is the people who are the point of reference in the study of Islam, like any religion or ideology.

Third, an important aspect of our approach is that we should not say in advance what Islam is and what it is not. Of course, as researchers into Islam we have studied its prescriptions and teachings, their development in history and their local variations. But against current assumptions, which exist even among Islamic scholars, I think that we should not posit in advance, for instance, that Islam by its nature is always a political religion, that the *Shari'a* as such always constitutes the core of Islam, or that Islam is always automatically opposed to development, democracy, and so forth. Our point of departure, rather, should be to see what specific Muslims say about Islam, their Islam, in specific circumstances, what they do with it, and what fruits it bears. This is basically the attitude of an intercultural student and interpreter.

To come back now to the reasons why there are so few studies, at least in the West, on Islam in present-day China. I mention just three:

1. There is a cruel lack of *sources*, written or oral, official or otherwise. An important element of this is the present near inaccessibility of Muslim regions to Islamicists, which makes carrying out fieldwork on the spot impossible.[48] This is a matter of priority for improving our state of knowledge.

2. There is an appalling lack of *craftsmanship and know-how*. Not many Sinologists and Uighur specialists are interested in Islam. Hardly any historians of religion are competent in languages like Chinese or Uighur. Hardly any ethnographers and anthropologists who know these languages are interested in religion in particular. In fact it would seem that the main group of researchers who pay attention to Islam in China at present are political scientists who tend to concentrate on the political aspect of it and are sometimes ideologically biased in that they give their own political interpretations.

3. There is a problem of *interpretation* which has not been solved so far and constitutes a challenge for the intelligence. Not only are there differences as to what researchers actually study (texts, social situations, subjective meanings, etc.), but — much more important — there are considerable variations in the interpretations offered by scholars, in particular when it comes to religion. Specifically, they may

— approach Islam on the analogy of what they know of Christianity or Judaism as 'Western' religion; this holds good for theologians and atheists
— idealise of denigrate Islam as a faith or particular elements of Islam as they see it
— impose different models of explanation, including schools which take Marx as their starting point
— apply various personal ways of understanding and hermeneutical techniques, if they happen to be more spiritually oriented
— bring with them a number of assumptions of which they mostly are not aware and which have to do with the time, society, norms of research, cultural and political situation of the researcher concerned.

The problems of the study of Islam in China are not confined, then, to sources, accessibility of people and technical know-how, but also, and perhaps much more importantly, it has to do with so many different approaches and interpretations. They lead to as many different views and images of Islam, in China or elsewhere, precisely when we have no opportunity to check such views with the people themselves and with new data generally.

As a consequence, a number of serious western scholars of

Islam do not want to become involved in Islam in China —
or the Soviet Union — as a research subject, on the grounds
that the conditions for a scholarly study of Islam in these
countries are not present.

In my view this goes too far. Briefly, the study of Islam,
and its religious aspects in particular, in China, but also in the
USSR and elsewhere, should encompass at least the following
data:

1 A survey of existing *institutions* (mosques, Islamic
teaching, religious personnel and leadership) and their
organisation.

2 A survey of specific Muslim *groups* and what they
make of their Islam, including the ways in which Islam
functions among them.

3 The study of specific *interpretations* of Islam and of
the groups and individuals where these interpretations
prevail, with particular attention being paid to what is
picked out from the many elements of the total tradition
of Islam.

4 Attention to *survivals* of earlier religious forms and
other symbolisms accepted in particular cultures, and
efforts made to *synthesize* Islam with other religions and
ideologies or to accentuate *differences*.

5 Attention to historical developments, revitalisation
and modernisation processes in Muslim societies with
their corresponding *emancipatory movements*, and the
impact these processes and movements have on them.

A scholar of Islam in China or elsewhere is not intent on
idealism or denigration, but he looks at what people make of
their Islam. That, at least, is the way I go about it.

5. Conclusion

A few years ago (1986) Françoise Aubin complained that
several studies on Islam in China were written by non-Islamici-
sts and arose in a non-scholarly context, inspired as they were
by political or missionary interests.

In the face of this situation, new extensive efforts must be
made, in particular by Islamicists and scholars of religion. They
have to familiarise themselves with Chinese and if possible a

Turkic language like Uighur, and they have to become acquainted with research carried out in history and anthropology. They should also be familiar with some leading models of interpretation, including those inspired by Marxist and Leninist thinking.

There are two extremes between which such an Islamicist will have to move. One extreme is the development of one general hypothesis or theory concerning the evolution of a Muslim community or of Islam. An example of such an approach is the work of Raphael Israeli, who stresses the continuity of the history of the Muslim minority community through the successive phases of the Empire, the Republic and the People's Republic.[49] Pretending to know what Islam is, throughout his work he contends that Islam was, is and will remain a stumbling block for any assimilation of Muslims under the official state ideology. Implicitly, Islam is held to undermine, for instance, the cohesion of the People's Republic and, although he does not put it as explicitly as, for instance, Alexandre Bennigsen does for Islam in the Soviet Union, he sees Islam as a potential danger for the Marxist regime. This does not mean that an Islamicist should not work with hypotheses but rather that he should not assume naively to know what Islam is and that he should not cling exclusively to one model of interpretation which serves certain political or ideological interests.

Another extreme is the painstaking work of creating an inventory of the sources available for our knowledge of Islam in China and of bibliographical work as such. Donald D. Leslie rendered a great service to the study of Islam in China by collecting source materials and composing an exemplary bibliography of them.[50] This, of course, need not be done by every Islamicist, but is an exceptional service rendered by a few scholars to the whole field.

An Islamicist then, whether working on Islam in China or in other regions, will work between the extremes of source collecting and hypothesis development, avoiding any pretension of knowing what Islam is and will be. To acquire further insight of a scholarly, rather than a political or religious nature, our access to sources of present-day Muslim life and of the history of Islam in China needs to be improved. Collaboration with Chinese colleagues in this respect is of vital importance.

For the interpretation of the materials acquired interdisciplinary work is an absolute requirement, and here, too, collaboration with Chinese scholars is indispensable.

Notes

1 The Hague and Paris: Mouton, 1963
2 For the materials contained in this contribution the author, who is an Islamicist without specialised knowledge of China or the Turkic languages, is especially indebted to the following publications and the bibliographies they include: Aubin (1982 and 1986), Dreyer (1981), Forbes (1976), Israeli (1979), Joyaux (1962), Rossabi (1987).
3 See for instance an early account by Isaac Mason, 'The Mohammedans of China — When and how they first came', *Journal of the North China Branch of the Royal Asiatic Society* Vol. 60 (1929), pp 43–78, and by the same: 'How Islam entered China', *The Moslem World*, Vol. 19 (1929), pp 249–263.
4 Huzzayin S A, *Arabia and the Far East. Their Commercial and Cultural Relations in Graeco-Roman and Irano-Arabian Times*, Cairo, 1942. Compare Tadeusz Lewicki, 'Les premiers commercants arabes en Chine', *Rocznik Orjentalistyczny* Vol. 11 (1935), pp. 173–186. See also the older account by Ch. Schefer, 'Notice sur les relations des peuples musulmans avec les Chinois, depuis l'extension de l'islamisme jusqu'à la fin du XVe xiècle', in *Centenaire de l'Ecole des Langues Orientales Vivantes 1795–1895* (Paris: Imprimerie Nationale, 1895), pp. 1–30.
5 Drake F S, 'Mohammedanism in the T'ang dynasty', *Monumenta Serica*, Vol. 8 (1943), pp. 1–40.
6 Gibb H A R, 'The Arab invasion of Kashgar in A.D. 715', *Bulletin of the School of Oriental Studies*, Vol. 2 (1923), pp. 467/8.
7 Rossabi Morris, 'The Muslims in the early Yüan Dynasty', in *China under Mongol Rule*, ed. by John Langlois. (Princeton: Princeton Univ. Press, 1981), pp. 257–295.
8 Canberra: Canberra College of Advanced Education, 1986.
9 Samolin E, *East Turkestan to the Twelfth Century*. The Hague and Paris: Mouton, 1964; Morris Rossabi, *China and Inner Asia: From 1368 to the Present Day*. London, 1975.
10 Bellew H W, 'History of Kashgar', in Sir T. D. Forsyth, *Mission to Yarkand in 1873*. London and Calcutta, 1875.
11 On the situation around 1800 see Joseph Fletcher, 'Ch'ing Inner Asia c. 1800', *The Cambridge History of China*, Vol. 10, Part 1, ed. by John K. Fairbank (Cambridge, 1978), pp. 35–306. Compare also by Joseph Fletcher, 'The heyday of the Ch'ing order in Mongolia, Sinkiang, and Tibet', in *the same*, pp. 351–408.
12 See for instance Joseph Fletcher, 'Central Asian Sufism and Ma Ming-hsin's New Teaching', *Proceedings of the Fourth East Asian Altaistic Conference*, ed. by Ch'en Chieh-hsien (Taipei, 1975), pp.

75–96. Comp. Josef Trippner, 'Die Salaren, ihre ersten Glaubensstreitigkeiten und ihr Aufstand 1781', *Central Asiatic Journal*, 9 (1964), pp. 241–276.

13 Lipman, Jonathan N 'Patchwork society, network society. A study of Sino-Muslim communities', in *Islam in Asia*, Vol. II: *Southeast and East Asia*, ed. by Raphael Israeli and Anthony H. Johns (Jerusalem: The Magnes Press, Hebrew University, 1984), pp. 246–274.

14 Forbes Andrew D W (1976), p. 76.

15 Rossabi Morris, 'Muslim and Central Asian revolts', in: *From Ming to Ch'ing*, ed. by Jonathan D. Spence and John F. Wills (New Haven: Yale Univ. Press, 1979), pp. 169–199.

16 Rocher E, *La province chinoise de Yun-Nan*. Two vols. Paris, 1879–80; Henri Cordier, *Les musulmans de Yunnan*. Hanoi, 1927. Comp. by the latter: 'Notes sur les musulmans de Chine (*Houei Houei Kiao*)" in *Mélanges Hartwig Derenbourg (1844–1908)* (Paris: Ernest Leroux, 1909), pp. 433–442.

17 Wen-Djang Chu, *The Moslem Rebellion in Northwest China 1862–1878. A Study of Government Minority Policy*. The Hague and Paris: Mouton, 1966. See also by the same author: 'The immediate cause of the Moslem rebellion in North-West China in 1862', *Central Asiatic Journal*, Vol. 3, No. 4 (1958), pp. 309–316. Compare also for the international background Hsü, Immanuel C. Y. *The Ili Crisis: A Study of Sino-Russian Diplomacy 1871–1881*. Oxford, 1965. On Tso Tsung-T'ang, see Bales W. L., *Tso Tsung-T'ang: Soldier and Statesman of Old China* (Shanghai, 1937), and Fields Lanny B., *Tso Tsung-t'ang and the Muslims. Statecraft in Northwest China 1868–1890*. Kingston, Ont.: The Limestone Press, 1978.

18 Kuropatkin A N, *Kashgaria*. Calcutta, 1882.

19 Boulger D C, *Yakoob Beg: Atalik Ghazi and Bedanlet, Ameer of Kashgar*. London, 1878.

20 Bonin, C E, 'Les mahométans du Kansou et leur dernière révolte', *Revue du Monde Musulman*, Vol. 10 (1910), pp. 210–233.

21 Vasil'ev Vasilij Pavlovich (1818–1900), *Islam in China*. English translation by Rudolf Loewenthal. (Central Asian Collectanea, No. 3). Washington, DC, 1960, 37 pp. The Russian original appeared in 1867 and was reprinted in 1900. A German translation *Der Mohammedanismus in China* appeared in 1909, as Ch. 4 (pp. 80–110) in Wassiljew W. P., *Die Erschliessung Chinas. Kulturhistorische und wirtschaftspolitische Aufsätze zur Geschichte Ostasiens*. Deutsche Bearbeitung von Dr Rudolf Stübe, mit Beiträgen von Prof. Dr A. Conrady. Leipzig: Dieterich Theodor Weicher, 1909, 236 pp.

22 Frechtling L E, 'Anglo-Russian rivalry in Eastern Turkestan', *Royal Central Asian Journal*, Vol. 26 (July 1939), pp. 471–489.

23 Two Vols. Paris: Ernest Leroux, 1878.

24 Fletcher Joseph, 'Les "voies" (*turuq*) soufies en Chine', *Les ordres mystiques dans l'Islam. Cheminements et situation actuelle*. Travaux publiés sous la direction de A. Popovic et G. Veinstein (Paris: Editions de l'Ecole des Hautes Etudes en Sciences Sociales, 1986), pp. 13–26.

25 Forbes Andrew D W, *Warlords and Muslims in Chinese Central Asia: A Political History of Republican Sinkiang 1911–1949*. Cambridge etc.: Cambridge Univ. Press, 1986; Jonathan N. Lipman, 'Ethnicity and politics in Republican China: The Ma Family Warlords of Gansu', *Modern China*, Vol. 10 (July 1984), pp. 285–316. On Feng Yu-Hsiang see J. E. Sheridan, *Chinese Warlord: The Career of Feng Yu-Hsiang*. Stanford, CA: Stanford Univ. Press, 1966.

26 Snow Edgar, *Red Star over China*. New York, 1938; J. Lindbeck, 'Communism, Islam and nationalism in China', *Review of Politics*, Vol. 12 (1950), 473–488. Compare also descriptions in Sven Hedin, *Big Horse's Flight*.

27 Forbes Andrew D. W. (1976), p. 78.

28 Andrew G. Findlay, *The Crescent in North-West China*. London, 1921; Isaac Mason, 'The Mohammedans of China', *Journal of the North China Branch of the Royal Asiatic Society*, Vol. 60 (1929), pp. 43–78. Compare also H. D. Hayward, 'Chinese-Moslem Literature. A study in Mohammedan education', *The Moslem World*, Vol. 23 (1933), pp. 356–377; and by the same author, 'Perplexing Sinkiang. Problems which now face Chinese Turkestan', *The Moslem World*, Vol. 25 (1935), pp. 182–195. See also the later description by Daoud Ting, 'Islamic culture in China', in *Islam: The Straight Path*. Ed. by Kenneth W. Morgan. New York, 1958.

29 One of the last western scholars who could do fieldwork in North-west China before the Second World War left a precious account: Joseph Trippner, 'Islamische Gruppen und Gräberkult in Nordwest-China', *Die Welt des Islams*, N. S., Vol. 7 (1961), pp. 142–171.

30 Lu D. J., *Moslems in China Today*. Hong Kong, 1964.

31 Kettani Ali M., *Muslim Minorities in the World Today* (Institute of Muslim Minority Affairs, Monograph Series Nr 2). London and New York: Mansell, 1986, p. 98.

32 Joyaux François, 'Les minorités musulmanes en Chine populaire', *L'Afrique et l'Asie*, Année 1964, 4e trimestre (no. 68), pp. 3–13. About the exodus of the Kazakhs, see p. 10.

33 On the situation of Islam in the PRC around 1953, see the chapter 'République Populaire chinoise (*Tchong-Hua Jen-Min Kung-Ho Kuo*)', in Louis Massignon (with Vincent Monteil), *Annuaire du Monde Musulman, statistique, historique, social et économique, 1954* (4e édition. Paris: Presses Universitaires de France, 1955), pp. 91–103. Further data on Islam in the PRC have been taken from the following publications: Aubin (1982), Dreyer (1981), Eberhard (1982), Forbes (1976), Israeli (1981, 1982), Joyaux (1962, 1964), Kettani (1986), Šilde-Karklinš (1975), Rossabi (1987). For details no specific references to these publications will be given.

34 See for instance Joyaux (1962) and Kettani (1986), pp. 90–94 (with reservations).

35 Moseley George, *A Sino-Soviet Cultural Frontier: The Ili Kazakh Autonomous Chou*. Cambridge, MA: Harvard Univ. Press, 1966.

36 Details are given in the brochure *Education in Xinjiang*, with a

Preface by the responsible Ismayil Amat, signed June 20, 1985 (11 pp.).

37 Dreyer (1981), pp. 225/6.

38 Forbes (1976), p. 79.

39 This was at least the case in the fifties. See Shichor Yitzhak, *The Middle East in China's Foreign Policy, 1949–1977*. Cambridge, 1977. For China's relations with (Muslim) African countries, see Larkin Bruce D., *China and Africa, 1949–1970*. Berkeley and Los Angeles: Univ. of California Press, 1971.

40 Yang i-fan, *Islam in China*. Hong Kong, 1958.

41 Rossabi (1987), pp. 388/9.

42 M. Ali Kettani (1986) estimates the number of refugees from Sinkiang residing abroad at about 250,000 people, of whom 220,000 are living in the USSR, 10,000 in Turkey, 10,000 in Saudi Arabia, and the rest scattered over various other countries (pp. 101/2).

43 Dreyer (1981), pp. 235–239; Kettani (1986), pp. 102–105.

44 Three booklets in English were edited by the China Islamic Association (*Chung-Huo I-ssu-lan-chiao hsieh-hui*) and published by the Nationalities Publishing House (*Min-tsu ch'u-pan-she*) in Peking: *Moslems in China* in 1953; *The Religious Life of the Chinese Moslems* (also in Chinese and Arabic) in 1956/1375; and *Chinese Moslems in Progress* in 1957. Publications in Chinese include Pai Shou-yi, *Hui-Min Qi-yi'* (The risings of the Hui people), 4 vols. in 1952; the same author with Ding Yi-min and Han Dao-ren, *The history and present circumstances of the Hui people* (Chin. 1967); Ding Yi-min, *The Muslim peoples of New China* (Chin. 1958), and Mao Xiao-shi, *The revolution of the North-western Muslim peoples. A brief history.* (Chin. 1951).

45 See Jin Yijiu, 'The Qur'ān in China', in *Islam in Local Contexts* (Leiden: E. J. Brill, 1982), pp. 95–101. The Quran translation by Muhammad (Ma Jian) Ma Chien (First Part) is entitled *Ku-lan Ching* (Shanghai 1952); the remaining part was published in 1981. See by the same author: 'How Muslims live in China', *China Reconstructs* (March-April 1953), pp. 13–15 and also much earlier 'Notizie d'un musulmano sui musulmani cinesi' (by Laura Vecchia), *Oriente Moderno*, Vol. 15 (1935), pp. 353–364, 425–434, and 483–487.

46 A critical account of PRC policies towards Islam is given by Yang i-fan in his *Islam in China* and *Muslim Unrest in China* (an.), both published in Hong Kong in 1958. A critical account of PRC policies toward all religions in the country is given by R. Bush, *Religion in Communist China*. Nashville, 1970.

47 Compare for the USSR: Jacques Waardenburg, 'Western studies of Islam in present-day Central Asia (USSR)', in *Utrecht Papers on Central Asia*. Proceedings of the First European Seminar on Central Asian Studies held at Utrecht, 16–18 December 1985. Edited by Mark van Damme and Hendrik Boeschoten (Utrecht Turcological Series No. 2; Utrecht: Institute of Oriental Languages, University of Utrecht, 1987), pp. 45–67.

48 In Islamic states like Saudi Arabia, Iran and Libya it is also impossible for Islamicists to carry out fieldwork on the spot.
49 Israeli Raphael, 'The Muslim minority in traditional China', *Asian
and African Studies*, Vol. 10, Nr. 2 (1975), pp. 101–126; 'Muslims in
China', *T'oung pao*, Vol. 63 (1977), pp. 296–323; 'The Muslim revival
in 19th century China', *Studia Islamica*, Vol. 43 (1976), pp. 119–138;
'Islam and Judaism in China: the merger of two cultural sub-
systems', *Asian Profile*, Vol. 5 (1977), pp. 31–42; 'Muslims versus
Christians in China', *Asia Quarterly*, 1976, pp. 327–335; 'Established
Islam and marginal Islam in China. From eclecticism to syn-
cretism', *Journal of the Economic and Social History of the Orient*, Vol.
21, Nr 1 (1978), pp. 99–109; 'The Muslims under the Manchu reign
in China', *Studia Islamica*, Vol. 49 (1979), pp. 159–179; 'Islamization
and Sinicization in Chinese Islam' in *Conversion to Islam*, ed. by
Nehemiah Levtzion (New York and London: Holmes & Meier,
1979), pp. 159–176; 'The Muslim minority in the People's Republic
of China', *Asian Survey*, Vol. 8 (1981), pp. 901–919; 'Islam in the
Chinese Environment', in *Islam in Local Contexts*, ed. by Richard
C. Martin (Leiden: E. J. Brill, 1982), pp. 79–94; 'Muslims in China.
Islam's incompatibility with the Chinese order', in *Islam in Asia*,
Vol. II: *Southeast and East Asia*, ed. by Raphael Israeli and Anthony
H. Johns (Jerusalem: The Magnes Press, The Hebrew University,
1984), pp. 275–304; 'Muslim plight under Chinese rule', in *The
Crescent in the East: Islam in Asia Major*, ed. by Raphael Israeli
(London/Dublin: Curzon Press, and Atlantic Highlands: Humani-
ties Press, 1982), pp. 227–245. For his book *Muslims in China*, see
the 'Selected Literature' at the end of this article.
50 Leslie Donald Daniel, 'Arabic Sources' in *Sources for Chinese History*.
Australian National University, 1973; 'Islam in China to 1800: A
bibliographical guide', *Abr-Nahrain*, Vol. 16 (1976), pp. 16–48; *Isla-
mic Literature in Chinese*. Canberra, 1981; together with Ludmilla
Panskaya, *Introduction to Palladii's Chinese Literature of the Muslims*.
Canberra, 1977. For his book *Islam in Traditional China*, see the
'Selected Literature' at the end of this article.
Other useful bibliographies on Islam in China are: Claude L. Pickens,
Annotated Bibliography of Literature on Islam in China. Hankow, Hupeh:
Society of Friends of the Moslems in China, 1950; Richard Loewen-
thal, 'Russian materials on Islam in China: a preliminary bibli-
ography', *Monumenta Serica*, Vol. 16, Fasc. 1 and 2 (1957), pp. 449–479,
and the same, 'Russian contributions to the history of islam in China',
Central Asiatic Journal, Vol. 7 (1962), pp. 312–315.

Bibliography

Aubin, Françoise, 'Chinese Islam: In Pursuit of its sources', *Central
Asian Survey*, Vol. 5, Nr 2 (1986), pp. 73–80.
The Cambridge History of China. Cambridge Univ. Press, Cambridge.

Forbes, Andrew D W 'The Muslim national minorities of China', *Religion. Journal of Religion and Religions*, Vol. 6 (1976), pp. 67–87.

Rossabi, Morris, 'Islam in China', in *The Encyclopedia of Religion* (New York: Macmillan and London: Collier Macmillan, 1987), Vol. 7, pp. 377–390.

China Before 1949

Andrew, G Findlay (1921), *The Crescent in North-West China*, London.

Broomhall, Marshall (1910), *Islam in China: A Neglected Problem*. Morgan & Scott and China Inland Mission, London.

Hartmann, Martin (1921), *Zur Geschichte des Islam in China*. Wilhelm Heims, Leipzig.

Israeli, Raphael (1979), *Muslims in China: A Study in Cultural Confrontation*. Atlantic Highlands, N.J.: Humanities Press (Scandinavian Institute of Asian Studies Monograph Series No. 29) London and Malmö: Curzon Press, 1980; New Delhi: Ambika Publications, 1980.

Leslie, Donald Daniel, *Islam in Traditional China: A Short History to 1800*. Canberra: Canberra College of Advanced Education, 1986.

Ollone, H. M. G. d' (Ed.) (1911), *Recherches sur les Musulmans chinois*. Ernest Leroux, Paris.

China Since 1949

Aubin, Françoise (1982), 'Islam et Etat en Chine populaire', in *L'Islam et l'Etat dans le monde d'aujourd'hui*, Oliver Carré (ed): Presses Univ. de France, Paris, pp 169–188.

Bush, R. (1970), *Religion in Communist China*, Nashville.

Davidson, Basil (1957), *Turkestan Alive: New Travels in Chinese Central Asia*. J. Cape, London.

Dreyer, June T. (1976), *China's Forty Millions. Minority Nationalities and National Integration in the People's Republic of China*. Harvard Univ. Press, Cambridge, MA.

— — 'The Islam community of China', in *Middle East Perspectives: The Next Twenty Years*. Ed. by George S. Wise and Charles Issawi: (The Darwin Press, Princeton, NJ: 1981), pp. 221–243.

Eberhard, Wolfram (1982), *China's Minorities: Yesterday and Today*. Wadsworth Belmont, CA.

Israeli, Raphael, 'The Muslim minority in the People's Republic of China', *Asian Survey*, Vol. 8 (1981), pp 901–919.

Joyaux, François (1962), *Les musulmans en Chine populaire (Problèmes politiques, sociaux et économiques des minorités musulmanes de la Chine Populaire, 1950–1960)*, Notes et Etudes Documentaires, No 2915 (20 août 1962), La documentation française, Paris.

Joyaux, François, 'Les minorités musulmanes en Chine populaire', *L'Afrique et l'Asie*, Année 1964, 4e trimestre (Nr. 68), pp 3–13.

Kettani, M Ali, *Muslim Minorities in the World Today* (Institute of

Muslim Minority Affairs, Monograph Series Nr 2). London and New York: Mansell, 1986.

Lattimore, Owen (1950), *Pivot of Asia. Sinkiang and the Inner Asian Frontiers of China and Russia*, Little, Brown and Company, Boston.

Lee, Fu-Hsiang (1973), 'The Turkic-Moslem Problem in Sinkiang: A Case Study of the Chinese Communist' Nationality Policy'. Unpublished Ph.D. Dissertation, Rutgers University, The State University of New Jersey.

McMillen, Donald H (1979), *Chinese Communist Power and Policy in Xinjiang 1949–1977*. Westview; Boulder, CO.

Massignon, Louis (with Vinvent Monteil), *Annuaire du Monde musulman statistique, historique, social et économique; 1954* 4e Edition. Paris: Presses Universitaires de France, 1955. (On the PRC, see pp. 91–103).

Šilde-Karklinš, Rasma, 'The Uighurs between China and the USSR', *Canadian Slavonic Papers*, Vol. 17 (1975), pp. 341–365.

Weggel, Oskar (1985), *Xinjiang/Sinkiang: Das zentralasiatische China. Eine Landeskunde*. (Mitteilungen des Instituts für Asienkunde, Hamburg, Nr 144), Hamburg.

18

CHANGE AND TRADITION IN EIGHTEENTH-CENTURY KAZAKHSTAN: THE DYNASTIC FACTOR

Alan Bodger

There is a 'black hole' at the heart of eighteenth-century Kazakh history. The metaphor is admittedly not exact in all particulars; in astro-physics a 'black hole' is presumed to be a phenomenon of such densely packed material and powerful internal gravity that nothing, not even light, escapes from it. The event in question, despite exerting an insistent pull on the course of Kazakh history for a hundred years, has certainly allowed little illumination to escape from it, although this is because it contains too little, not too much evidential material.

This event occurred in the immediate aftermath of the celebrated victory of the combined Kazakh Little, Middle and Great Hordes over their old western Mongolian enemies, the Jungars (Oirots), at the place called Anrakai, (Angkrai, Anrakhai), south-east of Lake Balkhash. There is no documentary evidence of the exact date of the battle, but it is presumed to have taken place in the spring of 1730. The only evidence for this lies in Kazakh oral tradition (Apollova 1948, p. 183).

Immediately after the victory something happened, what exactly is still unknown, but it led to the collapse of the military coalition of all three hordes against the Jungars which had been established between 1726 and 1730 (Tynyshpaev 1927, p. 67; Apollova 1948, p. 183). It heralded a bitter, century-long struggle for political supremacy among the Kazakh 'white bone' aristocracy. This struggle played an important part in eighteenth-century Kazakh history, setting its stamp on all the major crises in the Kazakhs' external and internal affairs.

Warfare with neigbours and within and between all seg-

344

ments of nomadic Kazakh society was a permanent feature of their particular patriarchal-feudal lifestyle, with its strong military-democratic aspects (Tolybekov 1971, p. 234). But I would suggest that the dynastic struggle which had its roots in the events of 1730 split the Kazakhs of the Little and Middle Hordes in a special way. It played a major role in the debates of the 1730s over Russian sovereignty; it seriously complicated relations between the Kazakhs and the Russian frontier administration in the 1740s, 1750s and 1760s; it showed itself in the period of increasing social and colonial unrest during the Pugachev revolt of the 1770s, and was a key issue in the struggle for national independence led by Batyr Srym between 1783 and 1797 (Apollova 1948, p. 225; Apollova 1960, p. 394; Vyatkin Batyr Srym, p. 213). It came to epitomise the conflict between change and tradition in eighteenth-century Kazakhstan (Tolybekov 1971, p. 277).

At the end of the seventeenth century the main migratory grazing territories of the three Kazakh hordes lay rather further to the south and south-east than they did from the early eighteenth century onwards. Their lands were bounded in the west by the Mugodzhar Hills, in the north by the Aral-Irtysh watershed, in the east by the Sary Su and in the south by the Syr Darya. Kazakhs and Jungars had been fighting for full control over these lands and the settled regions of the Syr Darya basin for over a hundred years, but the struggle had steadily intensified from the 1640s, as the Jungars were pushed westwards by the expanding Ching Empire (Tolybekov 1971, p. 241).

Towards the end of the seventeenth century the gravity of Jungar expansionism forced the three loosely connected Kazakh hordes into closer co-operation, bringing a shaky form of unity under Tauke Khan (1680–1718) (Istoriya 1979, III, p. 16). But in the last years of his khanate Jungar invasions became more destructive, pushing the Kazakhs into increasing conflict over essential grazing pastures with their other neighbours. According to a nineteenth-century Kazakh ethnographer and historian, 'The first decade of the eighteenth century was a dreadful time in the life of the Kazakh people. Jungars, Volga Kalmyks, Yaik Cossacks and Bashkirs attacked them from all sides, driving off cattle and taking whole families into captivity' (Valikhanov 1961, p. 426). The invasions culminated in a crushing defeat for the Kazakhs in 1723. The three hordes were scattered in all directions: the Little Horde partly into the borderlands of the Russian Empire along the Yaik, partly towards Khiva and Bukhara; the Middle Horde partly towards the Russian frontier on the Irtysh, partly towards Samarkand. The Great Horde milled around on their old territory and succumbed to Jungar overlordship (*Istoriya* 1979, III, pp. 18–20). This period became known in Kazakh history as the *Aktaban shubyryndy*, 'the age of the bare-foot flight', when to escape massacre the whole population fled, abandoning families, cattle, property and clothes (Tynyshpaev 1927). It was a time of disaster and tragedy not only for the Kazakhs, but for all their neighbours: Karakalpaks, Bashkirs, Kalmyks, Turkmens, the settled populations of Bukhara, Khiva, Samarkand, all suffered as the human waves of fleeing Kazakhs swept into their lands, seizing pastures and cattle and ravaging fields and gardens (*Istoriya* 1979, III, pp. 19, 20).

During the next few years the Kazakhs of the Little and Middle Hordes rallied. They gained victories in 1726 at Kara Siyr (Kalmyk kyrylgan) in the steppes of the south-east Turgai region, and most notably at Anrakai in 1730 (Apollova 1948, p. 183).

There were important changes in Kazakh military and political leadership during this period. Kazakh khans could only be elected from the 'white bone' aristocracy, claiming descent from Chingis Khan, and within that Chingisid aristocracy a tradition stretching back five generations gave precedence to the descendants of Zhadig. Tauke's authority dwindled in his last years and his son Bolat, his nominal successor as khan of all three hordes, was at best a shadowy figure (*Istoriya* 1979, p. 23). During the Jungar invasions the Kazakh hordes and competent segments were scattered and mixed. The 'white bone' aristocracy were fragmented and weakened and the Chingisids of the Zhadig line did not provide firm leadership. It was the representatives of the 'black bone' elite, the batyrs, standing close to the people, who led the struggle for independence (Vyatkin 1941, p. 121). While Kaip, like Tauke, a descendant of Zhadig's son Shigai, seems to have played the role of leading khan between 1716 and 1719, a sultan of the Little Horde, Abulkhair, came into increasing prominence as a military commander. He may even have been elected khan in 1710, and certainly emerged as khan in 1726. The sources speak of a 'struggle for supremacy' between Kaip and Abulkhair as a result of which Kaip left the steppe and established himself as khan of Khiva, presumably in 1719 (Apollova 1948, p. 134).

Abulkhair belonged to a cadet branch of the Chingisids, being descended from Osek, Zhadig's younger brother. But it was the Zhadig line which claimed to inherit power. No khan had ever been elected from the Osek line; indeed there is some doubt whether members of the Osek branch even had the right to consider themselves Chingisids (Apollova 1948, pp. 93, 94). Abulkhair owed his rise to a variety of factors. The Little Horde, being furthest from the centre of the Jungar attacks, was a natural focus of resistance. He was a shrewd and brave military leader, a batyr himself, and enjoyed the support of those 'black-bone' batyrs like Bukenbai and Eset and Janibek, who led large segments in both the Little and the Middle Hordes and who played such a large part in organising resistance to the Jungars (Apollova 1948, pp. 130, 31).

Despite the fact that Abulkhair's election as de facto senior khan in 1726 constituted a kind of 'dynastic revolution' the sources do not reveal any serious protests or hostility from the by-passed candidates of the Zhadig line. In Abulkhair's own Little Horde itself there was the powerful and ambitious Zhadig sultan Batyr, Kaip's son and for a while also khan of Khiva, while in the Middle Horde there were two Zhadig khans, Semeke the son of Tauke, and Kuchuk. There were also two Middle Horde sultans of influence, Abulmambet, Semeke's son and Barak, Kuchuk's brother. Kuchuk himself seems not to have played an important role in affairs as he resided in a remote part of the steppe (Apollova 1948, pp. 141, 2). In 1726 Semeke and Barak co-operated with Abulkhair in a campaign deploying 10,000 men against the Volga Kalmyks (Apollova 1948, p. 135, 36).

No doubt the Zhadig khans and sultans did resent the upstart Abulkhair, but this hostility presumably could not be expressed openly in a time of such national crisis, with Abulkhair enjoying the support of the leading batyrs. The death of Bolat, the nominal if passive senior khan, occurring more or less at the same time as the victory at Anrakai, would have raised the succession question (Tynyshapaev 1927, p. 67).

As mentioned above, we now come to the most enigmatic and most conjectural moment in modern Kazakh history. What appears to have happened is that Abulmambet was elected senior khan and that Semeke and Abulkhair, outraged at the decision, withdrew from the front. Semeke and the segments under his authority went into the northern steppe and Abulkhair moved north-west towards the Russian frontier. Abulmambet went to the town of Turkestan, the traditional residence of the senior khan. The break-up somehow precipitated a bitter feud between Abulkhair and the Zhadigid rulers (*Istoriya* 1979, III, p. 23).

Tynyshpaev writes, following Levshin:

Something happened which in an instant annihilated all the fruits of the heroic struggle of the last three or four years and disrupted the victorious campaign; something which brought the people not brilliant hopes for the future, but loss of political freedom and independence: incorporation in tsarist Russia on the one hand, and a life of servitude under the domination of the hated Jungars on the other . . . What caused this fateful denoument neither legend nor history relate. There are no hints or signs by which one might come to a conclusion. (Tynyshpaev 1927, p. 66)

This is perhaps too sweeping. We do not have any documentary evidence, but a power struggle clearly lay at the root of the break-up. A recent authority echoes Tynyshpaev: 'The rival feudal leaders again put their lust for power and their class interests above national interests; all the efforts and sacrifices of the people were lost' (Semenyuk 1973, p. 89).

Some months after he left the front Abulkhair sent an embassy to Russia placing himself and 'all the Kazakh people' under Russian sovereignty (*Kazakhsko-russkie otnosheniia* 1961, p. 35). This was the crucial first move in the incorporation of Kazakhstan into Russia, a process not completed until the middle of the nineteenth century (Semenyuk 1973, p. 111).

Now whereas all historians, irrespective of their methodology, agree that the cause of the break-up after Anrakai must have been the struggle for supreme power, the reasons for Abulkhair's approach to Russia, and the nature of that approach, have been much debated. Abulkhair had been authorised by an assembly of elders to negotiate with Russia only for an end to conflicts with Bashkirs, occasioned by Kazakh encroachments on pastures along the Volga and Yaik (Vyatkin 1941, p. 123). It was essential for the Kazakhs to obtain peace in their rear, to free their hands against the Jungars and gain access to the disputed pastures. The Anrakai victory had by no means removed the threat of new Jungar attacks and the grazing land question was a 'matter of life or death' for the Kazakhs. (Semenyuk 1973, p. 93; Istoriya 1979, p. 24). The Kazakhs desperately needed a 'single buttress against all their enemies' (Levshin 1832, II, p. 72). Although not much hard evidence is available it can also be conceded that it was essential for the Kazakhs to establish closer economic ties with Russia in view of the loss and disruption inflicted during the Jungar wars (Apollova 1948, p. 184; Semenyuk 1973, p. 111).

The elders' decision was therefore quite intelligible in terms of Kazakh national interests. There had been earlier feelers for Russian help against the Jungars and mediation in disputes with neighbours in 1716, 1718 and 1726 (Basin 1969, pp. 59–78).

However, the problem is that Abulkhair's embassy to Ufa of September 1730, while making the proposals specified by the assembly of elders, asked to be taken under Russian sovereignty. This was not, what he had been authorised to do. The Kazakh elders, the 'Black bone' tribal elite, the social category which, I suggest, in the specific Kazakh conditions of 'military democracy' or 'patriach-feudalism', more than any group can be argued to express the national will, did not want or ask to become Russian subjects. They wanted peace and assistance, but not Russian sovereignty over them. They did not want to surrender their independence (Vyatkin 1941, p. 123). Abulkhair had exceeded his authorisation in asking for Russian sovereignty not just for himself but for 'all the Kazakh people', although he only controlled a minority within his own Little Horde and had no status or influence at all in the Middle or Great Hordes (Vyatkin 1941, p. 123). Not only was he exceeding his authorisation, he was also exceeding his authority. Kazakh khans had extremely limited powers. They had no regular machinery of coercion, no absolute authority; in all important matters they had to consult and abide by the decisions of assemblies of elders (Vyatkin 1941, p. 106).

So the elders' decision to approach Russia should not be

confused with the form that approach took as mediated by Abulkhair. In Abulkhair's letter we see not simply a reflection of the national predicament but a reflection of Abulkhair's personal aims. He was exploiting the elders' decision in order, I suggest, to further his cause in the dynastic struggle launched by his election in 1726, by the death of Bolat and the election of Abulmambet as senior khan. By becoming a vassal of Russia he hoped to use Russian help to overcome his rivals, subjugate his neighbours to the south, the Khivans, Aralians and Karakalpaks, and eventually to recover his full independence (Alektorov 1900, p. 5).

This view is amply borne out by the subsequent course of events. The tsarist government decided it would be advantageous to accept the offer of allegiance by such a troublesome neighbouring people, whose territory Peter the Great had seen as the 'key and gate ' to 'all the countries and lands of Asia' (*VIMOIODR* 1852, p. 15).

An official, one Alexei Ivanovitch (Mamet) Tevkelev, a Tartar by birth, was sent in 1731 to administer the oath of allegiance. On his arrival at Abulkhair's camp he discovered that the khan had lied. He had not been authorised to appeal for Russian sovereignty either on his own account or on behalf of 'the Kazakh people'. He told Tevkelev exactly why he had done so. He wanted Russian protection because he was surrounded by enemies and wished to safeguard his rear while he sought his revenge against the Jungars who held the towns of Tashkent, Turkestan and Sayram, which he claimed his ancestors had ruled. He wanted to acquire real political power over his people and for this absolute power to be inherited by his sons. He wanted to be able to rely on Russian military help against his enemies just like other Russian subjects, the Bashkirs, Kalmyks and Cossacks (*KRO* 1961, pp. 49, 99).

The elders were infuriated. 'They said that it was an ancient tradition that the khans had no authority to do anything without consulting the elders. They argued that as Abulkhair had done this without consulting them he should be put to death'. They alleged that he was trying to lead them into slavery and said that although they wanted to be at peace with Russia, they did not want to become Russian subjects (*KRO* 1961, p. 53). Tevkelev used all his considerable powers of intimidation and persuasion to placate them, but to no avail. Fortunately for him a small number of influential batyrs, particularly Bukenbay and his relatives, supported the khan. Indeed Bukenbay turned out to be a more consistent advocate of Russian sovereignty than the khan himself. He and his associates were the same people who had championed Abulkhair's cause in the 1720s (Apollova 1948, p. 135; Vyatkin 1941, p. 127).

The 'hostile party', as Tevkelev calls them, steadily increased in number and activity until Tevkelev managed to escape from the steppe in November 1732, bearing with him oaths of allegiance from Abulkhair and his adherents, and accompanied by *amanats* — hostages — as guarantees of loyalty (Basin 1969), p. 97).

It is not possible to attribute this animosity to any one cause. The elders' outrage at Abulkhair's deviousness, ambition and violation of custom may be the most obvious factor, but there were several other strands in it. There was a fiercely independent spirit which saw Russian sovereignty as 'slavery'. It has been argued that the 'hostile party' were not objecting to Russian sovereignty as such, since it was not discussed as a separate issue (Apollova 1948, p. 243). But the elders made a precise statement, 'they did not want to become Russian *subjects*' (*KRO* 1961, p. 53). The elders were defending a system which favoured their interests. The Kazakh steppe was in complete turmoil, with small groups attacking their neighbours and each other with no overall authority. There were conflicts between Kazakhs and Russian subjects going on, while Tevkelev was in the steppe. Kazakh envoys had been detained in Russia. There were disputes over seizures of cattle and people. Some Kalmyk insurgents were trying to provoke the Kazakhs into anti-Russian actions. Khivan intriguers were also at work against Russian interests. The Kazakhs suspected Tevkelev of being a Russian spy, come to prepare the ground for a Russian invasion. Most of Tevkelev's party consisted of Bashkirs. Under such conditions there was bound to be hostility to the mission (Basin 1969, pp. 78–100; Apollova 1948, pp. 197–246).

Most surprisingly for the present-day observer was the virtual absence of any serious consideration of what most Soviet historians refer to as the gravest threat to the Kazakhs, the Jungar menace. This danger may have been fundamental, but the Kazakhs themselves show very little awareness of the fact. Only Bukenbay dwells on the dangers, and then more in the context of the totality of the problems besetting the Kazakhs. Even when Abulkhair attempts to justify his unilateral action to the assembly of elders he speaks only of his personal interests, as he does to Tevkelev too. There seems little to sustain the view that Abulkhair acted as he did out of a far-sighted concern for the common good (Bodger 1980, p. 51–6).

Finally, intertwined with the several strands of animosity towards Abulkhair was the dynastic problem. Batyr sultan, Abulkhair's son-in-law and the son of Kaip, Abulkhair's old rival, appeared on the scene. He was a key figure, controlling a large part of the Little Horde and had claims to the khanate. If he had joined the hostile party then Tevkelev would have been in really serious trouble (*KRO* 1961, p. 60). Abulkhair hated Batyr 'like a dog' because Batyr was urging the Kazakhs to kill him and to make him khan instead. He had a big following and only the support of the more eminent elders like Bukenbay and his associates saved Abulkhair (*KRO* 1961, pp. 80–81; Vyatkin 1941, p. 127).

Batyr was strongly influenced by his Khivan, hence anti-Russian orientation. By threatening Tevkelev he forced him to give him some modest gifts, in return for which he swore an oath of allegiance to the Empress! More than any other incident in the duration of Tevkelev's mission, I suggest, this reveals the shallowness, mercenariness and insubstantiality of these adoptions of Russian 'sovereignty'. Batyr was an enemy of Abulkhair and an enemy of Russia, yet he swore an oath of allegiance in exchange for R100 and a bolt of Damask, plus a further R50 and a bolt of Damask for his son! (*KRO* 1961, p. 61). Nevertheless, this was an important moment. If Batyr had put himself at the head of the 'hostile party' Abulkhair and his family could have been liquidated. It would be idle to speculate on how this might have affected future power struggles among the Kazakh elite, the nature of the khanate itself or the course of Russo-Kazakh relations, but all these questions would not have been exacerbated by the particular forms of dynastic conflict which took place between the 'house of Abulkhair' and the Zhadigid khans and sultans.

Under the terms of the oaths of allegiance the new Russian subjects promised to pay regular tribute in furs, to protect Russian merchant caravans passing through the steppe, to keep the peace with Russian subjects and to serve in any capacity when called upon to do so (*KRO* 1961, pp. 42–4). In fact these terms were honoured more in the breach than in the observance. The Kazakhs paid no tribute, performed no service, and in fact remained independent (Basin 1968, p. 30).

Abulkhair was unsuccessful in his aims. He had hoped that by placing himself nominally under Russian sovereignty he could become the sole ruler of Kazakhstan, and even of a considerable part of Central Asia. He had hoped Russia would provide him with the 'means of extra-economic coercion' to bring his own people to heel and to crush his rivals. Russia as it happened was not interested in creating a strong, central-ised state either in Kazakhstan or in Central Asia, and he had alienated large numbers of tribal leaders in both the Little and Middle Hordes by his violation of tradition and custom (Bizhanov 1967, p. 87).

Following the example of Abulkhair and his associates similar oaths of allegiance to Russia were sworn by the two khans of the Middle Horde, Semeke and Kuchuk (1732 and 1735) Khan Zholbarys of the Greater Horde (1738), Sultan Barak (1735) and Khan Abulmambet and Sultan Ablai of the Middle Horde together with four hundred elders (1740) (*Istoriya* 1979, III, p. 506). Their motives were similar to those of Abulkhair; they hoped to mobilise Russian help to strengthen their own power against their rivals, to keep their own 'restless' and 'disobedient' peoples under control, to gain access to the rich grazing lands along the frontier, to engage in lucrative trade with Russian subjects, and, of course, to secure Russian inter-cession and support against further Jungar invasions. (Basin 1969, pp. 106–18) Their disunity allowed the Russian authorit-ies to play off one against the other and thus prevent the emergence of a 'strong man' in the steppe who might become dangerously independent (Basin 1969, p. 114).

This policy of divide and rule was of course greatly facilitated in the case of the Little Horde by the dynastic question. The Russian authorities, while formally recognising Abulkhair as khan in fact entered into close relations with his Zhadigid rivals to balance his position (Apollova 1960, p. 394; Vyatkin 1948, p. 16).

Abulkhair in turn became disillusioned with his Russian overlords: they detained his *amanats* in retaliation for the mis-deeds of his subjects whom he could not control, they denied his people access to the much-sought-after grazing lands along the Yaik, they consulted with his rivals (Basin 1969, p. 125). On the credit side, Russian sovereignty did reduce the scale of border conflicts, and in 1740 the Russians did protect the Kazakhs from a massive Jungar invasion which swept through the steppe right up to the Russian frontier. Trade at the newly founded (1735) town of Orenburg must also have benefited some Kazakhs (Semenyuk 1973, p. 115). On balance though it is most probable that the position of the population of the Little Horde deteriorated as a result of Russian frontier policy (Asfendiarov 1935, p. 112).

As Abulkhair was increasingly unable to fulfil any expectations his people may have had of his policy of allegiance to Russia, discontent with him grew, and the popularity and influence of his Zhadigid rivals increased. They demanded that the whole *zhurt* (nation) move away from the Russian frontier and place themselves under Jungar sovereignty (Tolybekov 1971, p. 268; Vyatkin 1948, p. 16). In 1748, during a routine raid into Kara-Kalpak territory in the southern part of the steppe Abulkhair was killed by Barak, perhaps at Batyr's instigation (Basin 1969, pp. 142, 43; Tolybekov 1971, p. 269). The elimination of the 'great intriguer' brought a period of unprecedented calm in the Little Horde. While Batyr was elected khan by a large majority in the southern part of the steppe, his election was not recognised by the Russian authorities (Vyatkin 1947, p. 164). Although the Russians had found Abulkhair most difficult to deal with and had come to appreciate that his usefulness as an agent of influence was limited by the structure of Kazakh society, the illegitimacy of his dynastic pretensions and his personal characteristics, they decided on his death to continue to sponsor the Osek line and arranged for an 'election' of his son Nuraly. Nuraly in fact had little support, but in the interests of Russian policy the Little Horde was split in two khanates, thus finally asserting the principle of dynastic division (Apollova, 1960, p. 400; Vyatkin 1948, p. 21).

Unlike his father who had enjoyed considerable support and popularity before turning towards Russia, Nuraly was nothing but a creature of the Russian authorities. He was faced with intense hostility from the Zhadigid leaders; relations with Kalmyks, Bashkirs, Turkmens and Karakalpaks were, if anything, worse than before, and even his own relatives asserted their independence of him (Vyatkin 1941, pp. 154–63). Despite increasing dependence on the Russian frontier authorities Nuraly was impotent to solve problems vitally important to his people. In 1756 Russia even formally banned the Kazakhs from crossing the Yaik, and from 1759 took increasingly severe measures against illegal crossing. The Russians generally refused to return runaway Kazakh slaves. They encouraged hatred between the Kazakhs and their neighbours by urging Kazakhs to seize fugitive Bashkir insurgents in 1756, and to destory Kalmyks seeking to return to Jungaria in 1771 (Vyatkin 1941, pp. 156–71). As a result the Kazakhs of the Little Horde became increasingly alienated both from their nominal khan and from Russia; anarchy and violence within the horde, although necessarily expressed in patriarchal-clan form, have been described by a recent historian as amounting to a 'class war' (Semenyuk 1973, pp. 118–35). Kazakh hatred towards the Russians intensified too, due to Cossack punitive raids, extortionate traders, the crossing ban, the slave question and general increasing pressure and interference (Vyatkin 1941, p. 170).

During the Pugachev uprising Nuraly, after some initial equivocation, came out in support of the authorities. He collaborated with them in trying to stem the flood of Kazakhs taking advantage of the occasion in order to cross the Yaik and attacking Russian frontier posts. His position collapsed even further. His brother Aichuvak split away and his son Dosaly actually joined the insurgents (Bekmakhanova, 1973).

After the uprising had been suppressed Nuraly's reliance on and co-operation with Russia increased. By the beginning of the 1780s his authority was at an end (Apollova 1960, p. 404).

The breakdown in the institution of khanship affected only the north-western parts of the Little Horde. In the southern part of the horde the position of the Zhadigids remained strong. Distance from the frontier meant that they were not affected by the Pugachev disturbances, but Batyr and then his son Kaip ruled in conformity with a two-hundred-year-old tradition of authority. They maintained customary relations with their 'black-bone' elite, and adherence to the *adat*, which conferred legitimacy on the khan's demands. Dynastic legitimacy and observance of *adat* kept alive the dignity and popularity of khanship (Vyatkin 1947, pp. 139, 188, 365).

Batyr's and Kaip's Zhadigid khanate also had a more secure financial base. Regular taxes were collected, while in the Osek khanate the levying of any kind of regular dues had not been legitimised. (Vyatkin 1947, p. 95) This might suggest that of the two khanates it was the Zhadigid one which represented a more advanced stage in the evolution from a patriarchal-clan towards a feudal society and hence a more 'progressive' polity, not one of 'arch-reactionaries' as has been argued (Tolybekov 1971, p. 276).

Between 1783 and 1797 the accumulated grievances of the population of the Little Horde against Nuraly and the Russian frontier authorities led to a full-scale revolt, of which the best-known leader was Batyr Srym, a wealthy 'black-bone' elder.

> As the sultans of the house of Abulkhair turned into the executive apparatus of the tsarist colonizers this feudal group began to embody the system of dual exploitation . . . the struggle of feudal groups took the form of a struggle for independence and, drawing in wide circles of the Kazakh people, took on the features of a national liberation movement against feudal groups united by the house of Abulkhair, who appeared in the Horde as agents of tsarist colonisers (Vyatkin 1940, pp. 13, 14).

In 1783 an assembly of elders and 'the people' demanded the deposition of Nuraly whom they denounced as a 'bad khan' (Apollova 1960, p. 404). Batyr Srym wanted the complete abolition of the khanate, but the prevailing opinion in the Horde was for the khanate to be preserved but handed back to the traditional Zhadigid line. They wanted Batyr's son Kaip, a strong, popular and anti-Russian ruler, to become khan. This position was repeated at several assemblies throughout the duration of the unrest (Vyatkin 1947, pp. 212ff).

Although the house of Abulkhair had disgraced the dignity of khanship, it had been kept alive in the Zhadigid khanate of Kaip and in the Middle Horde, and both the Russian authorities and Batyr Srym eventually had to bow to its popularity. The Russian plan to abolish the khanate and introduce a system modelled on Russian local administration into the steppe (the Igelstrom Reforms) came to nothing; Catherine the Great's fear of anti-monarchical experiments also contributed to their demise (Apollova 1960, p. 408). Russia, however, refusing to consider the election of Kaip, known to be anti-Russian and connected with Khivan interests, persisted with sponsoring weak representatives of the Abulkhair dynasty. Nuraly, who died in 1790, was replaced by his brother Eraly, who died in 1794. His successor Esym was murdered in 1797 (Apollova 1960, p. 410). Kaip himself died in 1789, and his successor, Abulgazy, became the choice of the majority of the elders of the Little Horde (Vyatkin 1947, p. 317). Batyr Srym changed his position too and tried unsuccessfully to get himself elected khan (Vyatkin 1947, p. 345). His ambition brought about his political isolation and he was forced to flee the steppe in 1797. He died sometimes in 1802 (Vyatkin 1947, p. 357).

After his departure the disturbances slackened off, aided by a very severe winter. The elders mended their fences with the Russian authorities; the ancient and weak Aichuvak was appointed khan; the land question, so fundamental for the Kazakh people, was partially solved by the authorities allowing a break-away khanate to be set up between the Volga and the Yaik under Bukei, a son of Nuraly. Russian ascendancy over the Little Horde and its internal disintegration had reached the point when it was only a matter of time before they could abolish the khanate completely (Zimanov 1960, pp. 141, 142).

The dynastic factor played a prominent part in the politics of the Batyr Srym uprising. The basic struggle of ordinary Kazakhs was for land and against the depredations of the Russian authorities and Abulkhair's family (Vyatkin 1947, p. 380). But the anti-colonial and anti- feudal struggle had — at least in part — common roots in the almost mythical events of the 'black hole' after Anrakai, events which induced the khan of an upstart dynasty to place himself and his people under an alien and unpopular sovereignty in order to further his personal ambitions.

The purpose of this chapter has been to draw attention to a factor in Kazakh eighteenth-century politics which has not been the subject of much detailed research since the work of Vyatkin and Apollova in the 1940s. Eighteenth-century and nineteenth-century historians generally viewed Kazakh history, especially the history of the Lesser Horde, through the prism of dynastic struggles, but modern research has concentrated more of analysing the underlying social and economic forces of change. Zimanov, in his important work on the political structure of Kazakhstan at the turn of the eighteenth and nineteenth centuries, notes that 'the genealogies of the khanate dynasties had significance in the struggle for power', but does not thereafter pursue the matter in detail (Zimanov 1960, pp. 93, 94). He does not give it much consideration among the causes of the crisis and collapse of the Lesser Horde khanate, but rightly allows that the situation was very complex: 'Together with old institutions there appeared new forms of authority and administration. The mutual influence of the old and the new and their interweaving creates a diverse picture, which offers great interest for the researcher' (Zimanov 1960, p. 142).

Before the significance of the dynastic question can be fully appreciated much work has to be done on, for example, the way Batyr's and Kaip's Zhadigid khanate worked. That its structure differed from that of Abulkhair's and Nuraly's khanate has often been mentioned, but little detail seems to have emerged. Its popularity and integrity contrasted with the weakness and unpopularity of Abulkhair's and Nuraly's khanate. This was due in large measure to the involvement of Russia in Kazakh affairs, but the sources indicate that tradition and legitimacy played no small part.

Any future work in this area will have to tread carefully between two extremes. It will not do simply to label influences or individuals apparently identified with change as 'progressive' and countervailing traditional forces as 'reactionary'. At least one historian has taken a 'Whig interpretation' of Kazakh history to such extremes, contrasting the 'progressive' pro-Russian sultans of Abulkhair's family with the 'extreme reactionaries' of Batyr's family and deciding that the Batyr Srym movement was 'reactionary from start to finish' (Tolybekov 1971, pp. 276–80). This view would seem to be a hindrance to genuine historical understanding and has, fortunately, remained an eccentric position (Apollova 1960, p. 29). By the same token our recovery of the Kazakh past — which, like the past of all 'minority' peoples, has as much right to its autonomy and integrity as that of the 'historical nations' — will be equally impeded by idealisation of the old and traditional and anathematisation of all forces of change. Historical reality was forged in the continual interplay of contending forces; a backward-looking identification with a particular cause subordinates the past to our present purposes and conflicts with that aim of realising the autonomy and integrity of the past which should be the historian's real task (Butterfield, 1973 passim).

References

Alektorov A E (1900), *Ukazatel' knig i zhurnal'nykh i gazetnykh statei i zametok o Kirgizakh*, Kazan'.

Apollova N G (1948), *Prisoedinenie Kazakhstana k Rossii v 30kh XVIII veka*, Alma-Ata.

Apollova N G (1960), *Ekonomicheskie i politicheskie svyazi Kazakhstana s Rossiei v XVIII — nachale XIX v.*, Moscow.

Asfendiyarov S D (ed) (1935), *Istoriya Kazakhstana*, Alma-Ata.

Basin V Ya (1968), 'O sushchnosti i formakh vzaimootnoshenii tsarskoi Rossii i Kazakhstana v XVIII v.', *Izvestiya Akademii Nauk Kaz. SSR*, no 5, pp 26–34.

Basin V Ya (1969) 'Kazakhstan v sisteme vneshnei politiki Rossii v pervoi polovine XVIII v.', *Kazakhstan v XV -XVIII vekakh* (Suleimenov B S ed.), Alma-Ata.

Bekmakhanova N E (1973), 'Kazakhi v krest'yanskoi voine 1773–1775 godov pod predvoditel'stvom E M Pugacheva', *Izvestiya Akademii Nauk Kaz. SSR*, no 6.

Bizhanov M (1967), 'Dnevnik M Tevkeleva kak istochnik po istorii Kazakhstana', *Izvestiya Akademii Nauk Kaz. SSR*, no 4, pp 84–87.

Bodger A (1980), 'Abul'khair . . . and his Oath of Allegiance to Russia of October 1731', *Slavonic and East European Review*, vol 58, no 1.

Butterfield H (1973), *The Whig Interpretation of History*, London.

Istoriya Kazakhskoi SSR (1979), vol III Alma-Ata.

Kazakhsko-russkie otnosheniya v XV-XVIII vekakh (1961), Alma-Ata.

Levshin A A (1832), *Opisanie kirgiz-kaisatskikh ord i stepei* vol III, St Petersburg.

Semenyuk G I (1973), *Problemy kochevykh plemen i narodov perioda feodalizma*, Kalinin.

Tynyshpaev M (1927), 'Ak-taban shubryndy', *Bartol'du V V . . .* ed A E Shmidt, Tashkent, pp 57–68.

Tolybekov S E (1971), *Kochevoe obshchestvo Kazakhov v XVI nachale XX v.*, Alma-Ata.

Valikhanov, C C (1961), *Sobranie sochinenii*, Alma-Ata.

Vremennik Imperatorskago Moskovskago obshchestva istorii i Drevnostei rossiiskikh (1852), vol XIII, Moscow.

Vyatkin M P (1940), 'Politicheskii krizis i khozyaistvennyi upadok v Maloi Orde v kontse XVIII — nachale XIX vv', *Materialy po istorii Kaz. SSR*, vol IV, Leningrad, pp 3–39.

Vyatkin M P (1941), *Ocherki po istorii Kaz. SSR*, Leningrad.

Vyatkin M P (1947), *Batyr Srym*, Moscow & Leningrad.
Vyatkin M P (1948), 'K istorii raspada Kazakhskogo soyuza', *Materialy po istorii Kaz. SSR*, vol II, pt 2 (1741–51), Alma-Ata.
Zimanov S Z (1960), *Politicheskii stroi Kazakhstana kontsa XVIII i pervoi poloviny XIX vekov*, Alma-Ata.

19

THE ROLE OF THE HUI MUSLIMS (TUNGANS) IN REPUBLICAN SINKIANG

Andrew D. W. Forbes

During the Republican Period (1911–49) China's westernmost province of Sinkiang, literally 'New Frontier', romanised in Pinyin as *Xinjiang* remained essentially a Chinese colony in the heart of Central Asia, inhabited by heterogenous Muslim peoples (Uighur, Kazakh, Kirghiz, Tajik, Uzbek, Tatar and Hui) together with smaller, but still significant numbers of non-Muslim peoples (Mongol, Sibo, Solon, Manchu, Russian). Taken together, as recently as the late Republican period, these various 'minority' groups comprised an estimated 95 per cent of the total population of Sinkiang, whilst Han Chinese (including political exiles and their descendants, poor peasant settlers and administrative officials) made up the remaining five per cent. Thus, according to a survey made by the Sinkiang Provincial Police in 1940–41 (and considered by Owen Lattimore to represent 'the best available; figures for the late Republican period), provincial population estimates by linguistic group were as follows:[1]

Muslim		Non-Muslim	
1. Uighur	2,941,000	8. Mongol	63,000
2. Kazakh	319,000	9. Sibo	9,200
3. Kirghiz	65,000	10. Solon	2,490
4. Tajik	9,000	11. Manchu	670
5. Uzbek	8,000	12. Russian	13,000
6. Tatar	5,000		
7. Hui	92,000	13. Han	202,000

Whilst two of the smaller non-Muslim groups (the Mongols and the Russians) were certainly of economic and social sig-

361

nificance in the political fabric of Repubican Sinkiang, it is clear that the combined Muslim population — comprising seven 'nationalities' and numbering an estimated 3,439,000 (ca. 92 per cent) of the total population of 3,730,000 — was of overwhelming importance. It is this section of the Sinkiang population which forms the subject of the present paper, and more particularly the question of unity and diversity within the Muslim population with particular reference to the role and position of group 7 in the above table — the Chinese-speaking Hui Muslims, known to their Turkic co-religionists in Sinkiang as *Tuñgáni*, whence the English term 'Tungan', loosely applied to the Hui Muslims of Sinkiang, as distinct from the Hui elsewhere in China.[2]

Within Sinkiang — as, indeed, within the remainder of China — the role and position of the Chinese-speaking Hui Muslims has received relatively little examination, as a result of which various generalisations have come to be accepted and applied, with little variation, to China as a whole. Thus, the writings of earlier Christian missionary researchers such as Broomhall[3] tend to stress the inherent contradictions between Han and Hui, an emphasis continued in the work of perhaps the most prolific of contemporary 'Sino-Islamicists', Raphael Israeli, who writes at length of the 'incompatibility of Islam and the Chinese system'.[4] Yet it is also apparent that the Hui Muslim population, which must today (1987) number in excess of 10,000,000.[5] scattered throughout China from Yunnan in the south-west to Heilungkiang in the north-east, and from Sinkiang in the north-west to Hainan Island in the south-east, may be as diverse in aspects of its cultural and political heritage as the vast tracts of territory which it spans. Thus, what appears relatively 'incompatible' in Peking, may very well prove quite the opposite in Kashgar — as will be argued in the present paper.

Similar reservations should, perhaps, be applied to more restricted 'area studies' of Sinkiang. Thus, although no specific treatise on 'Islam in Sinkiang' has yet been written, serious studies of Republican Sinkiang (most notably those of Lattimore, Nyman and Whiting), whilst concentrating primarily on the 'Great Power' politics of the region, make some reference to the internal and regional Islamic politics of the province. Taken collectively, these passing references to Islam in Sinkiang (and especially to intra-Muslim relations within the province) tend, perhaps inevitably, to rest on stereotype rather than coherent analysis. Thus Lattimore, a writer of 'progressive' sentiment, tends to emphasise the linguistic, cultural, and ethnic diversity of the Muslim population of Sinkiang, stressing, for example, sedentary-nomadic dysfunctions (as exemplified by Uighurs and Kazakhs) in a general dismissal of Turkic nationalist aspirations;[6] it need hardly be noted that some Turkic nationalist studies of Republican Sinkiang adopt precisely the opposite standpoint, 'papering over' ethnic and cultural disparities which do exist, whilst emphasising the Turanian cultural identity of the region.[7] The present writer has argued elsewhere that such analyses are misleading, and that a better understanding of the Islamic politics of Republican Sinkiang may be attained by a study of regional, rather than ethnic, distinctiveness.[8]

Similarly, although Whiting recognises that within Sinkiang the Tungans 'seldom enjoyed the full confidence' of their Turkic (and Tajik) fellow-Muslims, and that very often 'racial animosities took precedence over religious identification',[9] the role of the Tungans as active supporters of the Chinese polity in Sinkiang has scarcely been elaborated, whilst the unifying force of shared Islamic belief has generally been over-stated and is frequently misunderstood.

Whilst the substance of the present paper is concerned with the role of the Tungans in Republican Sinkiang — between the overthrow of the Ch'ing Empire in 1911 and the establishment of the People's Republic in 1949 — it may first be useful very briefly to indicate the positon of the Tungans in Sinkiang during the latter half of the nineteenth century, during the great North-Western Muslim Rebellion (1862–78), and in the declining years of the Ch'ing Dynasty.

Following the usual pattern for Hui Muslim settlement in North-West China and Yunnan, the Hui of Sinkiang have for many years been linked with the caravan trade and its associated professions (as innkeepers, ḥlāl-butchers, etc.) and with the military calling so despised by the Han in traditional Chinese society, but which has almost come to exemplify the Hui in their role as frontiersmen. Indeed, whilst the Hui are unquestionably Muslim, proud of their position as part of the international Muslim community (*umma*) and always conscious of their spiritual links with the Hijaz, it must not be forgotten that they are also Chinese-speaking, proud of their position as _Chinese_ Muslims, and always conscious of their cultural links with Chinese civilisation. As such, they may act as agents of Sinification as well as of Islamisation — and, indeed, this has long been the case within the predominantly Turkic-speaking province of Sinkiang, as well as in the Yunnan-Southeast Asia borderlands.[10]

In terms of Sinkiang politics, this dual loyalty (to Islam and, at least when settled beyond the confines of exclusively Han civilisation, to China) has meant that Turkic-speaking Muslim and Chinese-speaking Muslim have rarely shared political aspirations or cultural objectives. Indeed, within Sinkiang, hostility between Turk and Tungan has generally (though not always) outweighed the shared spiritual convictions implied by common membership of the _umma_. To put it simply, whilst both Tungan and Turk, as Sunni H'anafī Muslims, may pray side-by-side in the same mosque, the predominant Uighur population of Sinkiang (and, to a lesser extent, the Kazakh, Kirghiz and other Turkic-speaking groups) have long aspired to autonomy or independence from China, if possible under their own Turkic-Muslim administration.[11] The Tungan/Hui population, by contrast, does not share this perception at all, but — whilst aspiring in spiritual terms to freedom of religious practice — would appear to prefer to live under a non-Muslim Chinese-speaking Han administration than under a Turkic-speaking Muslim administration.[12]

During Ch'ing times, the diverse political aspirations of Turkic-speaking and Chinese-speaking Muslim were best exemplified, in times of peace, by the role of the Hui as military garrison troops, loyal to the Manchu administration. This division was still further apparent in times of war — most particularly during the great North-Western Muslim Rebellion (1862–78), when Turk and Tungan, having simultaneously but separately thrown off the Ch'ing yoke, not merely failed to cooperate against the advancing armies of Tso Tsung-t'ang, but even engaged in a series of debilitating internecine conflicts which contributed directly to the re-assertion of Ch'ing power.[13]

It is noteworthy, too, that the victorious Tso, having crushed the secessionist regime of his main Turkic opponent, Yạqūb

Beg,[14] and having driven his main Hui opponent, Pai Yen-hu, across the frontier to Russian Central Asia,[15] dealt separately with his vanquished Turkic-speaking and Chinese-speaking enemies. Thus, Turkic-speaking Muslim rebels originating from Sinkiang were treated as subject peoples who had mis-guidedly rebelled against Ch'ing authority, who might now — if they lived peacefully in future — be forgiven; Chinese-speak-ing Muslim rebels were regarded as traitors to the Chinese polity, however, and as such generally given short shrift.[16]

Yet despite this distinction — and perhaps even because of it — within two decades of Tso's reconquest of the North-West, Hui Muslim troops were once again acting as the stan-dard-bearers of Han Chinese authority in Sinkiang. The reason for this was, simply, that not all Hui had been 'traitors' to the Ch'ing; indeed, the history of the Hui Muslim rebellions in Kansu, Shensi and Yunnan clearly indicates the presence of serious fissures within Hui society, which the Ch'ing were swift to amplify and to exploit. Thus, whilst the rebel Hui were seen as odious traitors to the Chinese polity who *ipso facto* merited extermination, those Hui who cooperated with or assisted the Ch'ing were seen as 'good' or 'loyal' Hui, properly conscious of their honoured position within the Chinese polity. Indeed, it is even possible that these 'good' Hui were seen as paragons of loyalty to China, for despite their outlandish and bizarre religion, which put them on the fringes of Chinese society, they had remained true. Finally, they were excellent soldiers, who generally mistrusted and looked down upon their Turkic-speaking co-religionists. What better material could there be for garrisoning the remote Inner Asian frontiers of China, a posting generally so abhorred by the Han?

During Republican times a similar pattern was to emerge. Thus Yang Tseng-hsin, the first Republican Governor of Sinki-ang, rose to a position of authority under the late Ch'ing on the strength of his ability to 'manage' the Hui Muslim popu-lation of Kansu and Ningsia. Subsequently, in 1908, he was transferred to Sinkiang where he built up a personal power-base which rested on his Hui garrison troops, who were the best in the province. In 1911, assisted by these troops, he assumed power in Sinkiang; for the next seventeen years he was to wield absolute authority over China's largest province, relying heavily for the greater part of this time on his efficient

Hui soldiery in the maintenance of Han power over an over-whelmingly Turkic-speaking population. Nor was the role of Yang's Hui supporters limited to the military field — in 1915 Ma Fu-hsing, a Hui Muslim from Yang Tseng-hsin's native Yunnan, was appointed _T'i-t'ai_ of Kashgar, the second most powerful post in the province. Fu-hsing — who proved to be a man of singular venality and incompetence — ruled over the Uighur heartland of southern Sinkiang until his dismissal and execution by Yang in 1924; yet it is noteworthy that his replace-ment, Ma Shao-wu, who continued the administration of the south until Sheng Shih-ts'ai's seizure of power in 1934, was also a Hui Muslim of Yunnan.

Throughout Yang Tseng-hsin's long period of adminis-tration,[17] therefore, his power was sustained not only by Hui Muslim troops, but also by Hui Muslim administrators — the first of whom, in Kashgar, was a sadistic incompetent, whilst the second, although a man of honesty and distinction, was characterised by an unswerving loyalty to Nanking. These facts were not lost upon the Turkic-speaking Muslims of southern and western Sinkiang who, as in Ch'ing times, continued to regard the Hui as colonial garrison troops of the Han Chinese, and not at all as Muslim brothers. Only in the Kumul region of Sinkiang's 'far east' did a different perception hold true, and this was because the Uighurs of Kumul Oasis had effec-tively come to terms with their _de facto_ position _within_ the Chinese polity, and as such rejected the secessionist aspir-ations of their Kashgarlik and Khotanlik bretheren.[18]

Passing over the relatively brief 'interregnum' of Chin Shu-jen — who assumed power in Sinkiang between 1928 and 1933, and whose tenure of office was undoubtedly shortened by the simultaneous alienation both of his Turkic-speaking and Chinese-speaking Muslim subjects[19] — we come to the period of Tungan invasions led by the young Hui Muslim warlord of north-western Kansu, Ma Chung-ying. It is in these invasions that we find, perhaps, our clearest indication of the traditional relationship between Turkic-speaking and Chinese-speaking Muslims within Sinkiang. Thus, although Ma Chung-ying ostensibly commenced his invasion of Sinkiang 'in the name of Muslim brotherhood' to help the Muslims of Kumul (Ha-mi),[20] it is in fact clear that Islam played little or no part in his thinking. Rather, Ma should be seen as a contemporaneous

Chinese Republican warlord who happened to be a Muslim. Accordingly, his troops sported KMT 36th Division insignia, and whilst Ma strongly denounced his arch-rival Sheng Shih-ts'ai for attempting to betray Sinkiang to the Soviet Union, he had no time for the Muslim secessionist camps in Kashgar and Khotan, and paid them scant attention. Only subsequently, when his forces retreated into south-western Sinkiang in the face of Soviet attack in 1934, did Ma turn his attention to the secessionist 'Turkish-Islamic Republic of Eastern Turkestan', and then his policy was dismissively to crush it, driving the Turkic-Muslim administration out of Kashgar and restoring the Yunnanese Hui, Ma Shao-wu, as China's representative in the far west. The Kuomintang flag was raised in Kashgar, statements of loyalty to the Chinese Republic were telegraphed to Nanking, Turkic-speaking Muslim secessionists were hunted down and executed and — to the horror of the Muslim Uighurs of Kashgar — Sun Yat-sen's portrait was raised in the 'Īd-Gah Mosque![21] In short, Chung-ying made it quite clear that his first loyalty (beyond, of course, loyalty to himself and, perhaps, to some of the 'Wu Ma' Muslim warlord clique)[22] was to China, and that he regarded the Soviet Union and the Turkic-speaking Muslim secessionists almost equally as his enemies. Of 'Muslim Brotherhood' little or nothing was said.

Following Ma Chung-ying's unexpected (and unexplained) decampment to the Soviet Union in July, 1934, a similarly pro-Nanking, anti-secessionist policy was followed by Chung-ying's successor, Ma Hu-shan, who in defiance of Sheng Shih-ts'ai and his Soviet backers continued to administer the southernmost part of Sinkiang until the collapse of his regime in the summer of 1937. It has been suggested that the motive force sustaining this isolated Hui fiefdom (aptly described, at least from a Turkic-speaking Muslim standpoint, as 'Tunganis-tan') was 'a spirit of militant Islam';[23] yet such was manifestly not the case. Rather, as the present writer has argued elsewhere,[24] the political standpoint and internal administration of 'Tunganistan' was of a pattern with other contemporaneous Chinese warlord regimes, but transferred westward from Kansu to the heart of Turkic-speaking Chinese Central Asia, where Hui Muslim troops (sporting KMT flags and insignia, and employing Chinese as the language of administration) served the Chinese polity (and, to be sure, themselves) as colonial rulers over Turkic-speaking Muslim subjects.

Yet, given the traditional relationship between Turkic-speaking and Chinese-speaking Muslims within Sinkiang, the attitude of Ma Chung-ying and the policies of the rulers of Tunganistan can have come as no surprise to the Turkic-speaking peoples of Sinkiang. Had not Sābit Dāmullāh, Prime Minister of the secessionist 'Turkish-Islamic Republic of Eastern Turkestan', denounced the Hui in the same way, and at the same time, as the Han in his 1933 'independence address'? Thus:

> The Tungans are no less our enemy than the Han Chinese . . . Neither the Han Chinese nor the Tungans have any legitimate claim to Eastern Turkestan. We, the people of Eastern Turkestan, no longer need foreigners to be our masters.[25]

Considered in historical perspective, therefore, it was Hui loyalty to Nanking — and at a deeper level to the Chinese polity as a whole — which distinguished Chinese-speaking Muslim from Turkic-speaking Muslim in Republican Sinkiang. Perhaps no better example of this dichotomy may be found than in the chaotic events surrounding the ill-fated 'TIRET' and the subsequent Hui administration in 'Tunganistan', when — at approximately the same time and in approximately the same place (Southern Sinkiang, 1933–37), Uighur, Kazakh and Kirghiz Muslims looked to Kabul and Ankara for recognition of their independence, instituted *Hijri* dating and *Islamic shari'a* law, and generally repudiated China and all things Chinese. By contrast, their Hui co-religionists responded by denouncing these developments, protesting their loyalty to Nanking, and festooning the cities under their control with posters (in Chinese) denouncing Japanese aggression in Manchuria and pledging support to the anti-Japanese war effort.

As a result of Stalin's intervention in support of the 'chameleon warlord', Sheng Shih-ts'ai, the aspirations of both Turkic- and Chinese-speaking Muslim were to suffer severe setbacks during the latter half of the Republican Era. Following the demise of the 'TIRET' in 1933, Turkic-speaking Muslim separatism — unless cautiously sponsored and controlled by the Soviet Union and its supporters, as manifested in the Ili-based 'East Turkestan Republic' ('ETR') of 1944–49 — became an unrealisable objective.[26] Yet Turkic-speaking Muslims continued to represent the overwhelming majority of the population of Sinkiang, and this demographic fact, combined with the general (although widely varying)[27] degree of hostility felt by the Turkic-speaking Muslims of Sinkiang towards the Chinese polity, ensured that both Sheng Shih-ts'ai and the Soviet Union continued to work with and through the Turkic-speaking majority in their manipulation of provincial politics.

Following the collapse of 'Tunganistan' in 1937, by contrast, Hui power in Sinkiang was very definitely, albeit temporarily, brought to an end. Thus, neither the Soviet Union (through its 'ETR' proxies), nor Sheng Shih-ts'ai (whether in 'progressive' or 'reactionary' manifestation) made any serious attempt to secure Hui support for their policies in Sinkiang. Rather, every attempt was made to exclude Chinese-speaking Muslims from the provincial (and 'ETR') administrations, simply because both Stalin and Sheng Shih-ts'ai realised that Hui loyalties lay primarily with Nanking, and that the Chinese-speaking Muslims of the North-West, almost without exception, considered Sinkiang to be an inalienable part of China.[28]

Fortunately for the Hui of Sinkiang, however, this loyalty to the Chinese polity was clearly understood and appreciated both in Nanking and — at one remove — in Yenan. Thus, with the downfall of Sheng Shih-ts'ai in 1944 and the extension (effectively for the first time) of Kuomintang rule to Sinkiang, Hui military units played a crucial role in those regions of the province under KMT control, whilst a Chinese-speaking Muslim, Wang Tseng-shan, was appointed (KMT) Commissioner of Civil affairs at Urumchi.[29]

The role of the Hui Muslims as supporters of the Chinese polity in Sinkiang may thus be seen as a continuation, from Imperial into Republican times, of a special relationship between successive Chinese national administrations and a Chinese-speaking Muslim minority which has generally (though in the opinion of the present writer, more often than not erroneously) been represented in Western writings as inherently 'rebellious', or anti-Han.

Finally, it can surely be no coincidence that, following the seizure of power by the Chinese Communists in 1949 and the entry of People's Liberation Army Units into Sinkiang during the same year, the first priorities of the victorious CCP in

China's far west proved to be the (comparatively simple) limitation of Turkic Muslim dissidence and the (much more difficult) elimination of Soviet influence from the region. By 1 October 1955, at the time of the establishment of the Sinkiang-Uighur Autonomous Region, both these aims had largely been realised. Yet, fully eighteen months earlier, in what may be interpreted both as an indication of the special Han-Hui relationship within Sinkiang and an implicit gesture of trust and reward, the first autonomous *hsien* in Sinkiang was established for the Chinese-speaking Muslims of Kara Shahr, an action which was followed within weeks by the establishment of similar autonomous counties near Kulja and at Bayan Gol for those other minority supporters of Han rule in the far west, the Sibos of the Ili Valley and the Mongols of the T'ien Shan.[30]

Notes

1 Lattimore, O (1950), *Pivot of Asia: Sinkiang and the Inner Asian Frontiers of China and Russia*, pp. 103–10, Little Brown & Co., Boston.

2 Raquette, G. (1927), *English-Turki Dictionary Based on the Dialects of Kashgar and Yarkand*, p. 74, C W K Gleerup, Lund. Whilst Chinese-speaking Muslims within China are generally distinguished by the generic term *Hui-hui* or *Hui-min*, the same people are known by a variety of other names beyond the frontiers of China — for example, 'Čhin-Hǫ˜' in Laos and Thailand, 'Panthay' in Burma, and 'Tungan' in Central Asia (cf. Russian 'Dungan'). In the present writer's recent study of Sinkiang — *Warlords and Muslims in Chinese Central Asia: A Political History of Republican Sinkiang*, (1986), Cambridge University Press, Cambridge. Republican Sinkiang is perceived as a Han Chinese colony in the heart of Asia, and an attempt is made to view the political history of the region from a Central Asian Muslim standpoint — hence the use of the Turkic term 'Tungan' rather than the Chinese 'Hui', a style continued in the present paper. It should be noted, however, that the terms 'Tungan' and 'Hui' are effectively interchangeable in application to Republican Sinkiang, whilst for studies of China post–1949 it would doubtless be more appropriate to use the term 'Hui-min' *passim*.

3 Broomhall, M (1910) *Islam in China: A Neglected Problem* (London: Morgan & Scott, London, esp. pp. 123–63; cf. Andrew, G F., *The Crescent in North-West China* (1921), China Inland Mission, London esp. pp. 63–75.

4 Israeli, R (1980) *Muslims in China: A Study in Cultural Confrontation* Curzon Press/Humanities Press, London, *passim*. See also *idem.*,

'The Incompatibility of Islam and the Chinese System', *T'oung Pao*, LXV (1977), pp. 296–323.

5 Estimate based on figures extrapolated from the 1953 Census. The 1982 census, which gives a figure of 7.2 million Hui, seems strangely low to the present writer, particularly in view of the fact that Hui, as a minority people, are not restricted to one child per family (as are the Han).

6 Lattimore, *Pivot of Asia*, pp. 103–51; cf. *idem.*, 'Sinkiang', in: *Studies in Frontier History: Collected Writings, 1928–1958* (1962), pp. 183–217, Oxford University Press, London.

7 See, for example, Isma'il, M.S., and Isma'il, M. A., 'Muslims in The Soviet Union and in People's China', *Joint Publications Research Services* No. 3936 (New York, 1960).

8 Forbes, *Warlords and Muslims*, pp. 229–32.

9 Whiting, A (1958) *Sinkiang: Pawn or Pivot*? Michigan State University Press, East Lansing, pp. 4–5.

10 For further details of the role of the Hui as cultural mediators in the Yunnan-Southeast Asia frontier area, see the present author's articles in the *Journal of the Institute of Muslim Minority Affairs*, VII, 1, pp. 173–86; VII, 2, pp. 384–94. A more detailed study, *Traders of the Golden Triangle: The Yunnanese Chinese Diaspora in Thailand, Burma and Laos*, is currently nearing completion.

11 Fletcher, J. (1978), 'Ch'ing Inner Asia, 1800–62', in: Fairbank, J K (ed.), *The Cambridge History of China, X, Late Ch'ing, 1800–1911*, Cambridge University Press, Cambridge pp. 35–91; Boulger, D C (1878) *The Life of Yakoob Beg; Athalik Ghazi and Badaulet; Ameer of Kashgar* Allen, London.

12 Forbes, *Warlords and Muslims*, pp. 34, 67, 80–89, 128–35, etc.

13 Boulger, *Yakoob Beg*, pp. 119–36 (Wars with the Tungani); Ho-dong Kim, 'The Muslim Rebellion and the Kashgar Emirate, 1864–1877', unpublished PhD thesis, Inner Asian and Altaic Studies, Harvard University, May 1986, esp. pp. 125–32. I am grateful to Jonathan Lipman for bringing this latter work to my attention.

14 Bales, Tso Tsung-t'ang: Soldier and Statesman of Old China (Shanghai: Kelly and Walsh, 1937); Wen-djang Chu (1966), *The Moslem Rebellion in Northwest China 1862–1878* Mouton The Hague pp. 163–96.

15 Svetlana Rimsky-Korsakoff Dyer (1979), *Soviet Dungan Kolkhozes in the Kirghiz SSR and the Kazakh SSR*, Australian National University Press/Faculty of Asian Studies, Canberra.

16 Lattimore, *Pivot of Asia*, pp. 49–50.

17 In 1926, towards the end of his rule, Yang turned against many of his Tungan subordinates, whom he suspected of conspiring with Ma Ch'i, Hui warlord of Tsinghai. This abrupt change of policy contributed greatly to Yang's downfall. Forbes, *Warlords and Muslims*, p. 35.

18 Forbes, *Warlords and Muslims*, pp. 229–34.

19 *Ibid.*, pp. 38–62.

20 Yao-lo-po-shi (Yulbars Khan), *Yao-lo-po-shih hui-i lu* ['Memoirs of

Yulbars' (Taipei: Chuan-ch'i wen-hsueh chu-pan she, 1969)] pp. 88–91.

21 Ma also lectured Turkic-Muslim worshippers on the importance of loyalty to Nanking after the 'Íd-Gah Friday prayers. Forbes, *Warlords and Muslims*, p. 124.

22 Forbes, *Warlords and Muslims*, pp. 55, 62.

23 Nyman, L E (1977) *Great Britain and Chinese, Russian and Japanese Interests in Sinkiang, 1918–34*, Esselte Studium, Malmo, p. 109; cf. Aubin, F (1981), 'Íslam et sinocentrisme: la Chine, terre d'Islam', in: *L'Islam de la seconde expansion*, Association pour l'Avancement des Etudes Islamiques, Paris, p. 10.

24 Forbes, *Warlords and Muslims*, pp. 128–35.

25 Chang Ta-chün, *Ssu-shih-nien tung-luan Hsin-chiang* ['Forty Years of Turmoil in Sinkiang' (Hong Kong: The Asia Publishing House, 1956)], pp. 52–3.

26 Forbes, *Warlords and Muslims*, pp. 128–62.

27 *Ibid.*, pp. 230–32.

28 In this context, It was indicated to me by Dr Jonathan Lipman, in conversation at his home in Mount Holyoke, Massachusetts, during April, 1987, that — in his experience — this attitude is shared by prominent Hui Muslim scholars in contemporary China.

29 Forbes, *Warlords and Muslims*, pp. 196, 214–5; Lattimore, *Pivot of Asia*, p. 144.

30 'The Evolution of Minority Nationality Regional Autonomy in Sinkiang', *Central Asian Review*, XV, 3 (1967), pp. 232–7.

Hann, C. M.
Dr Chris Hann is an Assistant Lecturer in Social Anthropology at the University of Cambridge, and a Fellow of Corpus Christi College. He spent the summer of 1986 in Xinjiang (Urumqi). Earlier fieldwork projects were located in Eastern Europe and the Black Sea coast of Turkey.

Jasiewicz, Z.
Professor Zbigniew Jasiewicz, ethnologist, b. 10 June 1934, Poznań. Ethnology and archaeology studies at Jagiellonian University, Krakow, and Adam Mickiewicz University, Poznań; MA 1955, PhD 1960, and habilitation 1969. Director of the Institute of Ethnology, Adam Mickiewicz University, Poznań. Two research visits to Uzbekistan and Tadzhikistan; in charge of Poznań Ethnological Expedition to Afghanistan, 1976. He has published numerous works on Central Asia problems, including traditional forms of production, especially handicraft, tradition and changes in the family, the *mahalla* in the contemporary social life and the situation of the Haydariha-endogamic group of blacksmiths. Other domains of research: Traditional village culture in Poland; processes of cultural adaptation and integration in the northern and western territories in Poland; the family and its culture in comparative perspective.

Jeziorska, Irena
Irena Jeziorska is a graduate of Cambridge University and wrote her PhD thesis on *Religious Themes in Contemporary Soviet Literature*. She is a research assistant at Keston College, Kent, and has published a number of articles on religious subjects.

Kirkwood, J. M.
J. M. Kirkwood is a Senior Lecturer in Russian Language at the School of Slavonic and East European Studies in the University of London. He has published a number of articles in the field of applied linguistics and is particularly interested in Russian language acquisition theory and Soviet language planning.

Momen, M.
Dr Momen is a private scholar primarily interested in the field of the history of religions and specialising in the Baha'i faith and Shi'i Islam. His books include: *The Babi and Baha'i Religions 1844–1944; Some Contemporary Western Accounts* (1981); *Introduction to Shi'i Islam; The History and Doctrines of Twelve Shi'isms* (1985). He has edited two volumes of *Studies in Babi and Baha'i History*, and published papers in the *International Journal of Middle East Studies, Iran*, and *Past and Present*, as well as contributing to the *Encyclopaedia Iranica*.

Montgomery, David C.
The author is Professor of History at Brigham Young University in Provo, Utah. He was Coordinator of the Near Eastern Studies Program from 1978 to 1985. He teaches Near Eastern and Central Asian history, and for a short period taught the Turkish language. In 1971 he received a PhD from Indiana University, where he studies Asian history as well as the Russian, Turkish, Uzbek and Mongolian languages. He has spent a total of a year in Soviet Central Asia (three stays during 1969–82). He is currently researching various aspects of the cultural history of the Uzbek Turks. He has published one book and several articles about the peoples along the Asian and Near Eastern borders of the Soviet Union.

Naby, Eden
Eden Naby is affiliated to the Center for Middle Eastern Studies at Harvard University where she researches, writes and teaches on topics related to ethnicity and cultural change in the Middle East and Central Asia. She has travelled and worked in much of the eastern Islamic world, including Soviet and Chinese Central Asia. Her publications include many articles and she is in the process of preparing a manuscript on Afghanistan.

Scarce, Jennifer M.
Jennifer M. Scarce is Curator of Eastern Cultures at the Royal Museum of Scotland, Edinburgh, and has travelled widely in the Muslim world. Publications include *Middle Eastern Costume from the Tribes and Cities of Iran and Turkey* (1981) and *The Evolving Culture of Kuwait* (1985).

Tapper, Nancy
Dr Tapper lectures in anthropology at the School of Oriental and African Studies, University of London. She has carried out ethnographic fieldwork in Iran, Afghanistan and Turkey, and has published numerous articles on gender, marriage, ritual and religion in Middle Eastern societies.

Tapper, Richard
Dr Tapper is Reader in Anthropology with reference to the Middle East in the University of London. He has carried out extensive field research in Iran, Afghanistan and Turkey, and his publications include *Pasture and Politics: Economics, Conflict and Ritual among Shahsevan Nomads of Northwestern Iran* (1979), and the edited volume *The Conflict of Tribe and State in Iran and Afghanistan* (1983).

Waardenburg, Jacques
Jacques Waardenburg is Professor of Comparative Religion at the University of Lausanne, Switzerland. His books include *L'Islam dans le miroir de l'Occident* (1961), *Les universités dans le monde arabe actuel* (1966) and *L'enseignement dans le monde arabe* (1983). He is the editor of *Islam: norm, ideal and reality* (1984 in Dutch) and he has published several articles on recent developments in Islam.